Alastair Sawday's

Special
places to stay

SPAIN

Edited by Guy Hunter-Watts

Typesetting, Conversion & Repro:	Avonset, Bath
Maps:	Bartholomew Mapping Services, a division of HarperCollins Publishers, Glasgow
Printing:	Stige, Italy
Design:	Caroline King & Springboard Design, Bristol
UK Distribution:	Portfolio, Greenford, Middlesex
US Distribution:	The Globe Pequot Press, Guilford, Connecticut

Published in March 2001

Alastair Sawday Publishing Co. Ltd
The Home Farm Stables, Barrow Gurney, Bristol BS48 3RW

The Globe Pequot Press
P. O. Box 480
Guilford, Connecticut 06437
USA

Fourth edition.

Copyright © March 2001 Alastair Sawday Publishing Co. Ltd

A catalogue record for this book is available from the British Library.

Alastair Sawday has asserted his right to be identified as the author of this work.

ISBN 1-901970-16-7 in the UK

ISBN 0-7627-0887-5 in the US

Printed in Italy.

The publishers have made every effort to ensure the accuracy of the information in this book at the time of going to press. However, they cannot accept any responsibility for any loss, injury or inconvenience resulting from the use of information contained therein.

Alastair Sawday's

Special
places to stay

Spain

"Travel is fatal to prejudice, bigotry, and narrow-mindedness."
Mark Twain

The Globe Pequot Press

Guilford
Connecticut, USA

ASP

Alastair Sawday Publishing
Bristol, UK

Contents

Contents

8

Acknowledgements

Guy Hunter-Watts has always done this book largely on his own. But for the first time he has summoned help. Is it that his earlier vitality was hard to maintain? Is it that Emma Baverstock and his wonderful B&B are hard to leave? Whatever, I don't blame him; those Spanish distances are huge, and gone are the days when sleeping under a 2CV in the vastnesses of Aragon was an attraction. So Sarah Lewis, with enormous skill, took on the whole province of Catalonia; Barry Birch criss-crossed much of Spain and even, because of an inspection trip, missed his daughter's birth by an hour. (I beg forgiveness.) Peter and Sheila Mills took care of much of Eastern Spain.

Emma deserves a special 'thank you' for her loyal behind-the-scenes support, tolerating Guy's long absences - whether on tour or downstairs in the office - and for rolling up sleeves to help.

Finding all these wonderful places in Spain was not easy. Now that 'Portugal' has split off to become its own book there was space for this book to grow. Guy has 'grown it' brilliantly and the result is a book that will bring enormous pleasure to thousands of readers, many of whom will make lasting friendships and discover a warmer and more open-hearted Spain than they ever thought possible.

Alastair Sawday

Series Editor:... Alastair Sawday

Editor:... Guy Hunter-Watts

Managing Editor:... Annie Shillito

Production Manager:.. Julia Richardson

Administration:.. Emma Carey, Kate Harris

Accounts:... Jenny Purdy

Additional inspections:....................................... Barry Birch
                                                                           Sarah Lewis
                                                                           Peter and Sheila Mills

Special thanks too, to the Rusticae group of small Spanish hotels. They helped us to find some of the places listed here and are mentioned in those texts.

Introduction

For centuries, until the Government introduced the wonderful parador system, few travellers came to Spain. Then came the invasion of the Costas, with the predictable result that there are stretches now where there is little left to admire.

However, pull back the sheet and you will find a vast country of ineffable beauty, depth and brilliance. Great swathes of the countryside are untouched by the ravages of this century. There are villages in the north that are uninhabited. You can walk for days alone, follow old pilgrim paths that wind from one moment of still-vivid history to another. It is a country where eagles still soar among mountains, where wild boar roam (and are eaten), whose wildlife shames those of us from a Europe already domesticated and intensively farmed. You will find villages whose post-prandial silence will be punctured by the revving of tractors as the farmers - all living in the village - slip out for an afternoon's work.

The contributions made by these books, in all their editions, is small. But they are an attempt to seek out those corners of Spain, those Spaniards (and non-Spaniards), that demonstrate Spain at its wonderful best. There are places lost within its deep folds where you find civilisation flourishing, with kindness, generosity and a sense of the mystery that it is to be human. We have sought beauty and authenticity, people whose contribution to this world is one we can admire. Another way of putting it is that we have tried to find the places that make you, the traveller, feel wholly human.

I experienced this last summer. One of the hotels gave me such a deep sense of gratitude to the owners for their originality and authenticity that I felt I would never want to leave. I came away richer for the experience. No doubt it was not perfect as a 'hotel', but it was perfect, to me, as a 'place to be'. Perhaps we should redefine 'hotel': why should it usually be a reception area, a dining room and a warren of bedrooms? Is there an argument for offering something else now?

Lots of people do so already. Come and see, for within these pages are people and places that you will be proud to have known. They are swimming against the current.

Alastair Sawday

Introduction

How do we choose our Special Places?

We look for owners, homes and hotels that we like - and we are fiercely subjective in our choices. 'Special' for us is not a measure of the number of creature comforts you get but relates to many different elements that make a place 'work'. Certainly the way guests are treated comes as high on our list as the setting, the architecture and the food. We are not necessarily impressed by high star ratings.

Expect this book to lead you to places that are original, individual and welcoming. We hope it will bring you closer to the Spain that we love, a country whose people are vibrant and spontaneous, incredibly friendly and - yes, the cliché is true - different.

So how how does this square with the foreign-run places in this book?

We don't search out ex-pats. But some of them have created marvellous places to stay and those we include have a proven track-record of commitment to their adopted land and people.

A word about the Balearic & the Canary Islands

Expect to pay about 50% more here than in the rest of Spain. We promise that we haven't sought out expensive places - that's just the way it is.

What to expect

The Spanish 'way of being' is hugely different from the British or the American one. One small scene illustrates the point. Imagine that you are standing at the counter of a bar in, say, the old town of Ronda. Two working men enter the bar, and one shouts at the barman. "*Oiga! Una cerveza*", - literally, "Here, give me a beer". The barman doesn't bat an eyelid and a beer is thumped down on the bar: not a 'please' nor a 'thank you' from either party. You might think that the two men are about to come to blows: why else would they be shouting at each other when standing just one foot apart? It gradually dawns on you from the smiles and laughter that this is simply a lively discussion and that daggers will not be drawn. Meanwhile, just behind the two men, an unwatched TV screams at full volume. You are both irritated and deafened. So you pluck up courage and ask the barman if he could just turn it down '*un poquito*'. "Of course, amigo", he replies, and turns it off, clearly bemused because he had not even noticed that it was switched on. The whole scene shows that you can't judge Spain by your own cultural yardsticks. So in hotels, bars and restaurants be quick to pardon what might at first seem a brash or an abrupt way of being. The Spanish are nearly always both kind and gracious, just not in the manner of the junior manager at the Dorchester!

Introduction

We have sought out beautiful homes and hotels throughout Spain. But, occasionally the 'charm' factor can be low: form often follows function and the Spanish like to get together in (very) large groups. Choose your hotel on looks alone and you will miss out on some remarkable places. Don't be too put off by, say, a cavernous looking restaurant. The food may well be tremendous. And likewise be prepared to tolerate a 'sugary' taste in decoration. The rooms will be comfortable and come with a low price tag.

Finding the right place for you

We want you to spend your time in places that you will like. We try to write honest descriptions and mention any misgivings in the text. Hotels, like people, are never perfect. So read the description carefully!

How to use this book

Maps

Look at the map at the front of the book, find your area then look for the places which are mapped. Note their numbers and look up the same entry number which you will find at the bottom of the page, in colour. The actual page number is different. If you prefer to browse through the book and let the individual entries make up your mind then simply check the map reference at the bottom of the page.

Rooms

We tell you the range of accommodation in single, double, twin, triple or quadruple rooms or in apartments, suites, cottages or houses. Extra beds can often be added for children. Check when booking.

Prices

The prices that we quote for rooms are exclusive of VAT at 7%. Prices are given for the room unless otherwise specified, ie p.p.= per person. When VAT and/or breakfast is included we let you know. The same applies to prices that we quote for meals. The symbols that we use are:

M = set menu. The price will generally include wine.
C = À la carte. This is an approximate price for a three-course lunch or dinner including a half bottle of inexpensive wine.

The prices we quote were applicable at the time that this book went to press. We publish every two years so expect prices to be higher if you are using this book in 2002 or early 2003.

Introduction

Symbols

There is an explanation of our symbols on the last page of the book. Use these as a guide, not as an unequivocal statement of fact.

Phones & Phone Codes

From Spain to another country: dial 00 then add the country code and then the area code without the first 0. Eg ASP in Bristol, from Spain: UK No. 01275 464891 becomes 00 44 1275 464891

Within Spain: All 9 figures are needed whether intra or inter-provincial.

Calling to Spain from another country:
From the USA: 011 34 then the 9 figure number
From the UK: 00 34 then the 9 figure number

Most mobile numbers begin with a 6. This is your best clue as to when you're dialling an (expensive) mobile number.

Telephone cards come from tobacconists or post offices (coin operated boxes are few). The cheapest starts at about £4 (US$6).

Abbreviations

C/	calle = street	Ctra	carretera = road
s/n	sin número = un-numbered	Pts	Pesetas

Types of properties

Mipect to find.

Can -	A farmhouse in Catalonia or the Balearic Islands. Often isolated.
Casona -	A grand house in Asturias (many were built by returning émigrés).
Cortijo -	A free-standing farmhouse, generally in the South.
Finca -	A farm; most of those included here are of the working variety.
Fonda -	A simple inn. It may or may nor serve food.
Hacienda -	A large estate. Originally a South American term.
Hostal -	Another type of simple inn where food may or may not be served.
Hostería -	A simple inn which tends to serve food.
Hostelería -	Another term for an inn which may or may not serve food.
Mas -	Another term for a farmhouse in the north-east of Spain.
Masía -	Another term for a farmhouse in the east of Spain.
Posada -	Originally it meant a coaching inn. Beds and food available.

Introduction

Parador - Originally another term for an inn. The one included here is not state-run.

Palacio - A grand mansion house.

Palacete - A slightly less grand version of the above.

Pazo - A grand country or village manor in Galicia.

Venta - A simple restaurant; rooms have often come later.

The spelling of proper names in Spain

Where there are two official languages (eg Galicia, the Basque Country, Catalonia) - place-names will often have two spellings. We try to use the ones that you are most likely to see in each instance: this may mean one version in the address, another in the directions on how to get there. We have no political agenda!

Practical Matters

Meals

Times - The Spanish eat much later than we do: breakfast often doesn't get going until 9am, lunch is generally eaten from 2pm and dinner is rarely served before 8.30pm.

Breakfast - The 'Continental' in larger hotels tends to be uninspired: coffee, toast (perhaps cakes), butter and jam. Marmalade is a rare sight and freshly squeezed juice is the exception. But few places would object if you supplement your meal with your own fruit.

Many Spaniards breakfast on pâtés and olive oil, perhaps with garlic and certainly with tomato in Catalonia. Your hotelier may assume that you prefer a blander, more northern-European offering. So do check.

Tea tends to be poor so take a few tea bags with you and ask for hot water. *Té* in Spain is normally served without milk. Ask for it *con leche* if you like it with milk or *con limón* for a slice of lemon. Bars nearly always serve camomile tea (*manzanilla*) - it can be a useful evening drink because coffee is nearly always very strong.

Lunch and Dinner - The daily set meal - *el menú del día* - is normally available at both lunch and dinner although waiters will often simply present you with the à la carte menu. But do ask for it: it tends to be great value and will often have fresher ingredients. Many restaurants serve only à la carte at weekends.

Tapas and raciones - A *tapa* is a small plate of hot or cold food served with an aperitif before lunch or dinner: it remains an essential part of eating out in Spain. It could be a plate of olives, anchovies, cheese, spicy chorizo

Introduction

sausage, fried fish... portions vary as does the choice. It is a delicious way to try out local specialities and even if your Spanish is poor, don't worry - *tapas* are often laid out along the bar for you to gesticulate at. If you would like a plateful of any particular tapa then ask for *una ración de* e.g. *queso* (cheese). Most bars will also serve you a half portion - *una media ración*.

The Spanish are not yet very vegetarian-conscious. Indeed, vegetables rarely appear and when they do they are often boiled beyond recognition. So do as the locals do and increase the salad and fruit intake to compensate.

Tipping

Leaving a tip is still the norm in Spain. In bars you are given your change on a small saucer; leave a couple of small coins. For lunch or dinner 5-10% is fine but you would rarely be made to feel embarrassed if you don't tip. Taxi drivers don't all expect a tip.

Bathrooms

In some of the simpler hotels in Spain baths vary from half to full length. And when packing do put in a bar of soap; the more simple 'hostal' type places often only have those minute throw-away soaps. Pack slippers too - winters, even in the south, can be very cold and buildings often have marble or tiled floors.

Seasons

When we give a price range the lower is the Low Season, the higher the High Season. There may also be a Mid Season price. In most of Spain, High Season includes Easter, Christmas, public holidays and the summer. Some hotels (especially those in the big cities) classify weekends as High and weekdays as Low.

Public Holidays

January 1st, January 6th, Good Friday, Easter Monday, May 1st, Corpus Christi (usually early June), June 24th, July 25th, August 15th, October 12th, November 1st, December 6th, December 8th, December 25th.

Booking

Try to book well ahead if you plan to be in Spain during holidays. August is best avoided unless you are heading for one of the more remote places in this book. Many hotels will ask you for a credit card number when you make your reservation. And remember to let smaller hotels and B&Bs know if you want dinner.

Introduction

There's a bilingual booking form you can use, at the back of the book. Hotels often send back a signed or stamped copy as confirmation. E-mail culture is still in its early days in Spain. Hotels don't necessarily assume that you are expecting a speedy reply!

Arrival/Registration/Checking out times

Many city hotels will only hold a reservation until the early evening, even though you might have booked months in advance. So ring ahead to let them know if you are planning to arrive late. (It remains law that you should register on arrival in a hotel. Hotels have no right, once you have done so, to keep your passport.)

Payment

The most commonly accepted credit cards are Visa, MasterCard and Eurocard. Larger places will probably take Diner's Club and Amex. Many smaller places don't take plastic because of high bank charges. But there is nearly always a cash dispenser (ATM) close at hand; again Visa, MasterCard and Eurocard are the most useful.

Euros

The Euro will be introduced into Spain during the period of this guide's validity and at first will operate in parallel with the peseta. By 2002 it will be fully operational. We include a conversion chart at the end of this book.

Plugs

Virtually all sockets now have 220/240 AC voltage (usually 2-pin). Pack an adaptor if you travel with electrical appliances.

Driving and car hire

Foreign number plates attract attention in the big cities so never leave your car with valuables inside. Use a public car park; they are cheap and safe.

It is compulsory to have in the car: a spare set of bulbs, a warning triangle and a basic first aid kit. (Spain has good terms for car hire - for a small one £100, or $140 US, for a week.)

Public transport

Trains, buses and taxis are very cheap in Spain. You meet people, and get much more of a feel for the country by travelling this way. Spain has a high-speed rail link between Madrid and Sevilla which gets you down South in under two and a half hours and a high speed link will soon be in place between Catalonia and Madrid. Some regional lines would bring a tear to any rail buff's eye; the journey between Ronda and Algeciras particularly.

Introduction

Spanish Tourist Offices

UK - 57/58 St. James Street, London SW1A 1LD. Tel: 0207 486 8077
USA - 665 Fifth Avenue, New York 10022. Tel: 212 759 8822

The Alhambra

A visit is a highlight of any trip to Spain. But tickets must be booked in advance.

Environment

We reduce our impact on the environment by recycling and:

- Planting trees to compensate for our carbon emissions (as calculated by Edinburgh University); we are officially a 'carbon-neutral company'.
- Encouraging staff use of bicycles (they're given free) and car-sharing.
- Celebrating the use of organic, home and locally produced food.
- Publishing books that support, in however small a way, the rural economy and small-scale businesses.

Subscriptions

Owners pay to appear in this guide; their fee goes towards the high production costs of an all-colour book. We only include places and owners that we find special. It is not possible for anyone to buy their way in!

Special Places to Stay on the Internet

8000 people a month 'visit' the site, and we think you should join them! Not only do they have access to honest and up-to-date information about hundreds of places to stay across Europe, but they can buy any of our books via our window on the world wide web: **www.sawdays.co.uk**

Disclaimer

We make no claims to pure objectivity in judging our Special Places to Stay. They are here because we like them. Our opinions and tastes are ours alone and this book is a statement of them; we hope that you will share them.

We have done our utmost to get our facts right but apologise unreservedly for any mistakes that may have crept in. Sometimes, too, prices shift, usually upwards and 'things' change. Please tell us about any errors or changes.

And finally

Thank you to all those who have taken the time to share your opinions with us. You have helped make this edition of the book even better than the last!

Please let us have your comments; there is a report form at the back of this book. Or e-mail us at spain@sawdays.co.uk

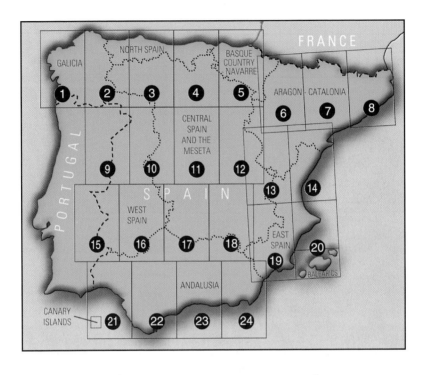

Guide to our map page numbers

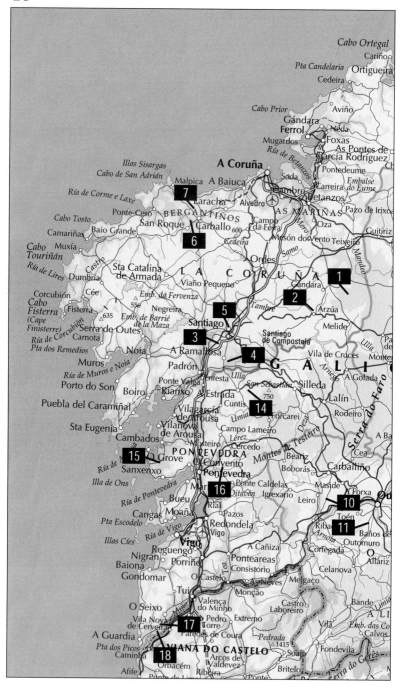

Map 1

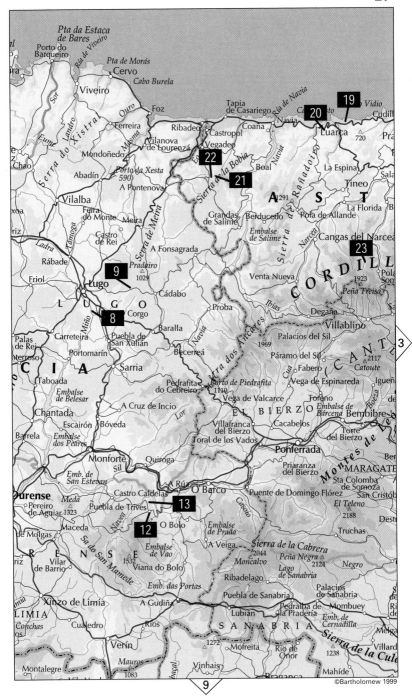

Map 2

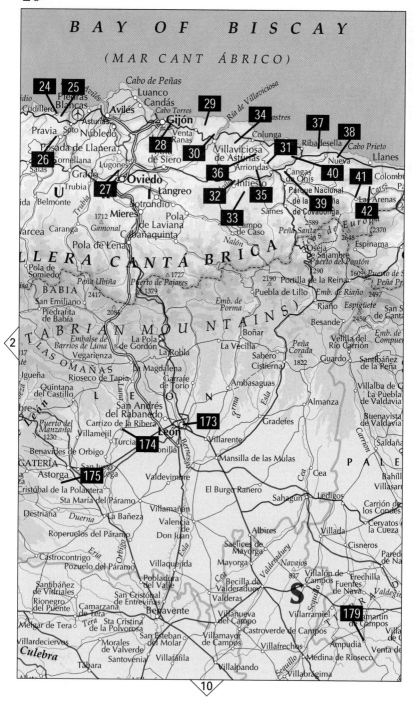

Map 3

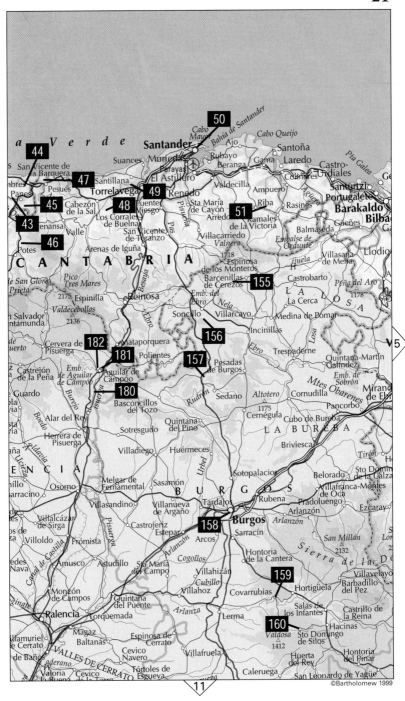

Map 4

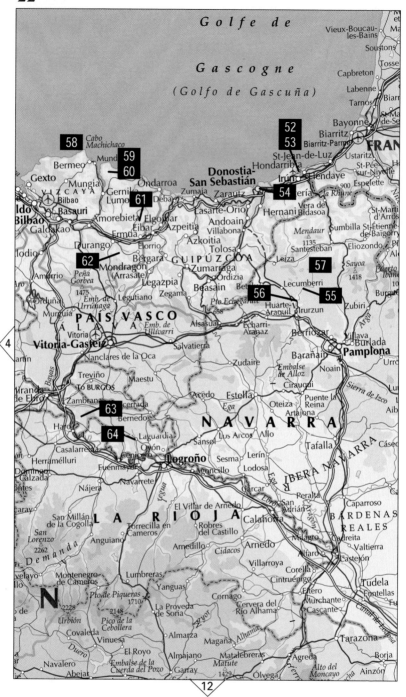

Map 5

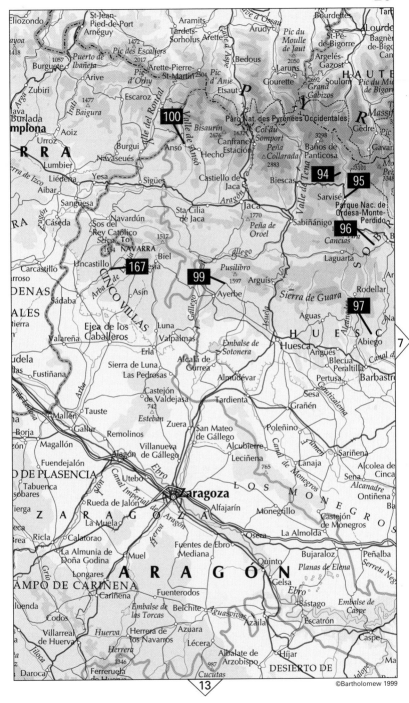

Eliozondo

St-Jean-
Pied-de-Port
Arréguy

Aramits
Tardets-
Sorholus
Arette

Vallée d'Ossau

Bourdettes

Pic du
Moulle
de Jaut

St-Pé-
de-Bigorre

Lourdes
Bagnères-
de-Bigor
Can

Arudy

1472
Pic des Escaliers
2017

Pic
d'Orhy

2504

Pic
d'Anie

Etsaut

Bedous

Larún

Laruns

Argelès-
Gazost

2050

2692

Grand
Gabizos

Soulon

Pic du Mi
de Bigor

HAUTE

P

Parc Nat. des Pyrénées Occidentales

R

Massif

1418

Zubiri

Puerto de
Ibañeta

Arive

1057

Arette-Pierre-
St-Martin

Escaroz

1477

Baïgura

100

Valle del Roncal

Ansó

Bisaurin
2676

1632

Col du
Somport

Canfranc-
Estación

Hecho

Peña
Collarada
2883

Castiello de
Jaca

3298

Peña de
Panticosa

Biescas

94

3101

Gavar

95

Mo
Per
3348

Burguete

Burlada

mplona

RRA

Urroz
Lumbier
Liédena
Aibar
Sangüesa

Navaseués

Yesa

Burgui

Sigües

Santa Cilia
de Jaca

Valle de Ansó

Aragón

Jaca

1770

Peña de
Oroel

Sabiñánigo

Sarvisé

Parque Nac. de
Ordesa-Monte-
Perdido

96

Cancias

Laguarta

Valle de Tena

Cáseda

Navardún

Sos del
Rey Católico

Selva To
1154

1517

NAVARRA

Biel

Gállego

Pusilibro

Arguís

Ayerbe

1597

167

Uncastillo

Sierra de Guara

Rodellar

97

Carcastillo

DENAS

ALES
tierra

Sádaba

Asín

Cinco Villas

Arba de

99

Luna
Valpalmas

Aguas

Abiego

Na

HUESC

Ejea de los
Caballeros

Gállego

Valareña

udela
las

Fustiñana

Sierra de Luna
Las Pedrosas

Erla

Alcalá de
Gurrea

Almudévar

Embalse de
Sotonera

Huesca

Angüés
Blecua
Peraltilla

Pertusa

Canal d

Barbastr

Mallén

Tauste

Arba

Castejón
de Valdejasa

742

Esteban

Tardienta

Sesa

Grañén

Gállego

Isuela

Gudialema

Borja
zón

Magallón

Remolinos

Zuera

San Mateo
de Gállego

Poleñino

Sariñena

Alcolea de
Cinca

Fuendejalón

Alagón

Villanueva
de Gállego

Alcubierre

Leciñena

Canal de Monegros

Lanaja

Sena

Alcanadre

Ontiñena

Ba

O DE PLASENCIA

Tabuenca
sobares

Utebo

Ebro

Canal Imperial de Aragón

Zaragoza

LOS

765

MONEGROS

Castejón
de Monegros

ierga

ZARA

Rueda de Jalón

Huerva

Alfajarín

Monegrillo

La Almolda

La Muela

eca
rea

Ricla

Calatorao

GOZA

Osera

Huerva

Muel

Fuentes de Ebro
Mediana

ARAGÓN

La Almunia de
Doña Godina

Longares

Quinto

Gelsa

Planas de Elena

Bujaraloz

Peñalba

Ebro

Serreta Neg

luenda

AMPO DE CARIÑENA

Cariñena

Fuenterodos

Codos

Villarreal
de Huerva

Embalse de
las Torcas

Belchite

Aguasvivas

Azaila

Sástago

Embalse de
Caspe

Caspe

Huerva

Herrera de
los Navarros

Azuara

Lécera

Herrera

1346

Albalate de
Arzobispo

Híjar

DESIERTO DE

Ma

Daroca

Jiloca

987

Cucutas

Ferreruela
de Huerva

7

©Bartholomew 1999

Map 6

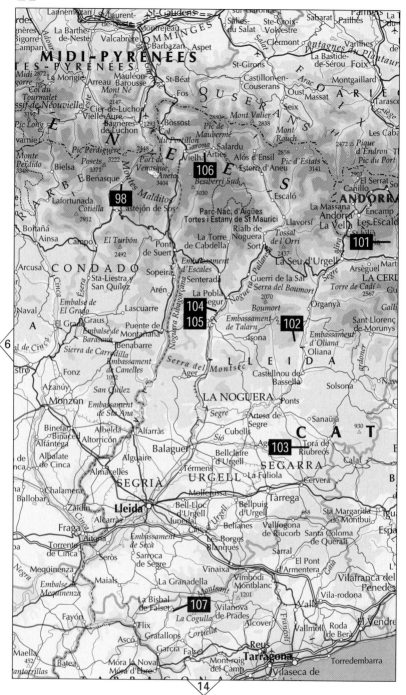

Map 7

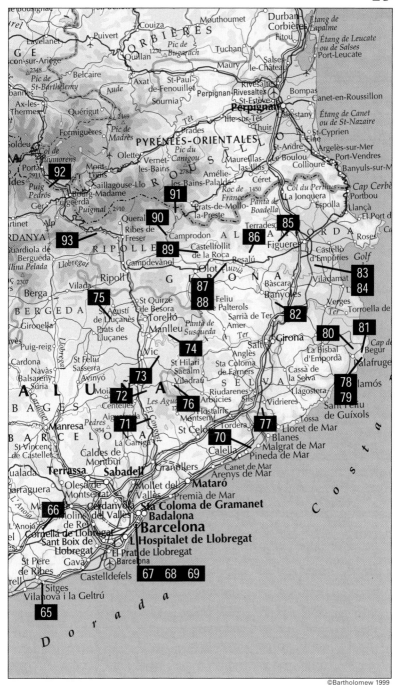

Map 8

This map page shows portions of Portugal and Spain including the regions of VILA REAL, BRAGANÇA, GUARDA, CASTELO BRANCO, and ABADENGO.

Selected place names visible:
Montalegre, Vila Verde da Raia, Chaves, Boticas, Vidago, Vilarandelo, Valpaços, Carrazedo de Montenegro, Ribeira de Pena, Vila Pouca de Aguiar, Murça, Vila Verde, Mateus, Sabrosa, Santa Marta de Penaguião, Favaios, Alijó, Peso da Régua, Armamar, Lamego, São João da Pesqueira, Tabuaço, Moimenta da Beira, Sernancelhe, Penedono, Meda, Sarzedo, Vila Nova de Paiva, Castanheira, Aguiar da Beira, Trancoso, Satão, Penalva do Castelo, Mangualde, Fornos de Algodres, Celorico da Beira, Gouveia, Seia, Guarda, Valhelhas, Manteigas, Belmonte, Teixoso, Covilhã, Unhais da Serra, Paúl, Silvares, Fundão, São Vicente da Beira, Orvalho, Alpedrinha, Medelim, Monfortinho, Escalos de Cima, Idanha-a-Nova, Alcains, Ladoeiro, Zebreira, Salgueiro

Vinhais, Bragança, Mahíde, Riofrío de Aliste, Trabazos, Alcañices, Edrosa, Rebordelo, Torre de Dona Chama, Quintanilha, Milhão, Macedo de Cavaleiros, Izeda, Vimioso, Miranda do Douro, Mirandela, Bornes, Peredo, Morais, Algoso, Fariza de Sayago, Sendim, Fermoselle, Trinidade, Mogadouro, Trabanca, Aldeadávila de la Ribera, Alfândega da Fé, Vila Flor, Carvalho de Egas, Carrazeda de Ansiães, Torre de Moncorvo, Carviçais, Fornos, Freixo de Espada à Cinta, Barruecopardo, Villase de los Rey, Vila Nova de Foz Côa, Touça, Longroiva, La Fregeneda, Barca de Alva, Vitigudino, Villasdar, Figueira de Castelo Rodrigo, Hinojosa de Duero, Cerralbo, Lumbrales, Bogajo, La Fuente de San Esteban, San Felices de los Gallegos, Vila Franca das Naves, Pinhel, Freixedas, Almeida, Castillejo de Martín Viejo, Sancti-Spiritus, Pinzio, Vilar Formoso, Fuentes de Oñoro, Ciudad-Rodrigo, Parada, Adão, Espeja, Ituero de Azaba, El Bodón, Alfaiates, Souto, La Albergueria de Argañán, Fuenteguinaldo, Nuñomoral, Villasrubias, LAS HURDES, Descargamaría, Caminomoris, Pinofranqueado, Gata, Valverde del Fresno, Eljas, Hoyos, Villanueva de la Sierra, de Granadi, Pozuelo de Zarzón, Capinha, Meimoa, Perales del Puerto, Moraleja, Emb. del Borbollón, Monteher, Penamacor, Aldeia de João Pires, Coria, Carcaboso, CASTELO BRANCO, EXTRE, Alcafozes, Zarza la Mayor, Torrejoncillo, Ceclavín, Puerto de los Castaños, Muradal

Route markers: 134, 133

Map 9

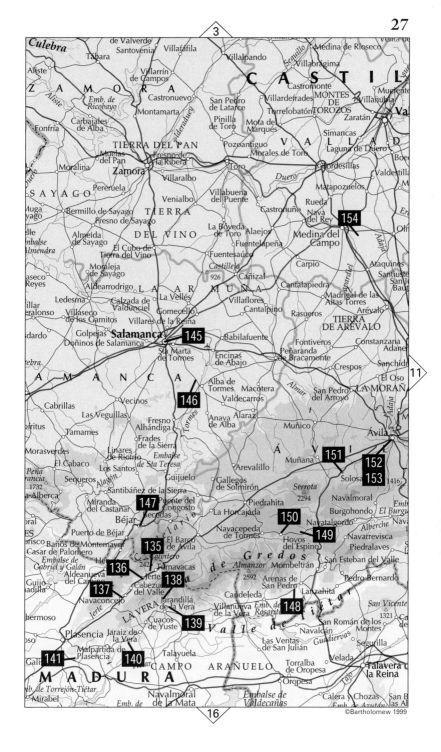

Map 10

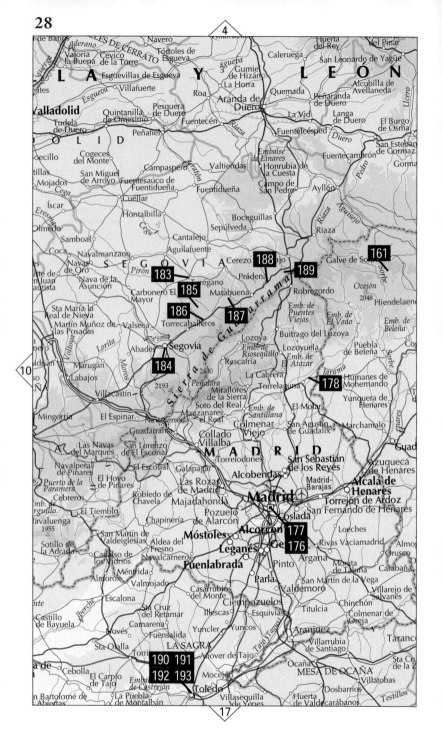

Map 11

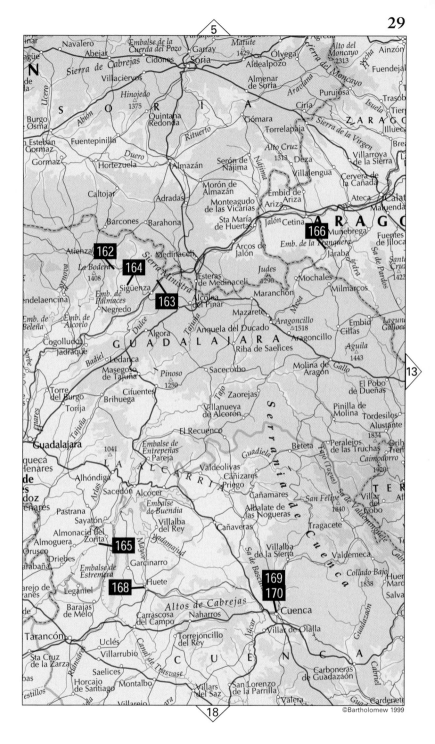

©Bartholomew 1999

Map 12

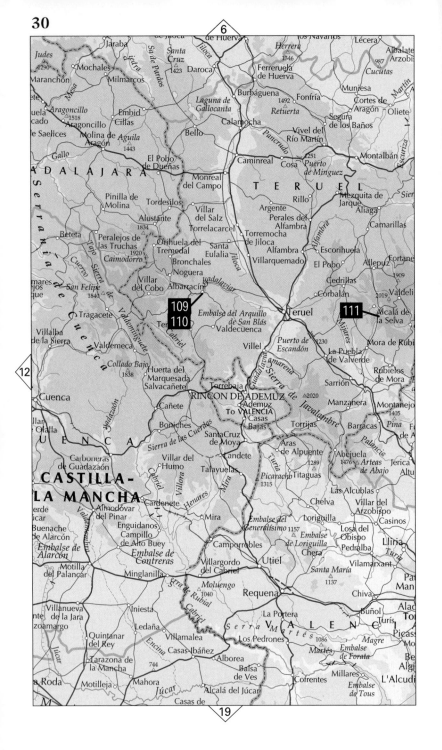

Map 13

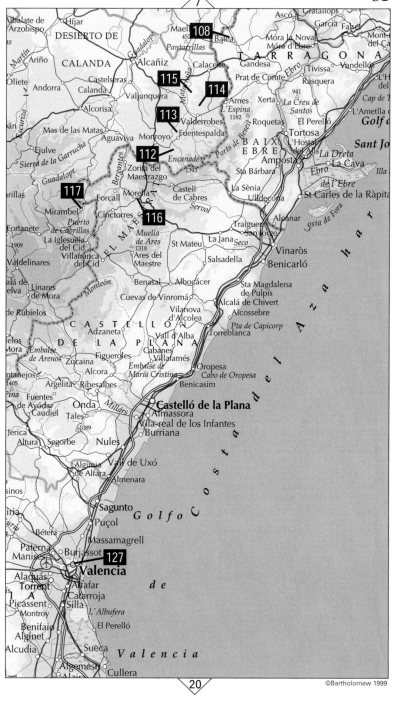

Map 14

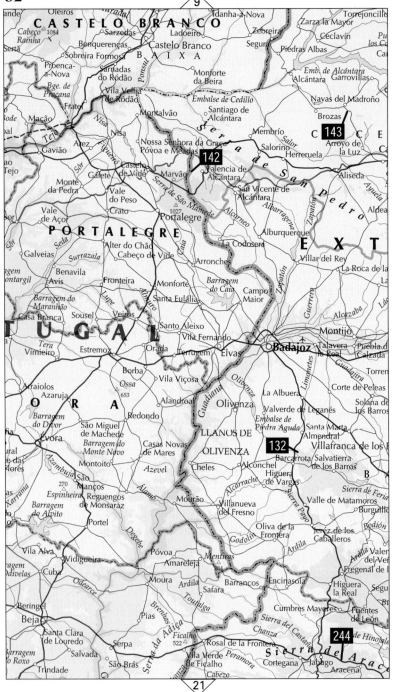

Map 15

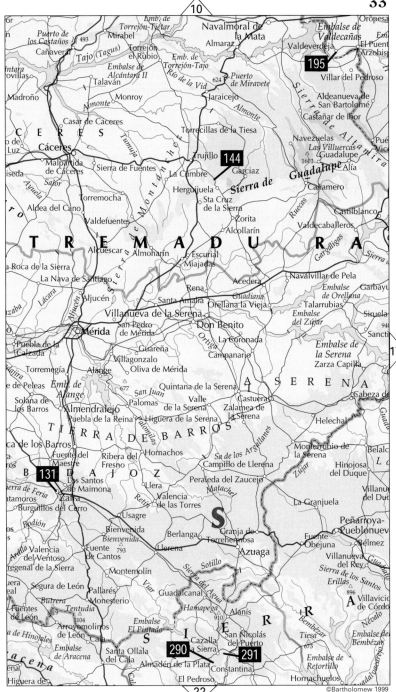

Map 16

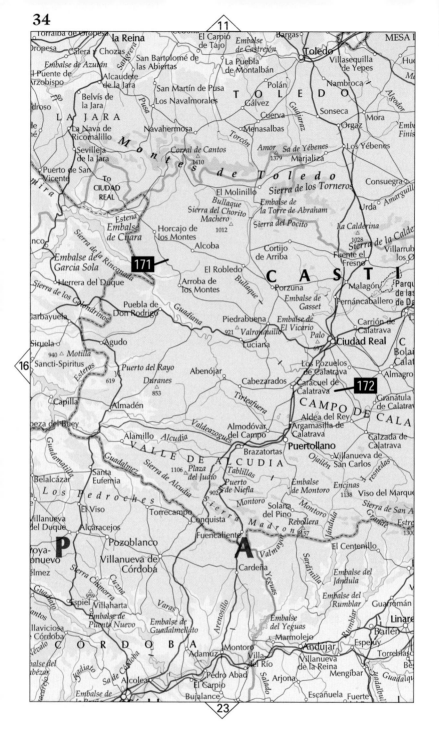

Map 17

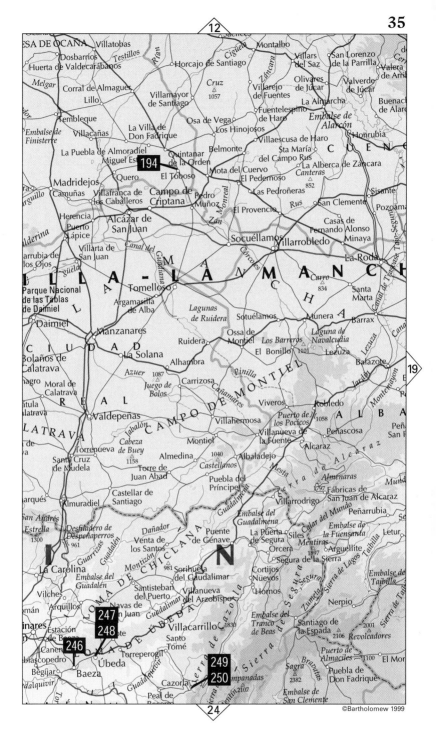

Map 18

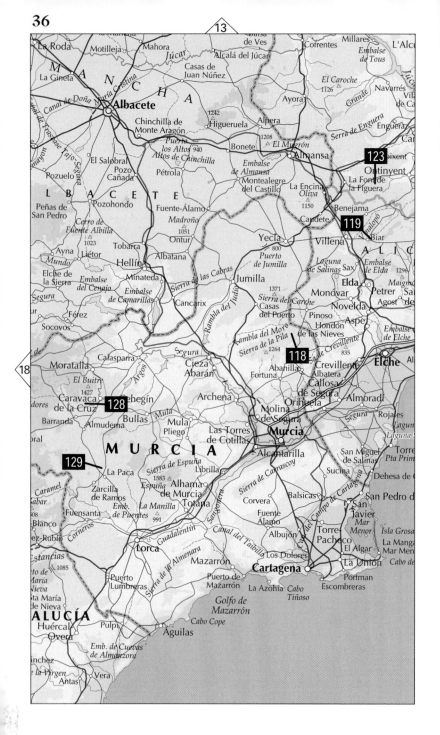

Map 19

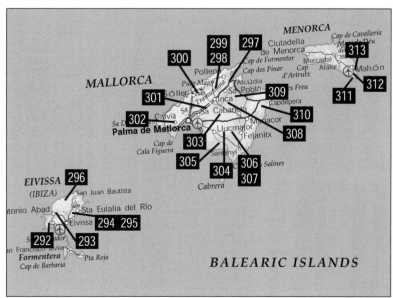

Map 20

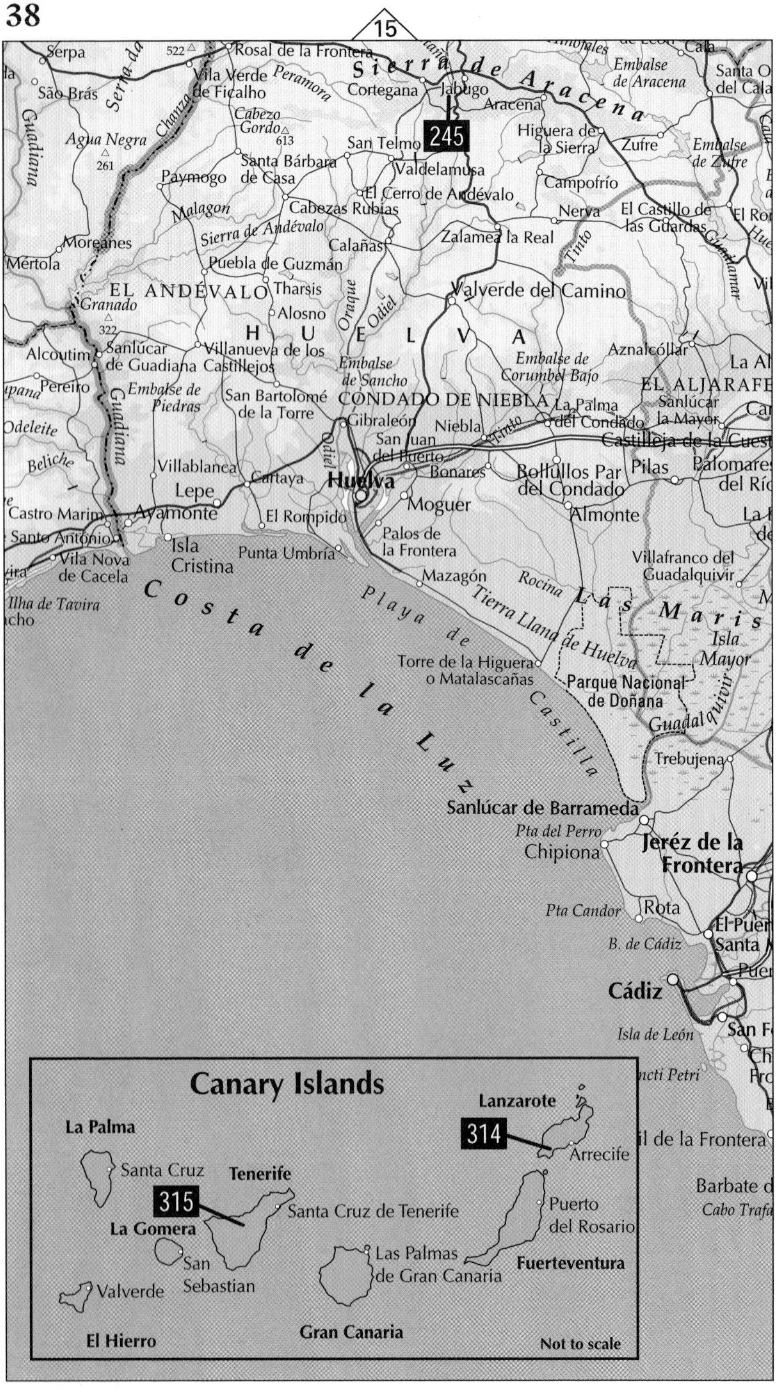

15

Serpa
São Brás
Agua Negra
261
Moreanes
Mértola
Granado
322
Alcoutim
Odeleite
Pereiro
Beliche
Castro Marim
Santo António
Vila Nova
de Cacela
Ilha de Tavira
acho

522
Rosal de la Frontera
Vila Verde
de Ficalho
Peramora
Cortegana
Jabugo
Aracena

Sierra de Aracena
Embalse
de Aracena
Santa O
del Cala

Cabezo
Gordo
613
San Telmo
245
Higuera de
la Sierra
Zufre
Embalse
de Zufre

Paymogo
Santa Bárbara
de Casa
Valdelamusa
Campofrío

Malagón
El Cerro de Andévalo
Nerva
El Castillo de
las Guardas
El Ro

Sierra de Andévalo
Cabezas Rubias
Zalamea la Real

Puebla de Guzmán
Tharsis
Calañas

EL ANDÉVALO
Alosno
Valverde del Camino

H   U   E   L   V   A

Sanlúcar
de Guadiana
Villanueva de los
Castillejos
Embalse
de Sancho
Embalse de
Corumbel Bajo
Aznalcóllar
La Al

Embalse de
Piedras
San Bartolomé
de la Torre
CONDADO DE NIEBLA
La Palma
Sanlúcar
la Mayor
EL ALJARAFE
Car

Villablanca
Gibraleón
Niebla
del Condado
Castilleja de la Cuest

Lepe
Cartaya
San Juan
del Puerto
Bonares
Bollullos Par
del Condado
Pilas
Palomares
del Río

Ayamonte
Huelva
Moguer
Almonte
La

Isla
Cristina
El Rompido
Punta Umbría
Palos de
la Frontera
Villafranco del
Guadalquivir

Mazagón
Rocina
Las   Maris

Playa   de
Tierra Llana de Huelva
Isla
Mayor

Torre de la Higuera
o Matalascañas
Parque Nacional
de Doñana
Guadalquivir

Costa   de   la   Luz
Castilla
Trebujena

Sanlúcar de Barrameda

Pta del Perro
Chipiona
**Jeréz de la
Frontera**

Pta Candor
Rota

B. de Cádiz
El Puer
Santa

Cádiz
Pu

Isla de León
San F

| **Canary Islands** | | |

La Palma

Lanzarote
314

Santa Cruz
Tenerife
Arrecife

315
Santa Cruz de Tenerife

La Gomera
Puerto
del Rosario

San
Sebastian
Las Palmas
de Gran Canaria
Fuerteventura

Valverde

El Hierro
Gran Canaria
Not to scale

il de la Frontera

Barbate d
Cabo Trafa

Map 21

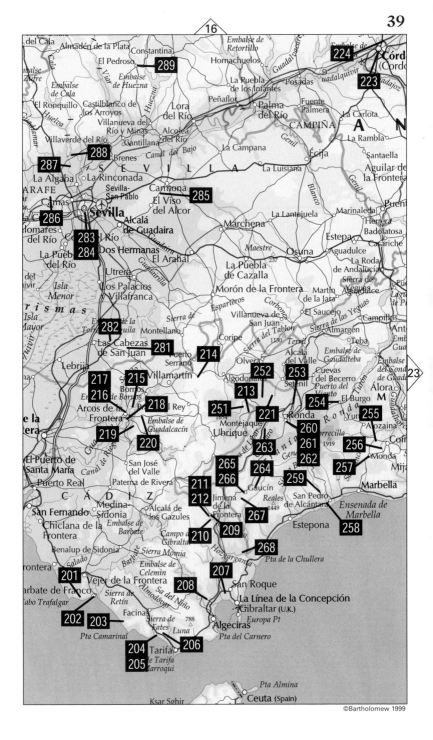

Map 22

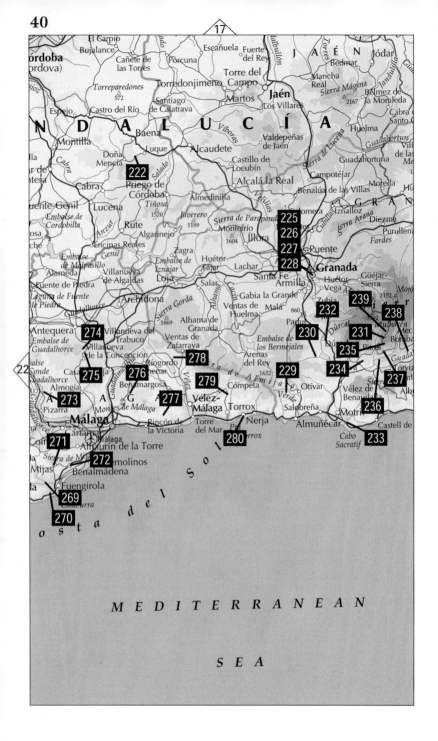

Map 23

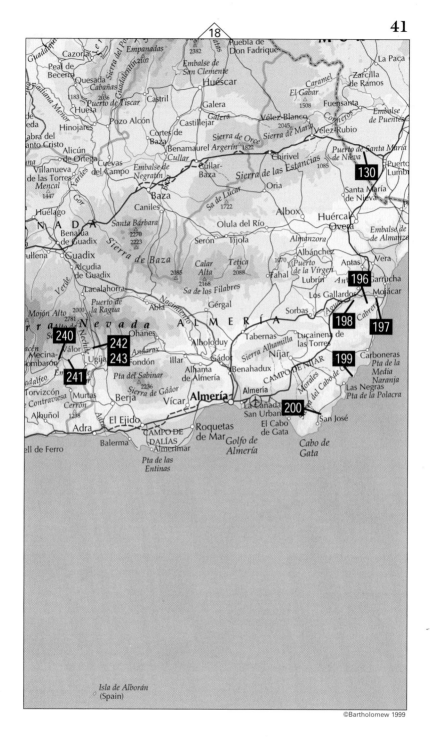

Map 24

La Coruña
•

Lugo
•

Orense
•

Pontevedra
•

Galicia

"The first condition of understanding a foreign country is to smell it"
Rudyard Kipling

Hotel San Marcus

Plaza Porta Sobrado de los Monjes	**Tel:** 981 787527
15132 Sobrado	**Fax:** 981 787680
La Coruña	

Manuel Carreira

Manuel's welcome is effusive and genuine. He loves Spain but after years in London loves the English and their language as dearly. He has now come home to create his Shangri-La beside the pilgrim's path to Santiago and opposite one of the oldest Cistercian monasteries in Europe. It is a smart, modern hotel of human proportions. Manuel treats every guest with the personal attention that he considers basic to the art of hostelry. His rooms are like wedding cakes – you might not choose the rather showy flourishes but few of us would fail to appreciate their comfort. Manuel thought long about every last detail when he designed and furnished the hotel. Furniture was specially made, bathrooms carpeted – and the Laura Ashley fabrics hark back to his days in Albion. Room 16 is particularly grand with a great canopied bed whilst another four rooms have a sitting area in the covered gallery. But what makes a stay here really memorable is the food – lots of Galician specialities with fish and seafood the mainstays. Those map-book people rate it and our readers do, too.

Rooms: 11 with bath or shower & wc; 1 suite
Price: Single 4000 Pts; Double/Twin 6000 Pts; Suite 8000 Pts.
Breakfast: 500 Pts.
Meals: Lunch/Dinner 2500 Pts (M), approx. 3500 Pts (C).
Closed: 22 December-1 March

From Lugo NVI west towards La Coruña.
At La Castellana, left onto LC231 to Tejeiro, and then Sobrado. Hotel opposite monastery.

Map no: 1   Entry no: 1

Pazo de Sedor

Castañeda
15819 Arzua
La Coruña

Tel: 981 193248
Fax: 981 193248

María Jesús Saavedra Pereira

One of a number of grand Galician manors (*pazos*) open to guests, Pazo de Sedor is a delectable place to stay if you're on the road to or from Santiago – or anywhere, come to that. It is an imposing, 18th-century country house surrounded by wooded hillsides and fields of maize and grazing cattle. Inside, you get a definite sense of its aristocratic past: the rooms are cavernous and a broad balustraded staircase joins the two floors. The building's most memorable feature is the enormous open fireplace (*lareira*) that spans one whole wall of the dining room with bread-ovens at each side. The bedrooms are a real treat; they are high-ceilinged, decorated with family antiques, have embroidered bedcovers and curtains and shining parquet floors. Half have their own balcony. One room has beautiful Deco beds; all are big enough to take an extra bed and the apartment has full facilities for the disabled. Meals are as authentic as the house: all the flavours of Galicia with many of the vegetables home-grown and meats free-range. Try the local cheese and cold sausage.

Rooms: 6 with bath & wc; 1 apartment.
Price: Double/Twin 11000 Pts incl. VAT.
Breakfast: 600 Pts.
Meals: Lunch/Dinner 2000 Pts (M) by prior arrangment.
Closed: Never.

From Lugo N540, then N547, towards Santiago de Compostela. 400m past km57 post, turn right to Pazo.

Casa Grande de Cornide

Cornide (Calo-Teo)
15886 Santiago de Compostela
La Coruña

Tel: 981 805599 or 981 505741
Fax: 981 805751
E-mail: casagcornide@teleline.es

María Jesús Castro Rivas

This very special B&B just 15 minutes drive from Santiago is surrounded by exuberant Galician green. Casa Grande might be likened to a good claret: refined, select and worth paying a bit more for. José Ramón and María Jesús are both lecturers (he writes books, including one called *The Way to Compostela*) and a love of culture is evident throughout their home. It has a large collection of modern Galician paintings, hundreds of ceramic pots, a huge library and decoration that is a spicy cocktail of old and new: exposed granite, designer lamps, wooden ceilings, and – all over – the paintings. A place to come to read, to paint in the beautiful mature garden (you may be surprised to see so many palms this far north) or to cycle out from the house (four bikes are provided free of charge for guests). The studied décor of the lounges and library is also in the bedrooms and suites, some of which are in a separate building. They have all mod cons and the same mix of modern and old furnishing; there are books, ornaments, more paintings and little details, like handmade tiles in the bathrooms, that all help create a special feel. "A glorious place" enthused one reader.

Rooms: 6 with bath & wc; 4 suites.
Price: Double/Twin 11000-13000 Pts; Suite 13000-15000 Pts.
Breakfast: 950 Pts.
Meals: None available.
Closed: January.

From Santiago N550 towards Pontevedra. After 7km, just after Cepsa petrol station, turn left and follow signs for 2km to Cornide.

Map no: 1

Entry no: 3

Pazo Cibran

15885 San Xulian de Sales (Santiago de Compostela)   **Tel:** 981 511515
La Coruña

Fax: 981 511515
E-mail: cibran@arrakis.es
Web: www.arrakis.es/~cibran

Carmen Iglesias Gaceo

We could tell you about the 18th-century history and period furniture of this house, its glorious 15,000-m² garden, its vine-covered walkways and bamboo woods, its entwined camellias and 200-year-old trees, its delightful chapel and library where you can look at ancient books. Maybe we should mention the works of modern art, the converted stables or the fresh flowers everywhere. But no. The true spirit of this elegant house is personified by Carmen, (Maica to those who get to know her), a relaxed and welcoming hostess. Here she is, sharing her family home with people who come as strangers but leave as friends. Her enthusiasm for Cibran and its surroundings is underpinned by a true love of the history and beauty of this area. She has excellent local information to guide you to the heart of nearby Santiago, to Pazo de Oca, the Versailles of Galicia, or on a country ramble. Although no dinner is available, eating at the Michelin-rated Restaurant Roberto only 50 metres away is a mouthwatering experience and Maica may well join you. A big and bountiful breakfast is served by Lola, the laughing, twinkling cook/housemaid. Your stay here will be as friendly and relaxed as she is.

Rooms: 11 with bath & wc.
Price: Double/Twin 13000 Pts.
Breakfast: 1000 Pts.
Meals: Dinner 2000 Pts (M).
Closed: Never.

From Santiago N525 towards Ourense. At km 336, by petrol station, right for San Xulian de Sales. Here, at end of village, Pazo Cibran is signposted to the right.

Entry no: 4   Map no: 1

Hotel As Artes

Travesia de Dos Puertas 2
15707 Santiago de Compostela
La Coruña

Tel: 981 555254
Fax: 981 577823
E-mail: recepcion@asartes.com
Web: www.asartes.com

Esther Mateos & Carlos Elizechea

Where would anybody, pilgrim or tourist, want to stay when visiting Santiago? As close as possible, of course, to the great Cathedral of Saint James. So look no further than this delightful small hotel 50 yards from the great edifice. The hotel is the creation of two exceptionally friendly Galicians, Esther and Mateos, inspired by a night they spent in an old Parisian hotel. They were so taken by the experience that they decided to open a similarly intimate hotel in Santiago. Their guest rooms look to the Seven Arts for their leitmotiv. No numbers here: instead choose between spending a night in the company of Rodin, Dante, Vivaldi, Gaudí, Picasso, Duncan or Chaplin. All rooms are stylishly furnished with parquet floors, repro wrought iron bedsteads, rugs, French café-style chairs and tables: print motifs and paintings evoke each particular 'art'. All are fantastic value but what makes this place 'work' is the care and generosity of your hosts. At breakfast you are treated to fresh orange juice, fruit salads, cold meats, cakes and different breads. For other meals there are dozens of restaurants just a short walk away. Brilliant value and an equally brilliant position.

Rooms: 7 with bath & wc.
Price: Double/Twin 9500-11000 Pts.
Breakfast: 900 Pts.
Meals: None available.
Closed: Never.

Arriving in Santiago head for the Praza do Obradoiro. Just to the left of Cathedral is Rua de San Francisco. Hotel 50m past cathedral on the right.

Pazo de Souto

Lugar de la Torre 1
15106 Sisamo-Carballo
La Coruña

Tel: 981 756065
Fax: 981 756191
E-mail: reservas@pazodosouto.com
Web: www.pazodosouto.com

José Taibo Suárez

Since Carlos and his father José opened their fine old Galician manor house to guests they have gradually established a reputation for being one of the very best places to stay in this little-known corner of Galicia. It has stood here for 300 years near the rugged north coast, lost among fields of maize and wooded glades. The vast sitting room has a *lareira* (inglenook) fireplace, exposed granite and heavy old beams. The dining area, similarly designed, has tables up on a gallery, all of it subtly lit and there is a very cosy bar area. Outside is a large garden and from the terrace there are fine views across the surrounding farmland. A splendid granite staircase leads up to the guest rooms – we preferred those on the first floor to the rather smaller attic ones. They are attractively furnished with a lot of twenties beds and dressers and it is all very spick and span. Lots of local folk were dining there when we visited (fresh fish daily from the nearby fishing village of Malpica), always a good sign. All this and the wild beauty of the north coast besides. Carlos is most helpful and has impeccable English. It is hard to find more charming or kinder hosts.

Rooms: 5 with bath & wc; 6 suites.
Price: Double/Twin 7500-10000 Pts;
Suite 9000-12000 Pts.
Breakfast: 600 Pts.
Meals: Lunch/Dinner 1750 Pts (M),
3500 Pts (C).
Closed: Never.

From Santiago C545 towards Santa Comba to Portomouro. Here follow signs to Carballo and in village centre at Plaza de Galicia follow signs for Malpica. Shortly, after passing petrol sation, turn left towards Sisamo. Here continue past church and Souto is signed to the right.

Entry no: 6   Map no: 1

Casa Entremuros

Cances Grandes 77   **Tel:** 981 757099 or 639 555440
15107 Carballo   **Fax:** 981 703877
La Coruña   **E-mail:** entremuros@eresmas.com
                                         Web: www.finisterrae.com/turural/muros.htm

Santiago Luaces de La-Herrán

The wild, indented coastline of the Rías Altas is little known beyond Galicia. But here are long stretches of fine, sandy beaches, hidden coves and a number of old fishing villages where the sea food is among the best in Spain. Santiago and Rosa will help to unlock the region's secrets for you if you stay at their solid old granite house which they have recently opened to their first paying guests. They have created four bedrooms and very handsome they are, too: shining parquet-clad floors, fitted wardrobes, carefully restored antique beds and good bathrooms. Number three is the best, we felt, with its antique trunk and two large wardrobes. There is a large, light-filled lounge with a wood-burner in the huge *lareira* (inglenook) and dresser. You breakfast in the old kitchen which still has the original granite sink; Rosa makes fresh fruit juices and there is local cheese and honey and cake. A warm, quiet and unassuming place to stay: no meals apart from breakfast but Casa Elias is only a mile away – you can have a memorable meal there at any time of year.

Rooms: 4 with bath & wc.
Price: Double/Twin 6000-8000 Pts.
Breakfast: 500 Pts.
Meals: None available.
Closed: Never.

From Santiago de Compostela, by the Alameda, take the road for 'Hospital General'. Continue on to Carballo, then on towards Malpica to Cances. House is signposted by petrol station.

Map no: 1   Entry no: 7

Casa Grande da Fervenza

A Fervenza-O Corgo   **Tel:** 982 150610
27364 Lugo   **Fax:** 982 151610
Lugo

Juan Pérez Orozco

The river Miño laps right up to the walls of Casa Grande de Fervenza and this ancient mill is girdled round by no less than 20 hectares of magnificent old woods of alder, oak and birch, beautiful and precious enough to have been declared a Nature Reserve. The dining room is in the oldest part and dates from the 17th century; most memorable is a rocky waterfall which provides a lovely visual backdrop to your meals (Fervenza comes from the Galician word 'ferver', the sound made by rushing water). The culinary philosophy is to give you the sort of food which was around when the building first saw the light like hearty Galician hot-pots or rich rabbit stews; wines are the region's best. Bedrooms are across the way in the house where the miller once lived. Restoration has been meticulous in its respect for local tradition and lore yet you get all your creature comforts. Antiques have been meticulously restored, rugs woven on local looms, there are linen curtains, chestnut beams and floors and hand-painted sinks: your room will be quiet, attractive and comfortable. Casa Grande is both museum and hotel and pays homage to the rich cultural traditions of Galicia. *A Rusticae hotel.*

Rooms: 7 with bath & wc; 1 suite.
Price: Double/Twin 10000 Pts; Suite 14000 Pts.
Breakfast: 700 Pts.
Meals: Lunch/Dinner 2000 Pts (M), 3000 Pts (C).
Closed: Never.

From Lugo NVI towards Madrid. After 4km in Conturiz turn right by Hotel Torre de Núñez towards Páramo. Continue for 11km then turn right at sign; 1km to hotel.

Pazo de Villabad
Villabad
27122 Castroverde
Lugo

Tel: 982 313000/313051
Fax: 982 312063

Teresa Arana

In a delectably quiet corner of Galicia, Pazo de Villabad is worth a long diversion. This fine old manor house is just beside the village church: it has a rather sober façade but once you pass beneath the fine granite entrance you enter a truly charming family home. All of the furniture and paintings that decorate the lofty bedrooms, sitting and dining rooms are family heirlooms. There are stacks of lovely pieces in the big, airy bedrooms – old brass or walnut beds, dressers and old tables; in the corridors there are statues, a *chaise longue* and family portraits above the grandest of stairwells. Endearingly, the bedrooms are named after beloved family members – Aunt Leonor, Great-grandmama. But most seductive is the breakfast room with its gallery and enormous *lareira* (inglenook) fireplace where you feast on cheeses, home-made cakes and jams and pots of good coffee. The heart and soul of it all is Señora Teresa Abraira, a hugely entertaining and sprightly lady, so determined to get it right that she studied rural tourism in France before opening her own house. Meet her and share a truly wonderful home and gardens. "Totally special, a fascinating place" wrote a reader.

Rooms: 6 with bath & wc.
Price: Single 10000 Pts; Double/Twin 12000-14000 Pts.
Breakfast: 800 Pts.
Meals: Dinner on request approx. 2500 Pts (M) exc. wine.
Closed: 15 December-15 March.

From Madrid towards La Coruña on the A6. Exit to Castroverde. There C630 towards Fonsagrada, and after 1km left to Villabad(e). House next to church.

Pazo Viña Mein

Lugar de Mein-San Clodio
32420 Leiro
Orense

Tel: 988 488400
Fax: 988 488732
E-mail: vinamein@wol.es

Javier Alen

Here, far off the beaten track and cradled among the steeply banked Ribeiro vineyards, an almost monastic silence and peacefulness await you. But don't expect to sleep in a cell: guest rooms are among the largest we have seen in Spain with beds and bathrooms to scale, terracotta floors, antique furniture and rich fabrics and prints. One has a double door leading to a private terrace where you can sit and soak up the quiet beauty of Viña Mein. In the living and dining rooms wood and granite have been harmoniously combined; the enormous lounge has a traditional *lareira*, a huge fireplace large enough to seat a whole family on its side benches during cold winters. Nowadays central heating means you won't feel the need to huddle in your inglenook but you can expect a fire to be lit. There are lots of books, too – Javier Alen owns a bookshop in Madrid. In the warmer months you breakfast out on the terrace and although no dinners are served, there are good restaurants in nearby San Clodio. There are mountain bikes if you feel like exploring the surrounding countryside and there is a pool, too. Be sure to visit Viña Mein's state-of-the-art *bodega*: the wine is superb.

Rooms: 4 with bath & wc; 1 two-bedroom apartment.
Price: Double/Twin 8000 Pts; Apartment 11000 Pts.
Breakfast: Included.
Meals: None available.
Closed: Never.

From Orense N120 towards Vigo. At km596 post right towards Carballiño. Continue for 10km, then right to San Clodio. There follow signs to Viña Mein.

Palacio Bentraces

Bentraces
32890 Barbadás
Orense

Tel: 988 383381
Fax: 988 383381

Angeles Peñamaría Cajoto

The old granite stones of Bentraces are steeped in history. Built for a bishop this delectable *palacio* was passed on to a noble Galician family who in turn sold it on and so on: there are no fewer than six different coats of arms on different parts of the building! Angeles will unravel the web of its history and tell of the three long years of restoration which have resulted in one of the most sumptuous and elegant manorhouse hostelries in Spain. The elegance within is hinted at by a Florentine-style southern façade and gorgeous formal gardens that lap up to the building. Push aside the heavy doors to discover an elegant world of books, rugs, engravings, parquet floors, marble staircases, all set off by the warmth of the colour schemes. Anyone with an interest in antiques would love it and no-one could fail to enjoy the choice of lounges, the enormous breakfast room in the palace's old kitchen and the sumptuous guest bedrooms: marble and bathrobes in bathrooms, top-of-the-range mattresses and bed linen, suites with room for a cocktail party. Romanesque chapels and monasteries are nearby and Santiago is an hour to the west. Book a suite, dine, and just luxuriate.

Rooms: 5 with bath & wc; 2 suites.
Price: Double 15000 Pts; Suite 20000 Pts.
Breakfast: 1200 Pts.
Meals: Dinner 4000 Pts (C). Book ahead. Not Saturdays and Sundays.
Closed: 22 December-22 January.

From Orense towards Madrid on N525, then (just past km7 post) N540 towards Celanova to Bentraces. Here at 'Bar Bentraces' turn right and house is beside the church. Ring bell at main gate.

Casa Grande de Trives

Calle Marqués de Trives 17
32780 Poboa de Trives
Orense

Tel: 988 332066
Fax: 988 332066
E-mail: casagtrives@tpi.infomail.es

Adelaida Alvarez Martínez.

Sometimes grand family homes converted to receive guests cease to be either 'grand' or 'family'. Not so Trives; here the balance between caring for you and respecting your intimacy is just right. This noble old village house (it has its own chapel) was one of the first in Galicia to open to guests. Like good claret it has improved with time. The rooms are in a separate wing of the main building, big and elegantly uncluttered with lovely wooden floors, the best of mattresses and wonderful cotton sheets. There is a sitting room where you can have a quiet drink, and a truly enchanting garden beyond for the warmer months. Breakfast is taken in an unforgettable dining room; here the richness of the furnishings, the cut flowers and the classical music vie with the grand buffet breakfast – a real feast. There are home-made cakes, fruit, big pots of coffee, croissants, and it all makes its way up from the kitchen via the dumb waiter. Fine bone china adds to the elegance of the meal. A marvellous place and a most gracious welcome by mother and son. *Grand Cru* Galicia!

Rooms: 9 with bath & wc.
Price: Single 6200 Pts; Double/Twin 7700 Pts.
Breakfast: 850 Pts.
Meals: None available.
Closed: Never.

From Madrid A6 towards La Coruña. Take exit 400 and continue on N120 towards Monforte de Lemos. At km468 branch off for A Rua/Trives then right at traffic lights on C-536 for Trives. House in centre of village on left.

Entry no: 12

Map no: 2

Pazo Paradela

Carretera Barrio km 2
32780 Pobra de Trives
Orense

Tel: 988 330714 or 608 777637
Fax: 988 330714
E-mail: pparadela@jazzfree.com

Mañuel Rodríguez Rodríguez

You are at the heart of Galicia's green interior, close to the sleepy village of Trives. Your home for the night is a 17th-century manor house with long views of the surrounding hillsides. Your host, Manuel, is a cheery fellow who speaks superb English: he grew up in the States where he dreamed of returning to his native soil and restoring these imposing old granite stones of the house his father bought some thirty years back. His natural generosity is reflected in the way the building has been restored and decorated; no corners have been cut here: "you have to be proud of your work," he says. So bedrooms were given only the best: chestnut floors and beds, marble-topped tables, rugs, beautiful antique mirrors and chairs, state-of-the-art heating and air-conditioning and Portuguese marble in the bathrooms. Views are long and green. The treats continue at table: in the vast granite-hearthed dining room, try the home-made honey at breakfast and for dinner expect the best of Galician country cooking with many of the veg freshly dug up from Paradela's kitchen gardens. This is real hospitality: share a Queimada with your hosts, the local hot brew that keeps the evil spirits at bay.

Rooms: 6 with bath or shower & wc; 2 suites.
Price: Double/Twin 8500 Pts; Suite 10000 Pts incl. VAT.
Breakfast: 850 Pts.
Meals: Dinner 3000 Pts (M). Restaurant closed weekdays in Low Season.
Closed: 22 December-2 January.

From Leon on the NVI to Ponferrada, then N120 into A Rua Petin and from here C536 to Trives. Through the centre of the town, cross bridge, then first right. Follow signs.

Map no: 2

Entry no: 13

Pazo A Nugalla

Pousada-Curantes
36686 A Estrada
Pontevedra

Tel: 986 591600
Fax: 986 588409

**Antón Rozas y
María Luisa Gil**

Nugalla is old Galician for laziness and refers to a nobleman who used to recline on the rooftop, hands clasped behind his head, watching the locals toil for him. His stone bust is still up there, surveying all who enter. Antón and María Luisa, ex-schoolteachers, are the antithesis of the previous idle owner. With designs by architect Pedro de Llano and a government grant, they have turned what was a 16th-century granite muleteer's inn, then the heart of a large 18th-century farm, into a stunning nine-bedroomed house. Inside, it is a mixture of rustic and modern. The big, three-level, skylit sitting room has a huge walk-in hearth, the television hidden in a piece of handmade furniture and a chess table. Bedrooms have lovely details: free-standing Victorian washbasins, oak beams, rugs! Antón creates a convivial atmosphere by gathering all his guests round the huge dining table, set with blue and white Galician crockery, or in the intimate courtyard and will often organise outdoor piano and violin recitals. Your hosts' cultural tastes also show in the often-renewed modern art that hangs on the walls. Everything is done without pretension and we highly recommend a stay here.

Rooms: 9 with bath & wc.
Price: Double/Twin 12000-15000 Pts.
Breakfast: Included.
Meals: Dinner 2500 Pts.
Closed: 23 December-31 January.

From Pontevedra A9-EI towards Santiago de C. Exit for Caldas de Reis then N640 through A Estrada towards Lalín. 8kms from A Estrada right for Curantes; after 1.5km, right and follow signs for Pazo A Nugalla.

Hotel Pazo El Revel

36990 Villalonga
Pontevedra

Tel: 986 743000
Fax: 986 743390

Luis Ansorena Garret

The caring eye of Don Luis Ansorena Garret, owner of this lovely old *pazo*, has watched over the Revel for the last three decades. This was one of the first palace-style hotels to open in Galicia and its reputation has grown with the years. The stately façade and huge gates greet you on arrival; and the surrounding gardens are a feast in themselves with exuberant stands of hydrangea. The palm, plum and citrus trees add an exotic touch and there's a bracing whiff of sea air penetrating this rich greenery. You enter the house via a grand entrance hall; here, as throughout the Revel, the granite, the beams and the tiled floors are warmly authentic. Sitting and dining rooms are large and airy and there is an attractive terrace with wicker furniture. The bedrooms are well furnished with tiled floors and 'rustic' style beds and dressers: they are good value. Both staff and owner take great care of their guests whilst remaining mindful of your intimacy. There is bar service here and plenty of good seafood restaurants just a short drive away, and at breakfast there is bread hot from the oven. But book ahead.

Rooms: 22 with bath & wc.
Price: Single 6650-7650 Pts;
Twin 10650-11650 Pts.
Breakfast: Included.
Meals: None available.
Closed: October-May.

From Pontevedra, Vía Rápida to Sanxenxo.
There, towards A Grove and A Toxa.
Through Villalonga; at end of village turn
left following signs to El Revel.

O Casal de Tenorio
36120 Cotobade
Pontevedra

Tel: 986 764141
Fax: 986 764141
Web: www.turgalicia.es

María José Gil Cons

High on a hill overlooking an old monastery in the Lérez valley, this 200-year-old family house has a pleasant, lived-in feel. María José is an attentive, genteel, somewhat matronly hostess with a great air of calm. Don't be put off by the unimpressive entrance: it yields to a most wonderful garden which has one of the best-positioned swimming pools we have come across. This could be the spot from where to take in the long view across the valley to the village of Tenorio, the spectacular sunsets or to wonder at the star-filled skys. For the more active there is tennis, either of the court or the table variety. On summer evenings barbecues can be served on the lawn and the large dining room is a wonderful setting for the sampling of fine Galician food and full-bodied Albariño or Ribeira wines. The interior may seem a bit cluttered and there is no particular style to the décor in the bedrooms – they have mahogany headboards and satiny bedspreads – but this is a home and not a hotel and if you treat it as such, you'll love it here and that pool-with-a-view is really quite something.

Rooms: 9 with bath & wc.
Price: Double/Twin 10000 Pts.
Breakfast: 750 Pts.
Meals: Dinner 2500 Pts (M).
Closed: Never.

From Pontevedra N541 towards Ourense. After 10km right for Tenorio. Into village and look for signpost on right for O Casal.

Finca Río Miño

Carril 6
Las Eiras
36760 O Rosal
Pontevedra

Tel: 986 621107
Fax: 986 621107
E-mail: finca_dawes@email.com

Tony & Shirley Taylor-Dawes

The green hills and rivers of northern Portugal and Galicia are dear to Tony and Shirley Taylor-Dawes. They know the people, villages, food and wines like few others. Perhaps their passion for fine wine led them to this 350-year-old farm with its terraced vineyards and *bodega* carved in solid rock. And what a position, up on the bank of the Miño with views across to Portugal. In the vast garden are two pine-clad lodges built by Tony. They are simply furnished, have their own small kitchen (although breakfast can be provided), lounge and two bedrooms. Best of all are the terraces which have the same wide view over the river. In the main house there is another room with bathroom, a sitting room with pretty Portuguese furniture, a breakfast room and an unforgettable terrace with a rambling passion fruit providing extra shade. Don't miss dinner if you happen to be here on a Sunday: it makes good use of port, whether in sauces for meat or in puddings like 'sozzled apricots' or 'Duero lemon haze'. There's a pool-with-a-view, river beaches at the end of the farm track and the Atlantic close by. *Minimum three night stay in July/August for lodges.*

Rooms: 1 with bath & wc; 2 lodges
sleeping up to 4 with bath & wc.
Price: Twin 8500 Pts; Lodge (for 2)
10000 Pts, (for 3) 13000 Pts
(for 4) 15000 Pts.
Breakfast: 700 Pts.
Meals: Sundays only. Gourmet dinner from
4000 Pts (M) inc. port tastings.
Book ahead.
Closed: 1 November-30 April.

From Vigo N550 to Tuy. La Guardia exit then C550 for about 15km. Just after km190 post, left at 'Restaurante Eiras' sign, over next crossroads, signposted to left after 1.5km.

Map no: 1   **Entry no:** 17

Hostal/Restaurante Asensio

Rua do Tollo 2   **Tel:** 986 620152
36750 Goian   **Fax:** 986 620152
Pontevedra

Dolores Martínez González and Fernando Asensio

Special it most certainly is although at first glance you may wonder how this simple
hostelry earns its place in the pages of this guide. But there are two very good
reasons for coming here. One: so you can meet Dolores ('Loli') and Fernando.
They lived for many years in the UK and they love to receive English-speaking
guests. Two: Fernando's gourmet cooking. No idle boast when Fernando claims
he can "satisfy even the most demanding of palates". With the Minho just a spit
away his food naturally gravitates towards fish: lamprey and elvers are house
specials, seafood too and to accompany there is a quality-rather-than-quantity wine
list (the wine from the village is superb). "Excellent meat dishes are also available"
wrote an enthusiastic reader. Tables are beautifully laid up in the small, pine-clad
dining room which leads off from the bar area (Loli's artistry with flowers is always
a feature) where you breakfast (see main photo). With food this good rooms could
be just an afterthought but they're as spruce as spruce can be, and comfortable
rather than memorable – our favourites are certainly the two new ones just recently
grafted on to the original building. But oh what food!

Rooms: 6 with bath or shower & wc.
Price: Double/Twin 6500 Pts.
Breakfast: 375 Pts.
Meals: Lunch 1200 Pts (M); dinner 3000-
4000 Pts (C). Closed on Wednesdays and
Sunday evenings.
Closed: 15 September-10 October.

From El Vigo to Tuy then exit at km172
post onto N550 towards La Guardia/A
Guarda. Continue for 15km and Asensio
on left as you pass through Goian.

Asturias
•
Cantabria
•

Northern Spain

"A good holiday is one that is spent among people whose
notions of time are vaguer than yours"
– J. B. Priestley

Hotel Torre de Villademoros

33788 Cadavedo-Valdés   **Tel:** 98 5645264
Asturias   **Fax:** 98 5645265
     E-mail: correo@torrevillademoros.com
     Web: www.torrevillademoros.com

Luis Antonio Alvarez-Santullano Martínez

On a cliff-top above the Cantabrian coast, this elegant retreat is a restored 18th-century Asturian house set in meadowland with its own medieval tower. Manolo, the owner's son, is the interior designer and your attentive host. The old granary and stones outside are in total contrast to the renovation inside. From the big lounge with its fireplace, sculpted lighting and sleek sofas to the glazed breakfast room with its slate floor and wide views, all is stylish minimalism with carefully-chosen colours and paintings to add depth. Manolo has achieved an intimate and relaxed atmosphere. The guest rooms are finely finished, mainly with polished chestnut and pine, and bathrooms have superb modern fittings. Most rooms look over the Sierra de Las Palancas and have their own sitting rooms. Dinner is an inexpensive and convivial affair with traditional food (stuffed tuna is a seasonal delicacy), good wine and fine desserts. But breakfast was our favourite meal: a hearty feast of pastries, cakes, crêpes and home-made jams (full cooked breakfast on request) with a glorious view of the tower and lush green countryside as a natural backdrop. *A Rusticae hotel.*

Rooms: 10 with bath & wc.
Price: Double/Twin 10000-14000 Pts.
Breakfast: 700 Pts.
Meals: Dinner 1600 Pts (M).
Closed: Never.

From Oviedo towards La Coruña on the E70-N632. Exit for Cadavedo then left at junction to Villademoros. Just before railway bridge turn right and follow signs to hotel.

Hotel Villa La Argentina

Villar de Luarca
33700 Luarca
Asturias

Tel: 98 5640102
Fax: 98 5640973
E-mail: villalaargentina@ctv.es
Web: www.ctv.es/USERS/villalaargentina/index.html

Antonio González Fernández

This flamboyant building was built in 1899 by a returning émigré who made his fortune in South America. It was abandoned and then rediscovered by the González Fernández family who saw in the crumbling building a brighter future; thanks to their gargantuan efforts it once again breathes an air of light-hearted elegance and optimism. The reception rooms are parquet-floored, high-ceilinged with pastel-coloured walls: their light and colour is enhanced by stained-glass windows, and fine net-curtaining. Enormous gilt-framed oil paintings, candelabras and tall mirrors add to the lofty, elegant feel of the rooms. The dimensions and style of the bedrooms is in harmony with the rest of the house. Your room will be large with a stuccoed and corniced ceiling, period furniture and a king-sized bed; really good mattresses and hydromassage tubs add to the feel-good factor. And La Argentina's low, slate-walled restaurant would be a perfect place to end your day. The González Fernández recommend that you try the turbot or their steak 'ultramar'. After dinner slip off for a game of billiards or wander the Villa's garden where you may stumble across the house's ornate little chapel.

Rooms: 9 with bath & wc; 3 suites.
Price: Double/Twin 7500-12500 Pts;
Suite 16000 Pts.
Breakfast: 800 Pts.
Meals: Lunch/Dinner 2000 Pts (M),
4000-5000 Pts (C).
Closed: Never.

From Oviedo towards Ribadeo via A66 then A8. Exit for Barcia/Almuña. At petrol station just before you reach Luarca right following signs Luarca por El Faro-Villar. Signposted.

Map no: 2

A Casoa

Santa Eulalia de Oscos s/n
33776 Santa Eulalia de Oscos
Asturias

Tel: 98 5626045 or
          98 5621233
Fax: 98 5626112

Francisco Castaño Pérez

A Casoa – simply 'The House' in Gallego – is a fine slate town house that has been well restored to make a five-bedroomed B&B with a self-catering cottage for four at the back. It is a splendid sight with its layered stonework interspersed with rustic shuttered windows; inside, the overall atmosphere is 'new traditional' and the welcome is relaxedly friendly. The main house contains a beautifully preserved Asturian kitchen – a *lareira* – with an open wood fire, a cookpot which swings on a wooden boom and a pitched ceiling lined with tin to prevent smoke damage and channel the smoke up through the chimney. In the past, this communal eating place must have produced many a *fabada* (bean stew with pork) and the walls have surely rung with the sound of women singing. If you want to eat in Santa Eulalia, try Pedro's restaurant down the hill. To catch a piece of local culture, visit the wonderful village shop *Tienda La Palma* where you can order wine or beer by the glass, sample local cheeses or sausage and buy... anything! The cottage is perfect for a family with a cosy living room, fully-fitted kitchen and two exquisite double rooms with open pitched ceilings.

Rooms: 5 with bath & wc; 1 cottage.
Price: Double 6000 Pts; Cottage 8000 Pts.
Breakfast: 500 Pts.
Meals: None available.
Closed: Never.

From Oviedo A66/A8 to Aviles then N632/634 along coast to Vegadeo. Here AS11 to Puerto de la Garganta; right at top to Santa Eulalia. A Casoa is in centre of village just behind Hotel Rural Casa Pedro.

Hotel Rural Casa Pedro

33776 Santa Eulalia de Oscos
Asturias

Tel: 98 5626097
Fax: 98 5626097

María del Mar Fernández López and Pedro Martínez Rodríguez

The Oscos are a group of high mountain villages in western Asturias that have only recently attracted walkers in search of new pastures. It is a lovely, deepest green land of gorse, heather, rushing streams and long views. In one of the area's more attractive villages, the Casa Pedro provides a safe port of call if you´re planning to explore the area. Modern it may be but this stone and slate house blends well with the village architecture; only traditional local building materials were used. The hotel sits high up above the road and has wonderful views. The young owners greeted us with genuine friendliness and we think you´ll agree that the rooms are worth every last peseta. They are medium-sized with smart, walnut furniture and good bathrooms; those at the front have the best views but all look out to the green beyond. The food is good and traditional: do try the lamb or the 'cachopo', veal stuffed with mountain-cured ham and local cheese. And eating here shouldn't break the bank. There are wonderful walks straight out from the village and bikes available at the hotel. Be sure to visit the local shop, Tienda la Palka, and have a glass of wine: real Spain.

Rooms: 6 with bath or shower & wc.
Price: Double/Twin 5000-6500 Pts.
Breakfast: 400-600 Pts.
Meals: Lunch/Dinner 1500 Pts (M), 2000-2500 Pts (C).
Closed: Never.

From Oviedo A66/A8 to Aviles then N632/634 along coast to Vegadeo. Here AS11 to Puerto de la Garganta; right at top to Santa Eulalia. Hotel in centre of village.

La Corte
33843 Villar de Vildas
Asturias

Tel: 98 5763131 or 985 463137
Fax: 98 5763131
E-mail: lacorte@grama.es
Web: www.gramacom.org/lacorte

Adriano Berdasco Fernández

Villar de Vildas is a tiny hamlet, literally at the very end of the road. At the western flank of the Somiedo park – where some of the last bears in Europe roam free – you could find no sweeter place from which to discover the beautiful walks of the Pigüeña valley. Your inn is a 19th-century farmhouse of wood and stone, reconverted by Adriano to create a small guesthouse and restaurant. You enter by a small courtyard and up old stone steps to a handsome wood-floored guest lounge (spot your host as a young boy in the photos). There are books, a handsome hearth and a galleried balcony that catches the afternoon light. A narrow wooden spiral staircase brings you up to your rooms; ask Adriano should you need a hand getting cases up. There are only five rooms (there's also an apartment next door) which vary in size; two have dormer windows looking to the stars and peaks, all have good bathrooms and comfy beds. There are durries, pine furniture; all of it sparkling clean. The restaurant is just as welcoming; low-ceilinged, beamed and with basket lamps. Expect to meet the locals who come for the Asturian cooking – or just a drink. A marvellous place for walkers.

Rooms: 10 with bath & wc.
Price: Double/Twin 7000 Pts.
Breakfast: 750 Pts.
Meals: Lunch/Dinner 1600 Pts (M),
3000 Pts (C).
Closed: Never.

From Oviedo take N634 west. Just before Cornellana left on AS15 to Puente de San Martín. Here AS227 south to Aguasmestas. Here, right to Pigüeña and climb on up via Cores to Villar de Vildas.

La Casona de Pío

Riofrío 3
33150 Cudillero
Asturias

Tel: 98 5591512
Fax: 98 5591519
E-mail: casonadepio@arrakis.es
Web: www.arrakis.es/~casonadepio/

Manuel Alfredo Valle

Cudilleros is one of the prettiest fishing villages of the Asturian coast, a huddle of houses around a sheltered cove where you can still watch the catch being landed first thing in the morning. When you enter this elegant little hotel (just one street back from the pretty main square), it is hard to imagine that Pío, a well-known local personality, once had his fish-salting factory here! But in a way fish is still the focus: this is one of the area's very best fish restaurants and it would be hard to fault it – beautifully presented tables and food, an extraordinarily crafted wooden ceiling, and a chef who is making waves. When we visited we were ushered through to the kitchen to see its all kinds of good things on the go in boiling pots and sizzling pans. Out of season Pío's charming owners will let you choose your bedroom. Ours might be 104 because of its private terrace or one on the top floor which gets more light. Most of the furniture is chestnut; there are crocheted linen curtains, beautiful taps and hydro-massage tubs. All of the rooms are very smart and amazingly good value at any time of the year. Picnics can be prepared for walks and other sorties.

Rooms: 10 with bath & wc; 1 suite.
Price: Double/Twin 7000-10000 Pts;
Suite 10000-13000 Pts.
Breakfast: 800 Pts.
Meals: Lunch/Dinner 3000 Pts (M),
4000 Pts (C).
Closed: Second half of January.

From Oviedo take the A66 motorway to Aviles; then on towards Luarca. Turn right off the road for Cudillero. The hotel is in the town centre, just off the main square.

Casona de la Paca

El Pito
33150 Cudillero
Asturias

Tel: 98 5591303 or
　　　98 5591316
Fax: 98 5591316 or
　　　985 590995
E-mail: hotel@casonadelapaca.com
Web: www.casonadelapaca.com

Montserrat Abad

La Casona de la Paca is one of Asturias' many *Casonas de Indianos*; these flamboyant edifices were built by émigrés who had made their fortune in the Americas then headed for home and local-boy-makes-good celebrity. Its strawberry coloured façade and exotic garden with many New World species immediately grab the eye – as was the intention. The atmosphere within reflects that of the building's early years; it is both elegant and opulent, lightened by a very contemporary idea of colour and distribution of space. Uniformed staff serve you in the dining room whilst the well-upholstered lounge is a lovely place to read: there are many books to choose from in the library. Bedrooms are in the main house and a purpose-built annex; the Tower Suite which is worth the extra for the privilege of having a wonderful wrap-around terrace. Colonial-style furniture is 'in synch' with the spirit of the place; mahogany and teak in abundance combined with contemporary fabrics and Deco-ish floor tiles. You are close to the fishing village of Cudilleros whose many restaurants, to quote the hotel's brochure, 'reveal the secrets of Cantabria and the sweetness of its customs'. *A Rusticae hotel.*

Rooms: 17 with bath & wc; 2 suites.
Price: Single 6900-9900 Pts;
Double/Twin 8400-11500 Pts;
Suite 10500-13500 Pts; Tower room
11500-15500 Pts.
Breakfast: 875 Pts.
Meals: None available.
Closed: 11 December-31 January.

From Oviedo A66 then A8 m'way towards Ribadeo/Galicia to Avilés. There N632 towards Ribadeo. Through Soto de Barco continuing west, then right at signs Cudillero for El Pito. House on right after approx 1km.

Hotel Casa del Busto

Plaza del Rey Don Silo 1   **Tel:** 98 5822771
33120 Pravia   **Fax:** 98 5822772
Asturias

Alberto Mencos Valdés

Parts of this fine old mansion – it has a rather South American, 'hacienda' feel to it
– date back to the XVIth century. After some lean years it has recently seen careful
and thorough renovation. It took several years and the owners now run courses in
furniture restoration – many of the pieces you'll see at the hotel come straight
from their workshop. Ceilings are high, floors of polished parquet, the staircase is
marble and, an unusual period feature, some of the walls are original *tabique*
(wattle and daub). Tapestries, sculptures and chandeliers embellish the whole and
– despite so much grandness – a relaxed, soothing atmosphere pervades the house.
The dining area is in an interior courtyard and guest rooms give onto the gallery
one floor up, each of them with stacks of period furniture: their decoration is a
harmonious potpourri of the grand and the simple. Pravia is an attractive village,
you are just 7km from the sea and the soaring grandeur of the Somiedo Park is
within easy driving distance. This was once was a favourite haunt of the famous
liberal politician Jovellanos who said of Busto "the food and the bed were always
to my liking". We think that you'll agree.

Rooms: 29 with bath & wc.
Price: Single 4500-7000 Pts;
Double/Twin 7000-9500 Pts.
Breakfast: 500-800 Pts; English breakfast
also served.
Meals: Lunch/Dinner 1300 Pts (M),
3000 Pts (C). Restaurant closed on Fridays.
Closed: Never.

From Oviedo, N634 to Grado. There take
AS237 to Pravia. In village centre.

Map no: 3   Entry no: 26

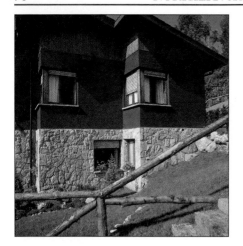

Casa Camila

Fitoria 28
33194 Oviedo
Asturias

Tel: 98 5114822
Fax: 98 5294198
E-mail: info@casacamila.com
Web: www.casacamila.com

Antonieta Domínguez Benito

There is one very good reason for visiting Oviedo; the exquisite churches of Santa Maria del Narranco and San Miguel de Lillo, built on a thickly-wooded hillside by the Asturian king Ramiro I in the ninth century. Visit and you'll understand why these diminuitive buildings have a grandeur far beyond their modest dimensions. Casa Camila shares the same magic mountain and has views out across the surrounding meadows to the distant Picos. Asturias has a tradition of innovative architecture (returning emigrants have always wanted to be noticed!) and the modern lines and rich pomegranate colour of this building strike a bold note of welcome. Within is a light, modern edifice; wood has been beautifully fashioned throughout the building, especially in the oak parquet of second-storey bedrooms. Camila's food is a match for its rooms; Asturias is its main inspiration but the Mediterranean tradition is also there, salads are interesting and the veggie side of things hasn't been neglected (stuffed onions and aubergines are specialities). This is an utterly peaceful spot; do come, walk from the hotel for a mile and a half or so and wonder at these early Romanesque churches.

Rooms: 6 with bath & wc; 1 suite.
Price: Single 8000-10000 Pts;
Double/Twin 10000-12500 Pts;
Suite 17000-20000 Pts.
Breakfast: 800 Pts.
Meals: Lunch/Dinner 2200 Pts (M), 4000 Pts (C). Restaurant closed on Mondays
Closed: Never.

From Oviedo, in area known as Pulmarin, take road towards Monte Naranco following signs for Fitoria. Hotel 1.5km after leaving town.

Hotel Quinta Duro

Cefontes
33394 Cabueñes
Asturias

Tel: 98 5371890
Fax: 98 5371890
E-mail: mpinilla@netcom.atodavela.com
Web: www.netcom.atodavela.com/mpinilla

Carlos Velásquez-Duro

Quinta Duro is just a couple of kilometres to the east of Gijón and overlooks the city; although it is just 800 metres from the main road it is quiet and secluded. The estate of the Velázquez-Duro family is a haven of greenery and mature trees, girdled round by a high stone wall. Carlos has recently refurbished the eleven guest rooms as well as the rest of the interior and the veranda at the rear; the result is both stylish and homely. Panelled walls, period Portuguese and English furniture show the family's love of quality and detail. The bronze statue in the garden is of Carlos' grandfather who casts a wistful eye on all those who visit; he would surely approve of his grandson giving the house a new lease of life. Only breakfast is served at the Quinta but there are two good restaurants very close but better still would be to head for the lively resort itself. The beach is clean but it can get busy, so carry on round the town to the harbour area where you'll find two Asturian specialities in abundance: fish and cider. The former comes in varieties distinct to the Cantabrian sea, the latter poured from a bottle held above the waiters head into a glass held at knee-height. Enormous fun.

Rooms: 11 with bath & wc.
Price: Double/Twin 12000-14500 Pts;
'Special' Double/Twin 14000-17000 Pts.
Breakfast: Included.
Meals: None available.
Closed: Mid-January-mid-February.

From Gijón towards Santander on motorway and then N632. Then right for Santurio/Cefontes. After 500m turn left; after 400m you will see the large entrance gates to Quinta on the right.

Map no: 3   **Entry no: 28**

La Quintana de la Foncalada

Argüero
33314 Villaviciosa
Asturias

Tel: 98 5876365 or 655 697956
Fax: 98 5876365
E-mail: foncalada@asturcon-museo.com
Web: www.asturcon-museo.com/inicial.html

Severino García & Daniela Schmid

You are welcomed with unaffected simplicity at this honeysuckle-clad farmhouse at the heart of the coastal *mariña* area of Asturias. Severino and Daniela are keen that their guests should learn about the people and traditions of the area; they encourage you to try potting (potters worked here in the 18th century) and help with the Asturian ponies or the organic veg patch. Nearly everything is home produced: honey, cheese, juices and jams. The inside of the house is what you might expect from such people; bedrooms are light, cheerful and uncluttered, with smallish bathrooms. Many of the fittings, like the unusual table lamps, were made by Severino. The atmosphere is relaxed; make yourself a hot drink in the large kitchen whenever the mood takes you. Upstairs there is a guest lounge with wicker furniture and masses of information on walks and visits. Severino will happily guide you towards some delectable beaches, good eateries and the best excursions from La Quintana by bike or pony. Equinophiles should know that Severino has created a museum dedicated to the Asturian pony, the *asturcón*. He also breeds them.

Rooms: 5 with bath & wc; 1 suite with bath & wc.
Price: Double/Twin 5000-7000 Pts; Suite 10000-13000 Pts incl. VAT.
Breakfast: 500 Pts.
Meals: Dinner 2900 Pts (M).
Closed: Never.

From Gijón N632 towards Santander. 23km from Santander turn for Argüero. Here follow signs for Foncalada/La Quintana de la Foncalada.

Hotel Casa España

Plaza Carlos I
33300 Villaviciosa
Asturias

Tel: 98 5892030/5892682
Fax: 98 5892682/5892682

María José Lorda

When rich emigrants came home after working in Central and South America many of them built grand houses with their earnings – these are the *Casas de Indianos* that you stumble across in far-flung corners of green Asturias. Casa España is one of them. It catches the eye with its display of colonial wealth in arched stone doorways, balconies and projecting eaves. It stands at the heart of the busy little town of Villaviciosa, looking out onto the main square, and was opened for paying guests in 1995. The rooms are on two floors, reached by the wide central staircase. They are mostly large, high-ceilinged and have shining wooden floors. The furniture is nearly all made of wood, too; many of the pieces are original, period antiques and there are original oils in some of the rooms. Bathrooms are big, all with full-length baths. The bar downstairs is lively throughout the day; this is where (Continental) breakfasts are served as well as snacks at other times. Although there is no restaurant there are lots to choose from close by. A comfortable and reliable, rather than remarkable, place to stay. *In August minimum stay 6 days.*

Rooms: 12 with bath & wc; 2 suites.
Price: Single 4800-8000 Pts;
Double/Twin 6000-10000 Pts; Suite 8000-12000 Pts.
Breakfast: 700 Pts.
Meals: Lunch/Dinner 1700 Pts (M). Closed Sundays.
Closed: Never.

From Santander A67/N634 towards Oviedo. Just after Infiesto (about 40km before Oviedo) right on AS255 to Villaviciosa. In centre of town.

Map no: 3

Entry no: 30

Hotel Posada del Valle

Collia
33549 Arriondas
Asturias

Tel: 98 5841157
Fax: 98 5841559
E-mail: hotel@posadadelvalle.com
Web: www.posadadelvalle.com

Nigel & Joann Burch

Nigel and Joann Burch's love of Spain is more than a passing romance; they lived and worked in eastern Spain for the best part of twenty years. But they longed for greener pastures and after two long years of searching the hills and deep valleys of Asturias they found the home of their dreams – a century-old farmhouse just inland from the rugged north coast with inspirational views out to rock, wood and meadow. And already they are nurturing new life from the soil whilst running a small guesthouse; the apple orchard is planted, the flock grazing on the hillside and their guests delighting in the sensitive conversion that has created one of the area's most beguiling small hotels. Rooms are seductive affairs with polished wooden floors below, beams above and carefully matched paint and fabric. Perhaps most memorable is the glass-fronted dining room – here the menu pays homage to the best of things local. You are close to the soaring Picos, the little-known beaches of the Cantabrian coast and some of the most exceptional wildlife in Europe. Do book a second or third night here. *No smoking is allowed in the hotel.*

Rooms: 8 with bath & wc.
Price: Double/Twin 7500-9500 Pts.
Breakfast: 850 Pts.
Meals: Dinner 2050 Pts.
Closed: 16 October-14 March.

N634 Arriondas, take AS260 signposted Mirador del Fito. After 1km right turn signposted Collia. Straight through village of Collia (don't take right-hand turn to Ribadesella). The hotel is 300m on the left after village.

Palacio de Cutre

La Goleta s/n
Villamayor-Infiesto
33583 Villamayor-Infiesto
Asturias

Tel: 98 5708072
Fax: 98 5708019
E-mail: palacio-de-cutre@hotelesasturianos.com
Web: www.hotelesasturianos.com/palacio-de-cutre

Alejandra Iglesias & Javier Álvarez

Javier worked for one of Spain's largest hotel chains but is now a firm convert to the 'small is beautiful' school of hostelry. He and his wife Alejandra have lavished energy and care on this intimate yet luxurious small hotel. Part of the spirit is captured by the leaflet describing the hotel: it's written as if all were seen by the old oak which towers gloriously over Cutre's lovely gardens. It tells that it was born in the same century as the palace – the sixteenth – and from its branches can look in on beautifully decorated guest rooms where no detail is lacking: it sees flounced and beribboned curtains, cushions on beds, Tiffany-style lamps, antique bedsteads, luxurious bathrooms and only the very best fabrics. It can also glimpse the cheerful dining room with its chequered table cloths and rush-seated chairs. But we give Alejandra herself the final word: she insists that what makes the place so special is Cutre's food, an innovative mix of traditional Asturian dishes with more elaborate dishes. And we would add that the wonderful Costa Verde coast is very close.

Rooms: 16 with bath & wc; 1 suite.
Price: Double/Twin 10950-17950 Pts; Suite 25000 Pts.
Breakfast: 1250 Pts.
Meals: Lunch/Dinner 4950 Pts (M), 5500 Pts (C).
Closed: 7 January-16 March.

From Santander towards Oviedo N634. At km356 post right towards Borines/Colunga. Cross railway line, then river, then turn right towards Cereceda and follow signs for 2km to Palacio.

Map no: 3

Entry no: 32

Los Cuetos
33537 Santianes (Infiesto/Pilaño)   **Tel:** 98 5710656
Asturias   **Fax:** 98 5710874
                                      Web: www.infiesto.com/loscuetos

Seila Sánchez Barro

Los Cuetos is a totally-rebuilt 16th-century farmhouse standing in a commanding position with wide views of the valleys and mountains of Asturias. The driveway, lined with flowers and fruit trees, brings you to the wooden façade, the house's most grand and striking feature. Inside, however, it is warm and friendly, furnishing and décor are 'designer smart' with lovingly-matched prints, warm-coloured fabrics, tiled and wood floors and pastel walls. It all blends serenely with the majestic setting. Seila, a great hostess, is happy in the kitchen cooking breakfast or creating one of her special fish dishes or meat casseroles for dinner. The sweeping curved staircase takes you up to the first floor where that great galleried window lets the light in, there's a sizeable sitting room and five very regal guest rooms. Each one is themed and utterly delightful, perfectly lit and furnished with good-looking wooden beds and rugs. *Les Mimoses* and its jacuzzi occupy one whole wing. The garden is memorable too, with a vast granary, while under the marquee you can sit at a great round table that comes from an old bread oven and spins! So watch your glass while watching the view.

Rooms: 5 with bath & wc.
Price: Double/Twin 7000-13000 Pts incl. VAT.
Breakfast: 500-800 Pts.
Meals: Lunch/Dinner 2000 Pts (M).
Closed: Never.

From Santander E70-N634 towards Oviedo. Exit at km363 to Infiesto and as you enter village left for Lozana on the PI-3. Los Cuetos is on right after 1.5km; large black entrance gate just beyond house.

El Correntiu

Sardalla 42
33560 Ribadesella
Asturias

Tel: 98 5861436
Fax: 98 5861436
E-mail: elcorrentiu@fade.es
Web: www.aritur.org/correntiu/correntiu.htm

María Luisa Bravo Toraño

One of the most original conversions we have come across in Spain: fancy spending the night in a converted grain silo? The buildings are off to one side of a traditional Asturian farm house that stands in nine acres of grounds. If you´re wondering about the abundance of fruit trees (even bananas) it's because the region has a microclimate and nearly everything seems to thrive. A stream babbles by just behind your dwelling: *escorentia* means 'place that collects rain water'. The renovation works surprisingly well: elegantly simple, rather Scandinavian in the crisp use of wood, ochre tones to impart warmth, discreet lighting and lots of space. Each apartment even has its own kitchen garden from which you may pick to your heart's content. One has a sitting room and fireplace; all have books, games, sheets and towels... everything you might need. If you´re more of a traditionalist there is also a little cottage in the grounds, fully equipped for self-caterers. You are close to the little fishing village of Ribadesella at the mouth of the river Sella, there are magnificent beaches and Maria Luisa (her English is excellent) can supply you with eggs and milk fresh from the farm.

Rooms: 1 cottage for 4; 2 apartments for 2/3.
Price: Apartment (for 2/3) 7000-9000 Pts; Cottage (for 4) 10000-12000 Pts.
Breakfast: Self catering.
Meals: None available – self catering.
Closed: Never.

From Ribadesella head for Gijón on N632. After bridge turn left for 'Cuevas-Sardalla'. From here it is exactly 2km to El Correntiu.

La Casa Nueva

33584 Cereceda-Infiesto   **Tel:** 98 5923737
Asturias

José María Muñoz Suárez & Purificación Pérez Pérez

Tick tock goes the clock. You feel time has come to a standstill in this quiet valley in the shadow of the Sueve Mountains. This is old Asturias, remote and magical with mysteries in every glade. The ancient region of Pilona is home to La Casa Nueva, a former village house where cattle were stabled and which had its own cider press. And apples are an important link to the past for present owner José María: he has planted big orchards that are now bearing fruit which, although only for personal consumption at the moment, will be a source of revenue in the future. Their house is coming to fruition, too, after a refit funded by a grant from Brussels. It has been simply laid out. The entrance hall is also the main guest sitting room – it has a lofty pitched ceiling, a wooden staircase and balcony and a big iron candelabra to light it all. We did feel that some of the detail was a bit twee but the bedrooms are simple and clean with only the odd creaking floorboard to break the silence. The Wild Horse Fair in August is an important fiesta, accompanied by many other local events, the wail of bagpipes *gaitas* and the rowdy consumption of free-flowing cider.

Rooms: 5 with bath & wc.
Price: Double/Twin 8500 Pts.
Breakfast: 650 Pts.
Meals: None available.
Closed: Never.

From Santander west on E70-N634. Pass Arriondas; at km 355, just before Villamayor, right on AS259 for Borines/Colunga. After 500m right on PI-II into Cereceda; house signposted on right.

Entry no: 35   Map no: 3

Hotel Halcón Palace

Cofiño s/n
Carretera AS260 Arriondas-Colunga
33548 Cofiño-Arriondas
Asturias

Tel: 98 5841312
Fax: 98 5841313

Leo Benz

This is a soul-stirring area of Spain cradled between the mighty Picos mountains to the south and the rugged coast to the north. Amazingly, a few years ago this 17th century palace was abandoned, overrun with vegetation and doomed to ruin... until this Spanish-Swiss couple arrived with the energy and conviction to create their dream hotel. The chief protagonist here is the incomparable view of the Cantabrian mountains and the mighty Picos de Europa. There are century-old trees in gardens dripping with colour – this part of Asturias enjoys a micro-climate. Indoors, the gentle good manners of your two hosts communicate themselves to the very building. The dining rooms are elegant but still conducive to long, lazy meals and here, as in other communal areas, antique and modern furnishings combine well. The bedrooms are smart, sparkling clean and have all-chestnut furniture; they have the best of mattresses and all have stirring views. And there is a cosy bar for an aperitif before dinner. "Leo is a super host" enthused one reader and many others have said how much they have loved staying here.

Rooms: 18 with bath & wc; 1 suite.
Price: Single 7000-1100 Pts;
Double/Twin 9000-13500 Pts; Suite
12000-16500 Pts.
Breakfast: Included.
Meals: Lunch/Dinner 1800 Pts (M),
4500-6000 Pts (C).
Closed: February & 24-27 December.

From Arriondas take SA260 towards
Colunga. After 5km turn left following signs for hotel.

Map no: 3

Entry no: 36

Casa El Ama de Llaves

Hontoria s/n
33593 Llanes
Asturias

Tel: 98 5407322 or 98 5407962
Fax: 98 5407697
E-mail: asturias@amadellaves.com
Web: www.amadellaves.com

Manuel Rodriguez

The senses are in paradise here. The exterior delights the eye, you can almost hear the sea in the distance, but the smell! – it's the smell wafting from the homely kitchen that really draws you. Manuel loves his food and takes huge pleasure in cooking for his guests: Asturian food at its best. The blue wash of the outside walls is perfectly set off by some of the deepest eaves you'll ever see. Generous use of chestnut wood on ceilings and floors lends warmth to the interior and Justine clearly has a great eye for fine antiques. In her passion for detail, she has studied every corner minutely and her choice of furnishings, fabrics and paintings enhances the utterly exquisite rooms. They are big and the beds sumptuous under their cascades of drapery. Bright ceramic tiles and modern fittings in the bathrooms make for a lively setting to your ablutions, all to the sound of music if you so choose! But relaxation is the main theme. Aromatic oils pervade the air (and can be purchased here) and the cosy, unhurried restaurant is another olfactory indulgence. Just sit there relishing good food and wine in congenial surroundings – not a care in the world can reach you. *A Rusticae hotel.*

Rooms: 6 with bath & wc; 2 suites.
Price: Double/Twin 9000-13500 Pts;
Suite 12500-16000 Pts.
Breakfast: 850 Pts.
Meals: Dinner 3000 Pts incl. wine.
Closed: Never.

From Oviedo east on E70-N634. Exit at km313 for Villahormes/Hontoria. Through Villahormes then right for Hontoria. Follow signs for Ama de Llaves.

La Montaña Mágica

El Allende
33508 Llanes
Asturias

Tel: 98 5925176
Fax: 98 5925780
Web: www.helicon.es/cuanda.htm

Carlos Bueno Sánchez

Thomas Mann's *The Magic Mountain* inspired this Alpine-style retreat. The rehabilitated farmstead perches on the hillside; the mighty Picos mountains rise up behind; you have an eagle-eye view of the valley below. Ecologically-minded Carlos, who has his own tree-planting programme, had experience of building and restoration for other people and decided to develop this ruined site to live and work in. The finish is rustic and cheerful with lots of stonework and old beams. The small reception area has an information centre, complete with topographical maps of the peaks, that leads to a log-fired sitting room/library. There are six rooms here, some are duplex with huge wood-burning stoves and all have stunning views of those mountains. The other, more recent, section has good, well-insulated, pine-finished rooms with large bathrooms. The dining room stands on its own beside the old *horreo* (granary), now converted into a children's playroom. The good-value lunches and dinners tend to be traditional Asturian with Riojan wine and there's a small bar to enjoy a digestif. There is superb walking and the staff will help organise a trek on one of the many ponies stabled nearby.

Rooms: 12 with bath & wc.
Price: Double/Twin 7200-11000 Pts;
Duplex 10500-13700 Pts.
Breakfast: 600 Pts.
Meals: Lunch/Dinner 1750 Pts.
Closed: Never.

From Santander west on E70 N634. Past Llanes and at km 307 right for Celorio then AS263 to Posada. Here left on AS115 towards Cabrales to La Herreria. Here right, cross Roman bridge and on past Allende.

Map no: 3

Entry no: 38

Hotel Aultre Naray

Peruyes
33547 Cangas de Onis
Asturias

Tel: 98 5840808
Fax: 98 5840848
E-mail: aultre@aultrenaray.com
Web: www.aultrenaray.com

Pilar Calleja & Fernando Mateos

Asturias' grand *casonas* date from a time when returning emigrants invested the gains of overseas adventures in fine, deliberately ostentatious homes. The transition from grand home to fine hotel has been a natural progression at Aultre Naray. The name comes from a medieval motto meaning, "I'll have no other" – as lovers would declare to their heart's desire. Pilar and Fernando, of course, would have you exclaim the same when you come to leave their hotel! Amid the greenest green, looking up to the high peaks of the Cuera sierra, this must be one of the loveliest places to stay in Asturias. Furnishing and decoration is designer-smart; the mood of the hotel is warm, relaxed and comfortable. Designerish print, fabric and furniture have been well married with the more rustic core elements of beam and stone walls. No expense was spared to get things just right; ever slept beneath a Dior duvet before? We marginally preferred the attic rooms but all are memorable. The biggest treat is to breakfast out on the terrace, with a choice of crêpes, home-made cakes, or even eggs and bacon to accompany the heart-stopping views. And there are lots of good places to eat nearby.

Rooms: 10 with bath & wc.
Price: Double/Twin 9000-12800 Pts;
'Special' Double 11000-14500 Pts.
Breakfast: 1000 Pts.
Meals: Dinner 2500 Pts (C) excl. wine.
Closed Wednesdays.
Closed: Never.

From Oviedo towards Santander on m'way, then N634. After passing Arriondas at km335 post turn right towards Peruyes.
Climb for 1km and the hotel is on left just before village.

Hotel El Carmen

El Carmen s/n
33567 Ribadesella
Asturias

Tel: 98 5861289
Fax: 98 5861248
E-mail: hcarmen@green-soft.com
Web: www.green-soft.com/hcarmen

José Ruisánchez Rodrigo

Two enthusiastic Sandras are your delightful hostesses should you stay a night at El Carmen. In the tiniest of hamlets (but there is a cheap and cheerful restaurant right next door) the hotel faces south towards the Sierra de Santianes: all the guest rooms were designed to catch the view when the building recently made the leap from farm to hostelry. The decoration has been a labour of love; one Sandra plied the antique shops in Madrid in the knowledge that her finds could be expertly restored by the other. Their combined female sensitivities have created the prettiest of bedrooms where stencilling and crocheted lace curtains perfectly complement the old dressers, trunks and wardrobes. Bathrooms and heating, on the other hand, are all state of the art. The sitting room and dining room have an open hearth, stone walls and terracotta floors; we enjoyed our breakfast here with choral music to accompany the home-made cake and excellent coffee. This would be an ideal place to stop for two or three nights and head either for the unspoilt beaches of the Asturian coast or up towards the magnificent Picos. And make sure to try a *fabada* (thick bean stew) at the restaurant next door.

Rooms: 8 with bath & wc.
Price: Double/Twin 7500-9500 Pts;
Triple 9500-11500 Pts.
Breakfast: 750 Pts.
Meals: None available
Closed: Never.

From Ribadesella N632 to the west. After 1km turn left on small road to El Carmen. Follow signs for 3km to hotel which is to the left of the road.

Hotel Torrecerredo

Barrio Vega s/n
33554 Arenas de Cabrales
Asturias

Tel: 98 5846705 or 98 5846696
Fax: 98 5846640
E-mail: torretours@fade.es

Pilar Saíz Lobeto

Torrecerredo is just outside the busy town of Arenas de Cabrales, a hub for walkers and sightseers visiting the Picos. The views are stunning – more so even than the photograph suggests – a 'double glory for hearts and eyes'. The hotel is a rectangular, modern building on a hillside just outside the town with a rather garish frontage. The bedrooms are simple, spartan affairs with no great charm; you should ask for one of those on the first floor at the front. But what lifts the hotel into the 'special' league for us is its pine-clad dining/sitting room where guests are treated to simple home cooking – the perfect thing when you return from a day in the mountains. Walking is the main activity here; Jim, Pilar's partner, is a mountain guide and when not leading group walks can take you out. Few know the area as intimately as he and Pilar; they are generous with time and advice on routes and can help plan excursions including nights in mountain refuges, canoeing, riding, climbing or caving. Good value but absolutely no frills. There is an excellent special offer in the low season: 3500 pts per person, room and half board!

Rooms: 19 with bath & wc.
Price: Single 5000 Pts; Double/Twin 7000-9500 Pts incl. breakfast. In winter (apart from Public holidays) just 3500 Pts half-board pp.
Breakfast: 500 Pts.
Meals: Lunch/Dinner 1200 Pts.
Closed: Never.

From Santander N634 towards Oviedo then left on N612 towards Potes. In Panes C6312 (AS114) to Arenas de Cabrales. Through town and right after Hotel Naranjo de Bulnes. Signposted.

Casa de Aldea La Valleja
Rieña
33576 Peñamellera Alta
Asturias

Tel: 98 5925236 or
98 5925320 or
689 183625

Paula Valero Saez

If you fancy turning your hand to preserve-making, cheese-culturing or mountain honey-gathering, then head for La Valleja. Tending the livestock and pottering in the garden are also a must: Paula, your hostess, is passionate about rural tourism and loves her guests to lend a hand. You'll probably pick up a few tips too. The house was built in 1927 and the original materials – bricks, tiles, stones and chestnut beams – used in its restoration maintain the rustic charm. Each bedroom has been named after one of the fruits used in the jam-making, and if your room seems a little sombre at first, throw open the windows and gasp at the glorious view. This is rugged terrain, well off the beaten track, and the walking in the Peñamellera Alta is superb. The best-known walk is that which takes you along the spectacular Cares gorge. You will be well fortified before any mountain trip: the food is all organic and lovingly prepared and vegetables do taste much better when picked straight from the garden. So whether you just want to sit and enjoy the scenery or go off yodelling on the slopes, this is the perfect place. Be sure to buy some of the home-made produce to take back.

Rooms: 5 with bath & wc.
Price: Double/Twin 5000-6000 Pts.
Breakfast: 500 Pts.
Meals: Dinner 1600 Pts.
Closed: Never.

From Santander N634 towards Oviedo for 67km; left to Panes. In Panes right after bridge towards Lagos de Covadonga through Niserias and Alles; on through Pastorias. 0.8km on, right up steep road to Rieña. Park at top of hamlet; house further up on right.

La Tahona de Besnes
33578 Alles
Asturias

Tel: 98 5415749
Fax: 98 5415749
E-mail: latahona@ctv.es

Sarah & Lorenzo Nilsson

In a valley of chestnut, oak and hazelnut with a crystalline brook babbling by, the Tahona de Besnes is a number of old village houses which have been carefully converted into a country hotel. The main building was once a bakery, another a corn mill, a third a stable. At the heart of it all, the bakery-restaurant is prettily decorated with dried flowers, chequered table cloths and old farm implements. Choosing from the menu will be hard; mention should be made of the *pote* (Asturian bean stew), regional cheeses, wild mushrooms and dishes cooked in cider. There is also a terrace up above the brook, a perfect place for a cool glass of cider after your journey or a pre-dinner drink. Rooms and apartments are decorated to match their rustic setting; there are comfy beds, good bathrooms and nothing too fancy. The hotel has plenty of literature on the area and can arrange for you to ride, walk, canoe, fish or take trips out by jeep. And when you finally drag yourself away, make sure you take a local cheese and a bottle of honey-liqueur, or other goodies from the bakery. Besnes is a comfortable, welcoming and beautiful place to stay.

Rooms: 13 with bath & wc.
Price: Double/Twin 7500-9500 Pts.
Breakfast: 750 Pts.
Meals: Lunch/Dinner 1850 Pts (M),
3500 Pts (C).
Closed: 10-30 January.

From Santander N634 towards Oviedo; after 67km left to Panes. In Panes right after bridge towards Lagos de Covadonga to Niserias. Here towards Alles and then follow signs.

Hotel La Casona de Villanueva

33590 Villanueva de
Colombres
Asturias

Tel: 98 5412590
Fax: 98 5412514
E-mail: casonavillanueva@inicia.es

Nuria Juez

Nuria left a city career in search of a quieter life and saw in the old stones of this solid, 18th-century village farmhouse, in the tiniest of hamlets close to the Cantabrian coast, a brighter future. Thanks to careful restoration and imaginative decoration she has created a truly exceptional place to stay. Rooms vary in size and configuration, as you'd expect in an old house, and have quite small bathrooms. There are warm pastel colours on the walls, rugs and cushions from Morocco, lots of paintings and etchings and heaps of antiques. Then there are a host of smaller details, like the home-made jams and flowers at breakfast or the music, mostly classical, which is a part of any meal. The food is good: there are often home-made soups, fish fresh from the slate and the wine list is about quality rather than quantity. But her passion is her walled garden, the most peaceful of retreats where you wander among fish ponds, flowerbeds and the vegetable gardens which supply your table. Nuria speaks excellent English and will help plan your sorties from Villanueva: visit Romanesque churches and sleepy fishing villages or walk along the rocky coastline and in the Picos de Europa Natural Park.

Rooms: 6 with bath & wc; 2 suites.
Price: Single 6500-8000 Pts;
Double/Twin 8000-10000 Pts;
Suite 13000-15000 Pts.
Breakfast: 900 Pts.
Meals: Dinner on request approx.
2500 Pts (C).
Closed: Never.

From Santander N634 towards Oviedo. At km283 post left towards Colombres.
Through village then 2km to Villanueva. Signposted in village.

La Posada de Tollo

Calle Mayor 13   **Tel:** 942 736284
39575 Tollo (Vega de Liebana)
Cantabria

Pepa Estevez Ortega

Imagine having the full majesty of the Picos de Europa at the bottom of your garden, then go to the Posada de Tollo and experience that very thing: Nature at her very boldest looms at the door of this 400-year-old house. Alfonso and Pepa live in the house, the guest quarters are in the former granary. High gates open on to a very Spanish garden with a fountain, a palm tree and stepping stones in the lawn while the full-length front window gives a hint of the rather cosmopolitan inside – and there is the most antiquated wooden balcony above it. The living room is modern and light with its polished oak floor and log fire; beyond is the towering heart of the house. Here, you find a super great mural of an American bar scene on one wall and black and white photographs of flamenco singers in the dining area. Pepa is a wonderful chef, dinner is beautifully presented and there is a good chance your hosts will sit and join you for a glass of wine. A central stairwell leads to the guest rooms which are light, airy and modern: no rustic furniture here but some interesting ornaments on shelves set into the walls. It is relaxed, friendly and the view from the back garden really carries the day.

Rooms: 7 with bath & wc; 1 suite.
Price: Double/Twin 6000-7000 Pts;
Suite 10000-14000 Pts.
Breakfast: 500-750 Pts.
Meals: Dinner 2000 Pts.
Closed: January & February.

From Santander A67/N634 towards Oviedo. Left at Unquera onto N621 to Potes. Here at Hostal Picos de Europa turn left for Tollo. Continue up hill for 2.6km then right at sign for Posada; house on right after 400m.

Casa Gustavo Guesthouse
Aliezo
39584 Tama-Potes
Cantabria

Tel: 942 732010 (Bookings UK 01629 813346)
Fax: 942 732010 (Bookings UK 01629 813346)
E-mail: istuart727@aol.com
Web: www.netizen.co.uk/holidaybank/canfab/accommodation.htm

Lisa & Michael Stuart

In the beautiful Liébana valley lies the tiny hamlet of Aliezo and the old farmhouse of Casa Gustavo. Lisa and Mike are not typical ex-pats; they obviously love their adopted land, have learned its language, know its history and its footpaths. Within the thick stone walls of their house are low timbered ceilings and wood-burning stoves and good smells wafting out from the kitchen. For home it is; don't expect hotelly trimmings like hairdryers, TVs or taped muzak. But walkers will be more than happy with the country cooking, hot showers and decent beds. The house is organic and shambolic; some rooms are small, some large, some have balconies. Redstarts nest beneath the eaves just outside and there are dogs and cats, a cosy lounge, magazines and books. But the main protagonist is Nature and her Picos mountains. Mike and Lisa know the best walks, will advise according to what the weather is doing and provide you with the best maps of the area. Casa Gustavo is a superb place for ornithology and botany – and there are ski-mountaineering courses in winter. Free transport to the beginning of walks is just one manifestation of your hosts' generosity.

Rooms: 1 with bath & wc; 2 twins, 1 double and 1 quadruple sharing bathroom.
Price: Single 2500-3500 Pts; Double/Twin 6000-8000 Pts incl. VAT.
Breakfast: Included.
Meals: Dinner 2500 Pts (M); packed lunch 500 Pts.
Closed: Never.

From Santander A67/N634 towards Oviedo. Left at Unquera onto N621 towards Potes. Shortly before Potes, through Tama, and after 200m left to hamlet of Aliezo. Follow tight bend up to top of village.

Map no: 4 **Entry no: 46**

Hotel Don Pablo

El Cruce   **Tel:** 942 719500 or 942 719523
39594 Pechón   **Fax:** 942 719500 or 942 719523
Cantabria

Pablo & Magdalena Gómez Parra

Don Pablo enjoys a beguiling spot between two estuaries on the outskirts of the hamlet of Pechón. The sea is just a few hundred yards away and a track snakes towards it through green fields from the hotel. This is all the creation of an exceptionally cheery and kindly ex-banker Pablo and his wife Magdalena who never faltered in their conviction that 'it could be done'. Don Pablo is a well-dressed hotel; downstairs is a spick and span little dining room where breakfasts include fresh fruit juices and Cantabrian cakes. Stone, antiques and oak beams decorate the inside, greenery adorns the outside where there is a terrace for sitting out when it's warm. There is a large sitting room with a television of enormous proportions. The bedrooms are medium sized with good wooden beds, chests, handsome oak ceilings and well-equipped bathrooms. We especially liked the attic rooms looking out to the Cantabrian Sea. This is a modern hotel with looks – and a heart.

Rooms: 30 with bath & wc; 4 suites.
Price: Single 6900 Pts; Double/Twin 8900 Pts; Suite 10500 Pts.
Breakfast: Included.
Meals: None available; restaurant next door.
Closed: Never.

From Santander A67/N634 towards Oviedo. 9km after San Vicente de la Barquera right to Pechón. Hotel on right as you leave Pechón.

Posada La Casona de Cos

Cos Mazcuerras   **Tel:** 942 802091 or 942 701550
39509 Mazcuerras   **Fax:** 942 802091
Cantabria

Natalia San Martín & Elias Puente San Martín

In a quiet village of Cantabria, just a short drive from Santillana this could be a super place to stay before or after you take the ferry. La Casona de Cos is small, family-run, unpretentious and a place where locals still far outnumber foreign visitors; in short, Spanish to the core. Bright-eyed, ever-smiling Natalia has built the reputation of the place over the past 33 years and what is so refreshing is not only her pride in her four (possibly five) hundred-year-old home but also the relish with which she greets you as hostess. Enter by way of a busy bar (where would the Spanish be without them?): beyond is the dining room. It feels as if it has always been there: low and beamed, it has marble-topped tables, a fire in the hearth and has a little of the atmosphere of a French bistro. The reader who discovered this place for us enthused about Natalia's home cooking and waxed more lyrically still about the delicious fruit juices at breakfast (e.g. a mix of apple, pear, grapefruit and lemon). Upstairs you'll find simple, spotless guest bedrooms: no frilly extras but it all feels just right. There's also a quiet lounge along the corridor from your room.

Rooms: 12 with bath & wc.
Price: Double/Twin 8000 Pts.
Breakfast: 500 Pts.
Meals: Lunch/DInner 2000-2750 Pts (C).
Closed: Never.

From Santander towards Oviedo, first on A67 and then on N634. In Cabezón de la Sal left onto C625 towards Reinosa, and then left at Puente de Santa C. to Cos. Posada on right in village.

Map no: 4   Entry no: 48

Posada Torre de Quijas

Barrio Vinueva 76   **Tel:** 942 820645
39590 Quijas   **Fax:** 942 838255
Cantabria

Pilar García Lozano

This is a superb little hotel within striking distance of Santander and only minutes
away from the beach. Along with a sizeable farm, it once belonged to a rich lawyer
who lost everything at cards – except the house. It fell into ruin, then Pilar and her
husband bought it as a family home before deciding to transform it into a hotel.
It's all splendidly furnished with fine antiques; fresh fruit and dried flowers give a
natural mood and the contemporary art reflects your hosts' flair and taste, as does
their simple, stylish interior design. A log fire and deep comfortable chairs in pale
cotton covers make the sitting room most attractive; polished chestnut floors
abound and the bedrooms are all white with a fresh cotton theme. Our favourite is
the Lemon Room, in the former chapel, carefully renovated so that original arches
still stand in the middle of the room. The upper part of the house shows off the
old oak beams and the rooms are more intimate up here. We liked the small bar
with its cane furniture and bright lace-covered lamps and the quiet patio full of
greenery. No dinners, but there's a choice of three good restaurants nearby. Great
for a first or last night in Spain.

Rooms: 16 with bath & wc; 4 suites.
Price: Double/Twin 8925-12400 Pts;
Suite 12600-17850 Pts.
Breakfast: 750 Pts.
Meals: None available.
Closed: 23 December-10 January.

From Santander A67/E70 towards
Oviedo. Exit at km 238 for Quijas. Into
village Posada on left, next to tower.

Hostal Mexicana
Calle Juan de Herrera 3
39002 Santander
Cantabria

Tel: 942 222350/54
Fax: 942 222350

**María Eufemia Rodríguez
and Caridad Gómez
Rodríguez**

The photograph says it all: at the Mexicana you feel you are in a different era. This modest little *hostal* first opened its doors in 1955 (when the picture was taken) – and has been run by the family of María Eufemia ever since. A kinder and more gentle family you could not hope to meet. You would probably not write home about the rooms but you WILL have a comfortable night here. The rooms are simple and the furniture is unmistakably Spanish, the bathrooms spic and span. The hostal is excellent value considering that you are right in the town centre. But what we liked most about the Mexicana was its tiny restaurant; it reminded us of an English seaside B&B with its cornices, deliciously dated '50s furniture and sense of timelessness. As you might expect, the food is simple home cooking. Do consider the Mexicana if you are looking for something not too grand. Santander has the charm of a slightly down-at-heel port; watch boats on the quay, admire the Cantabrian Cordillera on a clear day, eat fish-of-the-day in authentic sailors' restaurants.

Rooms: 27 with bath & wc.
Price: Single 3000-4500 Pts;
Double/Twin 4800-7400 Pts.
Breakfast: 400 Pts.
Meals: Lunch/Dinner 1800 Pts (M).
Closed: Never.

In town centre very close to Plaza del Ayuntamiento (town hall) right next to the Banco Zaragoza; underground parking in square with a reduction for Mexicana clients.

Map no: 4   Entry no: 50

Hotel Torre de Ruesga

39810 Valle de Ruesga
Cantabria

Tel: 942 641060
Fax: 942 641172
E-mail: reservas@t-ruesga.com
Web: www.t-ruesga.com

Carmen Caprile Stucchi

The Torre de Ruesga, a perfectly-renovated 17th-century palace surrounded by idyllic gardens, is owned and run by the Caprile family. Sitting on the banks of the river Asón, the historic building combines elegance and sobriety. You go through one of three glazed arches into a stone-finished hall with a cosy little bar to your right. This is a charming hotel and the feel is immediately informal and peaceful. The interior has been lovingly embellished with frescoes by the 19th-century Catalan painter Leon Criach – our favourite is in the pink-coloured banqueting hall on the first floor. On either side are the recreation rooms for board games or a quiet read. The bedrooms are palatially finished in stone and wood, with all the fittings of a modern hotel. In the ornate restaurant, dinner is a mixture of Cantabrian and international cooking accompanied by fine wines from the well-stocked *bodega* but you will get the best view of Torre de Ruesga when you take tea on the terrace or sit in the garden. The delightful grounds also house a large swimming pool with its own gymnasium and sauna – this is indeed the perfect place to relax and unwind. *A Rusticae hotel.*

Rooms: 6 with bath & wc; 4 suites.
Price: Double/Twin 13000-17000 Pts;
Suite 16000-19000 Pts.
Breakfast: 1000 Pts.
Meals: Lunch 2600 Pts (M),
Dinner 3500-4000 Pts (C).
Closed: 2 weeks in January

From Santander A8 towards Bilbao. Exit for Colindras then south on N629 to Ramales de Victoria. Here right on C530 towards Arredondo to Valle. Here right at sign for Torre de Ruesga.

Guipúzcoa
•

Navarre
•

Vizcaya
•

La Rioja
•

Alvara
•

Basque Country – Navarre – La Rioja

"The world is a book and those who do not travel read only one page"
– St. Augustine

Iketxe

Apartado 343   **Tel:** 943 644391
20280 Hondarribia
Guipúzcoa

Patxi Arroyo & Fátima Iruretagoiena

Another enchanting B&B in the rolling green Basque country. Very near the lovely town of Hondarribia yet entirely rural, Iketxe is a house that matches its owners: quiet, unpretentious and utterly Basque. You can only wonder at the energy of the engagingly enthusiastic owner, Patxi, who built his home virtually single-handed and made much of the furniture too. He finished it all just four years ago but you might not guess that Iketxe is a new house, so faithfully have local building traditions been respected. The rooms are beautiful; first there are the views and then the decoration – wood floors, bright kilims, handsome bathrooms and no two of them alike. Floors are terracotta and two of the upstairs rooms have their own balcony. It would be hard to choose a favourite but ours would probably be number 1. We were glad that there was no television to break the spell. Fátima will happily help at breakfast time when it comes to planning your visits or recommending one of the many restaurants in Hondarribia. Hats off to Patxi for realising his dream and sharing it with us: several readers have written to say how much they approve of the place and children would love it here too.

Rooms: 6 with bath & wc.
Price: Single 5600-6400 Pts;
Double/Twin 7000-8000 Pts.
Breakfast: 600 Pts.
Meals: None available.
Closed: Never.

From Irún towards Hondarribia. Just before airport left towards Arkoll, then follow signs to Iketxe.

Entry no: 52   Map no: 5

Caserío Maidanea

Barrio Arkoll   **Tel:** 943 640855
Apartado 258
20280 Hondarribia
Guipúzcoa

Rosamaría Ugarte Matxain

Maidanea, one of the first B&Bs to open in this beautiful corner of the Basque country, is a chalet-style farmhouse on a hill looking over the river to France. It is a traditional Spanish home with a mix of old and new furnishing, tiled floors, lace curtains, a collection of old plates and plants and books. It has been much restored – you probably wouldn't guess it was more than 400 years old. There is a big, galleried sitting/dining room for breakfast which is a relaxed occasion, served as late as you like; the silence of the place and good mattresses encourage late starts. When the weather is right you can breakfast on a beautiful terrace with wonderful views out across the surrounding hills. The bedrooms, on the first and attic floors, are modern and medium-sized. Señora has lavished much care on details such as her dried flower arrangements and her hand-embroidered sheets and cushions. Some rooms have the view across to France and number 4, our favourite, has its own balcony. The whole house is utterly spotless, there is a good mature garden and the old streets of nearby Hondarribia to discover: do stay for more than just one night. *Owners speak French.*

Rooms: 6 with bath & wc.
Price: Double/Twin 7000-8000 Pts.
Breakfast: 600 Pts.
Meals: None available.
Closed: Never.

From Hondarribia take Irún road and turn right just past airport. Through Amute, on towards Bekoerrota; signposted.

Map no: 5   **Entry no: 53**

Hostal Alemana

Calle San Martín 53
20007 San Sebastián
Guipúzcoa

Tel: 943 462544
Fax: 943 461771
E-mail: halemana@adegi.es
Web: www.hostalalemana.com

**Luis & Roberto Garagorri
Esnoz**

If visiting the North of Spain do spend at least one night in San Sebastián, one of
Spain's most attractive towns. La Concha, a marvellous sweep of golden sand, is the
centre of life and, just one street back from the promenade, Hostal Alemana is ideal
if the grander hotels are not your thing. The hostal occupies the upper floors of an
elegant turn-of-the century townhouse. The Garagorri family has run a hostal here
for more than thirty years and it was given a thorough face-lift just a couple of years
ago. Bedrooms have been designed with business folk in mind, with those credit-
card keys, trouser presses and minibars. But they are really roomy with good beds
and large bathrooms. The breakfast room is a lovely place to start your day with a
big buffet, good coffee and freshly squeezed orange juice: the light pouring in from
the three windows in its curved wall will take your mind off the taped music
pouring in from elsewhere. It would be tempting to use this as a last stop before
the ferry and have dinner at one of the seafood restaurants like 'La Nicolasa'. Or go
local and bar hop, feasting on any number of the delicious 'pinchos'.

Rooms: 21 with bath & wc.
Price: Single 7000-9000 Pts;
Double/Twin 9000-12000 Pts.
Breakfast: 700 Pts.
Meals: None available.
Closed: Never.

From motorway take exit 9 for Ondarreta;
continue towards town centre. Hostal is
2km from motorway exit.

Hotel Peruskenea

Beruete
31866 Basaburua Mayor
Navarre

Tel: 948 503370
Fax: 948 503284
E-mail: peruskenea@peruskenea.com
Web: www.peruskenea.com

José María Astíz & Conchi Amezkueta

The journey up to Peruskenea is by way of Navarre's deep forests; you are headed for a place of great natural beauty and tranquility. The old ruin of this country manor-house was rescued by Jose María Astíz and has undergone a complete metamorphosis to become one of the Basque country's most charming small hotels. The building stands alone with its whitewashed façade and bright wooden galleries looking out across the beautiful Basaburua valley. Breakfasts here are unforgettable; not just for the great spread laid before you but for those amazing mountain vistas. You may feel inspired to put your walking boots on and head off along one of the many pathways which criss-cross the countryside. The bedrooms on the first and attic floors have plumped pillows, large double beds and warm duvets. They have handsome oak parquet floors and are beamed; they feel light and airy and the bathrooms are excellent. There are two lounges, one on the first floor and the other up in the attic with a fireplace. The hotel's food is trad-regional; hearty soups, stews and roast meats. You are at the heart of the Navarrese vineyards where the tempranillo grape rules supreme so do choose a local wine.

Rooms: 9 with bath & wc.
Price: Single 7000-8000 Pts; Double/Twin 10000-11000 Pts; Room for 3 12000-13000 Pts; Room for 4 14000-15000 Pts.
Breakfast: 1000 Pts.
Meals: Lunch/Dinner 2500 Pts.
Closed: Never.

From Pamplona A15 towards San Sebastián. Exit at km118 then follow signs to Udabe. Continue on through Jauntsarats then left at sign for Hotel Peruskenea.

Map no: 5   **Entry no: 55**

Venta Udabe

Valle de Basaburúa
31869 Udabe
Navarre

Tel: 948 503105 or 609 440004
Fax: 948 503400
E-mail: udabe@jet.es

Juan José Mate López and Estela Gordo Juarez

On the edge of a tiny Navarrese village, Venta Udabe is a small country inn where every last detail of décor seems designed for aesthetic appeal. Juan José and Estela are young, friendly and very keen for guests to get to know this beautiful area. The cosy timbered dining room has ochre walls, a fireplace and stacks of antique pieces. There are two sitting rooms, one downstairs with a fireplace and one upstairs with peace and quiet. There are dried flowers and masses of old farm implements. The bedrooms have been designed with the same affection, books and flowers echoing the warmth of the wooden furniture and floors. Rooms at the front are slightly smaller and give onto a (quiet) road. Udabe's food has already won it laurels and is highly rated by all the food guides: Juan José formerly managed one of Vitoria's best restaurants. Specialities are *arroz con almejas y borraja*: rice with clams and borage, and *chuletón*, a superb beef steak served on a sizzling iron. The reputation is spreading and it is generously priced. Breakfast is a feast of fruits, yoghurt and home-made jams, after which you may ride out, on a bike or a horse, into the deepest green of the Navarre hills.

Rooms: 8 with bath & wc.
Price: Double/Twin 11000 Pts.
Breakfast: Included.
Meals: Lunch/Dinner 4000 Pts (C).
Closed Mondays.
Closed: 24 December-24 January.

From Pamplona N240A towards San
Sebastián. Then N130 still towards San
Seb. and at km117 post in Latasa Uriza,
take 2nd right following signs to Udabe.
On left as you pass through village.

Entry no: 56

Map no: 5

Venta de Donamaría

Barrio Ventas 4
31750 Donamaría
Navarre

Tel: 948 450708
Fax: 948 450708
E-mail: donamariako@jet.es

Elixabet Badiola & Imanol Luzuriaga

A mouth-watering address! Donamaría is hidden away off to one side of a pass through the mountains between France and Spain, within striking distance of Pamplona. The place has a long tradition of receiving travellers: there has been a restaurant here for almost 150 years. Your hosts are sophisticated, amusing folk whose love of the finer things in life is given ample expression in their guesthouse. These two old village houses (guest rooms in one, restaurant in the other) are packed full of *objets d'art*, antiques, old toys, dried flowers and a few surprises to boot; it all creates an intimate, relaxed atmosphere, much of it tongue in cheek. This is most certainly a place to linger over lunch or dinner; connoisseurs rave about the traditional Navarre dishes which has 'a French touch and modern elements' – and the foie gras is superb. The rooms are all that you'd expect – big, with antique furniture, timbered ceilings, lots of dried flowers and richly-coloured fabrics. Mother, father and daughter welcome you most graciously into their home. It is, by the way, set among old oak forests where the heart soars at every turn.

Rooms: 5 with bath or shower & wc.
Price: Double/Twin 8800 Pts.
Breakfast: Included.
Meals: Approx 2000 Pts (M); 3000-4000 Pts (C). No meals on Sunday evenings or Mondays.
Closed: Never.

From San Sebastián take motorway towards France, then N121 to San Esteban (Doneztebe). Here NA404 towards Oroquieta/Saldías. Venta in village of Donamaría on right.

Map no: **5**

Atalaya Hotel

Passeo de Txorrokopunta 2
48360 Mundaka
Vizcaya

Tel: 94 6177000/6876888
Fax: 94 6876899
E-mail: jomacsl@euskalnet.net

María Carmen Alonso Elizaga

Atalaya is one of the friendliest and most 'family' of Vizcaya's small hotels; the Spanish daily *El País* gives it no less than 10 out of 10 for service! You couldn't better its position, in the centre of Mundaka, a stone's throw from the lively fish market and just yards from a beach at the edge of a deep inlet carved by the Cantabrian sea. The house speaks of the optimism of the early years of the century; an open, galleried frontage lets in the ever-changing light and lets you contemplate sand, sea and the adjacent church tower of Santa María. The owners – kind, straightforward folk – care deeply for their hotel. You'll meet them when you arrive and they find time to help you plan your visits. The best rooms have sea views but they're all worth a night; medium-sized, carpeted and with modern prints, they are spick-and-span, quiet and comfortable. There are more gadgets than you need, plus king-size beds. This would be a marvellous place to spend a last night before the ferry (car and belongings safe in the free car park). There is good food in the recently opened restaurant: steaks and – of course – fish are the specialities. One of our favourites.

Rooms: 11 with bath & wc.
Price: Double/Twin 9300-12900 Pts.
Breakfast: 1100 Pts.
Meals: Tapas & light meals at lunchtime; Dinner 4000 Ptas (C).
Closed: Never.

From Bilbao take A8/E-70 motorway, leaving at Exit 18. Then BI-635 via Gernika to Mundaka; left into village centre. Hotel near Santa María church, 50m from ferry.

Entry no: 58

Map no: 5

Urresti

Barrio Zendokiz, 12
48314 Gautegiz Arteaga
Vizcaya

Tel: 94 6251843
Fax: 94 6251843
E-mail: urresti@nexo.es

María Goitia

One of the very latest Basque B&Bs to open, this is a dream come true for María and José María, Urrresti's two friendly young owners, who have completely transformed the ruins of this old farmhouse which they stumbled across in the deep greenery of the Basque countryside. Outside it still looks like a 17th-century farmhouse but inside it is has a much more modern feel. Breakfast is served in the large sitting/dining room, and good value it is too; cheese, home-made jam, fruit from the farm and plenty of coffee. For other meals guests have free rein in a fully-equipped kitchen. The smart, impeccably clean bedrooms upstairs have parquet floors and new, country-style furniture; some have their own balcony and number 6 is especially roomy with a sofa-bed. The house stands in beautiful rolling countryside with the sea not far away – and Gernika, too. There are old forests of oak and chestnut to be explored on foot or maybe on the bikes which are available for guests. The whole area is a Natural Park and many come here just for the birdlife. And there are good restaurants just 3km away.

Rooms: 6 with bath & wc.
Price: Double/Twin 6000-7000 Pts.
Breakfast: 600 Pts.
Meals: None available.
Closed: Never.

From Gernika take road towards Lekeitio and at fork continue on lower road towards Lekeitio. 6km from Gernika left towards Elanchobe. House on right after 1.2km at sign 'Nekazal Turismoa' (careful: there is another sign earlier for different B&B).

Map no: 5

Entry no: 59

Txopebenta

Barrio Basetxetas
48314 Gautegiz-Arteaga
Vizcaya

Tel: 94 6254923
Fax: 94 6254923

Juan Angel Bizzkarra

Between Gernika and the rugged north coast, in an area of great natural beauty, Txopebenta is one of the most remarkable of a growing number of first-class B&Bs in the Basque country. The house bears witness to the boundless energy and optimism of its owner Juan 'Txope' Bizzkarra. He decided that to create a guesthouse at his 19th-century farmhouse he would have to add another floor; he did so by careful use of old railway sleepers which he fashioned in every possible way: as lintels, stairs, roof supports, even as benches and tables. The sitting/breakfast room is ideal for a convivial breakfast with delicious local cheese and fresh fruit juice; a fire is lit in the hearth whenever it's cold. The rooms at the top are very small, low-ceilinged but cosy: light sleepers should know that insulation between rooms is minimal. There is a terrace where you can sit in summer. Your hosts love their native land and are keen that you should visit its every corner. Don't miss the 'painted forest' in the Oma valley and the Biosphere Reserve of Urdabai with its spectacular birdlife. There are beaches within easy walking distance.

Rooms: 6 with bath & wc.
Price: Double 7000 Pts; Triple 8000 Pts.
Breakfast: 700 Pts.
Meals: None available.
Closed: Never.

From Gernika take road towards Lekeitio and after 6km left towards Elanchobe. House on right after 0.8km.

Entry no: 60

Map no: 5

Ziortxa-Beitia

Goiherria 13
48279 Bolibar
Vizcaya

Tel: 946 165259
E-mail: zdiber@teleline.es

Francisco Rios

Our inspector arrived here with a bag of pears and green peppers and asked the owner – known as Paco to all and sundry – if they could be incorporated into his evening meal. Without batting an eyelid, Paco whisked the ingredients off to the kitchen whence the peppers later appeared with some freshly cooked pork and the wine-soaked pears were served with a smile. No, it wasn't a test of Basque hospitality: the fresh produce had come from the Paco's brother's garden and was in danger of spoiling (family loyalty runneth even unto pears). Nor is it an example of services offered to guests – it is just an illustration of your genial host's no-fuss-no-frills attitude. His old farmhouse sits in remote countryside below a Cistercian monastery on the famous pilgrim route to Santiago de Compostela. The rooms are basic modern-rustic but comfortable and very clean. Food is of the good home-cooked variety and although the bar can get quite lively in the evenings, the nights are blissfully quiet – just the hoot of the odd owl to serenade you. Nearby Bolibar is the birthplace of Simon Bolivar, the liberator of South America. The museum is well worth a visit, as is a walk round the grounds of the monastery.

Rooms: 6 with bath & wc.
Price: Double/Twin 5000-6500 Pts.
Breakfast: 600 Pts.
Meals: Lunch/Dinner 1200 Pts.
Closed: Never.

From Bilbao A8 towards San Sebastián; exit 17 to Durango and here BI633 towards Markina. In village of Iruzubieta, left to Bolibar. Here left towards Ziortxa/ Colegiata. House on right after 2.5km.

Map no: 5

Entry no: 61

Mendi Goikoa

Barrio San Juan 33
48291 Axpe-Atxondo
Vizcaya

Tel: 94 6820833
Fax: 94 6821136
E-mail: mendigoikoa@interbook.net
Web: www.mendigoikoa.com

Agurtzane Telleria & Iñaki Ibarra

"Donde el silencio se oye" – (where you can hear the silence) – is the way the owners like to describe their hotel. Peaceful it is, and utterly beautiful. Mendi Goikoa is one of a new breed of chic country hotels which provide *Cordon Bleu* cooking and a bed to match. The hotel is two 19th-century farms – big, handsome buildings in a huge meadow with wide views from every room. The main restaurant is vast and high-ceilinged – it was the old barn – and absolutely packed with antiques. The emphasis is on traditional Basque dishes with a few of the chef's own innovations. There is a smaller breakfast room and a real gem of a bar in the other building. It is a popular venue for the suit-and-tie brigade though you won't feel uncomfortable if you are not one of them. A wedding-feast place, in fact, but don't be put off. The guest rooms are as good-looking as the dining room with beams, exposed stones, some lovely old pieces, lots of carpet – and utterly seductive views. And there are lovely walks up to (or towards!) the surrounding peaks to work up an appetite for dinner: do check to see that it will be available when you make your booking.

Rooms: 12 with bath & wc.
Price: Single 9850 Pts;
Double/Twin 14500 Pts.
Breakfast: 1000 Pts.
Meals: Lunch/Dinner 3250 Pts (M).
Closed Sunday eve or Mondays.
Closed: Mid-December-mid-January.

From A8 exit 17 for Durango. From there
BI-632 towards Elorrio. In Atxondo right
to Axpe; house up above village,
signposted.

Entry no: 62

Map no: 5

Hospedería Señorío de Briñas

Travesía de la Calle Real 3
26290 Briñas-Haro
La Rioja

Tel: 941 304224
Fax: 941 304345
E-mail: hsbrinas@arrakis.es
Web: www.tecnitel.com/briñas

Angela Gómez & Pedro Ortega

Briñas is one of the prettiest villages of La Rioja. Its stately houses and ornate churches pay witness to its Golden Age, the 16th century, when the region reached its economic zenith and many noble families set up home. The façade of this 'casona' or mansion-house gives little idea of the artistic treat that awaits once you pass beneath its portal; its great idiosyncrasy is a series of *trompe l'oeil* frescoes which will have you groping for a walking stick, looking out of a window or pulling back a curtain, all of which only exist in paint and in the mind's eye of their Polish artist-creator. No surprise to learn, when faced with such decorative care-and-flair, that Angela and Pedro are interior designers. When they embarked on their own project the building was little more than a ruin: the previous owners had ransacked the place in search of a mythical hidden treasure trove! Treasures galore await you now; a vast, individually decorated and blissfully quiet parquet-floored bedroom, a breakfast which will include eggs scrambled with onions and freshly squeezed juices and a cosy bar where you can get to grips with Rioja's most famous export, its superb oaky red wine.

Rooms: 11 with bath & wc; 3 suites.
Price: Double/Twin 15500 Pts;
Suite 20000 Pts.
Breakfast: Included.
Meals: Light snacks available in evenings.
Closed: Never.

From A68 take exit 8 for
Miranda/Zambrana. Then follow N232
towards Logroño. Go through a tunnel
and then after 8km, after going up hill, left
for Laguardia, Labastida, Ábalos. You will see the hotel after 300m.

Map no: 5

Entry no: 63

Antigua Bodega de Don Cosme Palacio

Carretera de Elciego s/n
01300 Laguardia
Álava

Tel: 941 121195
Fax: 941 600210
E-mail: antiguabodega@cosmepalacio.com

Begoña Viñegra Uzquiano

So you like the best in food and wine? Then don't miss out on this double treat. Don Cosme Palacio is one of Rioja's most reputed *bodegas*: the tempranillo grape has been working its magic here, in casks of French oak, for more than a century. Visitors have been coming from all over the world to taste and buy the wine and it seemed right and proper that they should be offered food as delicious as the wine itself. Thus was born the restaurant where Jean-Pierre, Don Cosmé's French-Basque cook (what better credentials?), works his alchemy: he can turn the base elements (always fresh, always local) into such gourmet delights that the price seems almost a token payment. I had one of the most delicious meals of my years in Spain. Before or after dinner head down to the cellars where there is a bar for tastings and the main wine stores which have recently been decorated with a remarkable series of frescos depicting all things oenological: Dionysius, Noah (an early wine-buff), harvest time and so on. Bedrooms are named after a different grape variety and all are beautifully decorated. In short, superb: an obligatory stopover if visiting La Rioja: be sure to visit the winery.

Rooms: 12 with bath & wc; 1 suite.
Price: Single 8800-8900 Pts;
Double/Twin 9900-10800 Pts; Suite
12600-13900 Pts.
Breakfast: 925 Pts.
Meals: Lunch /Dinner 4000 Pts (M).
Closed Sun nights and Monday.
Closed: 23 December-23 January.

From A68 exit 10 for Lenicero. Through village and then left to Elciego and on to Laguardia. Hotel on right as you enter the village.

Aragón – Catalonia

"The traveler sees what he sees; the tripper sees what he has come to see"
– G.K. Chesterton 1874-1936

Hotel La Santa María

Passeig de la Ribera 52
08870 Sitges
Barcelona

Tel: 93 8940999
Fax: 93 8947871
E-mail: reservas@lasantamaria.com
Web: www.lasantamaria.com

Antonio Arcas Sánchez

Sitges has been a fashionable resort town with wealthier Catalans for many years. The crowd is more international now but the town has kept its intimacy and life centres on the promenade and beach. At the heart of it all is the Santa María. It is a cheery building; the pale peach façade is set off by a rambling bougainvillaea and a bright apricot and orange awning which covers its lively terrace; within is the dining room, a small sitting and bar area and the bedrooms – all under the caring eye of Señora Ute, the hotel's indefatigable owner who effortlessly switches between half a dozen languages. Some bedrooms have balconies and a view across the palm trees to the bay beyond and all are well furnished with functional wooden beds, tables and desks; one or two have their original tiled floors and older furniture. All, too, have prints of Sitges and there may well be fresh flowers. Downstairs the atmosphere is faintly redolent of a (smart) British seaside hotel and the food is good; as you'd expect, there is a lot of seafood and fish on the menu – the sea laps almost up to your table. You'll need to book ahead here, especially in season. The hotel has its own car park.

Rooms: 75 with bath & wc.
Price: Single 9000 Pts; Double/Twin
9500-12500 Pts.
Breakfast: 1300 (buffet).
Meals: Lunch/Dinner 1500-1800 Pts (M),
4000 Pts (C).
Closed: 20 December-20 January.

From Barcelona A16 motorway through
Tuneles de Garaf. Take the SECOND exit
for Sitges centre, follow signs to Hotel
Calipolis. The Santa María is on sea-front.

El Trapiche
Can Vidal
Els Casots
08739 Subirats
Barcelona

Tel: 93 7431469
Fax: 93 7431469
E-mail: michael-johnston@bmlisp.com

Marcela & Michael Johnston

A dream really: imagine waking from a deep slumber to see the crags of Montserrat silhouetted against a blushing dawn and vineyards all around... *cava* (Catalan bubbly) vineyards at that. It is easy to see what drew this couple to this old Masía. Michael is front of house and will probably be cook: he is gregarious, multilingual and fun and knows all the local lore that would be of interest to you. You'll probably meet the whole family because the focus of El Trapiche is relaxed and wholesome meals are eaten *en famille*: your hosts are too generous with the wine too. Bedrooms are large: two are twin-bedded with showers and the best, the Blue Room, is enormous with a table and chairs from where you can contemplate the lovely view. They have simple pine furniture, warm colours, darkened beams and wooden floors, all with central heating for the colder months. If you are interested in wine visit the Codorniu cellars which are just down the road and there's the wine museum at Vilafranca, just five miles away. And if you fancy a walk you can be picked up at the far end by this ever-obliging couple. Many readers have told us just how much they have enjoyed the Johnston's company.

Rooms: 3 with bath or shower & wc.
Price: Twin 12500 Pts; Blue Room 10000 Pts.
Breakfast: Included.
Meals: Lunch/Dinner 3000 Pts incl. wine.
Closed: Christmas & New Year.

From A7 exit 27 for Sant Sadurni. As you leave motorway immediately left towards Ordal. Continue for 3km to Els Casots, and take first track on left 600m beyond hamlet.

Map no: 8

Entry no: 66

Hotel Colón

Avenida Catedral 7
08002 Barcelona

Tel: 93 3011404
Fax: 93 3172915
E-mail: info@hotelcolon.es
Web: www.hotelcolon.es

Marina Canali

Grand and imposing, the Hotel Colón is at the heart of Barcelona, overlooking a magnificent square directly opposite the cathedral. To the right sweeps the Via Laietana, a bustling turn of the century artery leading to the Picasso Museum whilst a short walk to the left brings you to the dizzy delights of La Rambla, Barcelona's most famous street. Ahead lies the medieval 'gothic' quarter: designer emporia lure you from behind. The Colón lives up to its a four-star status. The elegant décor and muted gold/ochre colour schemes of the lounge and bar, their plants, chintzy sofas and subdued lighting, give off a whiff of 'old money' and easy comfort. The pale gold and cream dining room has an intimate feel for a large hotel; it has a traditional tiled fireplace paying homage to the hotel's namesake, Colón, (Columbus). The breakfast room is more homely, a Catalan rustic idyll, with terracotta tiles and traditional dark furniture. Cooking is regional Spanish with an emphasis on seafood, as you would expect in a coastal city. The bedrooms are comfortable and decorated in modern, low-key colours although some are in a more classical Regency style. A room with a view is worth the extra.

Rooms: 142 with bath & wc; 9 suites.
Price: Single 18000-22500 Pts; Double/Twin 27000-32500 Pts; Suite 47500-52000 Pts.
Breakfast: 2100 Pts.
Meals: Lunch 2600 Pts (M), 4000 Pts (C); dinner 3600 Pts (M), 4500 Pts (C):
Closed: Never.

Arriving in Barcelona follow signs for Puerto de Barcelona/Ciutat Vella and take the Via Laietana away from the sea then left into the Avenida Catedral; hotel is on the right. Three car parks right next to hotel: one in front and two behind. Space reserved for Colón clients.

Hotel Peninsular
Calle San Pablo 34
El Raval
08001 Barcelona

Tel: 93 3023138
Fax: 93 4123699

**Agustín Herrero &
Ernesto Catalan**

Once a convent, the Peninsular became a hotel in 1876. Run for over three decades by the Herrero family, the reception is still manned by their offspring. Their good nature is evident the second you enter this Art Nouveau delight. In a pedestrianised side street off the Rambla, the hotel is in the hub of what was the city's 'China town', once a byword for all things decadent. The area has seen much gentrification but it remains one of the city's more bohemian areas and still has a slightly dissolute air. Bedrooms are simply furnished in traditional Spanish style, with immaculate bathrooms, some of which are newish. While you won't get fabulous views, the sight and sounds of Mediterranean family life in neighbouring patios is charming. The dining room has unusual Moorish arches and finely crafted lamps which give it a stylish *fin de siècle* atmosphere. There is no lounge but the striking interior patio makes it an irrelevance: the refreshing pale green and white décor, the abundance of plants and wicker furniture may make older readers think of Raffles. Book well ahead – it's very popular.

Rooms: 59 with bath & wc and 21 sharing bath & wc.
Price: Double/Twin 10200 Pts; Double/Twin sharing bathroom 7500 Pts.
Breakfast: Included.
Meals: None available.
Closed: Never.

Calle San Pablo (Sant Pau) is off to the right of the Ramblas as you go from the Plaza de Cataluña to the Paseo Colón, next to the Liceo theatre. Easiest to leave car in underground car park in Plaza de Cataluña then take taxi or walk (5 minutes) to hotel.

Map no: 8   Entry no: 68

Regencia Colón
Calle Sagristans 13-17
08002 Barcelona

Tel: 93 3189858
Fax: 93 3172822
E-mail: info@hotelcolon.es
Web: www.hotelcolon.es

Marina Canali

In a quiet street behind its sister hotel, the Colón, the Regencia Colón may lack some of its sibling's grandeur but it is no poor relation. It shares its brilliant position, a stone's throw away from the enticing warren of streets of Barcelona's medieval quarter – and it is much less expensive. It could be a marvellous starting point to explore the city known as 'la gran encisera': the great enchantress. The '70's brick façade is a tad uninspiring but what it lacks in character is amply compensated by the friendly and helpful staff. The Spanish, bless them, are indomitably and vigorously talkative so its a relief to escape the streets into the hotel's serene, unaffected lounge, with its wicker chairs, floral sofas and greenery. The dining room is rather café-ish but agreeable nevertheless, with marble-topped tables, simple black furniture and vibrant lime green walls. Bedrooms are uncluttered and straightforward but pleasant: most have a muted ochre/peach colour scheme, chintzy bedspreads and framed prints. Bathrooms are spanking new in functional white with pretty floral framed mirrors. In a city which has beauty at every turn, a little unadorned simplicity is easily forgiven.

Rooms: 55 with bath & wc.
Price: Single 13500 Pts; Double/Twin 20500 Pts incl. breakfast.
Breakfast: 1350 Pts.
Meals: Lunch 1500 Pts.
Closed: Never.

Arriving in Barcelona follow signs for Puerto de Barcelona/Ciutat Vella then take Via Laietana away from the sea. Left into the Avinguida Catedral; Hotel Colón is on the right and Regencia Colón immediately behind it in Calle Sagristans. Two car parks right next to hotel; space reserved for Regencia Colón clients.

Can Rosich

Apartado de Correos 275
08398 Santa Susanna
Barcelona

Tel: 93 7678473
Fax: 93 7678473
E-mail: canrosich@teleline.es

Montserrat Boter Fors

You are very close to the beach, Barcelona and Figueres are an easy drive away and yet you're hidden away up a thickly wooded valley in 20 hectares of bucolic loveliness. You wouldn't think that this old *masía* is more than two centuries old: it's been completely rebuilt in recent years. To one side of the large hallway is a beamed dining room with six tables decked out in bright chequered cloths. Cooking is wholesome, delicious and amazing value when you consider that the price includes good Catalan wine. Among Montserrat's specialities are rabbit, pork from the farm and (order in advance!) *Asado de Payés*, a thick stew with three different meats, plums and pine nuts. Breakfast, too, is a hearty meal: cheese and cold meats, fruit and orange juice. Can Rosich's bedrooms are large and comfy and are named after different birds and animals of the region. Beds are antique but mattresses new and you'll find a beribboned, neatly ironed bundle of towels on your duvet, a nice touch. Most of the rooms have space to add a third bed. Just five minutes away are trains that can whizz you in and out of Barcelona in just one hour. A great favourite with our readers.

Rooms: 6 with bath or shower & wc.
Price: Double 6400 Pts.
Breakfast: 700 Pts.
Meals: Dinner 1700 Pts incl. wine.
Book ahead.
Closed: 20-27 December.

From A7 exit 9 for Maçanet. Then N2 towards Barcelona to Santa Susanna. Here, right at first roundabout for 'nucleo urbano', then follow signs for 2km to Can Rosich.

Map no: 8

Entry no: 70

El Folló

El Folló   **Tel:** 93 8429116
08593 Tagamanent
Barcelona

Mercè Brunés & Jaume Villanueva

It's hard to believe that El Folló, with its dramatic views of pine-clad mountains, fresh breezes and wild flowers, is only a hour from Barcelona. A traditional Catalan *casa pairal* ('father's house') it has been masterfully restored by Mercè and Jaume: their B&B is a triumphant mix of old and new. The bedrooms are exceptional with their original natural stone invigorated by bold colours, with a fruit and flower motif throughout. Hues range from the vibrant red of the 'strawberry' room to the gentler mauvish tones of the 'mallow' room. Lighting is subdued and complements the beamed ceilings, simple white curtains and fine bedlinen. Their bathrooms have free-standing tubs, natural wood surrounds and breathtaking views. Reminders of a rural past are never far away: the dining room, once a stable, now has a long wooden table as its focal point. A feeling of abundance and well-being abounds: the original trough now groans under piles of fruit and traditional kitchen tools. Mercè is proud of her cooking. Although a vegetarian herself she happily caters for meat-eaters, too. An unusual delicacy is her courgette bread and be sure to try her home-made *cava* (Catalan bubbly).

Rooms: 9 with bath & wc.
Price: Double/Twin Half-board 16000 Pts, Full-board 20000 Pts.
Breakfast: Included.
Meals: Dinner included (and lunch, if full-board).
Closed: Never.

From north A7 towards Barcelona then take exit 14 and pick up N152 towards Vic. At km 44 (opposite petrol station) turn right then go straight ahead at roundabout. Follow signs for approx 2km to El Folló.

Entry no: 71   Map no: 8

La Morera

08553 El Brull　　　　　　　　　**Tel:** 93 8840477
Barcelona

Ramón Casamitjana, Sergi Peytubi, Juan Carlos Cano, Xavier Villanueva

If you've dreamt of escaping the rat-race and heading for the hills, then La Morera is for you. This is precisely what the quartet who run La Morera did seven years ago. A gentler existence beckoned, centred on restoring a 17th-century *masía* in the Montseny massif. The relaxed atmosphere is palpable the minute you enter the walled courtyard and come across a pair of dogs dozing in the sun. The cosy, shambolic dining room is dominated by a long, communal dining table and a magnificent *llar de foc*, the traditional Catalan fireplace: it is given pride of place in winter when the aromas of home reared meats, good conversation and robust Priorat wine make for memorable evenings. The lounge is beguilingly unpretentious, furnished with a miscellany of old furniture, sofas and ancient chandeliers. Restoration is an still ongoing so unvarnished floors and exposed plasterwork are easily overlooked. Bedrooms are 'mezzanined' with old, carved beds and antique mirrors and steepish stairs leading down to the sleeping area. Bathrooms are newish with showers. Hearty dinners are eaten to the beat of Catalan rock whilst breakfast is simple but delicious.

Rooms: 8 with bath & wc.
Price: Double/Twin Half-board 11000 Pts, Full-board 13000 Pts; Triple Half-board 14500 Pts, Full-board 17500 Pts; Quadruple Half-board 18000 Pts, Full-board 22000 Pts.
Breakfast: Included.
Meals: Dinner (and lunch) included.
Closed: Weekdays from November to March apart from Bank Holidays.

From French border A7 south to Girona, then west on Eix Transversal. Exit for Viladrau. Continue on to Seva and then follow signs for El Brull. Just past village at km 30.5 La Morera signposted on right; 2km of track. Sign easy to miss.

Map no: 8　　　　　　　　　　　　　　　　　**Entry no:** 72

Mas Pratsevall

Mas Pratsevall s/n
Apartado de Correos 123
08522 Taradell
Barcelona

Tel: 93 8800880
Fax: 93 8850566

Ramón Godayol Vallmitjana

A number of fine old buildings in the village of Taradell are testimony to a once thriving weaving industry; mechanised looms put an end to its golden years but you still meet a number of well-heeled Catalans here. Nowadays they use the village as a hill-station during the hot summer months, a place where they can escape the noise and pollution of Barcelona. This imposing edifice sits proud on a hill looking out over the village. In summer, window boxes of geraniums lighten a rather sober façade; the mood of restraint is carried over into the cool uncluttered interior of the two guest apartments which are in the old granaries. Both are large enough for a family (each has two double bedrooms and one single) and have all the necessary bits and pieces for a comfortable week or two of self-catering – in addition to fridges, ovens and hobs, each has a washing machine and central heating. What brings them into the 'special' league is their lovely turn-of-the-century furniture which matches the beams and terracotta floors. Shuttered windows look to the large surrounding garden; beyond it is a stand of old oak and pine trees, a shady spot to wander or picnic on sunny days.

Rooms: 2 self-catering apartments sleeping up to 6.
Price: Apartment (for 2) 12500 Pts.
Minimum stay 2 nights. Weekly 75000 Pts for 2.
Breakfast: Self-catering.
Meals: None available – self-catering.
Closed: Never.

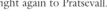

From Barcelona towards Vic on N152. Exit for Taradell/Centre Comercial. After approx. 4km right at junction then left into Calle Catalunya. Right at end then right again to Pratsevall.

El Jufré

08511 Tavertet-Osona
Barcelona

Tel: 93 8565167
Fax: 93 8565167

Josep Roquer & Lourdes Rovira

The medieval hilltop villages of this part of Catalonia rival some of those of Provence. Simply driving up to Tavertet (just recently declared a site of 'Cultural Interest') past craggy limestone outcrops and stands of forest is an adventure; once you arrive and look out over the plain far below you'll gasp at the magnificence of what lies before you. Stay with Josep and Lourdes and their two young children in their very old house: parts date back to 1100 and Lourde's family have been in residence for some 800 years! It was rebuilt in the 1600s then refurbished to create the guesthouse. You'll like your room; there are eight and they happily marry the old (beams, exposed stone) and the new (good beds, lighting and bathrooms). We would choose one that looks out over the craggy ledge on which El Jufré is perched. There is a terrace on which to linger over an aperitif to the sound of distant cowbells and good, simple food at dinner with most of the veg straight from Josep's vegetable garden – and at breakfast milk fresh from their own cows. El Jufré is for lovers of utter tranquility – there are only 40 full-time residents – and high places – and those glad to trade car for foot.

Rooms: 8 with bath & wc.
Price: Double/Twin 9000 Pts incl. VAT.
Breakfast: Included.
Meals: Dinner 2000 Pts (M).
Closed: 22 December-6 January,
1-15 September.

From Vic C153 towards Olot/Roda de Ter
to L'Esquirol/Santa María Corco. Here,
right to Tavertet. House on left as you
enter village.

Map no: 8

Entry no: 74

La Tria

08589 Perafita
Barcelona

Tel: 93 8530240
Fax: 93 8530240
E-mail: country@latria.com
Web: www.latria.com

Maite Tor Pujol-Galcerán

This area of the Pyrenean foothills remains puzzlingly 'undiscovered'; wandering through beautiful Perafita's back streets you meet few visitors. But it is lovely. Snug in the green countryside just a short walk from the village, this 17th-century Catalan *mas* will quicken your passion for the natural world. Gentle-mannered Maite is a painter and her sensitivity is reflected in the simple, country-style decoration; rooms are fresh, light and uncluttered. The place is really more geared to self-catering lets – there are two kitchens – but Maite will happily prepare you a Catalan (or Continental) breakfast and there are two cheap-and-cheerful restaurants in Perafita. In the main farmhouse are an enormous wooden-floored dining room and two lounges, one very cosy with open hearth. The whole place is blissfully quiet and would be ideal for families; there's an enormous, garden and the dairy farm to explore – Maite and husband Lluís enjoy showing guests round. Central heating means you'll be comfortable at La Tria in the cooler months, too. The area is known for its many Romanesque churches.

Rooms: 5 with bath & wc and 3 sharing bathroom.
Price: Double/Twin 7000 Pts incl. VAT.
Breakfast: 800 Pts, or self-catering.
Meals: None available.
Closed: First fortnight in July.

From Barcelona N152 to Vic. Bypass town to west then turn off for Sant Bartolomeu del Grau. There towards Perafita; La Tria signposted to left before arriving in village.

Entry no: 75

Map no: 8

Xalet La Coromina

Carretera de Vic s/n
17406 Viladrau
Gerona

Tel: 93 8849264
Fax: 93 8848160
E-mail: xaletlacoromina@teleline.es

Gloria Rabat

Viladrau is an elegant little town close to the stunning Montseny Natural Park. Its woodlands are grandiose, water flows and falls everywhere, indigenous trees and rare plants flourish. It is a wonderful place for walking. The building dates from the turn of the century when wealthy Catalans (they still come to Viladrau) built themselves summer retreats away from sticky Barcelona; the building looks more French than Spanish. It has kept its elegant exterior while thoroughly modernised inside. The ancient/modern mix is visible in the decoration too: the little sitting room has an old fireplace; all bedrooms have their own personality with antiques, English and French prints for curtains and bedcovers, good bathrooms and stupendous views. And the car rally memorabilia? Gloria's husband, Antonio Zanini, was one of Spain's most successful drivers. The Coromina prides itself on its food and on using local produce in season. Expect delicious mushroom dishes made with local *setas* when they spring up after the rain. A gentle small hotel which won its Michelin star for good food in its first year.

Rooms: 9 with bath & wc.
Price: Double/Twin 11400 Pts.
Breakfast: 1000 Pts.
Meals: Lunch/Dinner 2500 Pts (M), 3000-4000 Pts (C).
Closed: 2-26 January.

From Girona C25. Exit at km 202 then follow GI543 to Viladrau. In village towards Vic: hotel on right after 50 yards.

Map no: 8   Entry no: 76

Oriol Riera

Veïnat Pibiller 1
17412 Maçanet de la Selva
Gerona

Tel: 972 859099
Fax: 972 851316

Dolors Bosch Llinás

A special place, for those who are happy to forego some minor comfort in order to enjoy an authentic Catalan home. If you're happy to share a shower room and conversation at table, then stay as a guest of Dolors at her 200-year-old Catalan farmhouse. It is, she rightly points out, "una casa muy bonita". This is the antithesis of those credit-card hotels we so dislike; pull in off the busy NII and the ivy-clad frontage of Oriol Riera is a rest for sore eyes. Inside, decoration is as personal as in any family home: pictures of Dolors' family, sporting trophies on a shelf above a lace-clad dresser, dried flowers hanging down from the old beamed and planked ceiling. There are two dining rooms; dressers display the family china, there's a highchair for younger children and, in one corner, a stone staircase leads up to the bedrooms which are large enough to accommodate extra beds should the need arise. You'd be a fool to miss dinner; again we leave the last word to Dolors who describes it as, "traditional, family cooking with only the very best ingredients".

Rooms: 4 sharing bathroom & separate wc.
Price: Double/Twin 5200 Pts.
Breakfast: 800 Pts.
Meals: Dinner 1600 Pts (M) incl. wine.
Closed: Christmas.

From A7 take exit 9 for Massanet de la Selva. Towards Barcelona on NII; 500m after marker for km 691.5 turn left at sign (careful. brow of hill!) and you'll see Oriol Riera to the right.

Entry no: 77   Map no: 8

Hotel Sant Roc

Plaça Atlàntic 2
17200 Calella de Palafrugell
Gerona

Tel: 972 614250
Fax: 972 614068
E-mail: santroc@grn.es
Web: www.santroc.com

Teresa Boix & Bertrand Hallé

The Costa Brava remains, in many parts, a stunning stretch of coastline and this quiet little hotel could restore your faith in seaside holidays in Spain. It is very much a family affair – not just family-owned and run but also a place where guests are valued like old friends (many return year after year). The setting is marvellous: a perch at the edge of a cliff amid pine, olive and cypress trees. From terrace and dining room there are views across the bay and its brightly-painted boats to the pretty village beyond. The sea is ever with you at Sant Roc, its colours changing with every hour. The best rooms have seaward terraces but we liked them all: most striking are the hand-painted beds and abundance of original oil paintings. With Franco-Catalan owners you would expect something special from the kitchen and justifiably – the fish is excellent and there is a good range of fairly priced wines. There is a path from the hotel down to the beach and longer walks around the bay. Bertrand and Teresa remain humorous and charming hosts even in high season; their generosity seems to permeate this exceptional small hotel. And it is wonderfully child-friendly.

Rooms: 44 with bath or shower & wc;
4 suites.
Price: Single 7200-9600 Pts;
Double/Twin 9000-12000 Pts; Suite
25000-33000 Pts.
Breakfast: 1200 Pts.
Meals: Lunch/Dinner 3000 Pts (M),
4500 Pts (C).
Closed: Early November-mid-March.

From Barcelona A7 north to exit 6 (Girona Norte) then follow signs for La Bisbal via Palamos then on to Palafrugell; from here to Calella; hotel signposted.

Map no: 8 **Entry no: 78**

Hotel Llevant

Francesc de Blanes 5
17211 Llafranc
Gerona

Tel: 972 300366 or 972 300345
Fax: 972 300345
E-mail: hllevant@arrakis.es

The Farrarons-Turró family

On the pedestrians-only sea-front in the lively village of Llafranc, Hotel Llevant is a one of the Costa's most popular family-run hotels. The building is 60 years old but you could never tell; everything sparkles here from bathroom to crockery to the turquoise sea that almost laps its way to the door. The Farrarons family are proud of their creation, constantly improving and refurbishing; the bedrooms are all-white affairs, large and airy, with every mod con. But what makes it all special enough to earn a place in this guide is the restaurant/terrace. The promenade here is always animated, highly so at the evening *paseo* (stroll) time, and beyond all this the sea is a constant backdrop; what better place to watch the world go by than this terrace, with the hotel's prize-winning cooking as an accompaniment? The beach at Llafranc is sandy, clean and safe – we walked from end to end in September without seeing a scrap of paper! The Llevant is good value at any time of the year and it has recently been thoroughly refurbished. Note that in high season you are required to eat at least one meal apart from breakfast in the hotel.

Rooms: 24 with bath & wc.
Price: Single 6500-16000 Pts; Twin 10000-20000 Pts.
Breakfast: Included (buffet).
Meals: Lunch/Dinner 3100 Pts (M), 4500 Pts (C).
Closed: 2 weeks in November. Check!

From Barcelona A7 north to exit 9 (San Feliu); past San Feliu and Palamos to Palafrugell. Here follow signs to Llafranc; hotel in centre of village right on sea-front. Park in street.

Entry no: 79

Map no: 8

Hostalet 1701
Plaça Mayor s/n
17214 Regencós
Gerona

Tel: 972 303331
Fax: 972 304562

Xavi Roca Bassas and Nieves Artiga Llach

Just 5km from the Costa Brava, Hostalet 1701 is a welcome antidote to sun, sea and sand. Although Regencós is a simple working village, Xavi and Nieves' 18th-century house, once a coaching inn, is a treasure trove of the most amazing antiques. All are for sale whether in the rooms themselves or in the antique shop next door. As you'd expect of a couple dedicated to the pursuit of beautiful things, each room is exquisite. The bedrooms are quaint and simple with beamed ceilings, original floors, antique lamps and original prints: the translucent Empordà light filtering through antique muslin curtains gives a hazy, timeless quality. The lounge is large and light showing paintings by a well-known local artist. There are sofas, plants, books, a 17th-century pianoforte and other unusual *objets*. House rules are minimal: Nieves will serve you breakfast at 3 if you wish. And what a breakfast! You feast on a plethora of home-made goodies including plumcake, preserves and several different breads. Dinner is normally not provided unless specifically requested, but with so many restaurants nearby and an August wine festival in the medieval town of Pals, this is no great inconvenience.

Rooms: 3 with bath & wc.
Price: Double/Twin 18000 Pts.
Breakfast: Included.
Meals: Dinner 3500-4000 Pts.
Book ahead.
Closed: 2 weeks in November.

From France A7 south and the exit at junction 6 for Girona Nord. Follow C255 to Palafrugell. From here follow signs to Regencós. Hostalet 1701 is in the main square.

Map no: 8

Entry no: 80

Hotel Aigua Blava

Platja de Fornells
17255 Begur
Gerona

Tel: 972 622058 or 972 624562
Fax: 972 622112
E-mail: hotelaiguablava@aiguablava.com
Web: www.aiguablava.com

Joan Gispert-Lapedra

The Aigua Blava is something of an institution in Catalonia. It is a largish hotel but thanks to careful, friendly management and clever design it manages to remain both welcoming and intimate. The bedrooms are all decorated differently and ranged on several terraced wings which look out across the gardens to a delicious hidden cove – so rugged a piece of coast is almost unspoilable. Run by the same family (the manager started at 15), nourished by the same chef, tended by the same gardener for almost half a century, the hotel has a strong tradition of personal attention. Señor Gispert seems to genuinely care for each and every one of his guests; you are constantly made to feel that you are special, no groups are taken, and customer loyalty is strong. Breathe deeply in the sweet-smelling pinewoods, bask beside the huge pool, enjoy fresh lobster in the dining room whilst you look out across the incandescent waters of the small fishing port – or sip a cool drink at the snack bar on the uncrowded beach just beneath the hotel. The village, too, is one of the prettiest on the Costa Brava and you are close to Palafrugell which has a lively market and to the medieval town of Pals.

Rooms: 82 with bath & wc & 6 Suites.
Price: Single 10500-13300 Pts; Double/Twin 13100-15700 Pts; Double/Twin with terrace 15500-21000 Pts; Suite 17200-22500 Pts.
Breakfast: 1650 Pts.
Meals: Lunch/Dinner 3800 Pts (M), approx. 5000 Pts (C).
Closed: Early November-late February.

From Gerona C255 to Palafrugell. From there GE650 to Begur. Signposted on entry to village.

Entry no: 81   Map no: 8

Can Fabrica

17845 Santa Llogaia del Terri   **Tel:** 972 594629
Gerona   **Fax:** 972 594629

Marta Casanovas

On top of a gentle hill with wide, inspirational views all around this 17th-century *masía* (farmhouse) that has been restored and brought back to life by this young couple, not least by planting trees and farming their 17 acres of land. They have created a blissful corner of peace whence to explore the nearby villages and Romanesque churches. Ramón is an engineer, Marta a designer. They have environmentalist leanings and want you to discover the treasures of their area; there are four bicycles for hire and plenty of walking and cycling routes. Bedrooms are smallish, simply furnished with old pieces and lamps, while soft materials set off the bare stone walls. The food is good home cooking, often with produce from the farm, such as the honey at breakfast and the traditional Catalan ingredients of tomato, oil and garlic. Wine lovers will appreciate Marta's careful selections: she likes to give you two or three different wines at dinner. A lovely place with an exceptionally kind, vivacious hostess; without question this is one of our very favourite places to stay in Spain. If you are here in summer, do visit the Dalí museum by night!

Rooms: 6 with bath or shower & wc.
Price: Single 4000 Pts; Double/Twin 8000 Pts; Triple 11300 Pts incl. VAT.
Breakfast: Included.
Meals: Dinner 2300 Pts (M).
Closed: 7 January-Easter.

Leave A7 at exit 6 onto C150 towards Banyoles. After approx. 8km bear right towards Cornellà del Terri then at r'bout towards Medinya. After 2.5km left to Santa Llogaia; through village, 400m of track to house on left.

Map no: 8   Entry no: 82

El Molí

Mas Molí
17469 Siurana d'Emporda
Gerona

Tel: 972 525139 or 616 285024
Fax: 972 525139
E-mail: casaelmoli@teleline.es

Maria Sanchís Pages

Unusually for this guide, El Molí is a modern building; but it more than earns a place in the 'special' category alongside its older Catalan neighbours. Although only recently opened it has already been awarded a Diploma for B&B excellence. Its position couldn't be better; you are just 7km from wonderful Figueres and the Dalí museum, while just a ten minute drive will get you to the beach at San Pere Pescador. The house is modelled on the traditional Girona *mas*. It has tiled floors, wooden furniture and big rooms with views across the garden to the fields and woods beyond. Maria's food is exceptionally good value. Veg, chicken and beef come straight from the farm and are accompanied by a good local red wine as well as an infusion of *hierbas* to end your feast. At breakfast, try the home-made yoghurt and jams. This would be a good place to break the journey travelling north or south and Maria – she speaks excellent English – will help you plan your trips out, perhaps to the Dalí museum, the Roman ruins at Empuries or to the pretty fishing village of Cadaqués.

Rooms: 5 with bath & wc; 1 suite.
Price: Double/Twin 7000 Pts; Suite 8000 Pts incl. VAT.
Breakfast: 600 Pts.
Meals: 1400 Pts (M).
Closed: Never.

Coming from the North on A7 take exit 4 towards Figueres on the NII. After 3km right on C252 towards La Escala/Bisbal. Just after km post 32 turn right towards Siurana. El Molí signposted as you arrive in village.

Entry no: 83

Map no: 8

Can Navata

Baseia
17469 Siurana d'Empordà
Gerona

Tel: 972 525174
Fax: 972 525756
E-mail: apages@teleline.es
Web: wwww.entretodos.com/cannavata

Amparo Pagès

The village of Siurana is home to a small farming community and is close to Figueres and the Costa Brava. Amparo has lived here all her life and renamed this 19th-century farmhouse after her father's native village. You enter through an invitingly shady porch into the living areas: decorated in the colourful regional style they have low, arched ceilings and traditional Spanish furniture. All of the bedrooms are furnished with family heirlooms and four have a seasonal theme; we loved the 'summer' room: light and airy with an antique embroidered sheet for a curtain and lovely old mirrors. Another room and its bathroom have been converted for wheelchair access. This is an excellent place for children: they would like the playroom that Amparo has created on the ground floor, playing in the big garden and meeting the farm animals. She has also provided an elegant library as a peaceful refuge for parents. Ever obliging, Amparo will send you details of places to visit, make bookings and prepare cycling and walking routes. Can Navata is almost a home from home: indeed, among the 'facilities' offered you'll find 'amistat', the Catalan for friendship.

Rooms: 6 with bath & wc.
Price: Double/Twin 7600-9600 Pts.
Breakfast: Included.
Meals: Dinner (winter only) 1300 Pts.
Closed: Never.

From Figueres NII then C252 towards L'Escala. After 4km turn right for Siurana. Can Navata is on the left as you enter the village.

Map no: 8

Entry no: 84

Mas Falgarona
17742 Avinyonet de Puigventós
Gerona

Tel: 972 546628
Fax: 972 547071
E-mail: email@masfalgarona.com
Web: www.masfalgarona.com

Severino Jallas Gándara & Brigitta Schmidt

Severino and Brigitta spent a decade searching for Mas Falgorana and what a find it is. Built from pale, almost golden stone, the farm is said to be the oldest in the region, begun in 1098. Their restoration is a deft blend of ancient and modern achieved with flair and panache. Light, mood-enhancing colours lift the spirits as does their passion for old things and old ways. The result is a fresh, Mediterranean look, reinforced by the surrounding cypress, olive and palm trees. An aquamarine pool and stunning views over the Pla d'Estany almost gild the lily. The interior is a stylist's dream. Dominated by a beautiful arched ceilings, lounge and dining room have cool, neutral tones and their fabrics blend with the old flags and terracotta tiles. In contrast, a feast of colours runs riot in the bedrooms and bathrooms. A small, chic and cosy room has been set aside for aperitifs; a delightful place for a pre-prandial cocktail. Cooking is innovative and Mediterranean, based on aromatic herbs and olive oil, and includes many vegetarian dishes. After more than thirty years in the hotel business, Severino has achieved his dream, summarised by a favourite quote: "One eye sees, the other feels".

Rooms: 9 with bath & wc; 1 suite.
Price: Double/Twin 19000-21000 Pts;
Suite 24000 Pts.
Breakfast: Included.
Meals: Dinner 3800-5400.
Closed: First 3 weeks of January

From Figueres N260 towards Besalú/Olot. After 5km turn right to Avinyonet and follow signs to Mas Falgarona.

Mas Salvanera

17850 Beuda
Gerona

Tel: 972 590975
Fax: 972 590863
E-mail: salvanera@salvanera.com
Web: www.salvanera.com

Rocío Niño Ojeda & Ramón Ruscalleda

In a blissfully quiet part of the wooded Pyrenean foothills, Mas Salvanera – a solid 17th-century Catalan farmhouse – was transformed into the smartest of country hotels by this couple who still glow with enthusiasm for the project which changed their lives. Their guest rooms, in an old olive mill next to the main house, are named after signs of the zodiac: one contains the old bread oven which once fed the whole of the village. Rocío's decorative flair is on show throughout the house; beneath old, darkening beams the antiques (most of them restored by her), carefully arranged flowers and colourful fabrics have been stylishly combined. Our favourite is *Cancer* but all are large and elegant. The main building has an old well, vaulted ceilings, open hearths and lots of exposed stone. The dining room is up one level and its centrepiece is an 18-place dining table; everyone eats together at Salvanera. Many of Rocío's recipes at dinner are Basque (*paella* and rabbit are two of Rocío's specialities) and Rioja is de rigeur. Breakfasts are big and buffet, taken at any time you like. There is a library and a quiet walled garden with a pool sculpted in beneath the olive trees.

Rooms: 9 with bath or shower & wc.
Price: Double/Twin 13000 Pts.
Breakfast: 1200 Pts.
Meals: Dinner 3500 Pts (M).
Closed: 1-10 January, 1-10 July & 11-19 September.

From Gerona NII towards Figueres, then C150 via Banyoles to Besalú. Here right on N260 towards Figueres, then left for Maià de Montcal and then follow signs to Beuda; Mas Salvanera after 1.6km.

Map no: 8

Entry no: 86

Rectoria de la Miana
17854 Sant Jaume de Llierca
Gerona

Tel: 972 190190

**Frans Engelhard & Janine
Westerlaken**

In the middle of a vast stand of beech and oak, at the end of 6km of rough and winding track, La Miana sits in a fabulous setting. History is very present here: in the eighth century there was a fortified manor then in the 1300s a rectory was built complete with vaulted ceilings, escape tunnel and chapel. It took courage and vision for Frans to embark on its restoration and from the ruins has emerged an extraordinary and beautiful – and simple – hostelry. Much has been left as it always was; the original flagged walls and undressed walls. The old black and white photographs are touching in their directness; such as one of a group of people marvelling at the first radio to arrive at La Miana. Bedrooms vary in configuration and size; they have pastel walls, are furnished with antique furniture and bright kilims; each old handmade floor tile is a work of art. In the vaulted dining room downstairs, sitting on century-old pews, you will have a genuine Catalan breakfast and regional dishes for lunch or supper. Incomparable La Miana is not for those who are looking for standardised hotelly trimmings but poets, artists – or any true Romantic – would love it.

Rooms: 8 with bath/shower & wc.
Price: Double/Twin half-board 5000 Pts
p.p; Full-board 6800 Pts p.p incl. VAT.
Breakfast: Included.
Meals: Lunch and/or dinner included.
Closed: Never.

From Figueres N260 to Besalú and Sant Jaume de Llierca. Left into village, then 2nd left into Calle Industria. 6km along track to house following signs to Can Jou (marked at all junctions). Rectory just past Can Jou farmhouse.

Can Jou

La Miana
17854 Sant Jaume de Llierca
Gerona

Tel: 972 190263
Fax: 972 190444
E-mail: canjou@turismerural.net
Web: www.turismerural.net/canjou

Rosi Linares & Mick Peters

You'll long remember arriving at Can Jou: as you negotiate the long (6km), rough dirt track to the farm you sense you are leaving the mundane far behind you. You round a final bend and catch sight of the farm, high on a hill looking out over miles of thick forest of oak and beech. No wonder Mick and Rosa were inspired to revive this old Catalan farm in search of the 'good life'; first by working the land, then by giving the house a family (they have four children), thirdly by restoring the old barn so they could share the beauty of it all with their guests. Bedrooms are simply furnished with a mix of old and new and lively colour schemes; six of them have their own balconies. This could be a good place for a family holiday; there is the farm to explore, horses to ride (a perfect place for learners and there are marked forest bridle-ways for experienced riders). Rosa's cooking is excellent and many of the ingredients come straight from the farm; dinners are extremely friendly affairs around one huge table. Close to the house is a beautiful spring-filled rock pool – if you're heading back to Nature, and can do without the hotelly extras, head here.

Rooms: 11 with bath & wc; 1 suite.
Price: Full-board in Double/Twin 7300 Pts p.p; Full-board in suite 8300 Pts p.p.
Breakfast: Included.
Meals: Lunch and dinner included.
Closed: January & February.

From Figueres N260 to Besalú and to Sant Jaume de Llierca. Left into village, and then 2nd left into Calle Industria. Continue for 6km along track to house, marked at all junctions.

Map no: 8

Entry no: 88

Mas el Guitart

Santa Margarida de Bianya
17813 La Vall de Bianya
Gerona

Tel: 972 292140
Fax: 972 292140
E-mail: guitart@agtat.es

Lali Nogareda Burch

El Guitart is up with the avant-garde of a new, more dynamic approach to rural tourism that has emerged in Spain in the last couple of years. Lali and Toni are young, friendly hosts; he left television, she left designing, to launch themselves with gusto into the restoration of this old dairy farm. Thanks to their hard work (and stacks of good taste) they have succeeded in creating one of Catalonia's very best small B&Bs. We loved the rooms; each is decorated in a different colour with Lali's stencilling to match; there are wooden floors and beams, old beds and washstands, rugs, decent bathrooms and good views. The breakfast and sitting rooms are decorated in similar vein; breakfast is Catalan, with juice, jams and home-made sausage. Although no other meals are available there are two fully-equipped kitchens as well as a washing machine at your disposal: this would be an excellent choice for a longer stay. Take in the views from one of the hammocks or set out to on foot to explore the surrounding mountains: Toni has researched and marked new walking routes in the valley. Exceptional hosts, home and countryside and a wonderful place for families.

Rooms: 4 with bath & wc;
2 two-bedroom apartments.
Price: Double/Twin 6000 Pts; Apartment 11000 Pts incl. VAT.
Minimum stay 2 nights.
Breakfast: 650 Pts.
Meals: None available.
Closed: Never.

From Gerona C150 to Besalú. Continue on C150 to Castellfollit de la Roca. Here follow signs for Camprodón on the C153. House signposted in Vall de Bianya.

Entry no: 89   Map no: 8

Hotel Grèvol

Carretera Camprodón a Setcases s/n **Tel:** 972 741013/130130
Vall de Camprodón **Fax:** 972 741087
17869 Llanars **E-mail:** info@hotelgrevol.com
Gerona **Web:** www.hotelgrevol.com

Antonio Solé Fajula

Close to ski slopes, mountain trails and a whole series of Romanesque churches, your first glimpse of El Grèvol may make you wonder if you aren't in the Swiss Alps. Carved pine balconies, exposed stonework, slate and wood floors and wooden furniture all provide the perfect setting for the *après-ski*. But there are no cuckoo clocks here; instead there are high ceilings, a free-standing central hearth and lots of glass to bring the light flooding in. *Grèvol* means holly in Catalan (it is a protected species here) and the décor uses the leaf as its leitmotif. Guest rooms (each named after a different alpine flower) are four-star comfortable; those on the first floor give onto a balcony that runs round the building whilst attic rooms have pine ceilings, dormers and smaller stand-up balconies. The hotel has a warm, enveloping feel and food is a mix of regional, international and *haute cuisine* – "it tastes good and looks good" says Antonio and there is a vast choice of wines. The hotel – in season it fills with people heading off for the ski slopes in Vallter – also has an indoor swimming pool and a bowling alley; less seductive, perhaps, than the mountains which tower about you.

Rooms: 30 with bath & wc;
6 junior suites.
Price: Double/Twin 14500-18200 Pts;
Junior suite 19150-23150 Pts.
Breakfast: Included.
Meals: Lunch/Dinner 4350 Pts (M),
5500 Pts (C).
Closed: 2 weeks in May.

From Barcelona A7 towards France then N152 via Vic to Ripoll. There C151 to Camprodón. Hotel is 1500m from Camprodón on the road to Setcases.

Map no: 8 Entry no: 90

Hotel Calitxó

Passatge el Serrat s/n
17868 Molló
Gerona

Tel: 972 740386
Fax: 972 740746

Josep Sole Fajula

Molló is a pretty mountain village, over 3,000 feet up in the Pyrenees, just 5km from the French border. Hotel Calitxó has more than just a hint of the Tyrolean chalet: extraordinary to think that this building was once was a warehouse for the potatoes for which the village is famous. The hotel is set back from the road with an attractive balconied façade brightened by the pots of geraniums which adorn all the balconies. You enter through the rather barn-like restaurant; the day we visited there was a merry atmosphere and nearly all the diners were local – always a good sign. The menu is a mix of Catalan/trad Spanish and ingredients come fresh from the market. Ours might be the fillet steak in cream sauce with wild mushrooms; prices here are more than reasonable. The rooms are all you need: generous-sized with locally-made wooden furniture, and each has a view of the surrounding mountains. Some have their own balconies; when booking ask for one *con balcón*. We were won over by the Fajula family's easy cheeriness. There are walks through orchid-strewn fields, skiing and the beautiful Romanesque churches close by. And an attractive conservatory has recently been added.

Rooms: 23 with bath & wc; 3 suites.
Price: Double/Twin 10200 Pts; Suite 15500 Pts.
Breakfast: Included.
Meals: Lunch/Dinner 2600 Pts (M), 3500 Pts (C).
Closed: Never.

From Ripoll C151 to Camprodón, and continue on C151 to Molló. Hotel in village on the left.

Entry no: 91

Map no: 8

Can Borrell

Retorn 3
17539 Meranges-La Cerdanya
Gerona

Tel: 972 880033 or 629 794758
Fax: 972 880144
E-mail: info@canborrell.com
Web: www.canborrell.com

Laura Forn

Can Borrell was once the shelter of mountain shepherds who brought their flocks up to the high slopes of La Cerdanya for the rich summer grazing. High up on one side of a valley, this 200-year-old Pyrenean farmhouse of granite and slate is in the tiniest of villages with meadows in front and conifer-clad mountains beyond. Within, wood is all about you in beam, shutter and furniture while slate floors mirror the building's exterior. Its restoration and conversion from home to hotel have been sensitively accomplished; it is not over-prettified but very inviting and with the warmth and intimacy of a little Cotswolds pub. The rooms welcome you with fabulous views and excellent beds. They vary in size because they follow the idiosyncrasies of an old house and they are uncluttered by hotelly gadgetry. And expect something out of the ordinary at your (small) dinner table. The cooking here is, in the owner's words, "traditional Catalan – with a special touch": uniformed waiting staff add a more formal note. There are waymarked walks to neighbouring hamlets and cycle trails, too.

Rooms: 8 with bath & wc.
Price: Double/Twin 11000-13000 Pts.
Breakfast: Included.
Meals: Lunch/Dinner 3500 Pts (M),
5000-6000 Pts (C). Closed Monday nights
and Tuesdays.
Closed: 7 January-31 April, except Friday
& Saturday nights.

From Barcelona A18 via Terrassa and
Manresa then C1411 to Berga. Through Tunel del Cadí then on towards Andorra. After approx. 5km right towards Puigcerdá on N260 then left at Ger to Meranges. Signposted in village.

Map no: 8   Entry no: 92

Cal Pastor

Calle Palos 1
17536 Fornells de la Muntanya-Toses
Gerona

Tel: 972 736163
Fax: 972 736163
E-mail: ramongasso@logiccontrol.es

Josefina Soy Sala

Josefina and Ramón are quiet, gentle folk whose families have farmed this tranquil valley for generations. First two rooms next to their house were opened to guests and more recently Ramón's parents' former home was converted to create a further six guest rooms. These are spotlessly clean and simply furnished; all have tiled floors, a very Spanish choice of fabric and good beds. Our favourites were those in the attic where wooden ceilings create a cosier feel. The dining room is slightly soulless but don't be put off; you will be served a grand breakfast (eggs and bacon if you fancy it) and Josefina's dinners are hearty and wholesome – and she is happy to cook veggie dinners, too. Be sure to visit the *Museo del Pastor* (shepherd's museum) – a testimony to the work of four generations of Ramón's family on the surrounding mountainsides. The trans-Pyrenean, Mediterranean-to-Atlantic footpath runs right by the house and you may feel inspired to do part of it. In the evening, choose between Josefina's cooking and the quiet little restaurant next door. An unpretentious, authentic and peaceful B&B in a friendly hamlet; a perfect antidote to city life.

Rooms: 6 with bath or shower & wc.
Price: Double/Twin 6000 Pts.
Breakfast: 850 Pts.
Meals: Dinner 1700 Pts.
Closed: Never.

From Barcelona N152 towards Puigcerdà via Vic and Ripoll. Just past Ribes de Freser turn left at km133.5 post and then 2km to village. House by restaurant.

Hotel Villa de Torla

Plaza Nueva 1
22376 Torla
Huesca

Tel: 974 486156
Fax: 974 486 365

Miguel Villacampa

Torla lies at the heart of a spectacular walking wilderness and is the perfect base camp for any mountain forays. But it is essential to plan ahead as the weather can change dramatically. Miguel the hotel owner will gladly keep a watchful eye out during any planned excursions into the peaks and will also give you some very helpful hints on good routes and how to walk them. You are in capable hands, on all counts, at this homely, family-run hostelry. The simple, clean rooms with their wood-panelled walls and terracotta-tiled floors look good and have all you need for a comfortable and peaceful stay. The whole place is delightfully informal and has an excellent little restaurant to fire the furnace: as well as being incredibly good value, its full-length wall of window lets in the most sensational view and the red and white chequered tablecloths fit perfectly with the leafy-green furnishings. We had salmon cooked in cider and rich venison to delight our taste buds, some deep bodied wines to slake our thirst and home-made puddings that just melted in our mouths. It was all delicious. This is without doubt a good little hostelry.

Rooms: 38 with bath & wc.
Price: Double/Twin 5500-8000 Pts.
Breakfast: 700 Pts.
Meals: Lunch/Dinner 1800 Pts (M/C).
Closed: Never.

From Zaragoza N330 via Huesca towards Sabiñánigo then N260 via Biescas to Torla. Hotel in centre of village on main square.

Map no: 6

Entry no: 94

Casa Frauca

Carretera de Ordesa s/n
22374 Sarvisé
Huesca

Tel: 974 486353/486182
Fax: 974 486789

Carmen Villacampa & Francisco López

So close to the border, this delightful little roadside hotel could very well be a
French townhouse with its neo-classical pilasters, symmetrical design and pale pink
wash, but inside it is faithful to its Spanish Pyrenean environment with its timbers,
tiles, sloping ceilings and pieces of rustic furniture. The bedrooms are smallish
especially the ones beneath the eaves on the top floor but have a good feel to
them, nonetheless; we especially took to the round-windowed one with its two
semicircular shutters. There is an intimate, cosy little bar for close encounters with
the locals and a dining room where regional dishes will nourish the active visitor –
good stews and roasts, and plenty of everything. And vegetarians are well-catered
for with loads of salads and vegetable-based dishes like mushroom or onion tarts.
And a rich, very full-bodied Cariñena is the house red. Sarvisé is in an
extraordinary valley of abandoned villages that was due to be dammed... and never
was, thank heavens! Enjoy the wooded hillsides, rugged rocks and rushing streams,
or the snow and ice in winter.

Rooms: 12 with bath & wc.
Price: Single 3000-5000 Pts;
Double/Twin 4000-6000 Pts.
Breakfast: 475 Pts.
Meals: Lunch/Dinner 1600 Pts (M),
3000-4000 Pts (C).
Closed: Never.

From Lérida N240 towards Barbastro then
N123/C318 to Ainsa. Then N260 towards
Biescas to Sarvisé. Hotel on left in village.

La Abadía

Calle La Iglesia s/n
22349 Sieste
Huesca

Tel: 974 502044

Fernando Rodríguez Bielsa

Birdwatchers will love La Abadía in the high village of Sieste. Train your binoculars on the skyline and follow majestic birds of prey or, perhaps, the odd witch chortling by – but fear not, the hotel is armed with a pointed witch-scaring chimney (*espantabruja*) to stop them landing. This old manor has lintels dated 1571 and heraldic insignia from the Knights Templar. Solid stone walls support a stone roof with an amazing chimney – go into the sitting room, sit by the open plinth-like fireplace and look up: this astounding towering construction epitomises the quirkiness of the place. The hotel looks over forests filled with wildlife and clear, fish-teeming rivers, all set against the backdrop of the mighty Pyrenees: it is awe-inspiring. Rooms vary in size and numbers of beds; all have large bathrooms and some have air conditioning (check when booking). The restaurant is in the basement of the old stables: it is perfectly lit and serves hearty stews, roasts and steaks. Breakfast is Continental or cooked. And there's masses to do including rafting or floating down river canyons in a life jacket! *The village church is under restoration and work may continue for some time.*

Rooms: 13 with bath & wc.
Price: Double/Twin 5500-14000 Pts.
More details on request.
Breakfast: 700 Pts.
Meals: Lunch/Dinner 1400 Pts.
Closed: Never.

From Lérida N240 to Barbastro then C138 to Ainsá. There HU640 to Ainsá then N260 to Boltaña. Just before village turn left, cross bridge and follow signs to Sieste. La Abadía is just to the left of the church.

Map no: 6

Entry no: 96

La Choca

Plaza Mayor 1
22148 Lecina de Bárcabo
Huesca

Tel: 974 343070 or 689 633636
Fax: 974 343070

Ana Zamora & Miguel Angel Blasco

Lecina de Bárcabo is for lovers of high places: a tiny hamlet in a rugged, wild part of Huesca perched at the edge of a limestone outcrop. Miguel Angel and Ana left teaching to restore this several hundred-year-old fortified farmhouse and... to farm rabbits. But La Choca cried out to be shared so they opened the house: first as a farm-school and then later as a guesthouse. You will be captivated by the indescribable beauty of the views and the utter tranquillity of the hamlet. We fell asleep to the hooting of an owl and awoke to the sound of a woodpecker. The public rooms have stone walls and ancient timbers; the bedrooms are also rustically simple... and television-free. Three of them are big enough for a family and one has its own terrace. And you'll eat well here (often to the strains of classical music): home-made jams at breakfast, regional dishes with a French influence at other meals – and Ana's own recipes, too. Cave paintings nearby, bikes to be rented in the hamlet and gorgeous walks straight out from the house into the Sierra de Guara National Park. A favourite address, with two exceptionally kind hosts. Two self-catering apartments have recently been added.

Rooms: 9 with bath & wc; 2 apartments.
Price: Single 4000 Pts; Double/Twin 6500 Pts; Apartment (for 4) 5500-7500 Pts; Apartment (for 6) 7500-9500 Pts incl. VAT.
Breakfast: 550 Pts.
Meals: Dinner 1750 Pts (M); lunch 3500 Pts (C). (Except Thursday lunchtimes).
Closed: November & 24-27 December.

From Huesca on N240 towards Barbastro.
4km after village of Angües left towards Colungo. 15km after Colungo left towards Lecina de Bárcabo. House first on left entering village.

Hotel San Marsial

Avenida de Francia 75
22440 Benasque
Huesca

Tel: 974 551616
Fax: 974 551623
E-mail: sanmarsial@pirineo.com
Web: www.pirineo.com/hotelsanmarsial

The Garuz y San Martinet family

Benasque is a pretty place in the Aragonese Pyrenees, a centre for winter sports or for walking once the snows melt. The San Marsial is an immensely warm, friendly little hotel with a smile at reception and rooms of human proportions, all lovingly created thanks to a combined family effort. A sensitive commingling of slate floors, beamed wooden ceilings and rustic furniture makes it feel like a home from home, a place to linger over dinner (Aragonese) or a good book. Wood is the basic material: many of the pieces were made or installed by the carpenter owner. The bedrooms are very smart – many have attractive hand-painted bedheads; there are wooden floors and ceilings and matching curtains and bedcovers. Nine rooms have their own small terrace; all of them are light, medium-sized and have good bathrooms. In corridors, sitting and dining rooms there is a collection of old farm implements, skis, chests... and in the middle a hearth diffusing yet more warmth. The nearest ski stations are only 5km away and the hotel has special offers which includes lift passes and/or skiing courses. Ring or fax for details.

Rooms: 23 with bath & wc; 2 suites.
Price: Single 7000-10000 Pts;
Double/Twin 8000-12000 Pts; Suite
14000-18000 Pts.
Breakfast: 1100 Pts.
Meals: Lunch/Dinner 2200 Pts (M),
4000 Pts (C).
Closed: Never.

From Lérida N240 to Barbastro then
N123 to Graus. From here C139 to Benasque. Through village and hotel on left.

Map no: 7

Entry no: 98

Hospedería de Loarre

Plaza Miguel Moya 7   **Tel:** 974 382706
22809 Loarre   **Fax:** 974 382713
Huesca

Jorge Valdés Santonja

This fine 17th-century building graces the prettiest of main squares in the little village of Loarre. It was recently restored and given new life thanks to local government initiative: no corners were cut nor pesetas spared in this complete face-lift (cheering to see that the hotel has full facilities for the disabled). You'll probably mention the food before the rooms on the postcard home. Aragonese and French Basque cooking, seasonal veg and the best cuts of meat; stay in autumn when wild mushrooms and game dishes are on the menu. Do try one of the local Somantano reds (let yourself be guided by your waiter): they are all reasonably priced and honest, robust wines. Loarre's bedrooms are comfortable, clean and attractively furnished with pine beds and tables and the occasional antique. The best of them (three in all) have balconies giving onto the square whilst those at the rear get a view out over the rooftops to the almond groves beyond. Do come to visit the 12th-century castle (see photo) and the fabulous rock formations (and griffon vultures) of the nearby Mallos de Riglos range of mountains. Jorge and wife Anna are young and friendly: they'll advise on what to do.

Rooms: 12 with bath & wc.
Price: Single 4100-5100 Pts;
Double/Twin 6200-8200 Pts.
Breakfast: 600 Pts.
Meals: Lunch/Dinner 1800 Pts (M),
approx. 3000-4000 Pts (C).
Closed Mondays.
Closed: Approx 20 days in November.
Check when booking.

From Huesca take N240 to Ayerbe. Here
right on the HU311 to Loarre. Hotel is in
main square (with garage space for 3 or 4 cars).

Posada Magoría

Calle Milagro 32
22728 Ansó
Huesca

Tel: 974 370049

Enrique Ipas

"There's bears in them there hills!" You may not see one but do make a trip to this remote mountain village and stay a while. This 1920's family home has a genuine mood and has been caringly restored by the much-travelled Enrique. It's a well-insulated house with good winter heating, its pale-coloured interior finely finished with period furniture. Louvred shutters let in the most pleasing natural light, the austere bedrooms are uncluttered and finely attired, good-quality mattresses lie on 1920s beds and bathrooms have glass-brick walls to let the daylight in. The real heart of Posada Magoría is the communal dining area where a huge rock juts into the room beside the long table and the full-length wall tapestry lends the space weight. Here you will be served the most delicious vegetarian food – with lashings of organic cider. Breakfast is a selection of muesli, cereals and mountain honey with good tea and organic milk. But it's Enrique himself, with his intimate knowledge of the region and stories of foreign travel, who will deepen your understanding of this undiscovered peak. *Vegetarian food only.*

Rooms: 7 with bath & wc.
Price: Double/Twin 7000-8000 Pts.
Breakfast: 700 Pts.
Meals: Dinner 1800 Pts (M).
Closed: Never.

From Pamplona N240 towards Jaca. Left at Berdun on HU202 to Ansó. Here, second left into village past wood mill then bear left along narrow street up to church. Posada last house on right.

Cal Reí

25726 Lles de Cerdanya	**Tel:** 973 515213 or 659 063915
Lérida	**Fax:** 973 515213
	E-mail: cal.rei@lles.net
	Web: www.lles.net/cal.rei

Lluis Sellès & Piluca Gasch

Lluis' family has lived in the pretty Pyrenean village of Lles for generations. The house, once a cowshed, was bought by his grandfather half a century ago, and eventually left to Lluis who has done most of the restoration work. The adjective 'perfect' springs to mind: incomparable valley views are to be had from the magnificent flower-laden balcony, while the interior is an olfactory and visual delight. The scents of flowers and aromatic herbs linger in the rooms, which have been decorated with huge flair and imagination. The drawing room is a masterpiece, with nature lending a hand in the form of clear mountain light flooding through huge windows. Original touches abound such as a table made by Lluis incorporating thousands of dandelion puffs. The bedrooms and bathrooms are impeccable, full of carved rustic furniture, muted lighting and dried flowers. Piluca makes good use of local ingredients putting a fresh slant on traditional Cerdanya dishes, with vegetables from their own garden. She will provide vegetarian dishes if requested. Lluis, always there to help, will advise on walking and skiing and knows all the local artisans, from cheesemakers to herbalists.

Rooms: 6 with bath & wc.
Price: Double 7800 Pts; Triple 10250 Pts; Qaudruple 11850 Pts.
Breakfast: 900 Pts.
Meals: Dinner 1900 Pts.
Closed: 3 weeks after Easter & 3 weeks from 12 October.

From Barcelona A18 to Manresa. There C1411 north through Tunel del Cadí, then left on N260 towards La Seu d'Urgell to Martinet. Just beyond village right to Lles de Cerdanya; house signposted to left.

Can Boix
Can Boix s/n
25790 Peramola
Lérida

Tel: 973 470266
Fax: 973 470266
E-mail:
canboixperamola@infonegocio.com

Hotels Peramola S.L.

Ten generations of the Pallarés family have lived and worked at Can Boix; three of them have turned this seductively located inn into something of an institution in Catalonia. But this is not a family to sit back on its laurels; as you'll see from the photo, innovation and renovation have led Can Boix solidly into the new millennium thanks to the unflagging enthusiasm of Joan. Come, if only for the food; it is a celebration of what is locally grown or raised. Presentation is superb, and even if the dining room is big enough for a banquet the accompanying views are as scrumptious as the meal and it still feels welcoming. Guest bedrooms are big and modern, yet nevertheless cosy, thanks to the wooden floors and furniture; they all have terraces (see photo) – large, mirrored, fitted wardrobes and every mod con. Bathrooms are marbled, double-sinked, plush; tubs will hydro-massage you if the sauna and high pressure showers of the gym have not worked their magic. This is a blissfully peaceful spot; cycle or ride into the spectacular foothills of the Pyrenees. An immensely friendly and comfortable hotel which cares for both business people and travellers alike.

Rooms: 41 with bath & wc.
Price: Double/Twin 11800-16500 Pts.
Breakfast: 1200 Pts (buffet).
Meals: Lunch/Dinner 5000-7000 Pts (C).
Closed: 2 weeks November & 1 month in January/February. Check.

From Barcelona towards Lleida on N11. Exit for Cervera/La Seu d'Urgell, Andorra. Through Cervera to Ponts; there right on C1313 to Oliana. 3km after Oliana, after bridge, left to Peramola. 4km to hotel.

Map no: 7

Entry no: 102

Can Cuadros

Major 3
25211 Palouet-Massoteres
Lérida

Tel: 973 294106
Fax: 678 686201
E-mail: can_cuadros@airtel.net

Josep Arasa & Àngels Miró

Hidden in the Segarran countryside, Palouet is a minute village of fewer than twenty inhabitants. Arriving in the dreamy silence of siesta time, you'd never imagine that it could contain the wondrous Can Caudros. To describe this thousand year old castle as a mere hotel is to do it an injustice. Josep and Àngels are seeking not only to revive but to actually relive the traditions and culture of this pretty corner of Catalonia. Each room is a step back in time, devoid of intrusions from the electronic age. Bedrooms are full of fascinating artefacts and tapestries: nothing escapes the hand of history, not even the bathrooms which are wittily named Can Felip after the infamous oppressor of the Catalans. Each has antique fittings which blend in perfectly with the centuries-old atmosphere. The dining room is magical, like a medieval fairy grotto, with an old wine press for a fireplace. You dine on ancient recipes, expertly cooked by Àngels using organic produce: Segarran pancakes, nettle soup and medieval Jewish puddings, all washed down with organic wines and home-made laurel brandy. Josep's vast knowledge of Catalan folklore, local artisanal activity and walks add to the whole experience.

Rooms: 6 with bath & wc , 2 sharing bath & wc.
Price: Double/Twin 7000 Pts.
Breakfast: 750 Pts.
Meals: Lunch/Dinner 2000 Pts.
Closed: Never.

From Barcelona NII to Cervera. Here right to Guissona, then right to Massoteres, then follow signs to Palouet.

Entry no: 103   Map no: 7

Casa Mauri

Santa Engracia
25636 Tremp
Lérida

Tel: 973 252076 or 696 197404
Fax: 973 252076

Anne & Mike Harrison

Few villages in Spain can match spectacular Santa Engracia for setting; from its rocky ledge you look across to hill, lake and mountain – all of it changing with each passing hour. Just arriving here you feel a sense of adventure, of discovery. The heady magic of the place soon worked its spell on Anne and Mike who have gradually restored and renovated a group of 200-year-old houses. Guests can choose between the house and the *apartamento*. Either would be perfect for a family – or the house for a group of friends. Rooms come with radiators and wood-burners, attractive wooden furniture; pine and beam and pointed stone walls, rugs and bamboo lamps lend warmth. A place where you'd want to stay several nights. To do? – if you should tire of that grandest of views you could follow dinosaur footprints, visit Romanesque churches, bird-watch or, choose between any number of fabulous walks in the area – you may see wild horses and boar. Ask Anne and Mike for advice: they've written a walking book on the area. Rooms and dinner are both excellent value: from May to October weekly lets are preferred and you can choose between self-catering and catered-for.

Rooms: 1 house with 3 bedrooms sharing 2 shower rooms; 1 apartment with 2 bedrooms sharing 1 bathroom.
Price: Double/Twin 8000 Pts. House (for 4) 45000-80000 Pts per week; House (for 6) 55000-95000 Pts per week incl. VAT.
Breakfast: 1000 Pts (Eng) or self-catering.
Meals: Lunch/Dinner 2500 Pts (M) or self-catering.
Closed: Never.

From Tremp north towards La Pobla de Segur on C147. After garage on right, pass left turn to Talarn and after bends, left for Santa Engracia. Under railway, continue for 10km to village. Park and walk 300m up to house.

Map no: 7   Entry no: **104**

Casa Guilla

Santa Engracia
Apartado 83
25620 Tremp
Lérida

Tel: 973 252080 or 606 333481
Fax: 973 252080
E-mail: casaguilla@ctv.es
Web: www.ctv.es/users/casaguilla

Richard & Sandra Loder

This is a matchless position, a veritable eagle's nest. As you soar higher and higher
to the tiny hamlet perched high on a rocky crag you can only wonder at the
courage of Santa Engracia's earliest inhabitants. Richard and Sandra Loder have a
head for heights and after returning from Africa patiently set about restoring the
buildings that make up Casa Guilla – a fortified Catalan farmhouse parts of which
are nearly 1,000 years old. The house is a labyrinth: it twists and turns on many
different levels. There are two sitting rooms – one large with an open hearth,
another smaller with books and local info. The bedrooms are simply but cosily
furnished; there are terracotta tiles, heavy old beams, low ceilings... all deliciously
organic. And there are big breakfasts with home-baked bread, generous dinners
with lots of game and that incomparable view from both dining room and terrace
to accompany it. Caring and informative hosts in a fascinating part of Catalonia;
geologists, lepidopterists, ornithologists and botanists are in their element here! A
superb place. Many readers have written to say just how much they have enjoyed
their stays with the Loders.

Rooms: 1 double, 3 twins & 1 triple
sharing 3 shower rooms.
Price: Half-board only: 7000 Pts incl. VAT.
Breakfast: Included.
Meals: Dinner included; packed lunches
700 Pts.
Closed: December-February.

From Pobla de Segur C147 towards
Tremp. Continue north towards Pobla de
Segur for 1.5km then left at sign for Santa
Engracia. Continue for 10km to village. House next to church.

Entry no: 105   Map no: 7

Besiberri

Calle Deth Fort 4
25599 Arties-Valle de Aran
Lérida

Tel: 973 640829
Fax: 973 640829

Carmen Lara Aguilar

If you're headed for the Val d'Aran stay at the Besiberri: it is small, intimate and managed by the friendliest of families. This pretty, flower-clad building looked to the Alps for its inspiration and at first sight may remind you of sojourns in Switzerland, Austria or Germany. You enter through a small sitting room which has the dining area off to one side. There's an open hearth, beamed ceiling, Carmen's flower arrangements and a collection of pewter jugs. Wonderful to warm yourself in front of the fire after a day on the ski slopes or enjoy the light that streams in first thing. The sixteen smallish bedrooms are cheerfully decorated, clad throughout in wood with deeply comfortable beds and window boxes brimming with geraniums. Each floor has a balcony which looks out across the river which runs fast and deep past the hotel. Do splurge and take the suite at the top of the building; it has windows to both sides, its own balcony and a small lounge. No meals are served apart from breakfast but you are just yards from one of the best restaurants in the Pyrenees. You'll long remember Carmen's natural ebullience but do visit her before the village falls prey to further development.

Rooms: 16 with bath & wc; 1 suite.
Price: Double/Twin 8000-11000 Pts;
Suite 14000-16000 Pts.
Breakfast: Included.
Meals: None available.
Closed: May & November.

From Lérida N230 to Viella then C142 to Arties. Signposted to the right as you enter village.

Map no: 7

Entry no: 106

Cal Mateu

Residencia Casa de Pagés	**Tel:** 977 819003 or 977 819112
Calle Mayor 27	**Fax:** 977 819285
43372 La Bisbal de Falset (Priorat)	**E-mail:** casapagesmateu@terra.es
Tarragona	**Web:** www.agronet.org/agroturisme/cmateu.htm

Josep Carles Vicente Perelló

Every so often you meet folk who have taken on the role of 'mine host' for no other reason than the desire to share their wonderful homes with other people. To stay at Cal Mateu is rather like rediscovering a lost relative; Carmen says that her guests often cry when they take their leave! Hers is a warm, authentic and comfortable home in a quiet cul-de-sac in the medieval town of La Bisbal; the place is known for its ceramics and the old mansion houses built by a once-thriving Jewish community. Cal Mateu is of more recent construction but it has the spirit of a much older building. Its lounge, dining room and kitchen are all low, beamed and interlinked, separated just by stone arches; there are another two little lounges on each of the upper floors from where you have splendid views of the Sierra Montsant. The six guest rooms take their decorative cue from the rest of the house; they are smallish, beamed, and have simple red-chequered fabric for bedspreads, lampshades and curtains. The whole house seems to breathe an air of unaffected warmth and meals are, as you would imagine, simple and wholesome prepared by your most 'simpática' of hostesses. Extraordinarily good value, too.

Rooms: 6 sharing bathrooms & wcs
Price: Single 2500 Pts; Double/Twin 4000 Pts incl. VAT.
Breakfast: 600-800 Pts.
Meals: Lunch/Dinner 1200-1500 Pts (M).
Closed: Never.

From Reus N420 to Falset and there right on T710 to Gratallops then on to La Vilella Baixa. Continue on via Cabassers (Cabacès) to La Bisbal de Falset. House in centre on main street leading to church.

Venta de San Juan

43786 Batea
Tarragona

Tel: 649 644724
Fax: 93 4143854
Web: www.agroturisme.org/sanjuan.htm

Clotilde de Pascual

Wonderful, the sort of place that some of us dream of finding in this apparently
empty – and vast – Spanish countryside. If you begin your search for the house in
Batea you will be in benign mood, for it is a beautiful little town. Then there is the
long drive up to the house, ending with the sight of the solid old building,
apparently unoccupied, among fields and woods. But Jorge and Clotilde are filling
it with life, having inherited it from a grandfather who made his fortune in Cuba
but decided to cut his losses and return after Independence. If you love dilapidated
old houses then you'll love it here. The entrance is full of country clutter;
flagstone-floored with doors leading into ancient rooms still dressed in flock
wallpaper and just as they were when conversation first sparkled them into life.
Some might see so many minor inconveniences that they might not notice the
sheer authenticity of the house whilst others will thank us for bringing them here –
the food alone makes it worth it and much of what you eat will have been grown
on the farm. Jorge and Clotilde are young, modern, Catalan and charming – and
addicted to this mad, unkempt old house.

Rooms: 3 sharing bath & wc; 1 house
sleeping up to 6.
Price: Double/Twin sharing 6000 Pts;
House weekend 20000 Pts; week 50000
Pts, two weeks 80000 Pts.
Breakfast: 500 Pts.
Meals: Dinner 1500 Pts (M) incl. wine.
Closed: November-31 March.

From Barcelona A7 south towards Valencia.
Exit junction 38 for L'Hospitalet de L'Infant y Móra. Follow signs to Móra la Nova,
then Gandesa. There towards Alcañiz then right to Batea. Here P-723 towards
Nonaspe. At km 7.3 just before provincial boundary sign for Zaragoza turn left on
dirt track. At any fork keep left and after 2km you arrive at house.

Map no: 14   **Entry no: 108**

La Casona del Ajímez

Calle San Juan 2
44100 Albarracín
Teruel

Tel: 978 710321 or 978 700326
Fax: 978 700326
E-mail: c.ajimez@arrakis.es
Web: www.casonadelajimez.arrakis.es

Javier Fernández Martínez

Hidden in the heart of the old religious quarter of Albarracín, this 200-year-old house sits on ancient foundations. Javier has transformed it to remind one of the Muslim, Jewish and Christian communities who once lived here in harmony. The rooms fuse style with simplicity, each with its religious theme. *El Canónigo* was once a library and has a studious feel. *El Menora*, with its plush four-poster bed, has a Jewish candelabra as its headboard. The two *Muslim* rooms are duplex. And fine details: wrought-iron beds, hand-painted wall designs, wood impregnated with scented oils, warmly-lit and exquisitely-finished bathrooms. In the library-like dining room, writing desks become tables, the see-through kitchen lends an air of informality and delights such as partridge and lamb chops are served with good regional wines. You will need the fortifying breakfast of toast, honey, cakes and fruit if you are planning a mountain walk but if relaxation is all you want, sit and admire the old walled town from the terraced garden: the tiled cathedral roof is almost within reach. Excellent summer barbecues are prepared here and Javier also runs Restaurant Gallo, a short walk away.

Rooms: 6 with bath & wc.
Price: Double/Twin 10000-12000 Pts.
Breakfast: Continental 700 Pts or 'European' 1400 Pts.
Meals: Lunch/Dinner 3500 Pts (M), 5-6000 Pts (C):
Closed: In September for 5 days.

From Teruel N324 towards Calatayud then left on TE901 to Albarracín. Here, just before tunnel, left up hill to car park by Cathedral then up narrow cobbled street past museum towards church spire. House on left after 300m.

Entry no: 109   Map no: 13

Hostal Los Palacios

Calle Palacios 21   **Tel:** 978 700327
44100 Albarracín   **Fax:** 978 700358
Teruel

Valeriano Saez Lorenzo

Albarracín is one of Teruel's most attractive walled towns; its narrow streets tumble down the hillside beneath the castle and eventually lead you to a lovely main square and the medieval cathedral with its ceramic-tiled tower (a later addition). Los Palacios is a tall, balconied building just outside the city walls; its earthy colours seem to fix it to the hillside on which it stands. The 50-year-old building was just recently thoroughly refurbished and so was born this small *hostal*. The bedrooms, on the small side, are furnished with workaday wooden furniture; floors are decked in modern tiles. The fabrics are a shade satiny but forgive this little lapse: these are utterly Spanish rooms, impeccably clean and the views from their small balconies are second to none. It is good to escape from telephone and television; the owners are keen not to disturb their guests' utterly silent nights. The little breakfast room/bar area has views, too, and while busy preparing your breakfast the owners will happily chat about trips from the *hostal*. This little inn has few pretensions, is amazingly cheap and we recommend it wholeheartedly if you are happy with more simple accommodation.

Rooms: 16 with bath or shower & wc.
Price: Single 3000 Pts; Double/Twin 5000 Pts incl. VAT.
Breakfast: 250 Pts.
Meals: 1400 Pts (M), 2000 Pts (C). Restaurant closed 16 Oct-June 30th apart from Easter week.
Closed: Never.

From Teruel N234 north towards Zaragoza. After approx. 8km left on TE901 to Albarracín. Here through tunnel and right after 150m. Hostal is second house on right.

Map no: 13   **Entry no: 110**

Hotel Esther

44431 Virgen de la Vega   **Tel:** 978 801040
Teruel   **Fax:** 978 801059

Miguel Andrés Rajadel García

The high mountains and hilltop villages of the Maestrazgo have only recently begun to awaken the curiosity of those in search of new pastures to walk and ski. At the heart of this wild and beautiful area the modern little Esther is one of our favourite places. It is a purely family business – father, mother and son look after bar, reception and restaurant. The focus is the dining room; it is modern but a timbered roof, mounted ceramic plates and a lovely tiled picture of Jaca help to create intimacy. You can expect a memorable meal here; specialities are roast lamb and kid as well as jugged meats like turkey and rabbit. Try the junket with honey for dessert. There is a good choice of wines and you can trust Miguel's recommendations. Decoration is the same upstairs and down: tiled floors, simple wooden furniture. The bedrooms have small bathrooms and are irreproachably clean. Hotel Esther is another of the small hotels included here which prove that modern hotels can have a heart, too. Honest prices for rooms and food; you may well be the only foreigner staying here and if you're not we bet that they'll be travelling with this guide!

Rooms: 19 with bath & wc.
Price: Single 4000 Pts; Double/Twin 7500 Pts.
Breakfast: 650 Pts.
Meals: Lunch/Dinner 1800 Pts (M), 2750-3500 Pts (C).
Closed: 8-25 September.

From Valencia towards Barcelona; at Sagunto left on N234 towards Teruel. TE201 to Mora de Rubielos then TE201 towards Alcalá de la Selva. 2km before Alcalá on right.

Entry no: 111   **Map no: 13**

Masía Aragonés

44586 Peñarroya de Tastavins   **Tel:** 978 769048 or 978 896786
Teruel

Pilar & Manuel Andreu

Rising majestically above open pastures this lovingly-restored,16th-century
Aragonese farm has a three-storey stone tower with six guest rooms. It was once a
weekend retreat for wealthy locals but is now simply and pleasingly furnished. Its
airy, sitting/dining room has stone walls hung with old farm implements,
contemporary tiles, pine furniture and a fine wood-burning stove. This is where
you enjoy Pilar's cooking with nearly all ingredients home-grown or reared: she
prepares wholesome soups and stews and simple puddings accompanied by her
home-brewed wine and liqueurs. Although they are rather spartan, the bedrooms
are a good size and have iron bedsteads, homespun curtains and modern
bathrooms. With its arched windows and open-plan rooms, we best liked those on
the top floor where it would be wonderful to sit and decide which of the many
possible excursions to make into this historic and remote hinterland. The scenery is
epic, the mountains are home to ibex and eagles, there are crystalline rock pools
above Beceite and Valderrobres is worth a visit. And the Andreu family go out of
their way to make sure your stay is memorable.

Rooms: 6 with bath & wc.
Price: Double/Twin 4000-5000 Pts.
Breakfast: Included.
Meals: Lunch 1000 Pts; Dinner 1500 Pts.
Closed: Never.

From Barcelona A7 south then exit at junction 38 for
L'Hospitalet de L'Infant y Móra. Follow signs to Móra
la Nova, then Gandesa. There towards Alcañiz, but left
in Calaceite to Valderrobres. There left to Fuentespalda,
on towards Monroyo then left towards Peñarroyo de
Tastavins. After 500m right towards Herbes; signposted
on right after 1.6km, 3km of track to farm.

Map no: 14   **Entry no: 112**

La Torre del Visco

Apartado 15
44580 Valderrobres
Teruel

Tel: 978 769015
Fax: 978 769016

Piers Dutton and Jemma Markham

Bajo Aragón is one of Spain's best-kept secrets: beautiful, wild, unspoilt by tourism
and stacked with natural and man-made treasures. Stay with Piers and Jemma and
renew body and spirit in their superbly-renovated medieval farmhouse. Standards
of comfort, decoration and food are high yet the atmosphere at Visco is deeply
relaxing. Their farmland and forests protect the house from modern noise and
nuisance; peace is total inside and out with neither telephone nor television to
disturb you in your room. After a day of discovery – your hosts will advise you,
they have been here for years – settle with one of their 7,000 books in front of a
great log fire, delight in their eclectic taste where each piece of furniture, be it
antique, modern or rustic, Art Deco or Nouveau, fits with the old tiles, beams and
exposed brickwork. Dinner is a feast of own-farm produce, the Visco's *bodega* has a
fine selection of wines, breakfast in the great farmhouse kitchen is renowned. A
night at Visco is a treat never to be forgotten and it is refreshing to come across
ex-pats who have mastered the language of their adopted country and who are so
knowledgeable about its culture.

Rooms: 14 with bath & wc; 3 suites.
Price: Double/Twin 28000-35000 Pts;
Suite 45000 Pts (half-board).
Breakfast: Included.
Meals: Lunch approx. 5000 Pts;
dinner included.
Closed: 8-19 January.

From Barcelona A7 south towards
Valencia. Exit junction 38 for L'Hospitalet
de L'Infant y Móra. Follow signs to Móra
la Nova, then Gandesa. There towards Alcañiz, but left in Calaceite to
Valderrobres. There left towards Fuentespalda, and after 6km right. Follow track
to house.

Entry no: 113   **Map no: 14**

Mas del Pi
44580 Valderrobres   **Tel:** 978 769033
Teruel

Carmen & Ramón Salvans

This is the stuff of which back-to-nature dreams are made. High on a hilltop Mas del Pi is literally at the end of the road – a road to remember. Ramón and Carmen have worked their 70-hectare farm for nearly 20 years; there are vines, olives and almonds, ducks and chickens and a big vegetable garden. What better way for them to meet new people and share their love of the place than by setting up a small B&B? Thus an old tradition has been rediscovered: 200 years ago this was a coaching inn. Things here are definitely rustic; hosts and house are utterly unaffected. The Salvans are proud of their simple guest rooms with their tiled floors, old furniture and views across the farm. At breakfast there are home-made jams and cakes and newly-laid eggs. We have fond memories of sharing dinner (wonderful roast duck) and easy conversation; nearly everything from meat to veg to wine to liqueur is home-produced. Outside there is the farm to explore and glorious walks, with the Pyrenean sheepdog to accompany you if you want; children love it here. "We would readily stay here again" enthused one reader; "the perfect escape" wrote another. And a pool has just been finished.

Rooms: 6 with bath & wc.
Price: Double/Twin 5000 Pts p.p
(half-board).
Breakfast: Included.
Meals: Lunch 1700 Pts; Dinner included.
Closed: Never.

From Barcelona A7 south to exit 40 for
L'Aldea-Tortosa. C235 to Tortosa, then
C230 towards Mora la Nova. After 16km
left to Valderrobres. Just before village turn
right towards 'Ermita de los Santos'. Follow road for 4km then good track for
3km to reach Mas del Pi.

Map no: 14   Entry no: 114

Hotel La Parada del Compte

Antigua Estación del Ferrocarril   **Tel:** 978 769072/73
44597 Torre del Compte   **Fax:** 978 769074
Teruel   **Web:** www.rusticae.es

José María Naranjo & Pilar Vilés

The old railway station of Torre del Compte, hidden away in the valley below the village, has recently been given a new lease of life thanks to the dynamism of Pilar and José María who were convinced that rural tourism and modern design could be happy bedfellows. At the end of the road cutting down from the village a highly original ochre-and-Bordeaux-coloured hotel awaits you. It's about designer furniture, a bold use of glass and metal, and state-of-the-art bathrooms and beds, rather than rustic-style nostalgia. And it works wonderfully. Each bedroom's colour and decoration is inspired by a different town in Spain; thus Madrid is about classical elegance, Mérida inspired by Roman motifs, Valencia's whites and blues evoke the Mediterranean. It's hard to choose a favourite but we might go for França because it gets the sun first thing. All fittings and furnishings are top of the range throughout the hotel, from taps to beds to sofas. Relax in a light, airy reading room, dine on innovative and beautifully presented 'contemporary Mediterranean' food then head out (perhaps along the old railway track, by bike) to discover the wilderness and wonder of this part of Spain.

Rooms: 7 with bath & wc; 2 suites.
Price: Single 13000 Pts; Double/Twin 16000 Pts; Suite 25000 Pts.
Breakfast: Included.
Meals: Lunch/Dinner 4500-5500 Pts (C). Not available on Mondays.
Closed: 10-31 January.

A7 exit for Hospitalet Del Infante/Mora de Ebru. From Mora N420 towards Alcañiz. Just after Calaceite turn left to Torre del Compte.

Entry no: 115

Map no: 14

Hotel Cardenal Ram
Cuesta Suñer 1
12300 Morella
Castellón

Tel: 964 173085
Fax: 964 173218
E-mail: hotelcardenalram@ctv.es

Jaime Peñarroya Carbo

The whole of Morella is a national heritage site: you'll see why when you first catch sight of this fortress town girt about with its medieval walls. In one of its grandest mansions is a hotel as remarkable as the town. Just to one side of the colonnaded main street the proportions and arched windows of the Cardenal Ram give it a slightly Venetian air (when it was built there was a constant cross-cultural exchange between the Genoese and the eastern Spaniards). Enter through the 15th-century arched doorway beneath the coat of arms of the Ram family and you may well be greeted by genial Jaime Peñarroya. A vaulted stairwell sweeps up to the guest rooms – and what rooms! They are big, with polished parquet floors; bedheads, writing desks and chairs are all of carved wood. Bright bedcovers and rugs add a welcome splash of colour and the bathrooms are as good as they come. Do have dinner: truffles are a speciality, the meat is excellent and there are home-made puddings. Book several nights and discover the wild beauty of the Maestrazgo: there's a long distance pathway (GR route) linking these remote hilltop villages. Both food and rooms are amazingly good value.

Rooms: 17 with bath & wc; 2 suites.
Price: Single 5500 Pts; Double/Twin 8500 Pts; Triple/Suite 10500 Pts.
Breakfast: 800 Pts.
Meals: Lunch/Dinner 2000 Pts (M), approx. 4500 Pts (C). Closed Mondays and Sundays out-of-season.
Closed: Never.

From Valencia A7 towards Barcelona; exit for Vinarós. Here N232 to Morella. Up into old town (if lost ask for Puerta de San Miguel); hotel in main street 200m from cathedral.

Fonda Guimera

Calle Agustín Pastor 28
44141 Mirambel
Castellón

Tel: 964 178269 or 964 178268
Fax: 964 178293

Pedro Guimera

Mirambel is one of the most beautiful of the hilltop villages of the Maestrazgo, a place so well preserved that when Ken Loach came to film *Land and Freedom* it sufficed to move a few cars and the cameras were up and rolling for his 1930's drama. A lovely arch leads you through the town walls and straight into the village's main street; just along on your left is Fonda Guimera. The inn is just ten years old but you would never guess it; it is a lovely stone building that is utterly faithful to local tradition and fits perfectly between much older houses on both sides. On the ground floor are the bar and the restaurant which serves simple home-cooking. Upstairs the rooms are as unpretentious as your hosts but they lack nothing and are impeccably clean with simple wooden furniture and shutters. Bathrooms are smallish but have good-quality towels. The rooms at the back look out over terracotta roofs to the mountains beyond; a few have their own terrace. When leaving you may be tempted to question your bill; can it really be so little?

Rooms: 14 with bath & wc.
Price: Double/Twin 3500 Pts incl. VAT.
Breakfast: 300 Pts.
Meals: Lunch/Dinner 1200 Pts (M), 1500 Pts (C).
Closed: Never.

From Valencia A7 towards Barcelona; exit for Vinarós. Here N232 to Morella; just before Morella, CS840 to Forcall. Here road to La Mata de Morella, then Mirambel. Under arch and Guimera along on left.

Entry no: 117   Map no: 14

Alicante
•

Valencia
•

Murcia
•

Eastern Spain

"All travel has its advantages. If the passenger visits better countries, he may learn
to improve his own. And if fortune carries him to worse, he may learn to enjoy it"
– Samuel Johnson

El Fraile Gordo

Apartado 21
03650 Pinoso
Alicante

Tel: 968 432211
Fax: 968 432211
E-mail: david@fraile-gordo.com
Web: www.fraile-gordo.com

David Bexon

Multi-talented David Bexon – singer, interior designer, upholsterer and actor – moved on to a new career as innkeeper and chef-in-residence of El Fraile Gordo. He needed to draw on more of his Renaissance talents when he restored this old farmhouse. Why *El Fraile Gordo* (the fat Friar)? The house stands where Brothers of the Franciscan order once lived and worked. Hard to imagine what confronted David when you see dining and sitting rooms, kitchen and bedroom; everything feels much older, thanks to the many antiques and old materials that he searched out when nursing the building back to life. But this is more than a simple farmhouse; stained-glass windows, grand piano, statues, and original sculptures have added sophistication to lowly origins. Guest rooms are fresh and welcoming, with beds for big sleeps and glorious wrap-around views. There's a delightful walled garden, a terrace that captures the morning sun, inspired cooking (do buy David's cookery book!) and a host whose hospitality and kindness run far beyond the call of duty. "Bliss" wrote one of our readers. And David has recently added a self-catering cottage which can sleep up to five with full wheelchair access.

Rooms: 4 with shower & wc; 1 cottage.
Price: Double/Twin 7500-8500 Pts; Family room 10000 Pts; Cottage 18000 Pts.
Breakfast: Included or self-catering in cottage.
Meals: Dinner 3500 Pts (M) incl. wine.
Closed: Every Monday & 2 weeks in January after Epiphany.

From Alicante airport towards Valencia on A7/E15; first exit on N330 for Madrid. Exit to Novelda. In centre, left at second set of lights then right at island. On through Monovar to Pinoso/El Pino. Here C3223 towards Fortuna. After 8km right towards Cañada del Trigo; house in hamlet after 700m.

Entry no: 118   Map no: 19

Hotel Villa de Biar

C/San José 2
03410 Biar
Alicante

Tel: 96 5811304/5810055
Fax: 96 5811312
E-mail: hotelbiar@cvt.es

Manuel García Ortega

The monuments of Biar chart the history of the land and people; Moorish tower on top of its rocky pinnacle and below, among streets of lime-washed houses, several surprisingly ornate churches and chapels from the Christian period. The façade of this hotel is old, too, but this is all that is left of the nobleman's house. Behind its salmon-coloured frontage you find a hotel for both tourists and business people, this explains the muzak in reception and a slightly anodyne feel to bedrooms and dining area. We'd book one of the attic rooms: their wood-clad ceilings give them a cosier feel than those on the floor beneath. From here you can lap up the tranquility of the place: open your window wide to catch birdsong, the sound of church bells and views out across the garden. A large pool among pine and cypress trees could be the place to put a long, hot drive behind you. We were won over by the friendliness of the staff and the slant of the menu towards local Alicante dishes. Climb up to the castle for a stunning sunset and try to be here for the extraordinary festival when the Crescent and the Cross once more do battle and the whole town goes medievally mad!

Rooms: 40 with bath or shower & wc; 2 suites.
Price: Single 10400 Pts; Double/Twin 13000 Pts; Suite 16500 Pts.
Breakfast: 800 Pts.
Meals: Lunch/Dinner 2290 Pts (M), 3500 Pts (C).
Closed: Never.

From Alicante towards Madrid on A7, exit for Villena-Biar. Continue for 7km to Biar. Follow signs 'centro urbano' and then Hotel Villa de Biar.

Map no: 19

Entry no: 119

El Chato Chico
Plaza de la Iglesia 6
03788 Beniaya — Vall
d'Alcalá
Alicante

Tel: 96 551 4451
Fax: 96 551 4161
Web: www.terraferma.net/
chatochico/chatochicoing.html

Paul & Jakki Walmsley

Should you come and stay at the tiny hamlet of Beniaya don't expect the streets to be teeming with life: there are just fourteen inhabitants! Yet in the Middle Ages it was important enough for the Imam of the Moorish king Al-Azraq (the 'Blue-eyed one' – Jakki will tell you more about him) to have built himself a fine residence next to the mosque. It is this same building that the Walmsleys have nursed back to life and you can see one of the original Moorish arches in the beamed sitting room. The house has a snug, enveloping feel; bedrooms and public rooms (including a reading room) are smallish but your well-being is guaranteed thanks to good beds, central heating and the most peaceful of settings. At dinner don't expect purely Spanish food but do expect the lamb to be delicious: an enthusiastic reader wrote that "the quality of the food was outstanding, especially for the price". If you prefer holidays with a theme, make a note that your hosts arrange courses in cookery, Spanish conversation and painting. It is easy to see why the Walmsley's gave up their work in Benidorm to open this small inn which, incidentally, is surrounded on all sides by glorious walking country.

Rooms: 5 with bath & wc.
Price: Double/Twin 7000 Pts.
Breakfast: Included.
Meals: Dinner 2500 Pts incl. wine.
Closed: Never.

Round Valencia on A7/E15 then N430 towards Albacete. Bypass Xàtiva then exit on CV40/N340 towards Alcoy. Just after pass of Port d'Albaida left through Muro d'Alcoi, Benimarful/Planes then right to Margarida and there follow signs to Beniaia (Beniaya).

Hotel Els Frares

Avenida del País Valencià 20
03811 Quatretondeta
Alicante

Tel: 96 5511234 or 676 476151/148
Fax: 96 5511200
E-mail: elsfrare@teleline.es
Web: www.mountainwalks.com

Patricia & Brian Fagg

Brian and Pat left the UK to head for the Spanish hills. Herculean efforts have borne fruit at their village inn and restaurant which was a hundred-year-old ruin when they first set eyes on it. Now its attractive pastel frontage and a constant flow of visitors are adding life and colour to the village. Just behind the village, jagged peaks rise to almost 5,000 feet – the hotel takes its name from them. There are rooms with private terraces looking out across surrounding almond groves to those lofty crags. Good mattresses ensure deep sleeps, fabrics are bright, there are framed photos of the Sierra Serella, and some rooms have their original floor tiles. The cosy dining and sitting rooms are just right for the hotel; you'd look forward to returning here after a walk, perhaps with Brian as your guide – he knows the surrounding mountains better than the locals. At supper choose from a menu that celebrates local dishes and *tapas* yet still finds a place for imaginative veggie alternatives; many ingredients – from olive oil, to fruit, to herbs – are home-grown. Your immensely likeable hosts have made many Spanish friends. *No smoking allowed in hotel or restaurant.*

Rooms: 9 with bath & wc.
Price: Double (with terrace) 8500 Pts;
Twin 7500 Pts.
Breakfast: 500 Pts.
Meals: Lunch 2500 Pts (M); Dinner 2500 (M), 3000 Pts (C).
Closed: 8-25 January & 7-25 July.

From Alicante N340 towards Alcoy. 3km before Alcoy right to Benilloba. Then left to Gorga and from here to Quatretondeta (on map spelt Cuatretondeta).

Mas des Castellans

Ptda. Alcoies 25
03108 Torremanzán
Alicante

Tel: 965 619114 or 616 700252
Fax: 965 619074
E-mail: cesar.sempere@eper.upf.es

Jose Antonio & Cesar Sempere Olivar

The old farm of Mas des Castellans has recently been reborn as a country hotel-cum-activity centre thanks to the efforts of brothers Cesar and José Antonio, two young and exceptionally well-meaning hosts who like to refer to their revamped farm and outbuildings as an 'eco-rural' centre! Children would love it and quite a few grown-ups, too. Horseriding, cycling, walking, archery, pétanque, table tennis, football and volleyball are just a few of the activities on offer. By summer 2001 a large indoor pool will be up and running. Accommodation, too, is of many shades and hues; choose between self-catering or catered-for, a normal bedroom, a log cabin, a bungalow or an apartment. Whatever type of sleeping arrangement you opt for expect a clean and well-furnished living space; they are too diverse to describe here. Architecturally by far the most attractive bit of the farm is its *bodega* restaurant which has its original instrumentalia and wine press on display. Cesar, is a child psychologist; children will be kept entertained both physically and artistically; it is wonderful to see a place where they are celebrated and expected to be both seen and heard.

Rooms: 9 with bath & wc.
Price: Log Cabin 6000 Pts; Double 8000
Pts; House (for 4-6) 19000 Pts; House (for
6-8) 24000 Pts; House (for 10-12) 38000
Pts incl. VAT.
Breakfast: 500 Pts.
Meals: Lunch/Dinner 1900 Pts (M),
2000 Pts (C).
Closed: Never.

From N340 exit on AP1711 (formerly
CV785) to Benifalim then A161 (formerly CV780) to Torre de las Maçanes. Here turn left at sign for Mas des Castellans. 1.5km to Mas.

Entry no: 122

Map no: 20

Bodega Los Pinos

Casa Los Pinos
46635 Fontanares
Valencia

Tel: 96 2222090
Fax: 96 2222086
E-mail: pinos@jet.es

Madeleine & Manuel de Olaechea

The province is called Los Alhorines. The word comes from the Moorish period and means corn chamber: the rich agricultural lands have always provided bountiful produce. It seemed the perfect place for Madeleine and Manuel when they came to Spain in search of a house and land that they could farm organically. After just a few years the vineyards are planted and a visit here is a must for anyone who enjoys good wine. "The best organic wine in Spain," writes the magazine Vinum. The house has a truly Mediterranean feel: cypress trees suggest Provence, the elegant frontage evokes Tuscany. On the ground floor is the guest lounge with a wrap-around settee by the hearth and hand-painted plates and copper saucepans beneath the beams. Next door is a vaulted dining room and beyond the courtyard with an enormous bay, yuccas and palms. Choose between high-ceilinged guest bedrooms – you cross the corridor to your bath or shower room – and the enormous self-catering apartment. You can swim, play tennis, ride and visit the *bodega*. But do find time for a stroll through the vines with the dogs and do eat in: "I cook very well," says Madeleine matter-of-factly!

Rooms: 3 with bath or shower & wc; 1 apartment.
Price: Double/Twin 10000 Pts; Apartment 15000 Pts (min. 2 nights) incl. VAT.
Breakfast: Included.
Meals: Dinner 2000 Pts incl. wine.
Closed: 15 December-15 January.

From Alicante towards Madrid on N330. Exit for Fontanares (approx. 70km from Alicante). Los Pinos is 800m before Fontanares. Signposted on right.

Map no: 19

Entry no: 123

Masía la Safranera

Partida Serratella 13
46650 Canals
Valencia

Tel: 609 617280 or 609 608736
Fax: 96 2245383
E-mail: lasafranera@teleline.es

Rafael Llace Vila

You may have heard of Alcoy because of its annual *Fiesta de Moros y Cristianos* when the whole town dresses up and engages in mock battle until Saint George (Santiago) intervenes and puts the infidels to rout. You are less likely to have heard of La Safranera, a century-old farm and *bodega*. It is just five miles from the scene of the mock-medieval madness, protected by wooded hillsides and at the centre of a recently created Natural Park. The ever courteous Rafael Llace Vila and his extended family have vested much love and labour in nursing these old buildings back to good health. Simple guest rooms strike a balance between what is traditional and what is functional; they have old beams above, modern tiles beneath and decent beds and bathrooms. More striking is the dining room which has enormous old wine barrels and other oenological instruments on display as well as a mounted boar's head above the inglenook, one of Carlos' hunting trophies. The white plastic chairs feel incongruous but food is from the regional recipe book and there is excellent bottled cider. Come for the tranquility and be sure to walk from the house up to the old Sanctuary of Font Roja.

Rooms: 15 with bath & wc.
Price: Double 7560 Pts;
Quadruple 13440 Pts.
Breakfast: Included.
Meals: Lunch/Dinner 1500 Pts (M).
Closed: Never.

From Alcoy CV795 towards Banyeres. By km post 10 turn left and continue for 3km to La Safranera.

Entry no: 124   Map no: 19

Hostería de Mont Sant

Subida al Castillo s/n
46800 Xátiva (Játiva)
Valencia

Tel: 96 2275081
Fax: 96 2281905
E-mail: montsant@servidex.com
Web: www.servidex.com/montsant

Javier Andrés Cifre

The Arab castle is above and red-roofed city below, mountains and Mediterranean beyond, terraced gardens groaning with orange trees and 700 newly-planted palm trees. There is fascinating archaeology (Iberian and Roman shards, Moorish fortifications, Cistercian monastery walls – the history of Spain in a nutshell) and a Moorish irrigation system that has guaranteed water in all seasons since the 12th century. The mountain streams are channelled, refreshing the air as they go, into a vast cistern beneath the garden. Señor Cifre's old family house has cool, beamed living areas with unexpected nooks, charmingly undecorated guestrooms (just natural materials, old tiles, antique furniture and no pictures "because the windows frame pictures enough") and a see-through kitchen! Pity the exposed cooks but enjoy the delicious food: if you over-indulge there are gym, sauna and jacuzzi at your disposal. We enjoyed Mont Sant's balconies, terraces and quiet corners and next time resolved to book one of the log 'cabins' which have recently been built under the pines. A friendly, peaceful place to stay: 'The foie gras was out of this world and we enjoyed Javier's hospitality' enthused a reader.

Rooms: 11 with bath or shower & wc;
1 suite.
Price: Double/Twin 16000-20000 Pts;
Suite 22000 Pts.
Breakfast: 1450 Pts.
Meals: Lunch/Dinner 4500 Pts (C). 6000
Ptas (C).
Closed: 7-13 January.

From Valencia N340 towards Albacete.
X(J)átiva exit and here follow signs for 'Castillo'. Signposted.

Map no: 19   **Entry no: 125**

La Casa Vieja

Calle Horno 4
46842 Rugat
Valencia

Tel: 96 2814013
Fax: 96 2814013
E-mail: lacasavieja@xpress.es

Maris & Maisie Andres Watson

This most peaceful of houses combines 450 years of old stones with a very
contemporary idea of volumes and shapes. There are original arches, columns and
capitals (it was probably a nobleman's house), twisty beams, ancient floor tiles and
a well in the courtyard. In a more recent vein the swimming pool occupies most of
the remaining patio space and there are views to the orange grove-clad hillsides. A
double-height sitting area faces an immense inglenook where deep sofas hug you
as you sip your welcome sherry before dining, indoors or out. Many of the
antiques have been in Maris' family for as long as she can remember – like a 16th-
century grandfather clock, Persian rugs, hand-carved mahogany table and oil
paintings. Bedrooms are full of character, the beds firm, the night-time village-
quiet; kettles, tea and coffee remind you of home. Cooking follows the seasons;
expect market-fresh produce with interesting veggie alternatives but if there's some
dish you'd particularly like to try, just ask. The new restaurant is just the place for
your feast: we really enjoyed the grilled goat's cheese with fig and orange confit
and trust Maisie's recommendations when you choose your wine.

Rooms: 6 with bath & wc; 1 suite.
Price: Double 10000 Pts; Twin 11000-
12000 Pts; Suite 17000 Pts incl. VAT.
Breakfast: Included.
Meals: Lunch 1400 Pts; Dinner 3500 Pts
(M/C). Closed some days to NON-
residents. Check.
Closed: Christmas.

From Valencia A7 south then exit 60.
N332 towards Gandia/Alicante. Exit onto
CV60 towards Albaida. Exit for Terrateig/Montechelvo/Ayelo de Rugat/Rugat.
Through Montechelvo; Rugat is 2nd village to left, signposted.

Ad Hoc

Boix 4   **Tel:** 96 3919140
46003 Valencia   **Fax:** 96 3913667
Valencia   **E-mail:** adhoc@nexo.net

Eva de Roqueta

Valencia is a vibrant city, its old quarter brimming with fine old baroque-fronted mansion houses and its streets buzzing with life until the early hours: come for some of the best bar life in Spain. Ad Hoc is in a brilliant position at the heart of the old quarter in a quiet street and it's by far the best of the town's small hotels. The owner is in the art business and he lavished much care – and many of the paintings from his collection – on the building's restoration. Warmth is what Ad Hoc is about: in the way you are greeted, the choice of colour scheme and the general feel of the place. Wafer-bricking is the décor's leitmotiv: then there are handsome original floors, gilded mirrors, stencilled ceilings and barrel vaulting. The dining room is as intimate as they come with just a dozen tables: the set menu is particularly good value. The bedrooms are as carefully manicured as the rest of the hotel: rugs, writing desk and the same sensitive lighting. Do make sure you visit the Cathedral where you can see what Valencians claim to be the the chalice used by Christ at the Last Supper: the Holy Grail!

Rooms: 28 with bath & wc.
Price: Single 15800 Pts; Double/Twin 19900 Pts.
Breakfast: 1000 Pts.
Meals: Lunch/Dinner 2200 Pts (M), 3500 Pts (C).
Closed Sat lunchtime and Sundays.
Closed: Never.

Situated in historic centre of Valencia. On interior ring road, pass Torres de Serranos, Boix is third on the right.

Map no: 14   **Entry no:** 127

El Molino del Río
Camino Viejo de Archivel s/n
30400 Caravaca de la Cruz
Murcia

Tel: 968 433381 or 606 301409
Fax: 968 433381
E-mail: elmolino@molinodelrio.com
Web: www.molinodelrio.com

Carmen Alvárez

El Molino del Río is secreted away beside a rocky canyon cut by the Río Argos; its abundant waters explain why grain was milled here for nearly four centuries. Several generations of Carmen's family have lived here but it is just recently that she and her Swedish husband Jan restored and restructured the mill and its outbuildings to create a small hostelry. It could be a showcase 'eco' hotel; the earthy colour of the building was mixed to make the least impact on its physical setting, natural dyes were used for doors and beams, terracotta floor tiles were made locally by hand, and an organic orchard planted on the surrounding terraces. A lost tradition has been revived; in former times the mill became a kind of market-cum-inn when peasants came to barter their goods for flour. Nowadays you can exchange pesetas or euros for a beautifully-decorated apartment or room and excellent food, served in the low, beamed dining room. An enjoyable variant to dinner is the occasional crayfish and schnapps buffet supper; this tradition is slightly less local, being a variant on the Swedish midsummer shindig. An enchanting and blissfully quiet place and the kindest of hosts.

Rooms: 1 with bath & wc; 6 apartments.
Price: Double 6500 Pts; Apartment (for 4-6) 14900 Pts ; Apartment (for 4) 12900 Pts; Apartment (for 2) 9600 Pts.
Breakfast: 800 Pts.
Meals: Lunch/Dinner 2500 Pts (M).
Crayfish 'special' 5000 Pts. Book ahead.
Closed: Never.

Leave E15/N340 at km 595 then take C3211 to Caravaca de la Cruz. Here follow signs for hospital and El Carrascal. Continue for 9.5km (you'll see signs for Molino del Río) then turn right at another sign and follow track for 1km.

Hospedería Casazul

Ctra. Caravaca km 28
Finca 'Casas de D. Gonzalo'
30812 La Paca-Lorca
Murcia

Tel: 968 299163
Fax: 968 491595
E-mail: casazul-ucomur@coceta.com
Web: www.coceta.com/ucomur/casazul

Inés García

You won't miss the merry blue façade of Casazul as you approach along the road which leads to Caravaca. The house owes its origins to the spring waters which rise just behind it; legend has it that local folk who drank the water lived a hundred years and more. What is certainly true is that the old poplar next to the springs, with a trunk more than 3m round, is a good century old. So too Casazul which even at its birth as a country house in the mid 18th century sported its famous blue plumage. Changing fortunes meant it was used as a school and then abandoned until Carmen rediscovered it half a dozen years ago. Careful restoration in parts, sympathetic renovation in others, and a new build in the old grain stores has created a wonderful little inn. Bedrooms are large, beamed, with antique beds and modern bathrooms: they look out across fields of wheat and corn. There is a bar in the old *bodega* or wine store, a cosy lounge, a large dining room decorated with trophies from the hunt and a terrace leading to a spring-fed pool. Food is regional, vegetables home grown and game the speciality. Do visit nearby Caravaca and its medieval castle; at sunset it is an enchanting spot.

Rooms: 10 with bath & wc.
Price: Double/Twin 6500 Pts; 'Special' Double 7500 Pts.
Breakfast: Included.
Meals: Lunch/Dinner 3000 pts (C).
Closed: Never.

Leave N340 at km 595 then take C3211 towards Caravaca de la Cruz. Go through La Paca; Casazul is on the right after approx. 2km. Signposted.

Map no: 19

Entry no: 129

Hacienda Los Sibileys

Nogalte 84   **Tel:** 626 955346 or in UK 00 441934 520717
30800 Lorca   **Fax:** In UK 00 441934 520717
Murcia   **Web:** www.andalucia.com/accommodation/lossibileys/home.htm

Karl & Judith Lanchbury

One can't but be struck by the number of ex-pats who have made their homes in the remotest of places; the vastness of Spain makes this kind of frontier spirit possible. The Lanchburys are among them and built their 'hacienda' style country hotel around an old farmhouse, lost in a sea of olive and almond trees in the border territory between Andalucía and Murcia. They saved all they could of the original edifice; a timber-lintelled fireplace, old roof beams, a few of the original doors. The rough render of the newer parts makes it feel older; the house is a tribute both to Times Past and to the skill of local craftsmen who completed the project in just seven months! Bedrooms are large, light and beautifully upholstered; their Mexican beds, wardrobes, chests and bedside tables are well-suited to their rural, southern-Spanish context. The large lounge/diner also shows a will to get local craftsmen in on the act: a long eat-together dining table (there are separate tables if you prefer) is a copy of an English original, crafted by a local cabinet maker. *Tapas* lunches are full of local flavour whilst dinners are inspired both regionally and further afield – and puds are home-made.

Rooms: 5 with bath & wc.
Price: Double/Twin 12500 Pts.
Breakfast: Included.
Meals: Tapas-style lunches;
Dinner 3500 Pts (M).
Closed: Never.

From Murcia south on E15/N340 to
Puerto Lumbreras then west on N342
towards Granada. After 9km exit 93 for
Henares. At small r'bout take second exit,
signposted 'servicios'. Pass petrol station and after approx 1.5km go left over
m'way to r'bout. Here take last exit and after 100m right on dirt road and follow
signs for 3km.

Entry no: 130   Map no: 24

Badajoz
•
Cáceres
•
Salamanca
•

Western Spain

"There are no foreign lands. It is the traveler only who is foreign"
– Robert Louis Stevenson

Hotel Huerta Honda

Avenida López Asne 1　　　　**Tel:** 924 554100
06300 Zafra　　　　　　　　　**Fax:** 924 552504
Badajoz

Antonio Martínez Buzo

Travelling through western Spain do make a detour and visit Zafra; there is a castle, a beautiful arcaded main square and any number of churches to visit. Huerta Honda is the best place to stay in town. It is an unmistakably southern-Spanish hotel: geraniums, bougainvillaea, fountains in abundance and décor which is distinctly kitsch in places. There is a guest lounge where there are roaring log fires in winter and an extraordinary miscellany of styles: wicker furniture, balsa parrots, geometric tiles, a mounted deer's head, statue-lamps. The dining rooms feel really snug with their ochre walls, heavy beams and beautifully laid tables. Other parts of the hotel feel less intimate: it is often used for wedding parties and the hotel bar is always busy. The food is excellent: the cook is Basque and you might be tempted to splurge – but there's a cheaper menu if you prefer less elaborate food. Most bedrooms have balconies overlooking the plant-filled patio and are decorated with a whimsical mix of original paintings, hand-painted furniture, rugs and wickerwork. Three much grander suites have recently been added which take Moorish, Christian and Jewish Spain as their touchstone.

Rooms: 37 with bath & wc; 3 suites.
Price: Single 9592 Pts; Double/Twin 11990 Pts; Suite 25000 Pts.
Breakfast: 1000 Pts.
Meals: Lunch/Dinner 2500-3000 Pts (M), 4500(C). Closed Sunday evenings.
Closed: Never.

From Mérida south to Zafra. The hotel is in the city centre, near the Palacio de los Duques de Feria.

Rocamador

Apartado de Correos No. 7   **Tel:** 924 489000
06160 Barcarrota   **Fax:** 924 489001
Badajoz   **E-mail:** mail@rocamador.com
                                   Web: www.rocamador.com

Manuel Carlos Dominguez Tristancho

The monastery of Rocamador, long forgotten amid the wide spaces of
Estremadura, has had new life breathed into its old, old stones by its remarkable
owners, Carlos and Lucía. She is loathe to have it classified as a hotel: it is home
and hostelry and much more and, as for star ratings, "The stars are up above us
here," she quips. The labyrinthine buildings fan out around the cloister and chapel
which is now the setting for dinners where music and candlelight may accompany
you into the early hours. You may recognise some of your fellow guests: it's that
kind of place. Bedrooms are among the most extraordinary we've seen: most are
vast. So are the bathrooms, some have shower heads four metres up, some have a
chaise longue next to the bath! There are hand-painted tiles, enormous beds,
enticing views, three-piece suites, rich fabrics, wafer-bricking, vaulted ceilings,
open hearths. Each room is quite different from the next. The Rocamador is
luxurious, daring and unique and feels a long way away from the world in which
we normally live. *Note: the above address is for correspondence. The address the
hotel is: Ctra. Nacional Badajoz-Huelva km 41, Almendral.*

Rooms: 25 with bath & wc; 5 suites
Price: Double 24000 Pts; Suite 35000 Pts.
Breakfast: 2000 Pts.
Meals: Lunch/Dinner 6000 Pts (Gourmet
M), 5000 Pts (C). Closed on Mondays.
Closed: Never.

From Madrid take N5 and exit for La
Albuera (km382 post). Into village of La
Albuera, then towards Jerez de los
Caballeros. At km41 post turn right, cross
bridge and follow drive to Rocamador.

Finca El Cabezo
10892 San Martín de Trevejo   **Tel:** 927 193106
Cáceres   **Fax:** 927 193106
                               E-mail: correo@elcabezo.com
                               Web: www.elcabezo.com

Miguel Muriel & María Moreno

Although Finca El Cabezo is in one of Spain's furthest flung corners, do make the detour. It is an awe-inspiring journey across the western reaches of the province of Cáceres to the farm; rolling hills, cork oak forests, kites and eagles overhead and the road virtually to yourself for mile after mile. You will be headed for a working farm of more than 1000 olive trees and a hundred head of cattle but don't expect to cross a muddy farmyard; once you pass through the gates of this imposing granite-built farm you enter a magical inner courtyard, softened by a rambling virginia creeper and masses of potted plants. The guest rooms are in the house's eastern wing and their size and elegance comes as a surprise; the decoration stylishly mixes old granite and antiques with parquet, warm paint schemes and Modern Art paintings. The lounge, too, would have the designer-mag people purring; slate floors and granite walls juxtaposed by the warmth of the paintings and fabrics. Feast on eggs fried in olive oil, goat's cheese, home-made cakes at breakfast and at dinner-time choose between cheerful restaurants in San Martín or a Michelin-listed eatery just down the road. And find time to go for a walk.

Rooms: 5 with bath & wc; 1 suite.
Price: Double/Twin 10700 Pts; Suite 12840 Pts incl. VAT.
Breakfast: Included.
Meals: None available.
Closed: 31 December.

From Salamanca towards Ciudad Rodrigo. Here towards Cáceres and once you are over the pass of 'Puerto de los Perales' right towards Valverde del Fresno on Ex-205. House is on the left at km22.8 post. Signposted.

Entry no: 133   **Map no: 9**

Casa Manadero
Calle Manadero 2
10867 Robledillo de Gata
Cáceres

Tel: 927 671118 or 610 332628
Fax: 927 671115 or 927 671173
E-mail: casamanadero@wanadoo.es
Web: www.casamanadero.com

Caridad Hernández

What is so thrilling about Spain is the *space*. There are still vast, untamed parts of its interior. All-but-unknown Robledillo lies at the heart of the Sierra de Gata yet is still within easy reach of Salamanca and Portugal. The village's buildings make good use of the local dark slate; it is christened 'black architecture' by the locals but is not in the least bit gloomy: this is one of the region's prettiest villages and was recently declared a 'protected nucleus' by the regional government. It is surrounded by forests of oaks, olive groves and vineyards; no less a man than Cervantes was fond of the local wines. In the restoration of this tall building wood and slate have been combined to create a really warm, welcoming hostelry. The tiny restaurant has heavy old beams, delicate lighting and excellent regional food – "100% natural products" says Caridad who has pillaged the family recipe books for your benefit. Apartments vary in size and layout following the dictates of the original building; they all are centrally-heated, have views, fully-equipped kitchens, and the same warm-and-rustic style of décor. A place which is actively helping to preserve regional differences.

Rooms: 5 studios and apartments sleeping up to 4.
Price: Apartment (for 2) 6000-7000 Pts; Apartment (for 2) with lounge 8000 Pts; Apartment (for 4) 10000 Pts.
Breakfast: 550 Pts.
Meals: Lunch/Dinner 1600 Pts (M), 2250 Pts (C).
Closed: Never.

From Madrid NV to Navalmoral de la Mata, then to Plasencia on C551. Here C204 to Pozuelo de Zarzón and here, 100m after leaving village take turning for Robledillo. From here 30km to village.

Map no: 9   Entry no: 134

Finca El Carpintero

Ctra. N-110 km 360.5
10611 Tornavacas
Cáceres

Tel: 927 177089 or 659 328110
Fax: 927 177089
E-mail: fincarpi@teleline.es

Ana Zapatero de la Salud & Javier González Navarro

The Jerte valley is best seen in spring when the blossom of thousands of cherry trees turns the green sides of the valley a stunning hue of pink. Anna and Javier, an engaging young couple from Madrid, have turned these old farm buildings into a country B&B with a difference: a happy marriage of things rustic with turn-of-the-millenium creature comforts. Enter the building through a large terracotta tiled dining room, bar in one corner and 'Bigotines' the dog in another, then climb up to the enormous guest lounge of the photo: its most striking features are a wall of solid rock, huge granite hearth, high beamed ceiling and an enormous window that lets the light come streaming in. Here and in the bedrooms, too, are cut flowers, paintings and carefully matched prints. Ana's artistic flair is on show throughout the house and the hand-painted furniture, the bows on the sash windows, the drapes behind the beds are all her work. A first-class breakfast is included and you should give lunch or dinner a go: Ana and Javier's food follows the seasons and they buy local produce whenever possible. Both speak excellent English and take real pleasure in their newly-adopted profession.

Rooms: 8 with bath & wc.
Price: Double/Twin 9000 Pts incl. VAT.
Breakfast: Included.
Meals: Lunch/Dinner 2500-3000 Pts (C).
Closed: Never.

From Madrid NVI then N110 to Ávila and then on towards Plasencia. Pass village of Tornavacas; house on right after 1.5km.

Entry no: 135

Map no: 10

El Cerezal de Los Sotos

Camino de las Vegas s/n
10612 Jerte
Cáceres

Tel: 927 470429 or 607 752197
E-mail: lossotos@terra.es

Toñi Muñoz Vera y Gabriel Romero

Jerté is famous for its heroic uprising against the occupying French army in 1809. The rebellion was crushed and in reprisal the followers of Boney put the original settlement to the torch. Its more peaceful here now! People come to walk along the centuries-old transhumance routes, to fish in the deep-running waters of the Jerté river and to see the extraordinary annual show that Nature hosts when the cherry trees blossom. Should you visit Jerté do make El Cerezal de Sotos your home for a night – or more. The old farm lies across the river from the village: it has recently been converted by its young owners, Toñi and Gabriel. He is a man of the Great Outdoors: several of his framed photos of plants and birds and forests hang in the chestnut-beamed lounge/diner. It is an uplifting spot with cheery yellow lamps and prettily laid tables, one for each of the guest rooms which lead off from a long corridor. They have simple Mexican furniture and the lamps which Toni has made from tree roots with hand-painted pergamine shades – a nice touch. The price of your room includes a simple breakfast, picnics can be prepared and all of the dishes and wines on your dinner menu are from the area.

Rooms: 6 with bath & wc.
Price: Double/Twin 7500 Pts incl. VAT.
Breakfast: Included.
Meals: Dinner 2500 Pts.
Closed: 15 December-6 January

From Madrid AVI towards Ávila N110 to Ávila and then on towards Plasencia to Jerte. As you arrive in village, just after bridge, turn left at sign for 'La Ermita' and then follow signs to El Cerezal.

Map no: 10

Entry no: 136

Finca La Casería
10613 Navaconcejo
Cáceres

Tel: 927 173141
Fax: 927 173141
E-mail: daveymaria@jazzfree.com

David Pink & María Cruz Barona

This lovely old farmhouse has been the home of Señora's family for some 200 years. The cluster of old granite buildings stand in cherry groves to one side of the Jerte valley where a monastery once stood; be here at the end of March when blossom fills the valley or in early summer when you can help David to harvest the fruit. There are plums and figs and sheep and cows; between directing his guests to the extraordinary natural history or archaeological sites of the area David works hard at his smallholding. La Casería feels much more like a home than a hotel: there are dogs and nothing which feels remotely contrived. The huge sitting room has books and an open hearth and of the six guest rooms, which are mostly furnished with the family heirlooms, we preferred the upstairs room which has a screen and an old wrought-iron bed. Dinner or lunch is a relaxed occasion with home-made puddings to complement regional dishes. Many of the guests come for the walking but you can also fish for tench, swim in the nearby reservoir or just kick back. Very different from the designer-mag chic which characterises many of the newer rural B&Bs we loved La Casería's unstudied authenticity.

Rooms: 6 with bath & wc; 1 cottage.
Price: Double/Twin 6000-8000 Pts;
Cottage approx. 65000 Pts. *Minimum stay 2 nights.*
Breakfast: Included; cottage: self-catering.
Meals: None available.
Closed: Never.

From Madrid E90 to Navalmoral de la Mata; C511 to Plasencia; N110 towards Ávila. At km378.5 post (about 27km from Plasencia), right at small sign for La Casería (3km before Navaconcejo).

Entry no: 137

Map no: 10

Camino Real

Calle Monje 27
10459 Guijo de Santa
Bárbara
Cáceres

Tel: 927 561119
Fax: 927 561119
E-mail: caminoreal@retemail.es

Carmela Pérez Fontán

Guijo de Santa Barbara is one of the Gredos' highest, prettiest villages. It is famous for the springs which rise 1000 feet above it, a stopover for walkers heading up to the higher peaks and for shepherds and cowherds leading their livestock up to the summer pastures. Camino Real is at the heart of the village, named after the 'Royal Way', the route that the ailing Emperor Charles V followed as he made his way to the monastery at Yuste. It is a tall building with a new annexe just below. The six bedrooms are all in the older part of the house and named after species of tree. They are snug and prettily decorated with antiques, old prints and attractive fabrics which complement their dressed stone walls and tiled or planked floors. To reach the dining room and guest lounge you cross a terrace which looks out to the oak and chestnut forests to the Gredos. Here are more antiques and a small library; the generosity of your hosts is captured in a small sign which tells you that if you haven't finished a book just send it back when you have. The food is good, the staff friendly and the beautiful monastery of Yuste is close.

Rooms: 6 with bath & wc.
Price: Half board only: Double/Twin 14000 Pts for 2.
Breakfast: Included.
Meals: Dinner included.
Closed: Never.

From Madrid south-west on the NV then exit for Navalmoral de la Mata Este. Then right on Ex-119 to Jarandilla de la Vera. Here right to Guijo de Santa Bárbara.
House is signposted just to right of main street into the village.

Map no: 10   Entry no: 138

Antigua Casa del Heno

Finca Valdepimienta
10460 Losar de la Vera
Cáceres

Tel: 927 198077 or 609 603606
Fax: 927 198077
Web: www.pglocal.com/caceres/jarandilla/index.htm

Graciela Rosso & Javier Tejero Vivo

Casa del Heno stands superbly isolated on the southern side of the Gredos mountains, hidden away at the end of a 4km track that follows the river out from Losar. The 150-year-old farm has been sympathetically restored by its owners; granite, beams and cork are the recurring decorative leitmotifs. Eight guest rooms seem to get the balance just right; no tele, good beds and views across the farm. 150 yards away is a crystalline river and beyond are the mountains, criss-crossed with ancient footpaths. The whole of the valley is at its best in spring when the many thousands of cherry trees come into blossom but you'll need to book well ahead if you want a room during this annual spectacle. Ornithologists come to this area from all over Europe to focus their binoculars on azure-winged magpies, kites, vultures – and even great bustards. Java and Graciela are quiet and caring hosts. They offer their guests time-tried home cooking in Heno's slightly oversized dining room: the use only the very best cuts of meat. And by the time this edition of Special Places goes to print a reading room, with views down towards the river, will have been added. Horse-riding can be arranged, too.

Rooms: 8 with bath & wc.
Price: Double/Twin 8400 Pts.
Breakfast: 500 Pts.
Meals: Lunch/Dinner 2500-3000 Pts (C).
Closed: Christmas & for a month
after Epiphany.

From Madrid NV to Navalmoral de la
Mata. Right onto Ex-119 towards
Jarandilla to Losar de la Vera. Here, behind
the 'ayuntamiento' (town hall) to 'piscina
de Vadilla' then mountain track 3.5km to hotel; signposted.

Entry no: 139

Map no: 10

Hotel Rural La Casa de Pasarón

La Magdalena 18
10411 Pasarón de la Vera
Cáceres

Tel: 927 469407
E-mail: pasaron@pasaron.com
Web: www.pasaron.com

Susana Ayala

Susan Ayala's great-grandparents would surely have approved of the careful restoration that has recently given the 19th-century house where they once lived a new lease of life. An elegant portal of carefully-dressed sandstone in the building's unusual, russet-coloured façade leads you into the entrance hall with its original vaulted ceiling. The lounge, again vaulted, mixes old and new furnishings piecemeal; the old photographic portraits are touching, the standard Impressionist prints less so. But the dining room has a really nice feel to it with just five attractively laid tables and its old marble-topped dressers. It is a lovely spot to begin your day with a breakfast of oven-warm bread, local cheese and fruit compote made by the Ayala family. Things from-the-home rather than the supermarket are de rigeur at dinner, too; thick cream of vegetable soups, home-made meatballs or perhaps a kid stew. Of the bedrooms, reached by the heavy granite staircase, eight are on the first floor and four in the attic. They are simple, spotless and very quiet; those on the attic floor have just skylight windows. Do visit the nearby monastery of Yuste where Charles V spent his final months.

Rooms: 12 with bath & wc.
Price: Double/Twin 8560-10700 Pts incl. VAT.
Breakfast: Included.
Meals: Lunch/Dinner 1500 Pts (M) incl. wine.
Closed: 10 January-10 February & 2nd fortnight in June.

From Plasencia towards Jaraiz to Tejeda del Tietar. Here left to Pasarón. As you enter village take first turning to left. Signposted.

Map no: 10

La Posada de Amonaría

Calle de la Luz 7
10680 Malpartida de Plasencia
Cáceres

Tel: 927 459446 or 608 702070
Fax: 927 459446
E-mail: amonaria@inicia.es

Juan Tomé & Cruz Ibarra

Juan Tomé's feelings for Estremadura and its people run deep; he has named his house after Armonaria, his grandmother. The house is at the top of Malpartida: its meticulously restored chocolate-and-coffee coloured frontage is easy to recognise. Its walls bear the gentle finish which only countless layers of lime-wash can give, whilst beams have been treated with beeswax and floors with linseed oil in a conscious effort to use only natural finishes. The dining room is staggered on different levels with a handsome slate floor and an enormous hearth; it gives onto the house's original *bodega* where wine was once pressed: the huge amphorae are still in place and you could have a glass of wine and a *tapa* before dinner. Return to light, airy, antique-filled bedrooms which retain the original geometric floor tiles from the last century. Juan and Cruz have endeavoured to recreate the spirit of the age when the house was built; perhaps it is affection for that era which explains their love of ballroom dancing: you can learn to tango or fox-trot with them. A great place for a longer stay: don't miss Cáceres, Trujillo, the Jerté valley and the Monfragüe Park.

Rooms: 4 with bath & wc; 2 suites.
Price: Double/Twin 8300 Pts; Suite 9300 Pts.
Breakfast: 600 Pts.
Meals: None available.
Closed: Never.

N630 south to Plasencia and then onto C511 to Malpartida de Plasencia. The Posada is at the top of the village, next to the church; follow signs for 'Ayuntamiento'.

Casa Salto de Caballo

La Fontañera
10516 Valencia de Alcántara
Cáceres

Tel: (00 351) 245 964345 or 927 580865
Fax: (00 351) 245 964345
E-mail: saltocaballo@mail.telepac.pt

Eva Speth

An amazing place where it is hard to say which is the more beautiful: the journey there or the being there. Follow a narrow road across glorious, rolling hills to this furthest reach of the province of Cáceres and of Spain too: you are literally slap bang on its border with Portugal. This was where smugglers would ply their trade, saddlebags brimming with bread, coffee and garlic. In these days of pan-european markets you now walk straight out from the house (or ride) into Portugal's glorious São Mamede Natural Park along those same secret pathways – with not a thought for border patrols. Eva and Joaquín were so taken by it all they left Germany and restored this elegant village house: they were after good, solid comfort rather than gadgets and gimmickry. The old floor tiles are still there, "it is beautifully clean" wrote an enthusiastic reader, and there are lots of Achim's creations (he is a sculptor and artist). Eva prepares innovative vegetarian food (she is a nutritionist and dietician) and simple, *tapas*-style suppers – or you might prefer to walk into Portugal for dinner! Generous hosts, generous prices and as far from the madding crowd as you could hope to get.

Rooms: 3 with bath & wc & 2 sharing bath & wc.
Price: Double/Twin 5500 Pts incl. VAT.
Breakfast: Included. Special brunch: 750 Pts.
Meals: Lunch/Dinner 1500 Pts.
Closed: Occasionally in winter. Check.

From Cáceres N521 towards Portugal. Through Valencia de Alcántara, then right towards San Pedro. After 2km right again for La Fontañera. Last house on left in the village; signposted.

Map no: 15

Entry no: 142

El Vaqueril

Carretera Comarcal 523
10930 Navas del Madroño
Cáceres

Tel: 927 191001/223446
Fax: 927 191001

Beatriz Vernhes de Ruanu

The big skies and cork-oaked hillsides of Estremadura make it one of Spain's grandest visual feasts. Reached by a tree-lined drive, and in the middle of 320 hectares of cattle ranch, this old farmhouse stands amid carob, olive and palm trees. Its ochre and white frontage gives it a very southern face; the row of crenellations that top its façade look not a bit warlike. The house is classic *cortijo*; things gravitate towards a large central patio – the South's most effective technique for ensuring shade at any time of the day. No two bedrooms are the same; they are big, with domed ceilings and decorated with bright fabrics and family antiques. There are pretty hand-painted tiles in bathrooms, framed etchings and prints, open hearths. You sense a designer's hand has been involved. Downstairs is a vaulted lounge with a riotous ceramic hearth and a cavernous, beamed dining room; beef comes from the farm, of course. Breakfast is as generous as the evening meal – there may be home-made cake – and you may, once replete, cycle or walk out into the estate. Cáceres and Mérida are an easy drive. Some readers have felt that the greeting can be a little offhand: let us know.

Rooms: 6 with bath & wc; 1 suite.
Price: Twin 9500 Pts; Suite 14000 Pts.
Breakfast: Included.
Meals: Dinner 3000-4000 Pts (C).
Closed: Never.

From Cáceres towards Alcántara on C523. Just before village of Navas del Madroño turn left at sign for El Vaqueril and follow long track (have faith!) to the farmhouse.

Finca Santa Marta

Pago de San Clemente
10200 Trujillo
Cáceres

Tel: 927 319203 or 91 3502217
Fax: 927 319203 or 91 3502217
E-mail: henri@facilnet.es
Web: www.fincasantamarta.com

Marta Rodríguez-Gimeno and Henri Elink

Santa Marta is a fine example of an Extremadura manor house where the farmer
lived on the top floor and made olive oil below. It has been totally transformed by
interior designer Marta Rodríguez-Gimeno and husband Henri into a wonderful
country retreat. Each of Santa Marta's bedrooms has a character of its own; there
are antiques in some, hand-painted Portuguese furniture in others, and all of them
feel welcoming. Those which are in an adjacent building, the Finca Santa Teresa,
are more rustic with locally-crafted furniture: the effect is just as appealing. The
main building is a treasure trove of antiques, painting and good taste. In the
vaulted olive-pressing area is an enormous cool and elegant guest lounge and
library with *estera* matting, neo-*mudéjar* ceilings, antique furniture and sensitive
lighting. Why so many South American bits and pieces? Henri was Dutch
ambassador to Peru and it was the Latin readiness to share that inspired him to
open his home to guests. He and his wife are not always in residence but when
they are away a friendly housekeeper steps in. You are surrounded by thirty
hectares of peace and there is fabulous birdlife in this part of Spain.

Rooms: 14 with bath & wc.
Price: Double/Twin 10000 Pts.
Breakfast: Included.
Meals: Lunch/Dinner 2900 Pts. Book
ahead. Restaurant closed January 10th-
February 28th.
Closed: Never.

From Trujillo take Ex-208 towards
Guadalupe. After 14km Finca is on the
right where you see eucalyptus trees with
storks' nests (km89 post).

Hotel Rector

Paseo Rector Esperabé 10
Apartado 399
37008 Salamanca

Tel: 923 218482
Fax: 923 214008
E-mail: hotelrector@teleline.es
Web: www.teleline.terra.es/personal/hrector

D. Eduardo Ferrán Riba

A two-minute walk from the cathedral and close to the Roman bridge this *palacete* or town mansion is one of western Spain's smartest small hotels: it is a joy to come across it in a city of such interest and ineffable loveliness. Señor Ferrán is a man who like things to be 'just so' and his meticulous care is reflected in every corner of the hotel. Wood is used to good effect throughout the building; there are sparkling parquet floors in the public areas and inlaid bedside tables, writing desks and hand-crafted bedheads in mahogany and olive wood in the bedrooms. They have all the fittings of a five-star hotel: you might not need the telephone in the bathroom or the fax points but you'll probably appreciate double glazing, air conditioning and deeply comfortable armchairs. Bathrooms hold the same luxurious note – marble, double basins, thick towels. High standards at breakfast too: service and ingredients are excellent. You can leave your car safe in the hotel car park and head out on foot to explore the city: right next door is the wonderful Casa Lis, a museum dedicated to Spanish Art Deco and the incomparable Plaza Mayor is just minutes away.

Rooms: 14 with bath & wc.
Price: Single 13500 Pts;
Double/Twin 18000 Pts;
Larger Double/Twin 23000 Pts.
Breakfast: 1200 Pts.
Meals: None available.
Closed: Never.

Arriving from Madrid on N501 take the first right at signs for 'Centro Ciudad' . At r'bout turn left into Paseo Rector Esperabé. The hotel is in front of the two walls after approx 300m, very close to the Casa Lis museum. Drop bags at reception and they will advise where best to park.

Entry no: 145

Map no: 10

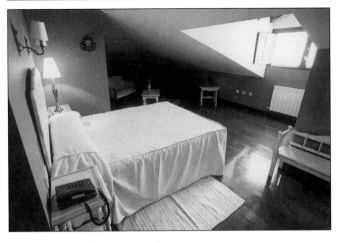

Hostelería Don Fadrique

Ctra. Salamanca-Alba de Tormes
37800 Alba de Tormes
Salamanca

Tel: 923 370076 or 923 370034
Fax: 923 370487

Familia Sánchez Monje

If religious relics are your thing you may have heard of Alba de Tormes; the heart and arm of Santa Teresa are on view in its Carmelite monastery. Don Fadrique is just outside of town on the road to Salamanca. When we visited the hotel had just opened and its hillside perch looked rather stark but gardens were being planted and once you get inside you'll be surprised at just what a handsome hotel and restaurant the Sánchez Monje family have created. The heart of the place is the large wafer-bricked and chestnut-beamed dining room; the family had already made a name for themselves at the bar they own in the town but now with a prize-winning chef in the kitchen, a wine list with more than 200 bottles and a policy of buying only the best meat and season-fresh vegetables the Michelin-man will surely soon be on his way. There is even an eight course *degustación* menu if you are up to it. A beautifully carved walnut staircase leads to your bedroom. Those on the attic floor have very low ceilings; all are unbelievably good value. A brilliant choice if you can't find lodgings in nearby Salamanca or are keen to see those religious bits and bobs.

Rooms: 21 with bath & wc.
Price: Double/Twin 9000-10000 Pts;
'Special' Double 15000 Pts.
Breakfast: 600 Pts or 1100 Pts (buffet).
Meals: Lunch/Dinner 1500 Pts (M),
4500-5000 Pts (C).
Closed: Never.

From Salamanca follow signs for Madrid and almost immediately turn right on the C510 towards Alba de Tormes. Don Fadrique is to the left of the road 1km before you arrive in the village.

Map no: 10

Entry no: 146

La Casa Inglesa
37700 Béjar
Salamanca

Tel: 923 404499 or 636 363476
E-mail: casa.inglesa@teleline.es

Anna Antonio

Anna Antonio is no typical ex-pat. Although she would be as at home at a dinner
party in Sussex as she would be at one in Madrid since setting up home in Spain
she has never been one to search out fellow compatriots. When we stayed with her
every other house guest was Spanish and they clearly love it here. They come to La
Casa Inglesa for good food, company and to escape the snarled-up roads and
frenetic pace of life in the capital. Because La Casa Inglesa is both a home and a
retreat, hidden away in a magnificent forest of chestnut trees (from which the
nearest village of El Castañar takes its name). Decoration has a distinct feel of
Kensington: drop-leaf tables, crystal decanters, books, candelabras and oriental
vases. Anna likes the finer things in life so expect candles at dinner, classical music
at most times and very good food: she had three restaurants in London during the
sixties when she fed everyone from Nuryev to the Rolling Stones. Her cooking
looks both west and east: dinners have a Lebanese slant and Anna is happy to
prepare you a cooked breakfast. A charming hostess and home: stay a couple of
nights and visit the beautiful village of Candelario, just minutes away.

Rooms: 4 with bath & wc.
Price: Double/Twin 8500 Pts.
Breakfast: 500 Pts.
Meals: 3250 Pts. Dinner on request.
Closed: Never.

From Salamanca south towards Cáceres.
Exit for Sorihuela/Béjar. In Béjar pass two
petrol stations then left for El Castañar.
There immediately opposite Hotel Los
Duques turn sharp left down steep cobbled
track. At third loop sharp left again to black entrance gate of house. Ring bell.

Entry no: 147

Map no: **10**

Central Spain

"It is not enough for a landscape to be interesting in itself.
Eventually there must be a moral and historic interest"
– Stendhal

El Canchal
Calle de La Fuente 1
05400 Arenas de San Pedro
Ávila

Tel: 920 370958
Fax: 920 370914
E-mail: elcanchal@autovia.com
Web: www.ciberestudio.com/elcanchal

Isabel Rodríguez

Arenas de San Pedro is an attractive little town, topped by a medieval castle and sculpted into the southern flank of the Sierra de Gredos. Walkers come for some of the most memorable paths in central Spain; the town is just a hop away from the main trailheads. El Canchal is in the middle of town. The original nobleman's residence dates from the Middle Ages but other parts are more recent; there was damage during the Peninsular War. Isabel is a perfect innkeeper; she is relaxed, flexible and eager to tell you about the history of the village and El Canchal. Each of her bedrooms is named after a variety of mushroom – the area is very popular with mycologists. They are smallish but feel homely thanks to their antique beds and dressers, lace-edged curtains, old washstands, parquet floors and low ceilings. The lounge and dining room feel similarly cosy. Try Isabel's home-made cake at breakfast and do have dinner with her at least once; meals are simple and wholesome and the house red is good. And be sure to visit the labyrinthine wine cellars deep beneath the building: one of Isabel's many projects is to fill them with her own selection of bottles.

Rooms: 4 with bath & wc & 2 sharing.
Price: Double/Twin 7500-8700 Pts; Double/Twin
sharing 7500 Pts.
Breakfast: 500 Pts.
Meals: Lunch/Dinner 2400 Pts incl. wine.
Closed: Never.

From Madrid NV south-west towards Badajoz. Exit for
Casar de Talavera then N502 to Arenas de San Pedro.
Here continue over r'bout towards 'Centro Urbano'.
Just before the castle right into C/ Isabel La Católica.
Round church then park in Plaza del Ayuntamiento.
Walk up C/ Cejudo, right and El Canchal
is on left.

Casa de Arriba

Calle La Cruz 19
05635 Navarredonda de Gredos
Avila

Tel: 920 348024
Fax: 920 348386
E-mail: reservas@casadearriba.com
Web: www.casadearriba.com

Teresa Pazos Gil

This 17th-century listed stone-built house is at the very top of the sleepy little village of Navarredonda and overlooks the wonderful mountains of the Gredos range. Push aside the huge old wooden entrance gates and enter a wonderful garden whose century-old trees protect the house from the harsh summer sun and throw dappled light across its warm façade. To either side of the main doorway are two simple stone benches; I sat here for ages and abandoned myself to the tranquility and beauty of the place. You enter the house by way of a large hallway; leading off from it the large lounge has incorporated the old kitchen and fireplace and has an area set aside for reading. Climb the original wooden staircase to your room; there are just eight and they have names which evoke the buildings past like *The Maid's Room, The room where bread was made* or *The Lumber room.* All have period furniture, attractive fabrics, and some have shining parquet floors. Breakfast will include freshly-squeezed orange juice and home-made cakes and jams; it may fortify you enough to strike out and climb the highest peak of the Gredos, the Almanzor, which towers 2592m above the valley. *A Rusticae hotel.*

Rooms: 8 with bath & wc.
Price: Twin 10000 Pts for one night stays; 9000 Pts if more than one night.
Breakfast: 850 Pts.
Meals: 2500 Pts incl. wine.
Closed: Never.

From Madrid A6 towards Valladolid then exit at Villacastín and take N501 to Ávila. Just past Ávila left on N502 to Venta Rasquilla, then C500 past Pardor to Navarredonda de Gredos. Calle La Cruz is at top of village.

Map no: 10   **Entry no: 149**

Hostal El Milano Real

Calle Toleo s/n
05634 Hoyos del Espino
Ávila

Tel: 920 349108
Fax: 920 349156
E-mail: milanor@santandersupernet.com

Francisco Sánchez & Teresa Dorn

If you insist on an historic building when sleeping out – Milano Real is not for you. But pass this small modern hotel by and you miss a very special experience. With the Gredos range all about, the hotel looks rather like a Swiss chalet; the feeling is heightened by the carved wood of the balconies and the cosy atmosphere within. Up beneath the rafters, is a huge lounge and down a floor is a second reading lounge. But festivities really get under way in the dining room. The food brings people all the way from Madrid; Basque/French influenced, with some fine regional dishes, the restaurant wins a mention in all the famous guide books, Michelin included. Francisco ('Paco') knows his wine; he has a selection of 135 of his favourites to choose from and alongside each wine lists year, *bodega*, D.O. – then gives each and every one his score out of ten! When you wend your way to your room more treats are in store: decorated by Madrid's best, the fabrics, polished wooden floors, antique prints and views set the rooms solidly in the special bracket. Food and rooms are incredible value; worth a VERY long detour and the Gredos are another of Spain's better-kept secrets.

Rooms: 21 with bath & wc; 8 suites.
Price: Single 8500 Pts; Double/Twin 9200-10500 Pts; Suite 13000-16500 Pts.
Breakfast: 950-1500 Pts.
Meals: Lunch/Dinner 3500 Pts (M), approx. 4500 Pts (C). Restaurant closed on Tuesdays in Low Season.
Closed: 10-30 November & 2nd week in January.

From Ávila N110 towards Bejar/Plasencia.
After 6km take N502 left towards Arenas de San Pedro and after 40km right on C500 to Hoyos del Espino; hotel to right.

Sancho de Estrada

Castillo de Villaviciosa
05130 Solosancho
Ávila

Tel: 920 291082
Fax: 920 291082
Web:
www.socranet.com/hotelesmayoral

Avelino Mayoral Hernández

Here, is a real 12th-century castle which just recently let down its drawbridge to paying guests. Avelino Mayoral is a man who likes to get things right. It took him 22 years of careful renovation and reconstruction before he felt ready to receive guests. Decoration is deliberately 'historical' with lances, suits of armour and heavy, Castillian-style furniture. At the building's centre is a galleried dining room where, as you might guess, medieval-style banquets are occasionally held. But most of the time the menu features the time-tried recipes of the Meseta; the roasted meats are memorable and the mark up on the wines is surprisingly little. To reach some of the guest rooms you wind up the original spiral staircases pushing aside heavy crimson curtains, all very cloak-and-dagger. Following the dictates of the original building some are large, others small, some have arrow-slit windows and a couple of them are in what was once the castle's prison. Last time we stayed some of the furnishings were beginning to look a little tired but a night at Sancho de Estrada remains a memorable and amusing experience.

Rooms: 10 with bath & wc; 2 suites.
Price: Double/Twin 9500-9900 Pts; Suite 13000-13600 Pts.
Breakfast: 900 Pts.
Meals: Lunch/Dinner 2800 Pts (M), approx 4000 Pts (C).
Closed: Never.

From Ávila N110 towards Plasencia. After 5km left on N502 towards Arenas de San Pedro. Arriving at outskirts of Solosancho hotel is signposted to the left.

Hostal Don Diego

Calle Marqués de Canales y Chozas 5
05001 Ávila
Ávila

Tel: 920 255475/254549
Fax: 920 254549

Miguel Angel Verguera

This sparkling little *hostal*, directly opposite the Parador and within the old city walls, is modest and unpretentious and here you'll find a clean room, a comfortable bed and a smile on arrival. The smallish rooms are on three floors, each one named after one of the owner Miguel's children. The *hostal* is named after his fourth child, Diegoe. The bedrooms combine pine furniture with modern brass bedsteads; there are good bedcovers and plenty of blankets in winter. All the fittings are modern; half the rooms have baths, the others small shower rooms. Light sleepers would probably prefer a room at the back of the *hostal*. It is all unmistakably Spanish with more than a hint of kitsch. Although the hostal has no breakfast facilities the Parador opposite serves breakfast in a setting which is far grander (but less friendly!). Or take a five-minute stroll up to one of the cafés in the *Plaza* to breakfast amid the hubbub of this lovely old town. A reliable, rather than remarkable, budget option from which to discover this fascinating city.

Rooms: 13 with bath & wc.
Price: Single 3500-4500 Pts; Twin 4900-5900 Pts; Double 5350-6990 Pts.
Breakfast: None available; Parador restaurant opposite.
Meals: None available.
Closed: Never.

Entering Ávila by Puerta del Carmen, follow signs to Parador Nacional. Hostal is opposite Parador.

Entry no: 152

Map no: 10

Hospedería La Sinagoga

Calle Reyes Católicos 22
05001 Ávila
Ávila

Tel: 920 352321
Fax: 920 353474
E-mail: lasinagoga@airtel.net

Borja Cermeño Sanchez

Hospedería La Sinagoga – it was indeed a synagogue which was built in the 15th century just years before the Jews were expelled from Spain – is plumb in the centre of the oldest, loveliest part of Ávila, just yards from the beautiful Plaza del Ayuntamiento. The entrance to the hotel is down a narrow side street; even though you are only yards from a busy, pedestrianised street, as soon as you pass under its old portal you are struck by the tranquility of the place. The building has been restored with great sympathy for the original walls and architectural features whilst incorporating a modern, minimalist decorative style; its seems fitting that its opening coincided with the new millennium. The inner patio area and dining room have large glass panels which bring the light streaming in; sienna colour washes and areas of exposed masonry add warmth. Each guest room is named after a Jewish person associated with the town's history; whether yours be *Samuel Cohen*, *Diego de Áyala* or *Ali Caro* you're bound to like their stylishness and tranquility. A marvellous place to stay in the city of Santa Teresa and marvellous prices, too.

Rooms: 21 with bath & wc; 1 suite.
Price: Single 6600 Pts; Double/Twin 9790 Pts; Suite 11550 Pts.
Breakfast: 880 Pts.
Meals: None available.
Closed: Never.

Entering Ávila by Puerta del Carmen, follow signs to Parador Nacional. Then continue on to the Plaza de la Catedral. Park here and walk 100m to the hotel.

Map no: 10   Entry no: 153

La Posada del Pinar

Pozal de Gallinas s/n   **Tel:** 98 3481004 or 639 394456
47450 Pozal de Gallinas
Valladolid

Ignacio Escribano

Exuding quality and charm, La Posada del Pinar captures the very essence of
Castilla-León. It is a plush hideaway, idyllically sheltered from any hubbub by over
300 acres of pine forest. Dating back to the early 17th century, the low vaulted
brickwork in the centre of the building is the oldest part but the whole place, built
with locally-fired bricks, is the colour of the earth in the fields, enhanced by the
light tones used inside. The public lounge with its enclosed log fire is relaxed and
intimate and leads through to the elegant arched dining room which has its own
wood-burning oven. Here, mouthwatering roasts are always part of the menu.
Behind is the old chapel whose airy grandeur now lives for wedding and
communion receptions and banquets. The guest rooms, each named after a local
town famous for its *mudejar* monuments, are large and well furnished. We did feel
the coloured mosaic tiles in some of the bathrooms were a bit garish but the
overall impression is pretty classy. The area is full of places and things of interest.
The nearby town of Olmedo is well worth visiting and there are plenty of natural
marvels to see. *A Rusticae hotel.*

Rooms: 11 with bath & wc.
Price: Single 6000-8000 Pts; Double/Twin 7000-9500
Pts; Quadruple 10500-14500 Pts.
Breakfast: 800 Pts.
Meals: Lunch/Dinner 1700 Pts.
Closed: Never.

From Valladolid N620 to Tordesillas and then NVI
towards Madrid. Exit at km 157 towards Olmedo to
Pozal de Gallinas. As you enter the village the Posada is
signposted to the right; continue for 3.2km to house.

Entry no: 154   **Map no: 10**

El Prado Mayor

Quintanilla del Rebollar 53
09568 Merindad de Sotoscueva
Burgos

Tel: 947 138689
Fax: 947 138689

Fernando Valenciano Velasco

After five years of devoted work at this 16th-century village mansion by Pilar, Fernando, Olga and Angel a dream of living and working in the Las Merindades region has come true. One of Spains' best-kept secrets, this lush landscape breathes culture and history, most significantly the 100km Ojo Guareña cave system, one of the biggest in the world, where you can trace humanity's religious expression from Paleolithic times. The impressive façade of the Prado Mayor hides behind a solid arched gateway. Go through into a small garden with a columned terrace – ideal for breakfast in summer – leading to what feels like a warm family home. Inside, the cream-coloured stone gives it a sheltered and peaceful air and its unfussy, stylish décor is in perfect harmony with the architecture: there are period antiques, colourful blankets and dried flowers; we particularly like the wooden cabinets under the basins, the marble tops and the ornate framed mirrors. Breakfast is a must – home-made cakes, biscuits, local bread from a wood oven and fresh organic milk. Lunch and dinner are stout affairs with home-grown vegetables and good local meats – the rabbit is rather special. A smashing place!

Rooms: 6 with bath & wc.
Price: Double/Twin 7500 Pts.
Breakfast: 750 Pts.
Meals: Lunch/ Dinner 1750 Pts.
Closed: Never.

From Burgos north on N623 towards Santander/Puerto del Escudo. At Cilleruelo de Bezana right for Soncillo. Through village then towards Argomeda to Quintanilla del Rebollar. Turn right at house no 52 to reach no 53.

Map no: 4

Entry no: 155

Posada Molino del Canto

09146 Barrio La Cuesta   **Tel:** 947 571368
Burgos   **Fax:** 947 571368

Javier Morala

This jewel of a place is remote and heavenly in an Eden-like valley, lapped by the River Ebro. It is a 13th-century mill, restored by the young owner Javier, and it is both authentic and exquisite. The stonework blends perfectly with its surroundings and the style of its simple façade is continued inside. The dark little entrance hall, cool in summer and warm in the colder months, takes you through a curtain to a cosy, low-beamed wood and stone sitting room with a log fire and handmade furniture. This is the only communal area but go up the old, wooden staircase to discover the bedrooms which are all duplex and a good size. They are a splendid surprise: all in much the same style, well thought out, each with a homely sitting room downstairs and an upper level where you find a very generous bed, a large classic wardrobe and a stylish bathroom. Sound, uninterrupted sleep is guaranteed. Breakfast here is a good start to the day and the home-cooked regional food is good too. Get Javier to show you the old mill house – it sits on a promontory down by the river and is, amazingly, 1000 years old. It still contains the old flint wheels which spin into action when the sluice gate is opened.

Rooms: 6 with bath & wc.
Price: Double/Twin 11500 Pts incl. VAT.
Breakfast: Included.
Meals: Lunch/Dinner 2000 Pts.
Closed: Never.

From Burgos N623 towards Santander. 6.5km north of Quintanilla de Escalada exit right for Gallejones. On towards Villanueva Rampally. There left for Arrepa. Posada signposted to right after 2.6km.

Balneario de Valdelateja

Ctra Burgos-Santander N-623
09145 Valdelateja
Burgos

Tel: 947 150220 or 942 318668
Fax: 947 150220
E-mail: grupocastelar@mundivia.es
Web: www.grupocastelar.com

Elena Cagigas

The original spa hotel at Valdelateja first opened its doors in 1872, when the well-heeled would ride up from Burgos or down from Santander to take the waters. But spas ceased to be fashionable; then came the war and, by the beginning of the decade, the site lay abandoned. But after the Dark Ages, the Renaissance! – total restoration of the two original buildings has produced a most interesting small hotel. The setting is wonderful; you look out to woods of holm and evergreen oak that cling to the sides of the canyon cut by the river Rudrón. The building is rather 'Swiss-chalet', with wooden balconies, galleries and ornately carved eaves; inside wood is again the primary element, whether in darkened beam or polished parquet floor. The lantern-ceiling of the lounge – the former ballroom – is a real beauty. No two guest rooms are the same; some have antique bedsteads of wrought-iron, other beds are of padded fabric; they have wonderful walnut floors and all have big bathrooms with full-length baths. The dining rooms looks out to the river, and the views are a wonderful accompaniment to the home-cooking. The staff are young, bright and friendly.

Rooms: 30 with bath & wc; 4 suites.
Price: Double/Twin 10000 Pts; Suite 12000 Pts incl. breakfast.
Breakfast: 800 Pts.
Meals: Lunch/Dinner 2700 Pts (M), 3500-4500 Pts (C).
Closed: 11 December-13 March.

From Burgos N-623 towards Santander. Through San Felices, and just before Valdelateja right to Balneario; signposted.

Map no: 4   **Entry no: 157**

Mesón del Cid

Plaza Santa María 8
09003 Burgos

Tel: 947 208715
Fax: 947 269460
E-mail: mesondelcid@sarenet.es

José López Alzaga

Few cathedrals match that of Burgos and if you come to see this marvel of the Spanish Gothic stay at Mesón del Cid; from the rooms at the front you can almost reach out and touch the buttresses, pinnacles and grimacing gargoyles. The building once housed one of the first printing presses in Spain, established by an acolyte of Gutenberg more than 500 years ago, and the hotel takes its name from an illuminated manuscript of *Mío Cid* displayed at reception. This fine old townhouse is quite naturally considered THE place to stay in Burgos. We liked the bedrooms; they are carpeted (right for winter), many have old wrought-iron bedsteads, all have prints, tables, plants and decent bathrooms. The suites are grander still; one has period furnishings, bronze taps and even an old-fashioned 'phone. If we were invited to choose a room it would be No. 302. Good things await you in the timbered restaurant where the setting is perfect for trying the traditional thick stews and roast meats that are so typical of this part of Spain.

Rooms: 44 with bath & wc; 3 suites.
Price: Double/Twin 18000 Pts; Suite 21500 Pts.
Breakfast: 1200 Pts.
Meals: Lunch/Dinner approx. 4000 Pts (M), 5000 Pts (C). Closed Sun eves.
Closed: Never.

In old town directly opposite main entrance to cathedral on Plaza de Santa María. Car park next door.

Hotel Arlanza

Calle Mayor 11
09346 Covarrubias
Burgos

Tel: 947 406441
Fax: 947 406359
E-mail: reservas@hotelarlanza.com
Web: www.hotelarlanza.com

Mercedes de Miguel Briones

Covarrubias is a charming old town, well off the tourist-beaten track and a must if you love places where tradition still counts. The heart of the old town is a wonderful colonnaded square – the Arlanza is on one side of it. Mercedes and Juan José, two of the friendliest hoteliers you could hope to meet, have created a hotel which matches the charm and intimacy of the town. You enter under the colonnade through an arched doorway. Inside, there are lovely terracotta floors, ceramic tiles from Talavera on the walls, old chandeliers, original beams and lintels. Downstairs it is all a little dark because little light enters through the small, original windows. By contrast, the bedrooms that give onto the square (see photo) are much lighter. All of the guest rooms are reached by an impressive staircase; they are large, with tiled floors, old lamps and rustic furniture. There is good regional food in the restaurant where you may well get a chance to talk with the owners; they visit the UK every year, know its farthest corners and speak the language, too.

Rooms: 38 with bath & wc; 2 suites.
Price: Single 5500 Pts; Double/Twin 9200 Pts; Suite 9700 Pts incl. VAT.
Breakfast: 650 Pts.
Meals: Lunch/Dinner 1900 Pts (M), 3000 Pts (C).
Closed: 15 December-1 March.

From Burgos N1 towards Madrid. In Lerma left on C110 towards Salas de los Infantes. Hotel in Covarrubias on Plaza Mayor.

Map no: 4

Entry no: 159

Hotel Santo Domingo de Silos

Calle Santo Domingo 14   **Tel:** 947 390053
09610 Santo Domingo de Silos **Fax:** 947 390052
Burgos   **E-mail:** hotelsilos@verial.es
                                                   Web: www.verial.es/hotelsilos

Eleuterio del Alamo Castrillo

The highlight of a stay in Santo Domingo de Silos is the Gregorian chant in the monastery chapel; you can hear it every day of the year and it is well worth a detour as you travel north or south. You may consider overnighting at this simple family hotel which has recently doubled in size thanks to a large extension. Its real *raison d'être* is its vast dining room; at weekends visitors come from far and near to eat roast lunch or dinner prepared by Eleuterio in a wood-fired oven. On weekdays you'd feel a bit lonesome in this large space so ask Nati to serve you dinner in a second, smaller dining area – or in the cosy bar next door. The cuts of lamb, kid and suckling pig are worthy of a medieval banquet and the prices are almost medieval, too. As far as the bedrooms go we'd recommend asking for one in the newly built extension: they are large and have fancy hydro-massage showers and tubs (ask for *"una habitación en la parte nueva"*). These are much bigger than the older rooms which are small and unremarkable. A friendly, unpretentious place where you come for the food, the value and the Gregorian chant.

Rooms: 38 with bath & wc.
Price: Single 3500-5500 Pts;
Double/Twin 4900-7000 Pts; 'Special'
Double/Twin 9000 Pts.
Breakfast: 425 Pts.
Meals: Lunch/Dinner 1400 Pts (M),
approx. 3000 Pts (C).
Closed: Never.

From Burgos N1 towards Madrid then
N234 towards Soria. Left in Hacinas on
BU903 to Santo Domingo de Silos. Hotel on right as you go through village.

El Nido de Valverde

Calle Escuelas 1
19224 Valverde de los Arroyos
Guadalajara

Tel: 949 854221 or 971 307448
Fax: 949 854221 or 971 307448
E-mail: conchamario@nidodevalverde.com
Web: www.nidodevalverde.com

Concha Sanz & Mario Alvarez

El Nido de Valverde is hidden away in one of Guadalajara's furthest-flung corners.
But make the effort to go here and you'll surely agree that there can be few nicer
places to stay in Spain. The home is the mirror of the soul; Concha and Mario are
sympathetic, sensitive, and care deeply for their guests – in the same way that they
cared for the children in the workshops that they used to organise and the fragile
ecosystems in whose defence they are so passionate. The village house which they
have restored is a wonderful example of Guadalajara's '*arquitectura negra*' which
uses the region's dark slate for walls and roofing ('which glint like fish-scales after
the rain' to translate Mario's phrase). The house wraps you in its warm embrace as
soon as you enter and catch a first delicious waft of linseed oil or perhaps of baking
bread. There is the cosiest of dining rooms and above it are two underfloor-heated
duplex-style suites whose decoration is as heart-warming as the rest of the house.
Nearly everything you eat at breakfast and dinner is home-made and much of it
organically grown. Stay at least a couple of nights but remember that the nearest
petrol station is some 50km away.

Rooms: 2 suites.
Price: Suite 21000 Pts; Suite for 2 or more
nights 18000 Pts.
Breakfast: 1100 Pts.
Meals: Lunch/Dinner 3400 Pts. Book
ahead.
Closed: Never.

From Burgos towards Madrid on the NI.
Exit for Riaza. Here to Santibañez de
Ayallón and then follow signs towards
Atienza. Turn right towards Cogulludo then right again to Valverde. El Nido is in
village square.

Map no: 11   **Entry no: 161**

Hospedería Rural Salinas de Imón

Calle Real 49
19269 Imón
Guadalajara

Tel: 949 397311
Fax: 949 397311
E-mail: sadeimon@teleline.es
Web: www.salinasdeimon.com

Jaime Mesalles de Zunzunegui

Salt is still produced at Imón: you'll see the crystallising beds as you arrive. Just
beyond is a tiny square and the salmon-pink Hospedería. This elegant house began
life as a convent in the 17th century then later became a lowly salt warehouse. The
heavy old studded door now opens onto another radical conversion – a mosaic of
different styles and atmospheres. An entertaining sitting room vibrates with bright
sofas, myriad antiques and ornaments, old dolls and books, framed prints and huge
repro paintings by Luis Gamo Alcalde, whose art is a thrill throughout the house.
A colourful stairway leads to the guest rooms, each differently themed. *Music* is
decorated with musical scores, instruments and signed photos of famous
musicians; *Keys* exhibits a collection of... old keys; *Chairs* has a Louis XVI style
cradle; *Carlos III* (they say he stayed here) has Empire beds and family photos.
Right at the top, a cosy little green, log-fired library leads to a patio and a peaceful
garden where the two towers of the original building rise and a secluded
swimming pool blends in seamlessly with its surroundings. A highly likeable place,
professionally run but with a personal touch.

Rooms: 11 with bath & wc; 1 suite.
Price: Double/Twin 9500 Pts; Suite
16500 Pts.
Breakfast: 800 Pts.
Meals: 2 restaurants in village.
Closed: Never.

From Madrid NII E90 towards Zaragoza.
Turn left to Sigüenza; here take CM110
towards Atienza to Imón. Hotel on main
square of village.

El Molino de Alcuneza

Carretera de Alboreca km 0.5
19264 Alcuneza
Guadalajara

Tel: 949 391501
Fax: 949 347004
E-mail: molinoal@teleline.es

Juan & Toñi Moreno

El Molino de Alcuneza is handsome proof of just what can be achieved when love and energy are present in great measure. Little remained of the 400-year-old mill buildings when Juan and Toñi fell for this swathe of delicious greenery whose rushing millrace promised soothing respite from the baking summers of Spain's vast Meseta. Originally it was to be a weekend bolt-hole for the family but then the idea of a hotel was mooted and Juan was hooked. All that could be saved from the old mill's installations was restored and every last detail of the interior decoration has been carefully mused upon: pine floors beneath darker beams above, rich fabrics, repro taps, trunks and cupboards that have long formed a part of the Moreno's collective memory, and, throughout the building, framed, pressed flowers (by an aunt). Our favourite rooms are 3 or 4 but all of them are special. Guests are allocated separate tables; at dinner there may be partridge with chickpeas, trout baked in Albariño wine, duck à l'orange or *cèpe* mushrooms. Breakfasts are hearty and picnic hampers can be arranged for *al fresco* lunches. Arrive as an appreciated guest; leave as a friend of this delightful family.

Rooms: 11 with bath or shower & wc.
Price: Single 8000 Pts; Double/
Twin 12000 Pts.
Breakfast: 850 Pts.
Meals: Dinner 3500 Pts (M).
Closed: Sundays.

From Sigüenza follow signs for
Medinacelli. The Molino is well signposted
just before you reach Alboreca on the
right-hand side.

Hotel Valdeoma

19266 Carabias
Guadalajara

Tel: 600 464309
Fax: 600 466921
E-mail: valdeoma@airtel.net
Web: www.valdeoma.com

Gregorio Marañon

Gregorio left a busy life in Europe and West Africa to restore a ruined house in the tiny village of Carabias, overlooking the mountains of Guadalajara. Now a small hotel, it is definitely modern with its large glass windows, stainless steel structures and minimalist interior but these original features blend beautifully with the older, base elements of wood and granite. The entrance, with its metal staircase and low reception desk, gives a lovely informal feel to Valdeoma: its parquet floor was made by Gregorio. Bedrooms, five of them on the raised entrance level, the rest at ground level, are finished with a warm choice of colours and bathrooms of earth-coloured marble. Both dining room and sitting room glow with period furniture and fireplaces and have large glass doors onto balconies: this is where you discover Valdeoma's most precious jewel – the view. Whether you're having breakfast or dinner or just lounging in one of the many comfortable chairs, those huge windows are calling you to live out there in that picture. Go down into it, into the medieval magic of the fine city of Sigüenza, only 10km away and worth visiting. *A Rusticae hotel.*

Rooms: 10 with bath & wc.
Price: Double/Twin 11000 Pts.
Breakfast: 750 Pts.
Meals: Lunch/Dinner 3000 Pts (M).
Closed: Never.

From Madrid NII E90 towards Zaragoza then left for Sigüenza; there take CM110 towards Atienza. After 7km left for Carabias/Palazuelos. In Carabias left past church, up hill; Valdeoma is at end of a narrow street on right.

Las Nubes

Camino de Cabanillas
Albalate de Zorita
Guadalajara

Tel: 949 826897 or 666 549968
or 610 552151
Fax: 949 826897

Carlos Sánchez

Clinging to a hilltop with breathtaking views of the Marques Valley and River Tagus, 'The Clouds' is well named. María Sol and Carlos have taken the lofty position, added a dash of Hollywood and created a conservatory sitting room whence you can follow the sun from its rising to its setting – MGM could never improve on this. Space and light and subtle neutral colours are the hallmarks of this splendid, peaceful hotel. Down from reception is the huge open-plan sitting area with a suspended canopy log fire in the middle and that vista beyond. And the dining room is on this floor where Valentin the chef serves lovingly-prepared regional dishes made with vegetables from the garden. The guest rooms are scented with lavender oil, their sliding windows open onto a communal balcony and, again, that staggering view. Each has an original headboard made with a large black and white photograph in a wooden frame, contemporary furnishings and perfect lighting. The suite has a four-poster bed as its centrepiece in a soft setting of cascading cream drapes and wheat-coloured walls. Go up to Las Nubes, breathe in the calm and get a birdseye view of the world. *A Rusticae hotel.*

Rooms: 5 with bath & wc; 1 suite with jacuzzi.
Price: Double/Twin 10000-12000 Pts; Suite 15000-18000 Pts.
Breakfast: 1000 Pts.
Meals: Lunch 3-4000 Pts, Dinner 5000 Pts incl. wine (M).
Closed: Never.

From Madrid NII towards Guadalajara; exit 23 to Alcalá de H., round town on M300 then M204 through Villabilla/Corpa/Fuentenovilla/Yebra. 2.5km after Yebra left towards Pastrana, right for Almonacid de Z. to Albalate de Z. Here follow signs for Ermita/Ruinas Históricas then signs for Las Nubes (8km from village, last 3.7km on track).

Map no: 12

Hotel Monasterio de Piedra

Afueras Nuévalos
50210 Nuévalos
Zaragoza

Tel: 976 849011
Fax: 976 849054
E-mail: monastpiedra@sta.es
Web: www.sta.es/monastpiedra

José Enrique Jirón Muntadas

Special place? Special special place! Prepare to enter a secret world of natural beauty. This 800-year-old monastery, a tranquil retreat in the hills above Nuévalos, is one of those gems of Spanish culture that simply ravish the senses and make you realise why exploring Iberia is such a joy. Your room is a converted monk's cell in an imposing vaulted building overlooking the quiet monastery gardens. Impressive corridors invite contemplation but it's not all horsehair mattresses and cold showers – the rooms are sumptuous and the restaurants excellent. So relax and take a guided tour of the cloisters, altars and tombs and the first European kitchen where chocolate was made! In one of the former cellars, the Wine Museum gives another glimpse of life in days gone by. Or there is the 'Life of the River' Centre with its three-dimensional audio-visual presentation of the life cycle of the trout. But the dense natural ecosystem of the park is the true jewel in this Aragonese crown. A 174-ft waterfall, a mirror lake, a sunken grotto: spellbindingly beautiful, it all awaits you – just go and lose yourself in the secret gardens and walkways.

Rooms: 62 with bath & wc; 1 suite.
Price: Single 8000 Pts; Double/Twin 10000-11000 Pts; Double/Twin (with terrace) 12000-13000 Pts; Suite 16000 Pts.
Breakfast: 600 Pts or 2100 Pts (buffet).
Meals: Lunch/Dinner 2950 Pts (M/C).
Closed: Never.

From Madrid N-II E90 towards Barcelona. Exit at km 209 for Nuévalos/Monasterio de Piedra. In Nuévalos follow signs for Monasterio de Piedra. Hotel is 2.5km outside village in grounds of monastery.

Entry no: 166

Map no: 12

La Pastora

Calle Roncesvalles 1
50678 Uncastillo
Zaragoza

Tel: 976 679499
Fax: 976 664188
E-mail: lapastora@lapastora.net
Web: www.lapastora.net

Inma Navarro Labat

Uncastillo, as the name implies, is an attractive castle-topped town just to the north of Zaragoza in the Sierra de Santo Domingo. It is all too often passed by; visitors to the area prefer to make for Sos del Rey Católico, another medieval town whose claim to fame is that the local-boy-made-good is no less a man than Fernando II whose marriage to Isabela would so radically change the course of Spanish history. Just behind the town's beautiful Romanesque church of Santa Marta this grand, eighteenth century house is by far the nicest place to stay in the area. The house's traditional elements of old flags, wrought iron window grilles, terracotta tiles and wooden beams have been preserved and restored. Massively thick outer walls mean that even at the height of the Spanish summer it remains cool inside; in winter a wood-burner keeps La Pastora's attractive little lounge as warm as toast. Guest rooms have no pretension to grandeur but with the same heavy stone walls, simple rustic furniture and antique washbasins they feel wonderfully snug. Inma is as charming and as unassuming as the delightful hostelry which she has created. *A Rusticae hotel.*

Rooms: 8 with bath & wc.
Price: Double/Twin 6500 Pts.
Breakfast: 600 Pts.
Meals: None available.
Closed: Never.

From Pamplona N121 south and then N240 towards Huesca then right on NA127 to Sangüesa. There take A127 to Sos del Rey Católico and as you leave village left to Uncastillo. Here go round the church of Santa María and park in a small cobbled square. Just 20m to Posada.

Casa Palacio Conde de Garcinaro

Calle Juan Carlos I, 19
16500 Huete
Cuenca

Tel: 969 372150
Fax: 91 5327378
E-mail: garcinar@teleline.es

Conchi & Ramiro Fernández

Antonio Reneses, the owner, spent his childhood just along the street from this imposing baroque mansion house; you wonder if he dreamed then that one day he would give the building back its lost dignity by its complete restoration. He has been helped with this formidable challenge by his wife Encarna, an artist and antique restorer by profession; every last corner of the palace shows an eye for detail, a feel for what is right. This is every inch a noble Castilian residence: fine portal of dressed sandstone, coat of arms above, grilled windows and beyond an enormous studded door leading through to the colonnaded courtyard. Climb a wide walnut staircase to the first floor; off to one side the old chapel is now home to a vast lounge decked out in rich burgundy colours. If it feels too imposing there is a second less formal lounge. Bedrooms are vast, high-ceilinged and in wonderful pastel colours. Old prints, window seats, cushions, easy chairs and hand-painted furniture; it's all surprisingly sumptuous given Garcinaro's more than modest prices. Breakfast in the old kitchen on bright chequered table cloths then head off to discover the delights of this wild and untouristy part of Castille.

Rooms: 10 with bath & wc; 3 suites.
Price: Double/Twin 8000-9500 Pts; Suite 10500-12000 Pts.
Breakfast: 750 pts.
Meals: None available.
Closed: Never.

From Madrid towards Valencia on N3. Exit for Tarancón, follow signs for Cuenca/Carascosa, then CM310 to Huete. The palace is in village centre next to Santo Domingo church.

Hotel Leonor de Aquitania

San Pedro 60
16001 Cuenca
Cuenca

Tel: 969 231000 or 969 231002
Fax: 969 231004
E-mail: reserleo@infonegocio.com
Web: www.hotelleonordeaquitania.com

Francisco de Borja García

A grand 18th-century townhouse is now home to Cuenca's smartest small hotel. Its position could hardly be more magnificent – a perch right at the edge of the deep gorge, next to the church of San Pedro and a few hundred yards from the main square and Cathedral. A well-known Spanish interior designer decorated the hotel, cleverly weaving innovation in and out of tradition. You see this immediately as you enter: first the heavy old wooden door, then a heavy modern glass door. In reception and bar, furniture that is unmistakably '90s goes well with terracotta floors and *estera* matting. In the dining room and bar, the lighting is subtle, diffuse and there are old tapestries and photographs – a lovely spot to dine. "Pricey but nicey" wrote one of our more poetical readers! The bedrooms are attractive, too, with hand-painted tiles, wooden beds, matching fabrics on bedcovers and curtains and exposed beams (rafters on the top floor). Some have a terrace, many a balcony; the view out across the gorge has to be seen to be believed. And the suite is one of the most enchanting in Spain.

Rooms: 46 with bath & wc; 1 suite.
Price: Single 9300-9950 Pts; Double/Twin 11950-14850 Pts; Suite 22000-25000 Pts.
Breakfast: 975 Pts.
Meals: Lunch/Dinner 3500 Pts.
Closed: Never.

From Madrid N111-E901 to Tarancón. Left on N400 to Cuenca. Follow signs to 'Casco Antiguo'. Cross Plaza Mayor; signposted (up Calle San Pedro. Hotel on right after 200m).

Map no: 12

Entry no: 169

Posada de San José
Calle Julián Romero 4
16001 Cuenca

Tel: 969 211300
Fax: 969 230365
E-mail: psanjose@arrakis.es
Web: www.arrakis.es/~psanjose

Antonio & Jennifer Cortinas

Cuenca is unique, a town that astonishes and engraves itself on the memory. Sitting on the rim of the town's unforgettable gorge, this is an inn to match the town. A sculpted portal beckons you to enter but you would never guess at what lies just beyond it. For this is a labyrinthine house and only from inside do you realise that it is multi-levelled. Staircases lead up and down, twisting and turning... the perfect antidote to the mass-produced hotels and their made-to-measure bedrooms. Every room is different, some small, some large, some with balconies, some without; most have bathrooms, a few share. Nearly all have old furniture, perhaps a canopied bed or a little terrace. We would ask for one that looks out across Cuenca's spectacular gorge but all of them, view or no view, are worth a night and are witness to Antonio and Jennifer's decorative flair who, like us, value a vase of fresh flowers more than satellite channels and trouser presses. In their welcoming little restaurant, with that heart-stopping view and a good meal to come, you'll be glad you cut across the Meseta to Cuenca. And whatever you do be sure to visit the town's wonderful museum of Contemporary Art.

Rooms: 22 with bath or shower & wc.
Price: Single 4500-5200 Pts;
Double/Twin 9000-10000 Pts; Triple
12250-16000 Pts. Prices approximate.
Breakfast: 550 Pts.
Meals: Snacks (good tapas!) always
available in evening except Mondays.
Closed: Never.

From Madrid N111-E901 to Tarancón.
Left here on N400 to Cuenca. Follow signs
to Casco Antiguo. Posada is just 50m from main entrance to Cathedral. Best to park in Plaza Mayor by Cathedral.

Entry no: 170

Map no: 12

Los Baños de Villanarejo Navalpino

Ciudad Real

Tel: 91 4488910 or 609 612659
Fax: 91 5933061
E-mail: acolomina@hotmail.com

Alvaro Colomina Velázquez-Duro

You won't want for space if you stay at Villanarejo; you are surrounded by 2,000 hectares of magnificent woodlands. Mineral water springs rise here and people have come to take the waters since Roman times. Old stands of olive, cork and evergreen oak are home to foxes, wild boar, mongoose, muflon and deer and although the Marquis and Marchioness of La Felguera have long received private hunting parties they only recently opened their home to paying guests, too. It does feel far more like a home than a hotel: sofas drawn up around the open hearth and the family coat of arms on the chimney breast. There are rugs and oils and – predictably – any number of hunting trophies. Twelve guest rooms have period furniture and rather less period tiles on the floors and in the bathrooms. Breakfast is a hearty spread of eggs and bacon, croissants, cakes and cold meats and at dinner you might be served pumpkin soup, game from the estate, and the dessert will be home-made; wine *à volonté* is included. As well as hunting activities on offer include archery, clay-pigeon shooting, horse-riding, cycling and ballooning. Note address for correspondence is: Calle San Bernardo 97-99, 28015 Madrid.

Rooms: 9 with bath & wc; 3 suites.
Price: Twin 15000 Pts; Twin sharing 10000 Pts; Suite 20000 Pts incl. VAT.
Breakfast: Included.
Meals: Lunch/Dinner 3500 Pts incl. wine.
Closed: Never.

From Madrid south on the NIV. Exit on N430 to Cuidad Real. Here continue on N430 to Piedrabuena then take CR721 via Arroba de los Montes and Navalpino towards Horcajo de los Montes; at top of pass turn left at green gate and follow track to house.

Map no: 17   **Entry no: 171**

Palacio de la Serna

Calle Cervantes 18
13432 Ballasteros de Calatrava
Ciudad Real

Tel: 926 842208
Fax: 926 842224
E-mail: palacioserna@paralelo40.org
Web: www.palaciodelaserna.com

Eugenio S. Bermejo

In the wide landscapes of Castilla-La Mancha the divide between vision and reality seems to blur – not just for hapless Quijotes lancing windmills. In a forgotten village of the province of Ciudad Real, this neo-classical palace may have you wondering if the sun hasn't got to you! Its unexpected opulence will remind you of a time when mining made many a fortune in the area. It was all abandoned to the Meseta, until designer Eugenio Bermejo saw in Serna a perfect outlet for his creative impulse. Two and a half years later nearly every corner of the Palace is embellished with his sculptures, paintings and eclectic taste in interior design. Each guest room is different, all are huge fun, with colour schemes to match paintings – or sometimes vice versa. Post-modern to the core. There are red roses in the gardens, music is ever-present – from Nyman to Bach – as are intriguing *objets* at every turn. Dinners are by torchlight; you might expect a Knight of the Calatrava Order to wander in. Fun, whacky, and *very* different; well worth a detour as you drive north or south.

Rooms: 19 with bath & wc; 8 suites.
Price: Double/Twin 15500 Pts; Suite 20000-25000 Pts.
Breakfast: 1500 Pts.
Meals: Lunch/Dinner 3500 Pts (M), 5000 Pts (C). Closed Mondays.
Closed: Never.

From Ciudad Real round town towards Puertollano then left on CR512 towards Aldea del Rey then right to Ballasteros de Calatrava. Palace to left, signposted.

Entry no: 172   Map no: 17

La Posada Regia

Calle General Mola 9-11
24003 León
León

Tel: 987 213173
Fax: 987 213031 or 987 251316
E-mail: regialeon@smonica.com
Web: www.si-santamonica.es/regialeon/

Angel Marcos Vidal Suárez

The stained-glass windows of Leon's Gothic Cathedral are reason enough to come to this lively provincial capital – and there is much more to do besides. By far the best place to stay here is the Posada Regia, plumb in the centre of the old town and one of the brightest stars in the firmament of newly-opened hotels in Spain. The building first saw the light in 1370 and it in turn had incorporated older elements: the dining room incorporates part of the old Roman wall. The warm ochre and beamed reception strikes a welcoming note as you arrive and the staff could not be more friendly. A fine old staircase leads up to the bedrooms which are some of the cosiest and most coquettish that you'll come across: soothing pastel shades, bright kilims, shining planked floors, old writing desks, brightly painted radiators, and really snazzy bathrooms which have all the extras like bathrobes, embroidered towels, hairdryers etc. The hotel's restaurant, La Bodega Regia, which predates the hotel by 50 years and was founded by Marcos' grandfather, is one of León's most renowned.

Rooms: 20 with bath & wc.
Price: Single 8500 Pts; Double/Twin 13000 Pts.
Breakfast: Included.
Meals: Lunch/Dinner 2200 Pts (M), 3500-4000 Pts (C). Closed Sundays, second 2 weeks January and first 2 weeks September.
Closed: Never.

Hotel is in town centre approx. 150m from the Cathedral. Best to park in Parking Ordoñez Segundo on Plaza de Santo Domingo and then less than 100m to walk to hotel.

Map no: 3   Entry no: 173

La Posada del Marqués

Plaza Mayor 4
24270 Carrizo de la Ribera
León

Tel: 987 357171 or 606 831337
Fax: 987 358101
E-mail: marques@aletur.es
Web: www.aletur.es/marques

Carlos Velásquez-Duro

There are few places to stay in Spain as special as this old pilgrim's hospital, originally part of the Santa María monastery next door. Pass through the fine old portal and discover a pebbled cloister and a lovely mature garden with a gurgling brook and big old yew and walnut trees. It is rather reminiscent of an English rectory with its high walls and rambling roses. Carlos Velázquez (his family have owned the *posada* for generations) and his wife graciously greet their guests before showing them to their rooms. These are set round a gallery on the first floor and are decorated with family heirlooms: Portuguese (canopied) beds, oil paintings, old lamps and dressers. One has a terrace over the cloisters; all are enchanting. The sitting and games rooms downstairs are similarly furnished with heavy old wooden doors, carved chests and tables and comfy armchairs and sofa in front of the hearth. At dinner there is good regional food and wine with a choice of two or three starters, main courses and puddings. Afterwards you might like to have a post-prandial game of snooker. Kind and erudite hosts and the most beguiling of settings. Be sure to visit the monastery for the plainsong.

Rooms: 11 with bath & wc.
Price: Double/Twin 11000-11500 Pts incl. VAT.
Breakfast: Included.
Meals: Dinner 2200 Pts. Book ahead.
Closed: 10 January-end February.

From León N120 towards Astorga. After 18km, right on LE442 to Villanueva de Carrizo. Cross river into Carrizo de la Ribera and ask for Plaza Mayor.

Guts Muths

Calle Matanza s/n
Barrio de Abajo
24732 Santiago Millas
León

Tel: 987 691123
Fax: 987 691123
Web: www.turismo.iranon.org/gutsmuths

Sjoerd Hers & Mari Paz Martínez

Santiago Millas and other villages in the area of La Maragatería drew their wealth from a virtual monopoly on the transport of merchandise by horse and cart throughout Spain. The coming of the railways put an end to all that. What remains of this past glory are some grand old village houses of which Guts Muths is a fine example. It is a big, solid house with a rather colonial feel; enter under an imposing arch to find yourself in a lovely flower- and palm-filled courtyard. It is utterly peaceful. Hats off to owners Sjoerd and Mari Paz for the easy-going intimate atmosphere they have created. Decorative flair-and-care is evident throughout the house – beds are of simple pine but a wacky feel has been created by interesting murals and paint techniques. Downstairs has a lot of exposed stonework, dried and fresh flowers and a dining room and well-stocked *bodega* with ceramic tiles, dark roof beams and an old bread oven: a proper backdrop for the honest regional dishes. Sjoerd is a no-nonsense sort: he loves to talk and will regale you with local history and folklore. He might take you out to explore the nearby gorges on foot, or mountain bike... or even attached to the end of a rope.

Rooms: 8 with bath & wc.
Price: Double/Twin 9000 Pts.
Breakfast: 750 Pts.
Meals: Lunch 17500-2300 Pts (M).
Closed: Never.

From Astorga LE133 towards Destriana. After about 10km, left towards Santiago Millas, Barrio de Abajo – signposted.

Map no: 3

Entry no: 175

Hotel Santo Domingo

Plaza de Santo Domingo 13
28013 Madrid

Tel: 91 5479800
Fax: 91 5475995
E-mail: reservas@hotelsantodomingo.com
Web: www.hotelsantodomingo.com

Antonio Núñes Tirado

Hotel Santo Domingo is larger than the other hotels in this book but we include it because, in spite of its size, it manages to retain an intimate and friendly atmosphere (many of the capital's chain hotels could heed the good example). It is right at the hub of old Madrid; close to the Opera, the Plaza Mayor and a stone's throw from the shops of the Gran Vía. Stepping in off the street it feels welcoming: reception and lounge are decorated in a warm, sandy tone; there are oil paintings and comfy sofas to flop into and a sparkling marble floor. And – take it in good faith – the décor in each of the 120 bedrooms is different. They contain all the extras you might expect given Santo Domingo's four-star status: mini-bars and TVs, bathrobes and stacks of toiletries, safety boxes, writing sets – hydro-massage baths in the 'superior' rooms. And the will to be as people-friendly as possible in the bedrooms holds true in the restaurant, too: even though you are in a large hotel there is "good home cooking" on the menu, in the words of Ana Hernández, the hotels ever-friendly manageress. Santo Domingo has long since won its laurels – but still aspires to be first past the post.

Rooms: 120 with bath & wc.
Price: Weekdays: Single 18650 Pts;
Double/Twin 23750-30300 Pts;
Weekends: Single 13525 Pts.
Double/Twin 17250- 24200 Pts.
Breakfast: 1625 Pts (buffet).
Included at weekends.
Meals: Lunch/Dinner weekdays 4350 Pts
(M), weekends 3550 Pts (M).
Closed: Never.

Head along Gran Vía away from Cibeles; pass Plaza de Callao then left into Calle San Bernardo to Plaza de Santo Domingo. Hotel on right. Pull up outside & porter will garage car.

La Residencia de El Viso

Calle Nervión 8
28002 Madrid
Madrid

Tel: 91 5640370
Fax: 91 5641965
E-mail: reservas@residensiadelviso.com
Web: www.resideciadelviso.com

Miryam Escudero

El Viso is one of Madrid's most chic areas, a quiet and leafy suburb surprisingly close to the centre. Until four years ago La Residencia was just one more of these smart private homes. Now, thanks to the efforts of its young and engaging owner, this interesting '30s-style edifice is a reliable port of call if you want to escape the noise and fumes of the city centre. Beyond a cheery façade and swing-glass doors is a marbled reception area where you are greeted by piped music, friendly staff. The long glass French windows bring in the light (there's no high-rise in this area to rob you of the sun) and draw your gaze out to a walled garden /patio area where you eat when it's warm, perhaps under the shade of the magnolia. The rooms are slightly faded around the edges but comfortable: some have carpet, others parquet and colours and fabrics have been well matched. All but two of the rooms look out across the garden: air-conditioning is a plus at the height of summer, sinks sparkle, floors shine, standards are high. In colder weather dine in the conservatory-style restaurant on good, traditional Spanish food and wines.

Rooms: 12 with bath & wc.
Price: Single 12000 Pts; Double/Twin 19500 Pts.
Breakfast: 1200 Pts.
Meals: Lunch 2550 (M) Dinner 5100 (C).
Closed: Never.

From Puerta de Alcalá take Calle Serrano towards Plaza de la Republica Argentina. Just before you reach the square turn left into Calle Nervión; hotel has a yellow awning.

Map no: 11

Entry no: 177

La Casa del Puente Colgante

Carretera a Uceda km 3   **Tel:** 91 8430595
28189 Torremocha de Jarama   **Fax:** 91 8430595
Madrid   **Web:** www.sierranorte.com/puentecolgante/

Silvia Leal

In this beautiful wooded spot on the banks of the Jarama river it's hard to believe that Madrid is less than an hour away. The name means 'the house of the suspension bridge': walk across it to discover a waterfall, a river pool for bathing and a grassy knoll from where to observe the exceptional bird life; you should see kingfishers and herons if you're patient. The peace and beauty of the setting continue on into the house: you'll find no TV here but classical music, the sound of the river, even the song of a nightingale in spring. Silvia loves the spot dearly, knows its every tree and shrub and hopes that her guests leave with something of the tranquility of her home deep within them. Bedrooms are medium-sized with no fussy extras but are sparkling clean with the best mattresses for comfort and eiderdowns for warmth. Silvia prepares simple lunches and dinners using organic fruit and veg, local cheeses and good cuts of meat. Do try her delicious apple cake: its recollection works the same magic for us as madeleine did for Proust! You can bus in and out of Madrid from here to avoid yet more driving. *A non-smoking household.*

Rooms: 5 with bath or shower & wc.
Price: Double 7500 Pts; Twin 5500-6500 Pts; Suite 7500 Pts.
Breakfast: Included.
Meals: Lunch/Dinner Monday-Friday 1700 Pts (M);
Weekends 3000-4000 Pts (C).
Closed: 23-25 December.

From Madrid N1 towards Burgos and exit at km50 post for Torrelaguna. Here towards Patones de Arriba then right to Torremocha. Through village following signs 'farmacia/turismo rural', continue for 3km until you see 'casa rural' sign on left by 2 white columns.

Entry no: 178   **Map no: 11**

Posada de la Casa del Abad de Ampudía

Pza. Francisco Martín Gromaz 12
34160 Ampudía
Palencia

Tel: 979 768008
Fax: 979 768300
E-mail: hotel@casadelabad.com
Web: www.casadelabad.com

Angel García

The impressive church of San Miguel beckons you into Ampudía, a village steeped in history. Known as *Fons Putida* (chaste spring) to the Romans, it has wooden colonnaded streets dating from the 1600s and a stunningly-renovated 17th-century abbot's house in the square. Angel García has blended authentic details with modern technology to create a wonderful, hedonistic hideaway. Beyond the stately porch is the six-metre vaulted orange hallway. The beams are original, the décor is contemporary; bright pinks, blues, greens and yellows mix with columns, arches, cornices and adobe walls to create an informal and hospitable atmosphere. The central patio, another riot of colour, is the place to enjoy an aperitif before settling into the distinctive wood-beamed restaurant where you will eat well and imbibe some of the rarer, more robust Iberian wines. There's an intimate little bar too, with its own entrance and garden. The bedrooms are individual masterpieces, a blend of antique wood and furnishings, sumptuous beds and superbly-finished bathrooms. There is a salt-purified, solar-heated swimming pool, a sauna, a gym and a tennis court – and friendly staff. *A Rusticae hotel.*

Rooms: 12 with bath & wc; 5 suites.
Price: Double/Twin 17870 Pts; Junior suite 20965 Pts; Suite with hydromassage bath 22960 Pts.
Breakfast: 1495 Pts.
Meals: Gourmet Lunch 7000 Pts (M).
Closed: 11-31 January.

From Burgos N620 towards Valladolid. 12km south of Palencia, right at km 92 to Dueñas. Here right to Ampudía; bear left at petrol station and follow wooden columns to square with large willow tree. Posada on left.

Map no: 3

Entry no: 179

Hostería 'El Convento'

Calle Convento s/n
34492 Santa María de Mave
Palencia

Tel: 979 123611/123095
Fax: 979 125492
E-mail: conventomave@airtel.net

Ignacio Antonio Moral

You leave traffic, city, and pollution far behind when you come and stay at El Convento. The Moral family laboured long and hard to nurse this vine-clad 18th-century Benedictine monastery back to good health and it is now classified as a national monument. On weekdays the cloister, gardens and the old stone walls remain as conducive to meditation as in the days when the brothers were here; at weekends the place's popularity means there are many more visitors. Some bedrooms (they are all named after other priories) are in what were once the monks' cells; they are medium-sized, simply furnished in the dark-wooded Castillian style and most give onto the cloister. The two suites have curtained four-poster beds and swish corner tubs. You dine in the old chapter house where heavy antique furniture, low beams and terracotta tiling are in keeping with the building's past. Food is traditional Castilian, thick chick pea or bean soups and many lamb-based dishes. Roast from a wood-fired oven is the house speciality, as are freshly-picked strawberries when in season. Don't miss the chapel; it dates from 1208 and is considered one of the finest of Palencia's many Romanesque edifices.

Rooms: 23 with bath & wc; 2 suites.
Price: Single 5000 Pts; Double/Twin 7000 Pts; Suite 11000 Pts.
Breakfast: 600 Pts.
Meals: Lunch/Dinner 1500 Pts (M), approx. 3000 Pts (C).
Closed: Never.

From Aguilar de Campo south towards Palencia on N611. After 5km, in Olleros de Pisuerga, left at sign for Santa María de Mave.

Entry no: 180

Map no: 4

Posada de Santa Maria la Real

Avenida de Cervera s/n   **Tel:** 979 122000/122522
34800 Aguilar de Campoo   **Fax:** 979 125680
Palencia   **E-mail:** posada@jazzviajeros.com
                                   Web: pagina.de/posadas.del.romanico

Elena Martín

In a wing of the Cistercian monastery of Santa María la Real, 18 guestrooms have
recently been created by the local *escuela taller* - a scheme that teaches traditional
skills to the young unemployed. While they have been utterly faithful to local
building and restoration techniques, they have dared to let '90s design play a part
too; the result is a hotel which is full of surprises. We were immediately struck by
the peacefulness of the place – presumably why the cowelled-ones came here in the
first place. A pebbled patio leads up to the entrance; the façade of timbers, stone,
wafer-bricking and eaves is a beguiling sight. Once you are inside the building the
mix of old and new works well: every last corner was carefully restored – and
considered. There are pebbled and parquet floors, designer chairs and lamps snug
beside hearth and beam. The design of the guest rooms follows the dictates of a
tall building: they are small and 'mezzanined' and attractively decorated; we feel
they work although one of our readers found them just a bit too small and
cramped. If you are sensitive to cigarette smoke then the low ceilinged dining
room could be an ordeal.

Rooms: 18 with bath & wc.
Price: Single 5600-6600 Pts;
Double/Twin 7700-8900 Pts incl. VAT.
Breakfast: Included (buffet).
Meals: Lunch/Dinner 1500 Pts (M),
4500 Pts (C).
Closed: 22-25 December.

From Santander A67 towards Oviedo, then
N611 south to Aguilar de Campoo. Posada
is on the left of the road that leads from
Aguilar to Cervera de Pisuerga.

Map no: 4   **Entry no: 181**

La Aceña

Ctra Aguilar-Cervera km 17   **Tel:** 979 870264 or 639 254090
34839 Quintanaluengos   **Web:** www.cyl.com/laacena/contactar.htm
Palencia

Angel Pérez Gutierrez

If you're looking for a stopover on the road to Santander and are tempted to explore the unknown pathways of the Río Pisuerga, look no further: this homely little B&B is a good place for both. Angel and Anna, the young owners, are enthusiastic and informative hosts who delight in sharing their local knowledge. Their oak-beamed house of patterned brick and stone stands at the edge of an unspoilt, deeply bucolic village. With old farm implements strewn around the garden, wheat threshers propped against the wall, young fruit trees and geraniums adorning the entrance, the atmosphere is a far cry from Angel's previous place of work: he was a miner who, after 14 years of hard toil, broke with family tradition and turned his talents to receiving guests. His energy is well placed and he is an excellent cook – we suggest you choose to dine in and try his food before he opens a restaurant! Guest rooms are rather basic with smallish bathrooms but the downstairs open-plan sitting/dining area is cosy with its pleasant fireplace and modern sofas to relax on. With an abundance of pine furniture and oak, it is well finished, clean and friendly so stay a while to explore this fertile region.

Rooms: 6 with bath & wc.
Price: Double/Twin 6500 incl. VAT.
Breakfast: 500 Pts.
Meals: 1600 Pts incl. wine (M).
Closed: Never.

From Burgos N627 north to Aguilar de Campo then left for Cervera. At km 17, as you enter Quintanaluengos, left for Barcenilla. Cross bridge, follow road round to left; La Aceña is last house on right as you leave village.

El Zaguán

Plaza de España 16
40370 Turégano
Segovia

Tel: 921 501165 or 921 501156
Fax: 921 500776
E-mail: zaguan@ctv.es
Web: www.ctv.es/USERS/zaguan

Mario García

Turégano gets forgotten as people flock by en route for nearby Pedraza. But this village is every bit as attractive. It has a porticoed main square and an enormous castle dominating the skyline: King Ferdinand rested here between Crusades to oust the Infidel. On the main square, El Zaguán is every inch the grand Castilian house: casement windows, dressed stone and its own stables, grain store and *bodega*. A warm, quiet and cosy hostelry awaits you. Downstairs is a lively bar and dining room: pine beams, wafer-bricks and terracotta floors, with beautifully dressed tables and sensitive lighting. There's a wood-fired oven where roasts are prepared: beef and lamb as well as (the ubiquitous) suckling pig. Here, in a lovely upstairs sitting room and in the bedrooms, you could be stepping into the pages of an interior design magazine and the underfloor heating is a real boon during the Castilian winter. The sitting room has comfy sofas, a wood-burner and a view of the castle and you sleep in style and comfort: no two bedrooms are the same and they are amongst the most handsome we've seen. A special hotel with hardworking, cheery and likeable Mario at the helm.

Rooms: 12 with bath & wc; 3 suites.
Price: Single 6000 Pts; Double/Twin 10000 Pts; Suite 15000 Pts.
Breakfast: 800 Pts.
Meals: Lunch/Dinner 2000 Pts (M), 3500-4500 Pts (C).
Closed: Christmas.

From Segovia take N601 towards Valladolid. After 7km right for Turégano/Cantalejo. Hotel in main square of the village.

Map no: 11

Entry no: 183

Hotel Los Linajes

Dr. Velasco 9   **Tel:** 921 460475
40003 Segovia   **Fax:** 921 460479
Segovia

Miguel Borreguero Rubio

Just a stone's throw from Segovia's Plaza Mayor and wondrous Cathedral, Los Linajes is cheek-to-jowl with the old city wall; the land drops away steeply here so the building is 'stepped' to give the maximum number of rooms with a view across the green valley of the river Eresma. Miguel Borreguero officiates in reception: this amiable gent has been in charge at Los Linajes for years and he constantly strives to improve the hotel. Parts, it's true, feel a little dated but a thorough revamp is under way. The oldest section of the building is 17th century: its portal of dressed sandstone leads to a beamed reception area where there's heavy Castilian-style furniture and oil paintings. What makes the rooms special are their views across the river valley: the best have terraces where you can breakfast if the weather's right. You're only really aware this is a 50+ room hotel in the rather cavernous dining room and bar. The food is classically Castilian-Spanish; if you prefer a cosier venue for dinner there are plenty of restaurants very close. A huge plus is the hotel's large underground car park.

Rooms: 44 with bath & wc; 9 suites.
Price: Single 8000-9400 Pts;
Double/Twin 11000-13200 Pts; Triple
13000-15200 Pts; Suite 14900-16900 Pts.
Breakfast: 975 Pts.
Meals: Lunch/Dinner approx.
3000 Pts (M).
Closed: Never.

As you arrive in Segovia from Madrid
follow signs for Zona Oriental/Acueducto.
By the Roman aqueduct follow signs for El Alcázar and then signs for hotel.

Entry no: 184   Map no: 11

La Abubilla

Calle Escuelas 4 posterior
40181 Carrascal de la Cuesta
Segovia

Tel: 921 120236 or 91 6617068
Fax: 91 6617268
E-mail: oneto@oneto.com
Web: www.oneto.com/abubilla/indice.html

Hermanos Oneto

The Oneto family have lavished love, care and much decorative *savoir-faire* on their latest project: the complete restoration of an old farmhouse in the tiny hamlet of Carrascal de la Cuesta whose daytime population numbered all of two at the last count! La Abubilla is a typical Segovian farm with main house and outbuildings wrapped around a sheltered courtyard where you breakfast in fine weather; a thick stand of shimmering poplars provides welcome shade during the Meseta's long, hot summer. Every detail of the guest room's decoration has been fussed over by Alfredo Oneto; even the light switches were individually crafted! Suites are in the old hay barn and here you'll sleep in one of the prettiest rooms imaginable where tiles are hand painted, beds are four poster and paint and fabric schemes are praised in all the coffee-table magazines. A split-level lounge and diner where a log fire roars in winter is every bit as special. Segovia is close by and you could easily visit Madrid, Ávila and Salamanca from here should you make the wise decision to stay for several nights. *A Rusticae hotel.*

Rooms: 1 with bath & wc; 4 suites.
Price: Double 13000 Pts; Suite 17000 Pts.
Breakfast: Included.
Meals: Dinner 2000 Pts.
Closed: Never.

From Segovia towards Soria on N110. In Sotosalbo turn left towards Turégano to Carrascal de la Cuesta.

Hostal de Buen Amor

Eras 7
40170 Sotosalbos
Segovia

Tel: 921 403020
Fax: 921 403022
E-mail: hosbamor@cempresarial.com
Web: www.cempresarial.com/hostaldebuenamor

Victor L. Soste and Dora P. Villamide

When Madrid folk tire of the capital they often head over the mountains to the green and fertile valleys of Segovia: tradition demands that a roast meal should complete the excursion. Dora and Victor's restaurant has long been famous, while their delightful small hotel, yards away, just recently opened its heavy old doors. Their niece, a designer, took charge of nursing the hamlet's finest old house back to good health: her creation is warm and intimate, a lovely blend of comfort and authenticity. The house is memorably silent: when sipping your aperitif you hear just the grandfather clock or perhaps distant church bells; the blaze from the central, suspended chimney warms all sides. Dora, a self-confessed antique shop addict, has waved a magic wand over the bedrooms: here you'll find old writing tables, cheery fabrics, superb mattresses and wooden beams. And those English engravings? Dora and Victor have both lived in England and speak English brilliantly. In this delicious hostelry of 'Good Loving' you are pampered in every way: underfloor heating to keep you warm when temperatures plummet in the wintertime and a breakfast that will send you contentedly on your way.

Rooms: 11 with bath & wc; 1 suite.
Price: Double/Twin 9500-14000 Pts;
Suite 20000 Pts.
Breakfast: 750 Pts.
Meals: Lunch/Dinner (in restaurant next door) 3500-4000 Pts (C).
Closed: Never.

From Madrid N6 towards La Coruña. After passing through tunnel, right towards Segovia. Here N110 towards Soria. Hamlet of Sotosalbos is on left after 18km.

Entry no: 186   Map no: 11

La Tejera de Fausto

Carretera la Salceda a Sepúlveda km 7
40173 Requijada
Segovia

Tel: 921 127087 or 619 240355
Fax: 91 5641520
E-mail: armero@nauta.es
Web: www.nauta.es/fausto

Jaime Armero

This is a gorgeous part of Castille: a fertile valley in the lee of the Guadarrama mountains which cut a jagged scimitar between Madrid and the Meseta. The stone buildings of the Tejera del Fausto stand in glorious isolation, a mile from the nearest village, close to the banks of the Cega river. It is no coincidence that the roofs are terracotta: tiles (*tejas*) were made here, hence the building's name. Decoration is warm, simple and appealing: bedrooms have simple wooden furniture and neither telephone nor TV to distract you from the views. What makes the place is the restaurant, a series of interconnecting rooms where fires blaze in colder months, as snug as an Irish pub; specialities are roast lamb, suckling pig and boar. Jaime is a gregarious host and regales you with nuggets of information about the area. He would have you visit the Romanesque chapel next door whose foundation stones were pillaged from a Roman villa. Walk out from La Tejera along the old transhumance routes that criss-cross the region: it is all Castillian to the core. There are often wedding parties at the weekend during the summer so visit on a weekday. "Very, very good" wrote a reader.

Rooms: 7 with bath & wc; 2 suites.
Price: Double/Twin 11000 Pts;
Suite 16000-22000 Pts.
Breakfast: 850 Pts.
Meals: Lunch/Dinner 4200 Pts (C).
Fri/Sat/Sun only.
Closed: Never.

From Segovia, N110 towards Soria to La Salceda. There, left towards Pedraza. Hotel on left after Torre Val de San Pedro.

Posada del Acebo

Calle de la Iglesia 7
40165 Prádena
Segovia

Tel: 921 507260
Fax: 921 507260
E-mail: acebo@tursegovia.com
Web: www.el-acebo.com

José Luis Martín Aranguez

Prádena sits snug in the lee of the Guadarrama sierra, the high chain of mountains that lie just north of Madrid. Its older houses are surprisingly grand: they are from an age when the villagers were granted royal privileges for the magnificence of their livestock whose meat and wool were famous throughout the land. Enter the house through the diminutive dining room-cum-lounge; the smell of seasoned timber, a fire in the wood-stove, photos of shepherds and their flocks and heavy bench seating feel truly snug. Ramón will show you upstairs by way of a fine old bannistered staircase – his great grandparents once lived here. The bedrooms are real gems; a lovely mix of the old (washstands, wrought iron bedsteads, lamps, prints) and the new (central heating, properly firm mattresses, double glazing to keep the fearsome Meseta winters at bay). There are mountain walks on your doorstep, the mighty Duratón river gorges to explore (on foot or by canoe), a feast of Romanesque churches and then dinner back in that cosy dining room. We think both rooms and food are worth every last peseta. If you're missing them, don't be afraid to ask for eggs and bacon first thing!

Rooms: 8 with bath or shower & wc.
Price: Single 6000 Pts; Double/Twin 8000 Pts.
Breakfast: 700 Pts.
Meals: Dinner from 1250 Pts inc. wine (M). Book ahead.
Closed: Never.

From Madrid take N1 towards Burgos. At km99 post exit towards Santo Tomé del Puerto and follow N110 towards Segovia. After 12km right into Prádena. House just off main square.

Entry no: 188

Map no: 11

La Posada de Sigueruelo

Calle Badén 40
40590 Sigueruelo
Segovia

Tel: 921 508135
Fax: 921 508135
E-mail: posada@situral.com
Web: www.situral.com

Concha Alarcos Rodriges

Concha was a social worker before she opened this tiny country inn in the mountains just to the north of Madrid. You arrive here by way of cobbled streets in the tiniest of hamlets; the outside of the building gives little away but once you get inside her 120-year-old farm is all homely comfort and warmth. A delicious smell of perfumed wood pervades the house; when renovating the building natural oils were used to treat rafters, doors and lintels. There are antique trunks, old wooden harvesting tools and six attractive bedrooms, one with Art-Deco furniture. Concha gradually gathered in the furnishings from the Madrid antique markets. The dining room is as cosy as the rest of the house and dinner is a chance to try good, Castillian home-cooking and there are interesting vegetarian dishes, too. Riding and canoeing (with the owner's son) in the unforgettable Duratón gorge can be arranged and there is free use of mountain bikes. It would be wonderful to return to the house's warm embrace and an open fire after a day of exploration. Readers have enthusiastically endorsed our opinions about Sigueruelo and all of them have enthused Concha's welcome.

Rooms: 6 with shower & wc.
Price: Half-board only: Double/Twin 15000 Pts.
Breakfast: Included.
Meals: Dinner included.
Closed: Never.

From Madrid N1 towards Burgos. At km99 post, exit towards Santo Tomé del Puerto onto N110 towards Segovia. After 3km left to Sigueruelo. Ask for Posada in village.

La Almazara

Carretera Toledo-Argés y Polan
Apartado 6
45004 Toledo

Tel: 925 223866
Fax: 925 250562
E-mail: hotelalmazara@ribernet.es

Paulino Villamor

One of Toledo's most illustrious *Cardenals* had this delectable house built as a summer palace in the 16th century; high on a hillside overlooking Toledo it catches the breezes that sweep in across the *Meseta*. He milled oil here: there are still huge vats of the stuff deep in the gunnels of the building. You arrive by way of a grand old portal and long drive to be greeted by Paulino: he is incredibly helpful and takes obvious pleasure in welcoming you and advising you on your forays. Downstairs is a large lounge with a fire in the hearth during the colder months but you may prefer to linger in the vaulted dining room which looks out over the fruit orchards to Toledo. Take a closer look at those oil paintings; these were all painted by Paulino's teenage daughter. We stayed in one of the rooms with views and sat enthralled on the terrace, contemplating the lights of the old town and lapping up the silence, almost uncanny so close to a city. Bedrooms are clean and comfortable and bathrooms have repro taps and gallons of hot water. A private car park is a real plus: leave the car and wander down to the town, about a 20 minute stroll. Brilliantly priced so book ahead.

Rooms: 24 with bath or shower & wc.
Price: Single 4200 Pts; Double/Twin (with view) 6900 Pts; Double/Twin 6000 Pts.
Breakfast: 500 Pts.
Meals: None available.
Closed: 10 December-1 March.

Arriving from Madrid turn right in front of town wall towards Navahermosa. After crossing bridge (Puente de San Martín) turn left; hotel on left after 2km (says 'Quinta de Mirabel' over entrance).

Entry no: 190   **Map no: 11**

Hostal Descalzos

Calle de los Descalzos 30
45002 Toledo

Tel: 925 222888
Fax: 925 222888
E-mail: h-descalzos@jet.es

Julio Luis García

Hostal Descalzos is very different from some of this book's grander hotels but having spent two happy nights here we feel that it, too, is 'special' enough to be included here – that is, providing you get a room with a view (ask for 'una habitación que tenga vista'). It sits high up by the old city wall, just yards from El Greco's house. There is nothing fancy about the place; fittings are modern and the combination of pine furniture and satiny curtains and bedspreads will win no prizes for (conventional) good taste. But the view – especially at night when the old bridge across the Tagus is illuminated – is what we will remember. When you book choose one of the smallish doubles at the front (like 31, 32, 41 or 42). The singles we saw were minuscule. The family who run the *hostal* are quiet, unassuming folk. They serve you breakfast in a tiny downstairs room; there is a photo-menu with 13 different breakfasts(!) and a cheap but adequate lunch and dinner are available in the recently opened cafeteria/restaurant. At the foot of the hostal is a pretty walled garden with a fountain and flowers, a place to sit out and watch the sun set over the Meseta after a day exploring the city.

Rooms: 12 with bath & wc.
Price: Double/Twin 6000-6500 Pts.
Breakfast: 500 Pts.
Meals: None available.
Closed: Never.

From Madrid N401 to Toledo, then follow signs to old town. At town walls (Puerta de la Bisagra) right; continue with wall on left until you see signs for Casa del Greco to left; hostal signposted off to right in front of Hotel Pintor El Greco.

Hotel Pintor El Greco

Calle Alamillos del Tránsito 13
45002 Toledo

Tel: 925 285191
Fax: 925 215819
E-mail: info@hotelpintorelgreco.com
Web: www.hotelpintorelgreco.com

Mariano Sánchez Torregrosa

At the heart of Toledo's old Jewish quarter, just yards from the El Greco house and synagogue museum, this small hotel, which was once a bakery, has had much praise heaped upon it – and rightly so. Restoration was completed less than ten years ago and both façade and patio have been handsomely returned to their former glory. Although the main building is 17th century, parts were already standing when Toledo was the capital of the Moorish kingdom; there is even an escape tunnel, built when the Inquisition was at work. The interior is cool, quiet and plush; most of the furniture is modern, there are lots of paintings and handicrafts by local artists, terracotta floors and plenty of greenery. Guest rooms are on three floors, wrapped around the inner patio; some have balconies. There are armchairs, thick Zamora blankets and more paintings; the colours are warm, beds have excellent mattresses and there is plenty of space to add extra beds if you are more than two. At breakfast there is fresh fruit juice, cheese and cold sausage as well as fresh bread – alas, no longer baked in situ. And there is a car park immediately in front of the hotel.

Rooms: 33 with bath & wc.
Price: Single 12080 Pts; Double/Twin 15100 Pts.
Breakfast: 850 Pts (buffet).
Meals: None available.
Closed: Never.

From Madrid N401 to Toledo, then follow signs to old town. At town walls right; continue with wall on left until roundabout. Left here and along to end of tree-lined avenue. Left through wall; along this street to Tránsito and hotel.

Entry no: 192

Map no: 11

Hostal del Cardenal

Paseo de Recaredo 24
45004 Toledo

Tel: 925 224900
Fax: 925 222991
E-mail: cardenal@macom.es
Web: www.cardenal.macom.es

Luis González

Bartolomé Cossio wrote of Toledo that "it is the city which offers the most complete and characteristic evidence of what was genuinely Spanish soil and civilisation". It remains a quintessentially Spanish place and it is tempting to stay at the Cardenal; like Cossio's city it seems to have absorbed the richest elements of Moorish and Christian Spain. It was built as a mansion house by the Archbishop of Toledo, Cardenal Lorenzana, in the 13th century. The gardens are unforgettable – fountains and ponds and geraniums and climbing plants set against the rich ochres of the brick. Go through the elegant main entrance to discover patios, screens, arches and columns. There are lounges with oil paintings and *mudéjar* brickwork. A peaceful mantle lies softly over it all; you hear the tock-tock of the grandfather clock. Wide *estera*-matted corridors and a domed staircase lead up to the rooms; they have latticed cupboards, tiled floors, sensitive lighting and heavy wooden furniture. You can choose between several small dining rooms where you can feast on roast lamb, suckling pig or stewed partridge. And the El Greco museum is just a short stroll away, through the fascinating streets of old Toledo.

Rooms: 25 with bath & wc; 2 suites.
Price: Single 6280-8500 Pts;
Double/Twin 10100-13700 Pts; Suite
13325-18700 Pts.
Breakfast: 975 Pts.
Meals: Lunch/Dinner 2675 Pts (M),
5000 Pts (C). Closed Xmas eve.
Closed: Never.

From Madrid N401 to Toledo. As you arrive at old town walls and Puerta de la Bisagra turn right; hotel 50m on left beside ramparts.

Map no: 11

Casa de la Torre
Antonio Machado 16
45820 El Toboso
Toledo

Tel: 925 568006
Fax: 925 568006
E-mail: info@casadelatorre.com
Web: www.casadelatorre.com

Isabel Fernández Morales

Recognise the chap beside the windmill in the photograph? It is, of course, El Quijote and many of his most famous misadventures are said to have taken place in this part of La Mancha; it was in El Toboso that he came to court Dulcinea, convinced she was a princess. Isabel Fernández is so passionate about the most universal of Cervante's literary creations that she organises "quixotic excursions" from her home, has dozens of paintings depicting events in his life and even recreates the sort of food that the knight errant might have eaten in her "literary cooking". In the best Spanish tradition dinner (accompanied by wines from the family *bodega*) is followed by a *tertulia* which means both 'chat' and 'discussion': the perfect occasion to quiz Isabel about the great bard. Afterwards, wend your way past family photographs via a cobbled inner patio, past potted aspidistra and family photos to your bedroom; it will have an antique bed, perhaps a marble-topped dresser or crocheted curtains and wonderful linen sheets. And at breakfast try Isabel's *arrope* on your oven-fresh bread, a spicy, honey-like condiment for spreading on toast. An unusual and fascinating stop-over.

Rooms: 8 with bath & wc.
Price: Twin 8000 Pts; Double 10000 Pts; Larger Double 15000 Pts.
Breakfast: Included.
Meals: Dinner 2500 Pts (M) incl. wine.
Closed: Never.

From Madrid NIV towards Córdoba. Exit towards Albacete. In Quintanar de la Orden right to El Toboso. As you arrive in village at fork by bar, right into Calle Antonio Machado. Straight along this road; house is on left.

Entry no: 194

Map no: 18

Casa Bermeja

Plaza del Piloncillo s/n
45572 Valdeverdeja
Toledo

Tel: 925 454586
Fax: 925 454595
E-mail: zabzab@arrakis.es

Angela González

Angela González happened upon this old house in a village that the twentieth
century seemed to have passed by. She'd found the place where a long-nurtured
dream could be realised: a house where her many friends could get together, far
from the noise and pollution of Madrid, to share food, conversation – and fun.
Luckily for us she later decided to share her home with paying guests too.
Architect brother Luis took renovation in hand: Angela, an interior designer, took
care of furnishings and fittings (you may not meet her unless you stay here at the
weekend). Beyond the exuberant red and cream façade with its stately entrance is a
truly coquettish home. The sun and red earth of Castille inspired the warm colours
chosen for paint and fabric. Antiques mingle with things 'designerish'; there's a
lofty lounge and dining room with beams above and terracotta beneath and
magazines and books in several languages. The apartments look onto the inner
patio; the rooms are in the main house: they are attractive, comfortable and
blissfully quiet. A wild and undiscovered corner of the Meseta and an
ornithological dreamland.

Rooms: 7 with bath & wc; 8 suite/studio
apartments.
Price: Double/Twin 11900-15200 Pts;
Suite/Apts 17000-26000 Pts.
Breakfast: Included.
Meals: Lunch/Dinner 2500 Pts (M).
Closed: Never.

From Madrid NV/E90 towards Badajoz.
Exit at km148 for Oropesa. From there to
Puente del Arzobispo and here, right to
Valdeverdeja. In main square, opposite 'Ayuntamiento', turn left to Casa Bermeja.

Map no: 16

Entry no: 195

Almería

•

Cádiz

•

Córdoba

•

Granada

•

Huelva

•

Jaén

•

Málaga

•

Seville

•

Andalusia

"As the Spanish proverb says, "He who would bring home the wealth of
the Indies, must carry the wealth of the Indies with him." So it is in travelling;
a man must carry knowledge with him, if he would bring home knowledge"
– Samuel Johnson

Casa Geminis

Carretera Mojácar-Turre
04638 Mojácar
Almería

Tel: 950 478013
E-mail: geha@computronx.com

Geoff & Eileen Howard-Ady

Mojácar, a pretty white hill village just back from the Med, was discovered in the sixties by a group of (mostly Spanish) painters. Anywhere you set up your easel was a 'cameo' view of a narrow street, a flower-filled balcony or a wonderful little square. Tourists followed, a resort was developed down by the sea, but the village has retained buckets of charm. Nowadays you are best visiting 'out of hours' so why not stay at this palm- and oleander-graced villa which is just a couple of miles out of town? The Howard-Adys are great entertainers and are legendary among their many friends for their hospitality. Eileen is a great cook whilst Geoff has an eye for what looks right in décor, design and presentation. Dinners are four courses-long and include wine and coffee; your hosts seem to enjoy these eat-togethers as much as their guests. There are just two guest rooms, each with its own entrance. They have bright duvet covers and curtains, rattan chairs and a host of electrical 'extras' like TVs, hairdryers, fridges, teas-mades and even an iron: the one at the back looks out to the mountains. If you prefer a day on the beach to one beside the pool a picnic hamper can be prepared.

Rooms: 2 with bath & wc.
Price: Double/Twin 7000-10000 Pts.
Breakfast: Included.
Meals: Lunch/Dinner 3000 Pts
inc. wine (M).
Closed: Never.

South on N340-E15 then exit 520
signposted Los Gallardos/Turre/Mojácar.
Then follow signs for Mojácar via Turre.
Casa Geminis is on right shortly before you
reach Mojácar.

Map no: 24

Entry no: 196

Mamabel's

Calle Embajadores 5
Mojácar Pueblo
04638 Mojácar
Almería

Tel: 950 472448
Fax: 950 472448
E-mail: mamabel@indalmedia.com

Isabel & Juan Carlos Aznar

Tourists discovered the charms of this pretty clifftop village long ago: it has become slightly touristy but it has kept its identity. So have Juan Carlos and his mother Isabel Aznar ('Mamabel') who always manage to greet you with a smile. Their small guesthouse has gradually been rebuilt and added to since Isabel came in the mid-sixties at the time when a growing number of artists were setting up home in Mojácar. The house is delightfully organic with stairways leading up and down and each room different from the next. They are prettily decorated with a rather feminine feel; number 1 is the grandest with its canopied bed, antique table and many knick-knacks; not a hint of 'hotel' here. But all of them are charming and we would all choose one of those with a terrace looking down to the glittering sea (our favourite is number 3). There is a cosy little dining room where there are stacks of paintings by Mamabel's husband, hand-painted chairs and simple food with an unmistakably Mediterranean flavour. If you head out for dinner there's lots of choice in the village. A casual and homely place: when you arrive drop your luggage at hotel and then look for a parking space.

Rooms: 8 with bath & wc; 1 'special' room.
Price: Double/Twin 7000-9000 Pts; Suite 8500-10500 Pts.
Breakfast: 800 Pts or 1100 Pts (full English).
Meals: Dinner 1800 Pts (M), 3000 Pts (C).
Closed: Never.

From N340/E15 exit 520 then towards Turre/Mojácar. Up into village of Mojácar; signposted to right.

Finca Listonero

Cortijo Grande   **Tel:** 950 479094
04639 Turre   **Fax:** 950 479094
Almería

Graeme Gibson & David Rice

Lovers of desert landscapes, their barrenness, aridity, sense of eternity and
proportion will be richly rewarded at the Finca Listonero with its wraparound
views of the Sierra Cabrera. For the sybaritic, this sensitively extended pink
(original colour) farmhouse has all the luxuries. David and Graeme, cultured and
gourmet Anglo-Australians, have lavished huge affection on this conversion. This
and their attention to guests make it very special. Bougainvillaea defies the dry
sierra with every flower; the delightful dining and drawing rooms, the fern-filled
atrium, the antiques and *objets* impose grandeur on lowly origins. Guest rooms are
all differently decorated and furnished. Breakfast is an easy-going occasion while
dinner is definitely a serious matter with a mix of regional and international dishes
(ingredients from the garden, fish delivered fresh from the port), great home-made
puds and a good selection of wines. There is good walking in the cooler months,
you are not far from the sea and horse-riding can be arranged.

Rooms: 5 with bath or shower & wc.
Price: Twin 14000 Pts.
Breakfast: Included.
Meals: Lunch light meals; Dinner 4500 Pts
(M). Closed on Sundays.
Closed: Never.

From N340/E15 exit 520 towards
Turre/Mojácar. 3km on, right through
entrance to Cortijo Grande. Finca
signposted on right after approx. 3.5km.

Hostal Family

Calle La Lomilla s/n
04149 Agua Amarga
Almería

Tel: 950 138014
Fax: 950 138070
E-mail: riovall@teleline.es

Marcos, René & Michèle Maingnon Salmeron

Gentle-mannered Frenchman René Salmeron came to Agua Amarga on holiday and, instantly seduced by what was then a little-known fishing village, dreamed of coming to live and work here. And here he is running this simple whitewashed *hostal* and restaurant and making new friends, just behind one of the area's most seductive beaches. A bumpy track leads you to the building which has recently acquired a second floor; rooms at the front have sea views. Downstairs and upstairs rooms are simply furnished with all-wooden furniture and thick, Alpujarran blankets as bedspreads. In the rather kitsch courtyard restaurant (covered in winter) you can expect to eat well; René's food is "Mediterranean with a French touch" – his home-made pâté makes a delicious entrée. There are decent breakfasts with home-made jams, yoghurt and fruit – or tortillas if you prefer. Do stay at least a couple of nights and explore the nearby Cabo de Gata National Park: the walking is wonderful. Even if Agua Amarga is is more developed than when René first came it remains an enchanting spot.

Rooms: 9 with bath & wc.
Price: Double/Twin 8000-12000 Pts incl. VAT.
Breakfast: Included.
Meals: Lunch/Dinner 2300 Pts (M); lunch weekends only.
Closed: Never.

From N344 exit 494 for Venta del Pobre/Carboneras. Continue towards Carboneras then right towards Agua Amarga. Signposted to right in village.

Entry no: 199

Map no: 24

Cortijo El Sotillo

Carretera de San José s/n
San José
04118 Nijar
Almería

Tel: 950 611100
Fax: 950 611105
E-mail: sotillo@a2000.es

María Torres

San José is one of the few village's on Andalusia's tourist-battered coastline which has managed to remain both attractive and, thank heavens, Spanish too. People come for its quiet marina, uncrowded beaches, coastal walks and the lunaresque landscapes of the Cabo de Gata Natural Park; the ornithologist count shoots upwards when migrating flamingos put on their annual display of pinkiness and grace. The old farm of El Sotillo is half a mile from the village, an attractive cluster of low, white, ranch-style buildings. The place is known for its equestrian centre but archery, tennis and cycling are also on offer. The lounge and restaurant are airy, high-ceilinged spaces; you dine on a mix of creative and traditional food with fish the obvious first choice. The adjacent bar/cafeteria has a cosier feel thanks to its old farm instrumentalia and tack, inglenook fireplace and locally-woven curtains and upholstery. Guest rooms are large, clean and functional with stable-doors leading out to a small patio. Walk along the rugged coastline, swim at near-deserted beaches (on a clear day you can see all the way to Africa) and visit Nijar if you like folksy ceramics.

Rooms: 17 with bath & wc; 3 suites.
Price: Double/Twin 16000 Pts.
Breakfast: 1000 Pts.
Meals: Lunch/Dinner from 1400 Pts (C).
Closed: Never.

From Murcia south on E15/N340 then E15/N344. Exit for Nijar, then follow signs for San José via Frailes de la Boca through El Pozo de los Frailes. El Sotillo signposted on left 1.8km after you leave El Pozo.

Map no: 24   **Entry no: 200**

La Fuente del Madroño

Fuente del Madroño 6
11159 Los Caños de Meca
Cádiz

Tel: 956 437067 or 649 780834
Fax: 956 437233
E-mail: karen@jet.es
Web: web.jet.es/karen

Karen Abrahams

Far less 'hotelly' than most places in this book, this could be a good place to kick back for a few days – or more. Karen worked in the music business before seeing in this group of old farm buildings an outlet for her desire to create something new and interesting. Her guest accommodation, set back from the Atlantic, has grown organically over the years and so you choose between several different types of living space. *Casa Karen 1 & 2* are more independent while rooms and apartments in the *Casa del Monte* and *Casa del Medio* are better if you want to be more sociable. Decoration takes its inspiration from the local surroundings; local here means Andalusian and Moroccan – the high mountains of the Magreb are visible on clear days from the garden. The place attracts people with a creative impulse and the atmosphere is very informal, like that of Caños itself, which is popular with young travellers. There is walking in the Natural Park just behind Caños and Karen will tell you where to eat the best fish. If self-catering seems daunting a friend can come and cook for you (veggie, organic) and a massage with aromatic oils is always available as well as reiki and yoga sessions.

Rooms: 4 houses, 1 studio & 1 trad. style thatched house.
Price: Double/Twin 5200 Pts; Studio 6600-9800 Pts; 1 bed house 7400-11000 Pts; 2 bed house 10400-15900 Pts; thatched house 6000-9000 Pts.
Breakfast: Self-catering.
Meals: Self-catering.
Closed: Never.

From Cádiz N340 towards Tarifa. At km35 turn right for Vejer de la Frontera and at first roundabout right towards Los Caños de Meca. Here pass turn for Faro Trafalgar and after approx. 500m turn left onto track at sign 'apartamentos and bungalows'. Signposted.

Entry no: 201   **Map no: 22**

Hotel Madreselva
Calle Real 1
11160 Barbate
Cádiz

Tel: 956 454033
Fax: 956 433770
E-mail:
hotel-madreselva@worldonline.es
Web: www.madreselvahotel.com

James Whaley

James Whaley has the alchemist's touch; a gift for turning that which at first seems uninteresting into something of a wholly different nature. He managed it brilliantly at the Hurricane Hotel (also in this book) and at Madreselva he has again turned a bog-standard *hostal* into a place where you'd want to stay. Barbate isn't known as a destination yet you are close to one of the coast's most beautiful stretches of beach and there are a couple of brilliant fish restaurants where you'll hear nothing but Spanish being spoken. Although one of the main roads through town wraps round two sides of the building good insulation means that traffic noise isn't a nuisance in the lounge or the bedrooms. Decoration is fresh, clean and simple with one of James' old-favourite surfboards adding a more exotic note – as do Moroccan lamps and the painted furniture. The bar serves breakfasts, drinks and *raciones* throughout the day. The hotel can organise tuition in wind or kite-surfing with their 'itinerant van' which takes you straight to where the waves are doing it. Madreselva, like Barbate, has an off-beat personality all of its own.

Rooms: 9 with bath & wc.
Price: Double/Twin 7500-9500 Pts.
Breakfast: Included.
Meals: Tapas and snacks in hotel bar.
Closed: Never.

From Cádiz south on N340 towards Algeciras. Just past Véjer de la Frontera right to Barbate. As you arrive in Véjer continue straight across at roundabout and on up hill to hotel.

Map no: 22   Entry no: 202

Hotel Restaurante Antonio

Bahia de la Plata
Atlanterra km 1
11393 Zahara de los Atunes
Cádiz

Tel: 956 439141/439346
Fax: 956 439135
E-mail: hotantonio@bbvnet.com

Antonio Mota

A short drive from the workaday little fishing village of Zahara de los Atunes, and with a garden that leads straight out to one of the best beaches on the Atlantic coast, Antonio Mota's hotel is in a very special position. Few foreigners seem to be in the know, but this family-run hotel is deservedly popular with the Spanish. It is an utterly southern hotel: repro prints of some rather sugary subjects (swans etc) and other rather grisly ones (bullfighting). Rooms and restaurant are light, clean and functional; expect the fish to be memorable and prices more than reasonable. It is unusual to come across so hearty a breakfast in Spain: eggs, fruit, cheeses and hams. Some rooms give onto an inner patio with fountain, palms and geraniums; pretty enough, but we'd prefer a room with a small terrace looking out over the palm-filled gardens to the sea. Some rooms have a lounge-cum-second bedroom, ideal for families. And there are horses for hire – try and stay at least two nights and ride (or walk) along the beach to Bolonia, where there are Roman ruins and more good restaurants. Old faithfuls return time and again.

Rooms: 25 with bath & wc; 5 suites.
Price: Single 52500-9250 Pts; Double/Twin 9000-13000 Pts; Suite 11000-16000 Pts.
Breakfast: 1200 Pts.
Meals: Lunch/Dinner 2500 Pts (M), 3500 Pts (C).
Closed: January.

From Algeciras E5/N340 to Cádiz. 25km after Tarifa take left turning to Barbate and Zahara on left after 10km. Hotel signposted in village.

Entry no: 203

Map no: 22

Valdevaqueros

Ctra Cádiz-Málaga km 74   **Tel:** 956 236705
11380 Tarifa   **Fax:** 956 236705 or 956 684919
Cádiz

José Ramón Vázquez Fernández

Valdevaqueros stands just yards back from a mighty sweep of surf and sand, right next to the Mistral surf school; if you fancy trying wind, kite or fly-surfing this is the place to stay. It is more *hostal* than hotel and would appeal to younger travellers rather than those who like things to be 'just so'; the atmosphere is very informal and laid-back, reminiscent of places you may have stayed at in south-east Asia. From the outside the building has a not-quite-finished look but the bedrooms feel just fine. They are high-ceilinged with Moroccan lamps, antique bedsteads and have bead curtains separating the bathroom from the main living space. If you can put up with a cracked tile or two for the pleasure of hearing the waves thumping down just yards away then you would like Valdevaqueros. Just outside is a bamboo-covered terrace, a great place for a sundowner and the restaurant/bar area also has a good feel with its driftwood sculpture, bench tables and good music; vegetarians will appreciate the high salad quotient. Let José Ramón know if you'd like a full meal; this quietly-mannered, very *simpático* Spaniard will get something good together.

Rooms: 7 with bath & wc; 1 apartment.
Price: Double/Twin 9000-12000 incl. VAT.
Breakfast: Included.
Meals: Lunch/Dinner 1000-1250 Pts (M),
2500-3000 Pts (C).
Closed: 1 November-Easter.

From Algeciras N340 towards Cádiz. Turn left for Valdevaqueros shortly after passing the Hurricane, opposite Restaurante Copacabana.

Map no: 22   **Entry no: 204**

Hurricane Hotel

Carretera de Málaga a Cádiz
11380 Tarifa
Cádiz

Tel: 956 684919
Fax: 956 680329
E-mail: info@hotelhurricane.com
Web: www.hotelhurricane.com

James Whaley

You could be on a film set as you look through the Hurricane's high arches to the palm trees, the glinting ocean and beyond to the Rif rising on the African shore. But despite echoes of Al Andalus, this place is anchored in surf culture – the best waves in Europe pound down just yards from the restaurant and there is a definite whiff of California (fully-equipped gym, two pools, windsurfing school, horses and mountain bikes). The feel of the East is strongest in the guest rooms. They are uncluttered, decorated with geometric designs and whirling fans: perhaps a keyhole arch over the bath or an oriental couch with cotton bolsters – reminiscent of palace hotels in Rajasthan. Sea-facing rooms are preferable: the busy N340 might disturb Arabian-night dreams on the other side. The food is an interesting mix of America, Spain and the East. Ingredients are fresh (fish of the day, home-made pasta, herbs from the garden), there are Louisiana prawns with basmati rice, spicy chicken with Peruvian sauce and good vegetarian dishes. The quality, the views, the furnishings make it worth the price and it would be wonderful to ride out from the Hurricane along the beach and up into the mountains.

Rooms: 35 with bath & wc.
Price: Double 11000-19000 Pts; Suite 20000-33000 Pts.
Breakfast: Included.
Meals: Lunch 2000 Pts (M);
Dinner 4000 Pts (C).
Closed: Never.

From Cádiz, N340 south. Hurricane is 7km before Tarifa on the right.

100% Fun

Carretera Cádiz – Málaga km 76
11380 Tarifa
Cádiz

Tel: 956 680330
Fax: 956 680013
E-mail: 100x100@tnet.es
Web: www.tarifa.net/100fun

Ula Walters & Barry Pussell

With a name like this you expect something out of the ordinary – and this young, distinctly wacky hotel should catch your imagination. The busy N340 lies between it and that oh-so-desirable surf but, in the exuberant greenery of the garden with thatched roofs overhead, we felt we were in deepest Mexico... or an Amazonian lodge... or was it Polynesia? Amazing to have transformed a bog-standard roadside hostel into something quite as spicy as this. The decoration is like the nearby Hurricane's, only simpler with a pleasing combination of floor tiles, warm ochres and fans to beat the sizzling summers. The rooms have a fresh, almost spartan feel, comfortable beds and terraces over the garden. There are gurgling fountains, a swimming pool and an airy restaurant serving spicy Tex-Mex dishes as well as some interesting vegetarian alternatives. It also has the best-equipped surf shop on the Tarifa coast, selling the owner's hand-crafted windsurfing boards. Especially good value out of (surf) season, this is a young, fun hotel!

Rooms: 16 with bath & wc.
Price: Single 6900-8900 Pts;
Double/Twin 8900-10900 Pts;
Quadruple 11900-15900 Pts incl. VAT.
Breakfast: 800 Pts.
Meals: Lunch/Dinner 2500 Pts (C).
Restaurant closed Nov-end March.
Closed: January & February.

From Cádiz N340 towards Algeciras. At beginning of Tarifa Beach, hotel flagged on left, next to La Enseñada (10km north of Tarifa) close to km76 post.

Hotel Casa Señorial La Solana

Carretera Cádiz-Málaga   **Tel:** 956 780236
N340 km 116.5 North Side   **Fax:** 956 780236
11360 San Roque
Cádiz

José Antonio Ceballos

An unmistakably Spanish house, La Solana was built for a noble family in the 18th century. It stands grandly in 14 hectares of lush gardens and parkland; brilliant southern blooms climb the façade. The beautifully glazed door beckons you in: it was restored just over a decade ago by the owner, an artist and sculptor, with great sensitivity. The house's overhanging eaves and the covered patio inside give it a distinctly colonial air. The interior is finely furnished with 16th-and 17th-century antiques from Spain's 'golden' age, a profusion of carved wood, rich rugs, velvets and brocades, crystal chandeliers and heavy wardrobes. Bedrooms are furnished with a mixture of old and less old pieces and the bathrooms are thoroughly modern. The bright 'white villages' of the Grazalema Sierra and the lesser-known beaches of the Atlantic coast are within reach: after a day of discovering these hidden treasures it is an extra joy to return to the secluded comfort of this country mansion. Although central heating has recently been added some readers have felt that a slight air of neglect is creeping in: please let us know.

Rooms: 18 with bath & wc; 6 suites.
Price: Single 8000 Pts; Double/Twin 10000 Pts; Suite 12000 Pts incl. VAT.
Breakfast: Included.
Meals: Dinner 3500 Pts. Closed on Mondays.
Closed: Never.

From Málaga take N340 towards Algeciras. Leave road at km116.5 and follow signs to hotel for 0.8km. (Or coming from Cádiz leave at exit 117, then U-turn).

Entry no: 207   Map no: 22

Monte de la Torre

Apartado 66
11370 Los Barrios
Cádiz

Tel: 956 660000
Fax: 956 634863
E-mail: mdlt@mercuryin.es
Web: www.andalucia.com/montedelatorre

Sue & Quentin Agnew-Larios

Quentin Agnew's family has farmed this estate for generations. It is puzzling to come across this utterly Edwardian building in the very south of Spain; it was built by the British when they were pushing the railway through the mountains to Ronda. This commingling of northern architecture and southern vegetation and climate is every bit as seductive as it is unexpected. The house stands alone on a hill, surrounded by palm trees, with views across the Gibraltar hinterland towards Morocco. The drawing room is panelled, the dining room elegant; there are masses of books, family portraits, a grandfather clock and dogs... this is a home, not a hotel. The bedrooms (reached by a grand staircase) are high-ceilinged, decorated with family heirlooms and have period bathrooms – a festival of tubs and taps. Each is different, all are lovely. The apartments are in the former servants quarters; lucky servants' if they could stay here now! Sue and Quentin are gracious hosts and although only breakfast is on offer, within the grounds of the estate, just 700m away, is a marvellous restaurant (shut on Sundays) which serves a fillet steak whose fame has crossed oceans.

Rooms: 3 with bath or shower;
2 apartments in house.
Price: Double/Twin 17000-20000 Pts;
Apartment (for 4/5) 85000-250000 Pts
weekly incl. VAT.
Breakfast: Included.
Meals: None available.
Closed: 15 December-15 January.

From Málaga N340 towards Algeciras.
8km after San Roque right on C440
towards Jerez; take first exit for Los Barrios and in town at roundabout with
fountains turn left and continue 3km; at stone marker right into main drive.
1km to house.

Map no: 22   **Entry no: 208**

El Antiguo Juzgado

Calle San Sebastian 15
11330 Jimena de la Frontera
Cádiz

Tel: 956 641317
Fax: 956 640944
E-mail: becko@mercuryin.es

Peter & Monica Becko

El Antiguo Juzgado was probably once a part of the church of Santa María whose tower stands alongside the building. It later became the local courthouse – hence the name. Peter and Monica Becko are musicians; between them they cover an impressive range of instruments and both give classes. Their home would be a perfect place for musicians to holiday: they love guests to join in with their choral and instrumental get-togethers, their motto being *música sin fronteras*. Of the four apartments (each named after a Spanish composer) the best are on the first floor which are high-ceilinged with marvellous old doors and retain their 18th century plasterwork. The very low ceilings of the attic floor apartment wouldn't be for everybody. They are decked out with durries, richly coloured bedspreads, books, country-style beds and chests and fully equipped kitchens. Although we don't usually list self-catering places, we happily include the Antiguo Juzgado because the Beckos provide you with all of the ingredients for a good breakfast. Non-musicians would enjoy it, too; the walking is marvellous and Jimena has some excellent restaurants. *No smoking in the house.*

Rooms: 4 apartments.
Price: *Minimum stay 3 days.* Double/Twin for 3 days 18000-22000 Pts; Double/Twin for 1 week 38000-48500 Pts; Double/Twin for 2 weeks 70000-90000 Pts.
Breakfast: Included.
Meals: Self-catering.
Closed: Never.

Arriving in Jimena continue up hill past Bar Cuenca. Opposite very first shops left into large parking area just beneath the church. Calle San Sebastian runs up hill just to left of church; house is on the right.

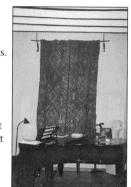

Rancho Los Lobos

11339 Estación de Jimena de la Frontera
Cádiz

Tel: 956 640429
Fax: 956 641180
E-mail: loslobos@teleline.es
Web: www.teleline.terra.es/personal/loslobos

Wolf & Esther Zissler

It's all about the great outdoors at Los Lobos, an old farmstead in a valley just outside the beautiful white village of Jimena de la Fontera (these 'de la frontera' villages once marked the boundary between Christian and Moorish Spain). Wolf and Esther came in the early eighties and gradually converted a series of outbuildings to house their guests and their horses: riding is their first love. Saddle up and head out through old oak forests, stopping to swim (with your horse) in deep river pools. If you're not horsey choose between mountain-biking, hiking, tennis, swimming and Russian bowling. You eat in the old farm kitchen around bench-tables – or across the courtyard in a larger dining room with a log fire in the colder months. Picnics can be prepared and dinner (perhaps after a sauna and an aperitif in the stable bar which has an unusual collection of memorabilia) combines Swiss and traditional Spanish food: it is wholesome rather than gourmet. Breakfast suffers because margarine rather than butter is on the table. Bedrooms are smallish, simply furnished with bright rugs and small bath/shower rooms. Wolf and Esther make a huge effort to make your stay a memorable one.

Rooms: 8 with bath or shower & wc;
1 apartment.
Price: Double/Twin 8000-12000 Pts;
Apartment (for 2) 12000 Pts incl. VAT.
Breakfast: Included.
Meals: Light lunches 550 Pts; dinner 2000
Pts (M).
Closed: Never.

Arriving in Jimena left at Bar Cuenca then
right past Guardia Civil building. Cross bridge and follow track until farm on right. (Phone and Wolf will fax you a map.)

Map no: 22

Entry no: 210

Hostal El Anón
Calle Consuelo 34-40
11330 Jimena de la Frontera
Cádiz

Tel: 956 640113/640416
Fax: 956 641110
E-mail: elanon@mx3.redestb.es
Web: www.andalucia.com/
jimena/hostalanon/info.htm

**Gabriel Delgado &
Suzanna Odell**

Five village houses and stables have been joined to make an organic whole of changing levels, interconnecting patios and intimate terraces. It is a delicious little piece of authentic Spain. Suzanna is warm, relaxed and welcoming. She has lived in Jimena for years and knows the people and country like her own. She will disentangle the rich web of local history for you while organising horse-riding or advising on painting, bird-watching, walking and flora-spotting expeditions. The countryside has treasures galore for nature-lovers. See it from the little rooftop swimming pool where the eye travels over the roofs of Jimena and across to Gibraltar. Dine off spare ribs or *tapas* among geraniums on the terrace. Enjoy the cool peace of the arched main courtyard and the exotic banana and custard-fruit trees, rejoice in the rich furnishings collected over the years (wall-hangings, paintings, imaginative sculptural bits and pieces) and the heavy beams and low ceilings of the old buildings. Come and soak up quantities of Spanishness in an easy-going, cosmopolitan, atmosphere.

Rooms: 11 with bath & wc; 1 suite.
Price: Single 4500 Pts; Double/Twin 8000 Pts;
Suite 9100 Pts incl. VAT.
Breakfast: 400 Pts.
Meals: Lunch/Dinner approx
3000 Pts (C). Bar snacks also available. Restaurant &
bar closed on Wednesdays.
Closed: 20 June-20 July.

From Málaga N340 towards Algeciras. At r'bout in Pueblo Nuevo de Guadiaro right for San Martín del Tesorillo and on to Jimena; in village centre left by taxi rank and 2nd right.

Entry no: 211

Map no: 22

Posada La Casa Grande

Calle Fuentenueva 42
11330 Jimena de la Frontera
Cádiz

Tel: 956 640578
Fax: 956 640491
E-mail: tcag@retemail.es
Web: www.posadalacasagrande.com

**Oonagh Luke &
Tom Andrésen-Gosselin**

Jimena is one of the most spectacular of the white villages: a cluster of whitewashed houses fan out around a limestone crag topped by a Moorish castle. The two Toms (father and son) have lived in the village for many years. The restoration of this grand old village house took eight years and hats off to them for creating a hostelry that feels much more home than hotel. There's an easy, informal atmosphere at La Casa Grande: you may well be greeted by loud pop music. Pass through a flagged courtyard with an exuberant honeysuckle to find an enormous guest lounge and, up another level, the reading room with hundreds of books. The base elements are those you expect in the south: wafer bricking, tiled floors, potted palms, heavy old beams. We liked the bedrooms: clean and comfortable and little matter that they share bathrooms. Breakfast is the only meal served but with a lively bar next door which serves the best *tapas* in the village (Tom would say "in Spain"!) you're off to a flying start and there are plenty of restaurants in the village. The mighty Atlantic is close by and the walking round here is fantastic: don't miss the climb up to the castle for an unbelievable sunset.

Rooms: 7 sharing 3 bathrooms & wcs; 1 suite.
Price: Single 3500-4000; Double/Twin 5000 Pts; Suite 8000-12000 Pts.
Breakfast: 750 Pts.
Meals: None available.
Closed: Never.

From Málaga N340 towards Cádiz. Right via San Martín del Tesorillo towards Ronda. In Jimena follow main street all way through village; last (sharp) right down to Casa Grande on right.

Map no: 22

Entry no: 212

Hostal Casa de las Piedras

Calle las Piedras 32
11610 Grazalema
Cádiz

Tel: 956 132014/132323
Fax: 956 132014/132238

Rafael & Katy Lirio Sánchez

Grazalema is one of the most dazzling of Andalusia's mountain villages, clinging to grey and ochre cliffs and dominated by craggy peaks that are home to eagles and mountain goats. A special place with a special *hostal*, half of which is in a grand 300-year-old house (witness to the days when a thriving weaving industry made many a Grazalema fortune) where rooms vary in size, are full of family antiques and loaded with charm. The new half, built and decorated in traditional style, has 16 simple and attractive rooms with their own bathrooms and central heating (temperatures can drop sharply during winter nights). Some have views across the terracotta roofs to the mountains beyond. Rafael and Katy are the nicest of hosts and serve much-appreciated local dishes in their lively restaurant. Don't miss the wild thistle or asparagus omelettes (in the right season), roast partridge or quail, or trout baked with a slice of mountain ham. This is a base for walkers with a healthy appetite and breakfast is appropriately hearty. An unassuming and charming place with owners who understand the art of good, old-fashioned inn-keeping.

Rooms: 16 with bath or shower & wc and 16 sharing.
Price: Double/Twin 5500 Pts incl. VAT.
Breakfast: 550 Pts.
Meals: Lunch/Dinner 1300 Pts (M), 3500 Pts (C) incl. VAT.
Closed: Never.

From Ronda, C339 towards Sevilla. After about 14km left to Grazalema. Enter main square & turn directly right up street beside Unicaja. Hotel is 100m up on right.

Entry no: 213

Map no: 22

Hacienda Buena Suerte

Apartado 60
11650 Villamartín
Cádiz

Tel: 956 231286
Fax: 956 231275
E-mail: hacienda@dysli.net
Web: www.dysli.net

Magda & Jean-Claude Dysli

What a grand arrival! As you pass under the great portal and up the drive you feel the marriage of Andalusia's past – the great estates or *latifundia* – and its present – Judas trees, bougainvillaea, palm trees, whitewash and terracotta tiles. All this in the loveliest of settings – the gently rolling olive groves and wheat fields of the foothills of the Grazalema mountains. But the real star here is the horse. Groups of riders come to learn with owners Jean-Claude and Magda Dysli who are rarely out of the saddle, either teaching in the riding school or trekking in the hills with their guests. Non-riders are also very welcome and there are lovely walks from the farm. The rooms, most of them in the converted granary, are large and simply furnished, decorated – naturally – with prints of horses and riders and with animal skins on the floors. You may find sweets on pillows or a candle in the corner. Meals, taken round the huge dining table, are 'international' – everything from goulash to bouillabaisse to couscous, all with organic ingredients.

Rooms: 12 with bath & wc.
Price: Single 7000 Pts; Double/Twin 12000 Pts.
Breakfast: Included.
Meals: Lunch 2500-3000 Pts (M/C).
Closed: Never.

From Ronda, C339 towards Sevilla. At junction with N342, left towards Jerez. 7km before Villamartín, left at sign for El Bosque and Ubrique. Buena Suerte is about 1.5km along on the left.

Map no: 22

Entry no: 214

Hacienda El Santiscal

Avenida El Santiscal 129
(Lago de Arcos)
11630 Arcos de la Frontera
Cádiz

Tel: 956 708313
Fax: 956 708268
E-mail: santiscal@gadesinfo.com
Web: www.gadesinfo.com/santiscal

Francisca 'Paqui' Gallardo

After many years of working with tourists Paqui and Rocío Gallardo, the dynamic managers of El Santiscal, had a very clear idea of what a small hotel should be. Much the sort of thing that we look for too. This grand old *cortijo* is a short drive from Arcos yet in a place of perfect quiet. The building has been sensitively converted from a forgotten family home into an elegant but simple hotel. The building is Andalusian to the core: an austere whitewashed façade, a grand portal and then the blissful peace and cool of the inner sanctum of the central courtyard. Each of the rooms leads off the patio (and nearly all have views out across the estate too). All have a slightly different feel, but scrupulous attention to detail is a leitmotiv: matching fabrics, lovely old beds, terracotta floors and good bathrooms. The suite was really special, we thought, and probably worth the extra if you are feeling flush. Either dine in on classical Andalusian dishes or head up to wonderful old Arcos where there are loads of interesting *tapas* bars and a couple of good restaurants.

Rooms: 11 with bath & wc; 1 suite.
Price: Twin 10000-16000 Pts; Suite 16000-24000 Pts.
Breakfast: 1250 Pts.
Meals: Lunch/Dinner 3500 Pts (M).
Closed: 10-20 January.

From Arcos C334 towards El Bosque. 1km after crossing bridge turn left into Urbanización Dominio El Santiscal and follow signs (carefully) to El Santiscal.

Entry no: 215

Map no: 22

Hotel Los Olivos del Convento

Paseo de Boliches 30
11630 Arcos de la Frontera
Cádiz

Tel: 956 700811
Fax: 956 702018
E-mail: mmoreno0237@viautil.com

María Moreno Moreno & José Antonio Roldán Caro

Just off a street leading to the old quarter of Arcos, Los Olivos is an unmistakably Andalusian townhouse. A huge oak door leads you into the hotel and a cool wicker-furnished lounge; beyond it is an arched inner courtyard with geraniums, aspidistra and palms: rather colonial in feel. The bedrooms all give onto this light, airy courtyard and some have views across gentle hills and olive groves, down towards the Atlantic. If you're a light sleeper choose a room at the back; they are very quiet. All the bedrooms have high ceilings and a pleasant mix of old and modern furniture. You can breakfast on the patio until the hotter summer days chase you indoors – to the air-conditioned lounge. The staff seem to genuinely enjoy their work and their eagerness to help you is reflected in the hotel's participation in the scheme offering visitors free guided tours of Arcos (twice daily in season). The old town with its arches (*arcos*) and narrow winding streets is just a short walk from Los Olivos and so too is the restaurant 'El Convento' which is also managed by the hotels owners: the food is excellent and has won many prizes. *The hotel has its own car park.*

Rooms: 19 with bath & wc.
Price: Single 5000-6000 Pts;
Double/Twin 8000-10000 Pts incl. VAT.
Breakfast: 900 Pts.
Meals: Sister restaurant – Lunch/Dinner
2500 Pts (M), 3000-3500 Pts (C).
Closed: Never.

In Arcos, follow signs for 'Conjunto Monumenta'/Parador. As you climb up into town following one-way system, hotel is on left of road parallel to main street.

El Convento

Calle Maldonado 2   **Tel:** 956 702333
11630 Arcos de la Frontera   **Fax:** 956 704128
Cádiz

María Moreno Moreno & José Antonio Roldán Caro

Arcos is spread like icing along the top of a craggy limestone outcrop. It was a great stronghold when Moors and Christians fought over the ever-shifting *frontera*. The Convento, a former cloister, is perched right at the edge of the cliff in the centre of the old town. Behind the plain white façade is a deliciously labyrinthine hotel some of whose rooms have terraces over the cliff where watching the sun set will make your heart soar. José Roldán Caros is proud of his home town and he and his wife have filled their hotel with works by local artists. Decoration varies in the original part of the hotel while in the newly opened annexe just across the rooftop terrace, furnishings are much smarter. Breakfast is served in an attractive beamed dining room-cum-bar and there's a large terrace above – a perfect spot for a sundowner and for watching the aerobatics of the kestrels which nest in the cliffs below. José Antonio and María own a restaurant in the covered colonnaded patio of a 16th-century palace just up the road (see photo) where you can taste some of the best food in the Province of Cadiz.

Rooms: 11 with bath & wc.
Price: Single 5000-8000 Pts; Double/Twin 7000-12000 Pts.
Breakfast: 800 Pts.
Meals: Sister restaurant – Lunch/Dinner 3000 Pts (M), 4000 Pts (C).
Closed: Never.

In Arcos, follow signs to Parador/Plaza del Cabildo. Here park in front of Santa María church then walk along Calle Escribanos and at end turn right into Calle Maldonado.

La Casa Grande
Maldonado 10
11630 Arcos de la Frontera
Cádiz

Tel: 956 703930
Fax: 956 703930
E-mail: lacasagrande@lacasagrande.net
Web: www.lacasagrande.net

Elena Posa

Arcos, like the better known 'white town' of Ronda, is strung out along the top of a high limestone cliff. La Casa Grande nudges right up to its very edge and you couldn't wish for a more spectacular position: from its terrace-of-terraces at night you look out to two floodlit churches and for mile after mile across the surrounding plain. The house is almost three hundred years old and many of the original features have survived to tell the tale. In true *Andaluz* style a central, colonnaded, plant-filled patio is the axis around which the house turns; vaulted reception rooms lead off to all sides. A cosy lounge doubles as a library; there are thousands of books, some of them written by Elena who is a journalist and who has also worked in theatre, radio and TV. The decoration of the house reflects her and her husband's cosmopolitan taste. Moroccan lamps, prints by Hockney or Bacon, perhaps a Habitat lamp or chair or a woven rug from Arcos: it feels both stylish and homely. The guest rooms do too; antiquey bits and pieces like a Deco writing table might be topped by a designerish lamp. How wonderful to breakfast or have a light *tapas* supper on that unforgettable roof terrace!

Rooms: 1 with bath & wc; 2 suites.
Price: Double 11000 Pts; Suite (sleeps up to 4) 11500-14000 Pts.
Breakfast: 750 Pts.
Meals: Tapas-style lunches and suppers.
Closed: 15 December-15 February.

Arriving in Arcos follow signs to Parador. Park in square immediately in front of Parador and then walk to end of Calle Escribano (just to left of Parador), turn right, pass Hotel El Convento then turn left. La Casa Grande is on the right.

La Casa del Curandero

Urbanización San Marcos /
Cuesta de la Escalera
Ctra Arcos-El Bosque km 5.5
Arcos de la Frontera
Cádiz

Tel: 956 231204
Fax: 956 231204
E-mail: arcosexp@viautil.com
Web: www.whitevillagewalks.com

Anne Lacy and David Lanfear

La Casa del Cuandero is in the last reaches of the rolling Jérez campiña: its landscape is much gentler than the jaggedy limestone and dolomite of the Grazalema Park which lies just beyond. David and Anne came to Spain in the mid-eighties and for many years ran a language school in nearby Arcos. He is one of the few official non-Spanish park guides in Spain, no mean achievement in a country with a long tradition of nepotism. The rustic-style furniture, Moroccan lamps and farmhouse-kitchen of the main house feel snug and authentic; large picture windows lead to a terrace from where there are views up to Arcos. Guest rooms have been set among the surrounding pines and orange orchard; they look poolwards, their decoration again mixes things Spanish and North African and they have simple tiled shower rooms. Life at La Casa del Curandero is lived *en famille* with the Lanfears and their young children; they find time to help you plan your forays (guided by David or with walking notes provided) or onward travel from them. The house takes its name from the natural healer who once lived here; these alternative doctors are still a part of life in the sierras of the south.

Rooms: 2 with bath & wc; 1 apartment
Price: Double/Twin 6000 Pts;
Apartment 7000 Pts.
Breakfast: Included.
Meals: None available.
Closed: 21 December-6 January.

From Arcos A382 towards Antequera and then almost immediately right towards El Bosque/Ubrique on A372. Pass lake and petrol station and continue along a very straight section of the road. At beginning of lane for slow vehicles right at sign for 'Girasol' onto old road and after 300m at another 'Girasol' sign right again along track. House is the 5th on left.

Cortijo Barranco

Apartado de Correos 169
11630 Arcos de la Frontera
Cádiz

Tel: 956 231402
Fax: 956 231209

María José Gil Amián

Barranco stands alone, high on a hillside, across from the lovely 'white' town of Arcos de la Frontera. Getting here is quite an adventure: once you leave the main road and follow the winding track up through the olive groves you feel you are leaving the real world behind. This is every inch the classic *cortijo* – private living quarters and (former) stables wrapped around a sheltered courtyard. The farm's guest rooms and apartment are soberly decorated with terracotta floors, wrought iron bedsteads, heavy linen curtains and hand-crocheted and knitted bedspreads. The whole place is uncannily quiet: pin back your ears to hear the owls hoot or the birds hymn the dawn. The sitting room is enormous with space for a billiard table and most memorable of all is the dining room with a gallery, a lofty beamed ceiling and an open hearth at one end. Breakfast at Barranco is disappointing and when you stay here you have little contact with the owners who prefer to get on with their own lives. But it is wonderful to stroll out from the farm at sunset and abandon yourself to the beauty of the surrounding hills. *The above address is for correspondence and is not that of the farm.*

Rooms: 8 with bath & wc; 1 apartment.
Price: Double/Twin 12000 Pts;
Apartment 20000 Pts incl. VAT.
Breakfast: Included.
Apartment: self-catering.
Meals: None available.
Closed: 15 December-15 February.

From Arcos de la Frontera A372 towards El Bosque. After 5.7km, at end of long straight section, left at sign onto track – 2km to farm.

Map no: 22

Entry no: 220

El Gallo Andante

Calle de la Pluma 7
00073 Pico de la Frontera
Cádiz

Tel: 734 973884
Fax: 743 973884
E-mail: elgalloandante@ave.es
Web: www.itsa.con

Ana María & Juan Kikiriki

Ana María, Juan and their extended family (it numbered seventy four at the last count) welcome guests to an unaffected, simple and unique living space. The philosophy here is very *laissez-faire*: you simply pick a spot that looks comfortable and bed down. El Gallo's most memorable feature is its large, communal feather-and-straw mattress. It is not only a deeply comfortable cradle for the night but also provides for your supper in the form of the eggs laid by your fellow guests (yes, they are free range). At supper they come scrambled, poached, sunny-side up or fried: egg nogs are *the* alternative drink. One of the place's most original features is a nightly show after supper when various members of the Kikiriki clan balance, asleep, on a number of high perches and old farm machinery. Late sleepers should note that the family are early risers and that alarm calls will never be the same once you have heard Juan crowing his guests awake. Prices, it must be said, are paltry, as it were.

Rooms: 1 sharing bathroom and wc.
Price: Double/Twin 350 Pts.
Breakfast: Included and inevitable.
Meals: Lunch/Dinner 25 Pts per egg.
Closed: Never.

Follow your nose.

Hotel Zuhayra

Calle Mirador 10   **Tel:** 957 694693 or 957 694694
14870 Zuheros   **Fax:** 957 694702
Córdoba   **E-mail:** zuhayra@teleline.es

Juan Carlos Ábalos Guerrero

The rather monolithic structure of the hotel might at first have you wondering. But do visit this small village which lies at the heart of the virtually unknown Natural Park of Subbetica: 3,000 hectares of wilderness await you. Zuheros is quintessentially Andalusian: its houses hug the hillside beneath the old castle. Up above are the greys and ochres of the mountains while below are mile after mile of silver-green olive groves. Two gentle-mannered brothers and their wives manage the hotel and they are exceptionally kind hosts. Zuhayra's downstairs café-cum-bar is vast but climb up to the first floor to find a cosier dining room where local specialities include partridge, *clavillina* (thick stew served with a fried egg on top) and delicious *remojón* (potato, onion and pepper salad with oranges). Wonderful bread, too, from the local bakers. Bedrooms are functional rather than memorable: modern pine furniture, hot-air heating and really comfy beds: bathrooms are surprisingly plush. Second floor rooms have the best views. Footpaths galore radiate out from Zuheros; there are cave paintings at 'The Cave of the Bats' just outside the village and Córdoba is just an hour's drive.

Rooms: 18 with bath & wc.
Price: Double/Twin 6500-8000 Pts.
Breakfast: Included.
Meals: Lunch/Dinner 1700 Pts (M), 2500-3000 Pts (C).
Closed: Never.

From Málaga towards Cordoba on N331and just past Lucena right to Cabra. On towards Dona Mencia then right towards Luque/Zuheros. Here through village to Castillo – same street 200m down hill.

Map no: 23   Entry no: 222

Los Omeyas
Calle Encarnación 17
14003 Córdoba

Tel: 957 492267/492199
Fax: 957 491659

Juan de la Rubia Villalba

You couldn't hope to find a better-positioned hotel than Los Omeyas. Just a few yards to the east of the great Mezquita in a narrow street of the old Jewish quarter, beyond dozens of souvenir shops, this plexus of mystic alleys is one of Andalusia's most alluring urban experiences. The building is in harmony with much older neighbours; the whitewashed façade, with its wrought iron balconies and wooden shutters, is classic Cordoban architecture. And so too within, where a small patio gives access to bedrooms on two levels. The design may seem a bit theatrical – the mezquita-style arches in reception, the marble staircase – but then we are in the larger-than-life south and the whole hotel is as clean as the newest pin. Marble floors throughout the building and whitewashed walls are the perfect foil for the summer heat and there's air conditioning, too. The hotel perhaps belongs more in the 'safe' rather than the 'remarkable' category, a few of the bathrooms are very small but many of our readers have endorsed our views on Los Omeyas. "The best of all our stays" wrote one; "excellent coffee at breakfast" wrote another.

Rooms: 38 with bath & wc.
Price: Single 5000-6000 Pts; Double/Twin 8000-10000 Pts.
Breakfast: 500 Pts.
Meals: None available.
Closed: Never.

Entering Córdoba follow signs for centre then Mezquita. In a street just off north-east corner of the Mezquita. Nearest parking by Alcázar de los Reyes Católicos.

Entry no: 223

Map no: 22

Hotel Los Abetos del Maestre Escuela

Calle Santo Domingo km 2.8
14012 Córdoba
Córdoba

Tel: 957 282132/282105
Fax: 957 282175
E-mail: hotelabetos@teleline.es

Rafael Jurado Díáz

Los Abetos (a type of yew) is in a quiet residential area to the north of the city, just at the foot of the Sierra Morena and a ten-minute drive from the centre. The 200-year-old colonial-style hotel, named after a famous schoolmaster who once took up residence here, stands among palm and cypress trees; these and the hotel's pink and white façade give it a distinctly colonial air. There is a peaceful pebbled courtyard with wicker chairs for sitting out and other equally attractive spots beneath the palms. The restaurant and lounge have much less of a period feel: the hotel was renovated with business folk in mind and seminars and banquets are often held here. The guest rooms are currently undergoing a (timely) refurb: we certainly preferred those with views across the estate towards Córdoba which come with Provençal-style furniture and modern tiled floors. In spite of the muzak and a definite 'hotelly' feel, this is a good place to stay if you want to be just out of town. The Jewish quarter and the Mezquita is an easily-arranged taxi ride away and there is a beautiful swimming pool discreetly sculpted into the hotel's terraced gardens.

Rooms: 34 with bath & wc; 2 suites.
Price: Single 7900-10600 Pts;
Double/Twin 10800-14000 Pts;
Suite 13000-16000 Pts.
Breakfast: 750 Pts.
Meals: Lunch/Dinner 2000 Pts (M),
3000 Pts (C).
Closed: Never.

Coming from Madrid take the first exit for Córdoba: 'Córdoba Norte'. Follow this road round the town's eastern and then northern edges and soon you will see signs for Hotel.

Map no: 22   Entry no: 224

Hotel Carmen de Santa Inés

Placeta Porras 7
C/San Juan de los Reyes, 15
18010 Granada

Tel: 958 226380
Fax: 958 224404
E-mail: sinescar@teleline.es
Web: www.madeinspain.net/hotelesgranada/carmen

Nicolás Garrido Berastegui

El Carmen de Santa Inés is a deliciously intimate hotel, right at the heart of one of
the city's most beautiful quarters. Push aside the heavy old studded door to
emerge into the small flagged patio. Here to greet you are a tinkling fountain,
potted aspidistra and deeply comfortable sofas. Marble columns still support the
original three hundred year old beams and off to one end, beyond another fine old
door is a small formal garden, the most romantic spot imaginable: there are roses,
a lemon tree, a vine, gold fish and a view up to the Alhambra. Climb up a marble
staircase, pass the tiny chapel and know that you'll love your room – even if it
might be a little small. Or opt for a suite: El Mirador is the loveliest, with its own
private terrace, but I liked all the rooms and their potpourri of antique and
modern art, fine fabrics and lovely tiles. Breakfast in the honeycomb-tiled dining
room where there are just three tables, then wander the Albaicín's labyrinthine
streets by way of other 'Carmens': this is the name given by the people of Granada
to these fine old houses with a walled garden. A favourite: our congratulations to
Nicolás!

Rooms: 5 with bath & wc; 4 suites.
Price: Double/Twin 16000 Pts;
Suite 20000-30000 Pts.
Breakfast: 800 Pts.
Meals: None available.
Closed: Never.

Go to sister hotel, El Palacio de Santa Inés (see our
description), staff will park car & accompany you to
hotel. Easier still, park in Parking San Agustín and
take a taxi.

Entry no: 225

Map no: 23

Hotel Reina Cristina
Calle Tablas 4
18002 Granada

Tel: 958 253211
Fax: 958 255728
E-mail: clientes@hotelreinacristina.com
Web: www.hotelreinacristina.com

Federico Jiménez González

The Reina Cristina is a grand 19th-century townhouse, close to the Cathedral and the lovely pedestrianised 'Bib-Rambla' square. Legend has it that Lorca spent his last night here, hidden by his friend Rosales. The hotel sits comfortably astride time past and time present, quite able to please the most demanding of modern travellers. The very dapper rooms (20 more are planned as we go to press) are set round a cool courtyard (it has a *neo-mudéjar* ceiling, a fountain, geometric tiles, aspidistras and marble columns), all of it utterly in sympathy with tradition and climate. In one corner is a repro of the painting depicting the rendition of Granada. The downstairs dining room is a good venue for dinner: it has the original Art Deco fittings and a series of photos from the period when Lorca was around. Make sure you eat at least once at the Cristina whose Rincón de Lorca restaurant was recently voted the top hotel eatery in town. It serves a mix of local dishes and those "we create ourselves" and the wines have been intelligently selected and honestly priced. There are also excellent *tapas* in the café as well as home-made cakes. A favourite Granada address.

Rooms: 43 with bath & wc.
Price: Single 9700 Pts; Double/Twin 15000 Pts.
Breakfast: 1000 Pts.
Meals: Lunch/Dinner 2300 Pts (M), 4000 Pts (C).
Closed: Never.

From A92 exit 131 onto Mendez Nuñez which becomes Avenida Fuentenueva. Just before the Hotel Granada Center turn right into Melchor Almagro which soon becomes Carril del Picón. Turn left at end into Calle Tablas. Hotel on left.

Map no: 23   Entry no: 226

Palacio de Santa Inés
Cuesta de Santa Inés 9
Barrio del Albayzín
18010 Granada

Tel: 958 222362
Fax: 958 222465
E-mail: sinespal@teleline.es

Nicolás Garrido Berastegui

Just yards from the Plaza Nueva, off to the side of a quiet and leafy square at the heart of the Albaicin (the hill rising opposite the Alhambra was recently declared a World Heritage Site by UNESCO), is this 16th-century palace. The building came to be known as 'The House of the Eternal Father' after the frescoes that surround the inner patio; perhaps the creation of a pupil of Raphael. Above them, two storeys of wooden galleries lead to bedrooms or suites. These are the delight of owner Nicolás Garrido. His love of antiques, modern art and interior design has been given free rein; his creation is elegant, southern and unique. Hang expense and book one of the suites with small terraces looking straight out to the Alhambra; ask for *Morayma* or *Mirador de Daraxa* or the *Alhambra* suite which has a wonderful 16th-century *mudéjar* panelled ceiling. But come also to meet the delightful manageress, Mari-Luz; her warmth makes a stay at Inés a double treat. She serves you breakfast in a cosy breakfast room. There is also a large lounge with a *mudéjar* ceiling, a quiet retreat for musing over the wonders of the Alhambra.

Rooms: 13 with bath & wc; 5 suites.
Price: Double/Twin 16000 Pts;
Suite 20000-35000 Pts.
Breakfast: 800 Pts.
Meals: None available.
Closed: Never.

Into centre to Plaza Nueva; then Carrera del Darro and, by FIRST BRIDGE, best to leave car, walk to hotel just up to left; someone from hotel can show you where to park. Or easier: any central public car park then taxi to hotel.

Entry no: 227

Map no: 23

Hostal Suecia

Calle Molinos (Huerta de los Angeles) 8   **Tel:** 958 225044/227781
18009 Granada   **Fax:** 958 225044

Mari-Carmen Cerdan Mejías

Hostal Suecia is hidden away at the end of a quiet little street at the foot of the Alhambra hill. It seems hard to believe that you're in the city and just a few hundred yards from one of Europe's architectural wonders. The Suecia is most seductive too, every inch a southern house with terracotta roof tiles, arched windows and an old sharon-fruit tree (that of the photo) in the front. But don't get the idea that the Suecia pretends to anything: inside it feels like a family home. There is a pretty sitting room downstairs, a tiny breakfast room up above and bedrooms which vary in size and comfort, like those of your own house. The beds are comfortable, the rooms are spotless. Come for the most peaceful spot in town, the rooftop terrace (no better place to read *Tales from the Alhambra*) and leisurely breakfasts. Or to relax in the nearby 'Campo del Príncipe' where you can sit in a café and think of the generations who have fleeted across this lively square.

Rooms: 8 with bath or shower & wc and 3 sharing.
Price: Single 6000 Pts; Double/Twin 7000 Pts; Double/Twin sharing 5000 Pts.
Breakfast: 500 Pts.
Meals: None available.
Closed: Never.

Entering Granada follow signs for Alhambra via the 'Ronda Sur'. Near Alhambra Palace hotel (by Alhambra) turn down Antequerela Baja which becomes Cuesta del Caidero. At bottom turn right into C/Molinos. After 30m right under arch to Suecia. If you get lost pay taxi to guide you.

Map no: 23   Entry no: 228

Palacete de Cazulas

Caserío de Cazulas s/n
18698 Otívar
Granada

Tel: 958 644036 or 619 040309
Fax: 958 644048
E-mail: info@hotel-cazulas.com
Web: www.hotel-cazulas.com

Brenda Watkins & Richard Russell-Cowan

The oldest deeds of Cazulas date back to 1492 and are in Arabic! The main
building came later but its debt to 'Alhambra' style, to things Moorish, is manifest.
Wafer brick, terracotta, fountain, clipped hedge and palm combine exquisitely in
this utterly southern, seductive summer palace. Hidden away at the end of a
subtropical valley, the setting could not be more peaceful. It is like being in a time
warp; the shepherd passing with his flock is the only traffic you'll see here. Rooms
are plush, the furnishing antique; there are sparkling new bathrooms, four-posters,
views out across the estate. There is a columned and vaulted lounge with books, an
honesty bar and a grand, panelled dining room decorated with old pieces. Dinner
is a labour of love for Brenda and served with great panache by Richard. And
Cazulla is much more: there is a private chapel, hidden corners of the garden, a
spring-fed swimming pool, a tennis court and a heavenly walk along the valley
floor to a towering gorge where rock-pools are fed by crystalline water. Granada is
close and you'll soon warm to your genial hosts. Several readers have written to say
how much they have enjoyed staying at Cazulas.

Rooms: 7 with bath & wc; 2 suites.
Price: Double/Twin 18000-19000 Pts;
Larger Double 21000 Pts; Suite 22000 Pts;
Suite with 4-poster 27000 Pts.
Breakfast: Included.
Meals: Lunch, summer only, from 2000
Pts; Dinner 4950 Pts (M). Book ahead.
Closed: Never.

From Almuñecar follow old road towards
Granada via Jete to Otívar. Continue on for
5km then left at sign 'central Cazulas'. Continue for 1.5km until you see the twin-
towered house.

Entry no: 229   Map no: 23

El Cortijo del Pino
Fernán Nuñez 2
La Loma
18659 Albuñuelas
Granada

Tel: 958 776257 or
607 523767
Fax: 958 776257

**James Connel &
Antonia Ruano**

Although it is just a short drive away from the Costa few people have heard of Albuñuelas – it is a fetching little place surrounded by citrus groves with wonderful walks along the rocky canyon which cuts south from the village. El Cortijo del Pino sits high on a bluff above the village and takes its name from the gargantuan two hundred year-old Aleppo pine that stands sentinel over the house and valley. The sober lines of the building have a rather Italian feel and the sandy tones which soften its façade change with each passing hour. Perhaps it was these constant changes of light which attracted James Connel; he is a painter and his artist's eye, combined with his wife Antonia's flair for interior decoration, has helped create a gorgeous home-from-home for guests and friends. Bedrooms are big, beamed and terracotta-tiled with really comfortable beds and excellent bathrooms. Dinner strikes the right balance between formality and relaxed enjoyment; James and Antonia are entertaining hosts and the food and wine are first class. And if you should feel inspired to grab a canvas and an easel you can make use of James' studio. But collectors should be warned: you'll want to buy one!

Rooms: 5 with bath & wc; 1 apartment.
Price: Single 5000 Pts; Double/Twin 10000 Pts.
Breakfast: Included.
Meals: Dinner 2000 Pts (M).
Closed: Never.

From Málaga towards Granada. Just before arriving in Granada pick up motorway to Motril then exit for Albuñuelas. Here, opposite the bus stop, turn right and follow steep road up to house.

Las Terrazas
Plaza del Sol 7
18412 Bubión
Granada

Tel: 958 763252/763034
Fax: 958 763034
E-mail: terrazas@teleline.es

Francisco Puga Salguero

You are high up in the Alpujarra, so high that on a clear day you can see down to the coast, across the Mediterranean and all the way to Africa. Las Terrazas, as the name implies, stands on a terraced hillside on the southern edge of Bubión. You enter by a quiet bar; this is the only place in Spain apart from monasteries and churches where we have ever seen a 'Silence Please' sign on the wall. This is where you breakfast; unusually for a simple place like this, it includes cheeses and cold sausage. No other meals are served but there are plenty of places to eat in the village. The rooms are nothing fancy but with their terracotta floors, locally-woven blankets and framed photographs they have simple charm. Even if they are smallish those with their own terrace are remarkably inexpensive. (There are also self-catering apartments at Las Terrazas.) Your hosts are the kindest of folk; they have 13 mountain bikes and happily help you plan your sorties on two wheels – or two feet.

Rooms: 20 with bath or shower & wc incl. apartments.
Price: Single 2750 Pts; Double/Twin 3950 Pts; Apartment (for 2) 6000 Pts; Apartment (for 4) 8000 Pts; Apartment (for 6) 12000 Pts.
Breakfast: 300 Pts.
Meals: None available.
Closed: 7 January-7 February.

From Granada N323 towards Motril; C333 through Lanjarón; just before Orgiva take road to Pampaneira and then left to Bubión. In village on left.

Entry no: 231

Map no: 23

El Molino del Puente

Puente de Durcal s/n **Tel:** 958 780731 or 687 430910
18650 Durcal **Fax:** 958 780731
Granada **E-mail:** biodurc@teleline.es

María Dora Tello & Francisco Marato

Durcal lies between the fertile Lecrín valley and the Alpujarras just off to one side of the motorway which cuts down from Granada to the 'tropical coast' of the Mediterranean. The abundant water which runs off the high Sierras is the *raison d'être* for this old mill and it also explains its lush greenery and prolific birdlife. Dori and Victor first established a cottage industry here making organic biscuits and jams. Thanks to its success they have been able to convert the remainder of this rambling building into a small hotel and restaurant. As you would imagine, the sound of rushing water is never far away (you also hear cars crossing the bridge above). Our favourite room is 102 which has a waterfall plummeting down just outside the window. All the bedrooms have warm colour washes, repro prints of the usual Impressionist stuff and smallish shower rooms. Because of the proximity of the river a first floor room might be a wise choice during winter. The rather cavernous restaurant has only recently opened but it has already made a name for itself: the food is trad-Andaluz, the oven wood-fired, deserts and liqueurs home-made and at breakfast you can sample those fabulous organic jams.

Rooms: 8 with bath & wc;
1 apartment for 4.
Price: Double/Twin 9000 Pts;
Apartment 9000 Pts.
Breakfast: Included.
Meals: Lunch/Dinner 1800 Pts (M),
4000 Pts (C).
Closed: Never.

From Motril take motorway north towards Granada. Exit for Durcal/Cozvijar. Follow signs towards Durcal. Just after crossing bridge turn sharp right down hill to Molino del Puente.

Map no: 23 **Entry no: 232**

La Casa de los Bates

Ctra Nacional 340, km 329.5 Tramo Motril-Salobreña   **Tel:** ~~958~~ 349495
Apartado de Correos 55   **Fax:** 958 349122
18600 Motril
Granada

958 349122
349122

Borja Rodríguez Martín-Feriche

La Casa de los Bates dates from 1898; it was a bad year for Spain with the loss of
its last American colony but you don't sense a hint of depression in this flamboyant
Italianate villa. It stands far enough back from the coastal highway for noise not to
be a nuisance. Surrounded by one of the most fabulous gardens in the South the
exuberance and size of the palms, catalpas, magnolias and Atlas cedars will make
any plant-lover's heart beat faster. Many of the trees and fishponds pre-date the
present villa. When the Martín-Feriche family acquired the house it had long lain
empty but thanks to careful restoration and a well-known interior designer it is
once again an elegant, beautifully furnished home-and-hotel. There are Deco
lamps, marble floors, Japanese lacquered tables, screens and oils; a Bechstein piano,
family photos and a harp; books, gilt mirrors and a butterfly collection. The
mahogany table in the dining room sits up to 20. Give your charming, blue-
blooded hosts enough warning and a candlelit dinner can be prepared. Bedrooms
are as fabulous as you'd expect and this would be a fantastic venue for a really
special occasion. *A Rusticae hotel.*

Rooms: 3 with bath & wc; 2 suites.
Price: Double 16000-18000 Pts;
Junior suite 25000-30000 Pts;
Master suite 35000-40000 Pts.
Breakfast: Included.
Meals: 7500-9000 Pts.
Closed: Never.

From Málaga N340 towards east. Pass
Salobreña and after approx 2km you will
see large warehouses on the right of 'Frutas
de Cara'. Exit here and then take the N340 back towards Salobreña; after 200m
turn right for Casa de los Bates.

Hotel Rural El Montañero

Carretera Orgiva-Pitres s/n   **Tel:** 958 787528 or 657 857671 or 606 032005
18410 Carataunas   **Fax:** 958 787528
Granada   **E-mail:** edelamonja@terra.as

Enrique de la Monja & Carolina Pavageau

El Montañero is an unexciting building at first sight: it sits just off to one side of
the road which leads up to the high Alpujarra with large plastic-lettered signs
announcing your arrival. But if you want an active holiday you might consider a
stay here. On offer are guided walks, horse-riding, canoeing, scuba-diving (just
three-quarters of an hour gets you down to the Med and Enrique is a qualified
teacher) plus mountain biking for the really energetic. Bedrooms here are
functional rather than memorable: they give onto a central lounge and are simply
furnished with bright bedspreads of local weave and with small bathrooms. But do
ask for one of those with views over the valley. The restaurant-cum-bar looks out
across a long rectangular pool that runs the length of the building. Enrique's
kitchen produces a mix of traditional Andalusian and Moroccan-inspired dishes
and good vegetarian food. We leave the last word to two readers who both
recommended the place to us: "Friendly owners, good food and all very
reasonably priced" said one; "we'll definitely be back" promised another.
(Alternative therapies can be arranged: ask for more info.)

Rooms: 7 with bath or shower & wc;
1 apartment.
Price: Single 3000-4200 Pts;
Double/Twin 4500-6900 Pts; Suite 6900-
7900 Pts, Apartment 5900-7900 Pts.
Breakfast: 750 Pts.
Meals: Lunch/Dinner 1900 Pts (M),
3000 Pts (C).
Closed: November.

From Granada towards Motril then left on A348 via Lanjarón & just before
Orgiva left towards Carataunas. Hotel on right just after entrance to village.

Map no: 23   Entry no: 234

Sierra y Mar

Calle Albaycín 16
18416 Ferreirola
Granada

Tel: 958 766171
Fax: 958 857367
E-mail: sierraymar@hotmail.com

Inger Norgaard & Giuseppe Heiss

Take the blue door for paradise; enter a sunny/shady, flowery/leafy walled garden, a magic world apart. Mention breakfast; you will eat a minor feast under the spreading mulberry tree. This is a gorgeous place run by two northerners (Italian and Danish) who know and love their adopted country. They are relaxed, intelligent and 'green'. They have converted and extended an old Alpujarran house with total respect for its origins; they like things simple, the emphasis being on the natural treasures that surround them, not on modern gadgets or plastic paraphernalia. The house is furnished with old rural pieces, lovely materials for curtains and bedcovers, all in good simple taste. Fear not, there are modern bathrooms and central heating. José (Giuseppe) and Inge organise walking tours: there is a beautiful half-day circular walk which begins and ends at the house. Head out to the nearby villages for your meals; there is a marvellous family-run restaurant within walking distance and two newly-opened veggie restaurants nearby. The atmosphere at Sierra y Mar is relaxed and your hosts know the Alpujarras like few others. In short, a wholly special B&B but try and book well in advance. *Minimum stay 2 nights.*

Rooms: 9 with bath & wc.
Price: Single 5000 Pts; Double/Twin
8000 Pts incl. VAT.
Breakfast: Included.
Meals: None available; kitchen for guests.
Closed: December & February.

From Granada N323, towards Motril, then
C333 through Lanjarón. Just before
Orgiva take road to Pampaneira. Just
before Pitres turn right towards Mecina;
through village to Ferreirola.

Albergue de Mecina

Calle La Fuente s/n
18416 Mecina Fondales
Granada

Tel: 958 766254
Fax: 958 766255
E-mail: alpujarr@ctv.es
Web: www.ctv.es/alpujarr

Encarna Ortega

The tiny hamlet of Mecina Fondales sits high on the southern flank of the Sierra Nevada, a cluster of whitewashed houses with the flat slate roofs and rounded chimney stacks which give the villages of the Alpujarra their unmistakable identity. The walking here is wonderful and this small, modern hotel would be a great place to return to after a day of trail-bashing. It looks out across Guadalfeo valley; read more about the area and its people in Chris Stewart's delightful 'Driving Over Lemons'. In spite of a puzzlingly large reception area, the hotel has a cosy, inviting feel; best of all is the dining room which has dark chestnut beams, cheery curtain fabrics and naïve paintings. In winter a fire burns in the hearth. If you don't need to worry about cholesterol try the *plato alujarreño*, a sort of glorified fry-up: it has several local variants but will certainly include spicy black-pudding and 'poor-man's potatoes', fried in olive oil with sweet green peppers. Bedrooms are medium to large, as clean as clean can be, and also have an attractive choice of fabric; insist on one with a view. All are centrally heated, well furnished and great value. And the staff are very kind.

Rooms: 21 with bath & wc.
Price: Double/Twin 8500 Pts;
Quadruple 12000 Pts.
Breakfast: 825 Pts.
Meals: Lunch/Dinner 2000 Pts (M),
2500-3000 Pts (C).
Closed: Never.

From Granada N323, towards Motril, then C333 through Lanjarón. Just before Orgiva take road to Pampaneira, then continue on towards Pitres. 1km before village right towards Mecina; hotel is at top of village, to the right as you arrive.

Map no: 23   **Entry no: 236**

Los Tinaos
Calle Parras s/n
18412 Bubión
Granada

Tel: 958 763217
    or 958 763192
Fax: 958 763192
E-mail: lostinaos@teleline.es

Isabel Puga Salguero

If you plan to visit the Alpujarra for a few days consider staying in one of the 12 'apartments' at Los Tinaos. They are built on terraces at the bottom of Bubión in local style; slate walls, flat-topped roofs and rounded chimney stacks with potted geraniums brilliantly contrasted against whitewashed walls. What lifts these simple self-catering houses into the 'special' bracket is their position, close to the village church and looking out over terraced groves of cherry, pear and apple all the way to the Contraviesa Sierra; on a clear day you can see passing ships on the Mediterranean! Each house has a kitchen/sitting/dining room giving onto a small terrace, a wonderful spot for meals and sundowners. They have open hearths, workaday pine furniture, smallish bedrooms and bathrooms: the locally-woven curtains and bedspreads add a welcome splash of colour. You are well away from the lively village centre so won't hear much apart from the murmur of the Poqueira river and the tolling of the church bells. Wood is available in winter and Isabel and José (who also own a gift shop) will advise on what to do and see.

Rooms: 12 self-catering apartments.
Price: Apartment (for 2) 8500 Pts;
Apartment (for 4) 10700 Pts; Apartment
(for 6) 12840 Pts incl. VAT.
Breakfast: None available.
Meals: None available.
Closed: Never.

From Motril towards Granada on N323.
Exit for Vélez Benaudalla. Here to Orgiva
and there right to Bubión. As you enter
village left into Calle Lavadero. After just
25m take first (sharp) turning to left and at
small fountain right to Los Tinaos.

Alquería de Morayma

A348 Cádiar-Torvizcón
18440 Cádiar
Granada

Tel: 958 343221/343303
Fax: 958 343221
E-mail: morayma@arrakis.es
Web: www.alqueriamorayma.com

Mariano Cruz Fajardo

Mariano's commitment to the Alpujarra and its people runs deep and he hopes that guests leaving La Morayma do so with a deeper understanding of the traditions of these high mountain villages. He and his family built this small hotel entirely in the local vernacular and have created a series of rooms and buildings which have the feel of an Alpujarran village. The main farmstead and the individual houses (one in the old chapel) are set amid olive groves, vineyards and vegetable plots, all of it farmed organically. Decoration is in the same vein as the architecture: old brass bedsteads, bright Alpujarra bed covers, marble-topped dressers, grilled windows, old paintings, and a large collection of photographs of a different age. Each room is differs to the next, all of them feel warm and cared-for. The food, too is a celebration of things local: olive oil and tomato, fennel, wild capers, goats cheese, thick stews and *migas* (semolina cakes to accompany tomatoes and peppers or fish) and organic wine from Morayma's *bodega*. There is wonderful walking, the chance to see olives being milled during the winter and you could even join in with the grape harvest or the sausage-making!

Rooms: 8 with bath & wc; 5 houses.
Price: Double/Twin 7500 Pts; House (for 2) 9500 Pts; House (for 4) 12500 Pts.
Breakfast: 500 Pts.
Meals: Lunch/Dinner 1600 Pts (M), approx. 3500 Pts (C).
Closed: Never.

From Granada N323 south towards Motril then A348 via Lanjarón, Órgiva and Torvizcón. 2km before Cádiar, signposted to left.

Map no: 23

Entry no: 238

Hotel La Fragua

Calle San Antonio 4
18417 Trevélez
Granada

Tel: 958 858626/858573
Fax: 958 858614
E-mail: lafragua@navegalia.es
Web: www.lafragua-navegalia.com

**Antonio y Miguel
Espinosa González**

Just to the south of the towering peak of Mulhacén (at 3,481 metres the highest in the Sierra Nevada), Trevélez is one of the prettiest villages of the Alpujarra. You climb steeply up to the middle of the village to find La Fragua, shared between two old village houses next to the town hall. In one building there is the friendly little bar and above it a real eagle's nest of a pine-clad dining room with a terrific view across the flat rooftops. A wonderful place to sit and gaze between courses. The food is just like the place – simple and authentic. The locally-cured ham is utterly delicious and whatever you do leave some space for one of the home-made puddings. Just a few yards along the narrow street is the second house where you find your room; no fussy extras here, just terracotta floors, timbered ceilings and comfy beds. Up above is a roof terrace with tables and the same heavenly view. Your host, Antonio, knows walkers and their ways and will gladly help you plan your hikes. Visit the Alpujarra before it gets too well known!!

Rooms: 14 with bath & wc.
Price: Single 3200 Pts; Double/Twin 5000 Pts.
Breakfast: 350 Pts.
Meals: Lunch/Dinner 1500 (M), 1500-2000 Pts (C).
Closed: 10 January-10 February.

From Granada N323 towards Motril; C333 through Lanjarón; just before Orgiva take road to Trevélez. Up into village asking for 'barrio medio'; park in or near to Plaza Las Pulgas. La Fragua is next to Town Hall (Ayuntamiento).

Hotel Los Bérchules

Carretera de Bérchules 20
18451 Bérchules
Granada

Tel: 958 852530
Fax: 958 769000
E-mail: hot.berchules@interbook.net
Web: www.berchules.com

Alejandro Tamborero

I was lucky to came across Los Bérchules when walking in the area. As a walker it was all that I wanted; cosy, inexpensive with good food, wine and a genuine welcome from Alejandro and his mother Wendy. The hotel is just beneath the village of Bérchules which is 1322 metres above sea level; thought-provoking to think that you'll be sleeping at about the same height as the summit of Ben Nevis! Things are on a human scale at Hotel Los Bérchules: there is a small, pine-clad bar-cum-lounge with a hearth and a small collection of walking guides and novels. This leads through to a beamed dining room where you choose between a staggeringly cheap *menú del día* or eating à la carte. If you enjoy rabbit then be sure to try Wendy's *paella*. The ten guest rooms are simply furnished with bright Alpujarra-weave curtain and blankets and the central-heating is a boon during the colder months. The long distance footpath which runs the length of the southern flank of the Sierra Nevada passes right beside the hotel and Wendy knows many other footpaths and will even run you to and from your walks. A hostelry which proves that special doesn't have to be synonymous with grand.

Rooms: 13 with bath & wc.
Price: Single 4000-6000 Pts;
Double/Twin 5500-7500 Pts incl. VAT.
Breakfast: 500 Pts.
Meals: Lunch 900 Pts (M), Dinner 2000
Pts (C).
Closed: Never.

From Málaga east on N340. Pass Motril then turn left to Albuñol. Just after Albuñol right on GR433 to Cádiar. Here towards Mecina then left to Bérchules. Hotel on left as you enter village.

Map no: 24

Entry no: 240

El Rincón de Yegen
Camino de Gerald Brennan
18460 Yegen
Granada

Tel: 958 851270/ 851276
Fax: 958 851270/851068

Agustín & Mari-Carmen Rodríguez

Yegen is the village where Gerald Brennan came to live: required reading before, during or after your stay here must be his *South from Granada*. Getting here is much easier than in Brennan's day and although the twentieth century has caught up with the villages of La Alpujarra there is still beauty in great measure to be found here. The recently built hotel fits well with its older neighbours thanks to the architects sticking to the dictates of local tradition: thus local slate, beam and bamboo are used in abundance throughout the building. Agustín is a trained cook who likes reworking local dishes in a more "modern" (read 'slightly lighter') way. His onion and goats cheese tart makes a heavenly starter and his braised lamb with grapes is excellent. Bedrooms are to the back of the restaurant, built high to catch the views from the hotel's 3,500-foot perch: they are large, with loads of space, pine furniture, bright bedspreads, shining floor tiles and it's all as spick and span as can be. You'll certainly appreciate the underfloor heating if you travel through the Alpujarras in winter and if you prefer self-catering the apartments have all you need and more.

Rooms: 4 with bath & wc; 3 houses.
Price: Double/Twin 6000 Pts; House (for 4) 9000 Pts or 50000 Pts weekly incl. VAT.
Breakfast: 600 Pts.
Meals: Lunch/Dinner 1300 Pts (M), 2500-3000 Pts (C). No meals on Tuesdays.
Closed: From 1st to 3rd Tuesday in June.

From Málaga N340 towards Almería. Exit for La Rábita/Albuñol. Here on to Cádiar, then on via Mecina Bombarón to Yegen. Signposted on left as you go through village.

Entry no: 241

Map no: 24

Casa Rural Las Chimeneas

Calle Amargura 6
18493 Mairena
Granada

Tel: 958 760352
Fax: 958 760004
E-mail: dillsley@moebius.es
Web: www.moebius.es/contourlines

David & Emma Illsley

Mairena lies at the eastern end of Sierra Nevada and is one of the first of the Alpujarran villages that you encounter if you take the high pass of La Ragua across from Granada. The village hasn't suffered any obvious changes since the advent of tourism; most visitors pass it by as they head for Trevélez and Bubion. David and Emma are both keen walkers and many of their guests come to explore the little-trodden paths which lead out from the village. Their old village house has been restored with particular sensitivity and the feel-good factor soars as soon as you enter the beautiful guest lounge/diner. It is a light, high-ceilinged room with rocking chairs around a hearth, potted aspidistra, masses of books and views out across the terraced hillside beneath the village. A plant-filled terrace with a tiny plunge pool shares the same view: you can see North Africa on a clear day! The bedrooms feel as special as the shared space; they have plants, old dressers, antique beds (but modern mattresses) and attractive bathrooms. Dinner and breakfast is eaten *en famille* and the spirit of Las Chimineas is relaxed and friendly. A perfect place for a long, deeply relaxing stay.

Rooms: 5 with bath & wc; 2 studio-apartments.
Price: Double/Twin 8000-10000 Pts.
Apartment 8000-10000 Pts.
Breakfast: Included (apart from in apartment).
Meals: Packed lunch 500 Pts; Dinner 1500 Pts.
Closed: Never.

From Granada A92 east towards Almería. Shortly past Guadix turn for La Calahorra then continue over pass of Puerto de la Ragua to Laroles. There right to Mairena. Take second right into village by weeping willows, park in square and go down narrow street at south-east corner of square. 100m to Las Chimeneas.

Map no: 24

Entry no: 242

Refugio de Nevada

Carretera de Mairena s/n
18493 Laroles
Granada

Tel: 958 760320/760338
Fax: 958 760304
E-mail: alpujarr@ctv.es
Web: www.ctv.es/alpujarr

Victor M. Fernández Garcés

More proof: small IS beautiful. The Refugio de Nevada opened just two years ago but it already has a growing number of old faithfuls. The building makes much use, inside and out, of local slate – entirely in keeping with traditional Alpujarran architecture – and it sits well among the older village houses of Laroles. The lounge and bar area is a perfectly cosy spot and the restaurant even more so: here there are just half a dozen tables, crocheted lace curtains, cut flowers, rush-seated chairs and old prints of Granada. The bedrooms have the same quiet intimacy about them: beams and terracotta, chimneys in the studios (open plan with a lounge area), feather duvets, and simple wooden tables and chairs. They aren't enormous but it all works perfectly. They are light, too: the hotel faces the south so the maximum sunlight is captured. Rooms and food are very reasonably priced: the set menu particularly so. Try the roast goat with garlic and perhaps some wild asparagus as a starter. This is a hotel of very human dimensions, the staff are young and friendly, and the Alpujarras are waiting to be walked: book a studio in winter and hunker down by a blazing fire.

Rooms: 5 with bath & wc; 7 studios.
Price: Double/Twin 6800 Pts;
Studio 8750 Pts.
Breakfast: 650 Pts.
Meals: Lunch/Dinner 1800 Pts.
Closed: Never.

From Granada A92 to Guadix, then right towards El Puerto de La Ragua and continue to Laroles. Signposted to right as you reach village.

Entry no: 243

Map no: 24

Finca Buen Vino

Los Marines
21293 Aracena
Huelva

Tel: 959 124034
Fax: 959 501029
E-mail: buenvino@facilnet.es
Web: www.buenvino.com

Sam & Jeannie Chesterton

After many years in the Scottish Highlands, Sam and Jeannie knew that to settle happily in Spain they would need to find a place of wild natural beauty – so they chose this divinely isolated spot amid the thick oak and chestnut woods of the Aracena mountains. Many of the materials used were old, shipped in from far corners of Spain: you would never guess Buen Vino was built just a dozen or so years back. The panelled dining room, the arched doors and the wooden staircase leading to the guest rooms all have that seductive patina that only time can give. The house's decoration is unaffected yet elegant; just the right balance between comfort and authentic Andalusian style. Jeannie is a *Cordon Bleu* cook and the candlelit dinner with quail and *Cerdo Ibérico* (Iberian pork with woodland *setas*) was unforgettable (starlit on the terrace in summer). The guestrooms are all different: the 'Pink' room has a bathtub with a view, the 'Yellow' room a sitting-cum-dressing room, the 'Bird' room its own hearth. In each you find books, cheery oil paintings, family memorabilia. There are also independent cottages that can be rented, hidden away at the edges of the estate, each with its own pool.

Rooms: 4 with bath & wc; 3 cottages.
Price: Double/Twin 27000 Pts.
Cottages: ring/fax for details.
Breakfast: Included.
Meals: Lunch, in summer, only on request, 2500 Pts (M). Dinner 3500 Pts.
Closed: July & August, Christmas & New Year.

From Seville N630 north for 37km then N433 towards Portugal/Aracena. Los Marines is 6km west of Aracena. Finca Buen Vino is 1.5km west of Los Marines off to the right at km95 post.

Map no: 15

Entry no: 244

Finca la Silladilla

21290 Los Romeros
Huelva

Tel: 959 501350 959 501184
Fax: 959 501351
E-mail: silladi@teleline.es

Juan Manuel Borrero Bustamante

Just to the west of the market town of Aracena lies the Natural Park of the same name. A staggering 90% of it is forested and it embraces some of Andalusia's prettiest villages. Finca La Silladilla stands in glorious isolation at the very western end of the park in the midst of a deep forest of century-old oak trees. You couldn't wish for a more peaceful, pastoral setting. Choose between a room in the old house (it was once a textile mill) or in two nearby farmhouses which are more isolated still. The decoration of the rooms can be described as 'smart-rustic'; each is different with old brass bedsteads, perhaps a Deco table, parquet floors and stylish bathrooms. Colours and fabrics have been thoughtfully combined: the views out to the forest are gorgeous. Unusually there is no dining room in the main house and breakfast is delivered to your room in the colder months. In the other farmhouses the same arrangement applies or there are kitchens for self-catering: there is a small farm-shop where you can buy the makings of a meal. It also doubles as a tiny bar. A perfect place for people who are happy with just Nature for company. *A Rusticae hotel.*

Rooms: 2 with bath & wc; 4 houses.
Price: Double/Twin 10000-12000 Pts; Suite 12000-15000 Pts; House (for 4) 20000-24000 Pts; House (for 6) 30000-36000 Pts.
Breakfast: Included.
Meals: None available apart from snacks; self-catering.
Closed: Never.

From Sevilla N630 towards Mérida then N433 through Aracena towards Portugal. Just past El Repilado left towards Los Romeros. La Silladilla is signposted to the left, just past the cemetery.

Hospedería Fuentenueva

Paseo Arca del Agua s/n
23440 Baeza
Jaén

Tel: 953 743100/243200
Fax: 953 743200
E-mail: info@fuentenueva.com
Web: www.fuentenueva.com

Victor Rodríguez

There is a good reason for Fuentenueva's rather forbidding façade; it was once a womens' prison. Both sexes are now welcome – and unshackled to boot. Under the aegis of the town council it was converted into an open, airy, friendly hotel run by a co-operative of five enthusiastic and professional young people. Inside, the arches and vistas, the marble floors, the tinkling fountain and the neo-Moorish cupola create impressions of space and gentle cool. Exhibitions of works by local artists and craftsmen are held in the salons. The bedrooms are mostly large and light with modern, locally built, furniture and fittings, bright bedcovers and plush bathrooms. On summer evenings drink in the outside bar in the shadow of the old prison tower then dine in the patio on local fish specialities. When all the windows are opened in the morning, the characteristic scent of high-quality olive oil will drift in and envelop you. Visit unsung Baeza (guided tours daily, in English), revel in her exuberant Renaissance palaces and richly endowed churches and don't miss the Cathedral's silver monstrance (hidden behind St Peter...). Fuentenueva is a great place to serve time!

Rooms: 12 with bath & wc.
Price: Single 6400 Pts, Double/Twin 10500 Pts.
Breakfast: Included.
Meals: Lunch/Dinner approx. 2500 Pts (M), 3000 Pts (C).
Closed: Never.

From Granada N323 to just before Jaén and then N321 to Baeza. On far side of Baeza on left as you leave in direction of Úbeda.

Map no: 18

Entry no: 246

Palacio de la Rambla

Plaza del Marques 1
23400 Úbeda
Jaén

Tel: 953 750196
Fax: 953 750267
E-mail: rusticae@rusticae.es
Web: www.rusticae.es

Elena Meneses de Orozco

The old towns of Úbeda and nearby Baeza are often missed as travellers hurry
between Madrid and the Costa. They are two of the brightest jewels in the crown
of Spanish Renaissance architecture. At the heart of old Úbeda, the exquisite
Palacio de la Rambla dates from this period and has never left the Orozco family.
You enter the building through an ornate Corinthian-columned portal into the
main patio; colonnaded on two levels, ivy-covered and with delicately carved
lozenges and heraldry, its opulence takes you by surprise. Lounge, dining room
and bedroom are a match for their setting; there are antique beds, chests, lamps,
claw-footed bath tubs, oil paintings of religious themes and – as you might expect
– the family portraits. Native terracotta is softened by *estera* matting. An attentive
member of staff may will be the only person you get to meet apart from other
guests. You will be served a full Andalusian breakfast: eggs, toast with olive oil,
fresh orange juice with nice touches like a glass of chilled water in summer and
lace-edged napkins. Palacio de la Rambla has a long tradition of regal welcoming;
King Alfonso XIII stayed here when he was in town.

Rooms: 8 with bath & wc; 1 suite.
Price: Single 12000 Pts; Double/Twin
15500 Pts; Suite 18000 Pts.
Breakfast: Included.
Meals: None available.
Closed: 15 July-15 August.

From Madrid south on NVI. At km292
take N322 to Úbeda. There, follow
'Centro Ciudad' until Palace in front of
you between C/Ancha and C/Rastro,
opposite cafetería 'La Paloma'.

Maria de Molina

Plaza del Ayuntamiento s/n
23400 Úbeda
Jaén

Tel: 953 795356
Fax: 953 793694
E-mail: hotelmm@hotel-maria-de-molina.com
Web: www.hotel-maria-de-molina.com

Juan Navarro López

Úbeda is one of Andalusia's most beautiful towns and a wander through its old quarter once night has fallen feels like a step back in time. You will come upon a number of grand old houses, built by descendants of the Christian knights who were given land in the city by king Fernando 'el Santo' following the Reconquest from the Moors. The very heart of the town is an imposing Renaissance square and its finest *palacete* (a small palace) has recently been converted into a small, coquettish and very comfortable hotel. The building is wrapped round an inner courtyard; to one side is an enormous dining room that can seat up to 600 but you will dine in a much smaller, more intimate one or in the fountain-graced patio when its warm. Although you are miles from the sea the restaurant serves excellent fresh fish as well as the roast meats for which the area is known. Bedrooms are superb. Each has been individually decorated with repro antiques, warm colour washes and beautiful lamps, cushions, linen and prints. The hotel's staff are attentive and charming: this newly opened hotel is already making waves and we recommend it wholeheartedly.

Rooms: 18 with bath & wc; 2 suites.
Price: Single 7000-8000 Pts;
Double/Twin 11000-13000 Pts;
Suite 20000 Pts.
Breakfast: 1000 Pts.
Meals: Lunch/Dinner 2500 Pts (M),
4000 Pts (C).
Closed: Never.

Arriving in Úbeda follow signs for 'Centro Histórico'. Hotel next to the town hall ('el ayuntamiento') and Plaza Vázquez de Molina. Signposted.

Map no: 18

Entry no: 248

Hotel La Finca Mercedes

Ctra de la Sierra km 1   **Tel:** 953 721087
23476 La Iruela
Jaén

Mercedes Castillo

La Iruela is a tiny village just outside of Cazorla on the road leading up to the
Natural Park of the same name. Its literal crowning glory is the castle-fortress
which was built by the Templars; slog up to the top for an amazing view. La Finca
Mercedes is just out of the village, a simple roadside hotel and restaurant which
takes its name from its gregarious, charming and attractive owner who is helped by
her two young daughters. Although you are just next to the road there is little
passing traffic and rooms and restaurant are on the far side of the building. The
dining room is as cosy as a Cotswold pub, even in the winter (it can get really cold
here) when a fire burns in the corner hearth throughout the day. The food is
simple, regional, flavourful and very good value. So too are the guest rooms which
are medium-sized with good bathrooms, simple pine furniture and wonderful
views across the olive groves which surround the village; nothing is fussy but
nothing is missing, either. The Castillo family have just completed a further six
bedrooms at 'Cortijo Berfalá' which you reach in just five minutes down a very
steep track. A great place to stay for walkers.

Rooms: 9 with bath & wc.
Price: Double/Twin 5000-5500 Pts;
Suite 6000 Pts.
Breakfast: 400 Pts.
Meals: Lunch/Dinner 1750 Pts (C).
Closed: Never.

As you arrive in Cazorla follow road up
into the centre of village and at large square
turn left for La Iruela. Follow road round
the bottom of La Iruela: La Finca
Mercedes is just to the left of the road after approx 1km. Signposted.

Molino La Farraga

Calle Camino de la Hoz s/n
Apartado de Correos 1
23470 Cazorla
Jaén

Tel: 953 721249 or 610 737661
Fax: 953 721249
E-mail: farraga@teleline.es

Nieves Santana Martín

The setting one of great beauty: a deeply verdant river valley just beneath the rocky crests of the Cazorla mountains. This two hundred year-old mill's gardens are an Ode to Water which is everywhere in ponds, channels, races and falls; they were planted by an English botanist, nurtured for years by an amiable American and now lovingly tended by the kindliest Spanish woman you could hope to meet. Nieves left her native Canary Islands for this corner of Paradise and visitors here can revel in simple comfort, wholesome food and buckets of caring: it came as no surprise to learn that she was once a nurse. A delicious waft of linseed oil pervades the house; its architecture is an organic, interlocking puzzle of stairways, corners, niches and turns. The bedrooms are 'just right', some have fireplaces, another a small terrace and all are spotlessly clean. The price of your room includes a generous breakfast and don't miss dinner: it's a friendly, relaxed affair, often organic and served around one big table in winter or on a gorgeous riverside terrace on warm, summer nights. Unforgettable; do go to La Farraga, one of the brightest stars in the places-to-stay firmament!

Rooms: 7 with bath & wc; 1 suite.
Price: Single 5300 Pts; Double/Twin 9100 Pts; Suite 10700 Pts.
Breakfast: Included.
Meals: Picnic lunch 800 Pts; Dinner 1500 Pts.
Closed: 15 December-1 February.

Arriving in Cazorla follow signs for Ruinas de Santa María. Here pass between ruined church and Cueva de Juan Pedro retaurant towards 'Castillo'. Park on left by sign for La Farraga. Cross river (on foot), house on right after 100m.

Map no: 18

Entry no: 250

Cortijo El Horcajo

Carretera Ronda-Zahara
de la Sierra
29400 Ronda
Málaga

Tel: 95 2184080
Fax: 95 2184071
E-mail: info@elhorcajo.com
Web: www.elhorcajo.com

Luis González

The old farmstead of El Horcajo lies at the northern boundary of the Grazalema Natural Park; you reach it via a long track which snakes down to the bottom of a deep valley. This is every inch the classic Andalusian *cortijo*: outbuildings are wrapped around a sheltered inner courtyard. This is partly designed not only for aesthetic appeal but also as a means of escaping the heat of the Andalusian summer. Things 'rustic' are prominent in cobble, beam, tile and ceramics. The large lounge, dining room and reception area are in the converted cattle byre; the original vaulting has been preserved and new windows opened to bring light into a rather dark space. Bedrooms are comfortable, if a little bare, and many of them have small terraces looking out to the hills. We would prefer one of the courtyard (patio) rooms, which are quieter than those above the restaurant. There are good walks close by and pretty Grazalema is just 20 minutes away by car. The housekeepers, 'Mari' y Bernabé, are friendly and even if their English is 'basic' they make a huge effort.

Rooms: 14 with bath & wc;
10 apartments.
Price: Double/Twin 11500 Pts;
Apartment (for 4) 16000 Pts.
Breakfast: Included.
Meals: Dinner 2300 Pts (M); 3600 Pts (C).
Closed: Never.

From Ronda A376 towards Sevilla. After approx. 15km left towards Grazalema. Don't take next left turn for Grazalema, continue towards Zahara and at km95.5 post turn left and down track to the farm.

El Tejar

Calle Nacimiento 38
29430 Montecorto
Málaga

Tel: 95 2184053
Fax: 95 2184053
E-mail: eltejar@mercuryin.es
Web: www.sawdays.co.uk

**Emma Baverstock &
Guy Hunter-Watts**

El Tejar looks out from the forest above Montecorto, just a short drive from Ronda, looking out to a heavenly panorama of mountain, hill and wooded slopes. Emma and Guy have lived long in Spain; she managed some of the area's best restaurants, he has written books on walking and places to stay(!) in the area. The house is built on several levels and the decoration is simple, stylish and southern. An open hearth, whitewashed beams and terracotta tiles impart an authentically *Andaluz* flavour whilst bright textiles and rugs collected in Asia, Africa and South America add spice and colour. The sitting room has French windows and a large collection of books on Spain. Three big bedrooms share the view and have more books, bright bedspreads and kilims. Dinner is a relaxed occasion; food has an Andaluz/Moroccan slant, the wines are excellent and you eat with your hosts round a candle-lit table (there is a wonderful little *venta* nearby if you prefer eating out). Guy can take you walking in the Grazalema Park; Emma will accompany you on her horses to a Roman theatre hewn out of solid rock. Intimate, fun and friendly there is nowhere we would rather stay.

Rooms: 2 with bath & wc; 1 suite.
Price: Double/Twin 9500 Pts; Suite 10500 Pts.
Breakfast: 600 Pts.
Meals: Dinner 3250 Pts (M) incl.all drinks.
Closed: Never.

From Málaga towards Cádiz on N340, then A376 to Ronda. Continue round Ronda on A376. After 20km right into Montecorto. El Tejar is at top of village via track through pines. Ask for 'la casa del inglés' if lost!

La Fuente de la Higuera

Partido de los Frontones   **Tel:** 95 2114355 or 610 847731
29400 Ronda   **Fax:** 95 2114356
Málaga   **E-mail:** lafuente@ncs.es

Christina & Pom Piek

Pom and Tina have travel in the blood; he chartered yachts, she worked for one of
the big airlines. But then the magic of the Ronda mountains put them under its
spell and they saw in this old mill a new dream; of a luxurious retreat where good
food, wine and company could ease away urban worries. Tina is the 'spark' – an
enormously vivacious and likeable woman, it was she who chose the furnishings
and fabrics which add so much razzmatazz to the rooms. Pom is born to the role
of host; a raconteur by nature he has a dry humour born – perhaps – of many years
in the UK. The conversion of this old mill has been accomplished with style by the
local craftsmen; good plastering and planked floors give the place a manicured and
stylish look and make a nice change from the usual beam and terracotta.
Indonesian beds, lamps, chairs and tables add a rich, exotic feel. The focus of the
house is poolwards; beyond groves of olives and the changing colours of the
mountains are a great backdrop for your sun-downer. At dinner feast on locally
inspired food and good wines: the staff are very friendly and Pom will be around
to share a yarn and/or a glass or two.

Rooms: 3 with bath & wc, 6 suites
& 1 apartment.
Price: Double/Twin 16500 Pts;
Junior Suite (for 2) 21500 Pts; Suite
(for 2) 23000 Pts; Deluxe Suite 25000 Pts;
Double Suite (for 4) 31500 Pts;
Apartment 21500 Pts.
Breakfast: Included.
Meals: On request 3700 Pts (M).
Closed: Never.

From Málaga N340 then m'way towards Cádiz. Exit for Ronda then bypass Ronda
on A376 towards Sevilla. Pass turning to Benaoján and turn right at sign for hotel.
Under bridge then left at first fork, over bridge, left after approx. 200m.

Hotel Posada del Canónigo

Calle Mesones 24   **Tel:** 95 2160185
29420 El Burgo   **Fax:** 95 2160185
Málaga

María Reyes

Your arrival in the mountain village of El Burgo will be memorable: it is a splash of brilliant white amid the ochres and greys of the surrounding limestone massif. Little visited, it will give you as essential a taste of Andalusian mountain life as can be found anywhere. This grand old village house is another good reason for coming. It is very much a family affair; 13(!) brothers and sisters helped restore and decorate the house. Bedrooms are simply furnished in local style with tiled floors, old bedsteads and lots of family things: prints, paintings and dried flowers have been lovingly arranged by María Reyes. It is all spotless and the owners are visibly proud of every last corner of this inn. There is a small dining room leading to a little patio where you breakfast in the morning sun and a newly opened *bodega*-style restaurant where only local dishes are on offer. Both sitting rooms have open hearths and exposed stonework and the whole place is uncannily quiet by Andalusian standards. Stay two nights to walk or let the owners take you riding in the virtually unknown National Park of the Sierra de la Nieves above Ronda.

Rooms: 12 with bath & wc.
Price: Double/Twin 6795-7865 Pts.
Breakfast: 700 Pts.
Meals: Lunch/Dinner 1500 Pts (M), 3000 Pts (C).
Closed: 24 December.

From Torremolinos to Cártama then continue to Calea, Alozaina, Yunquera and El Burgo. Turn right into village and ask; hotel is next to church of San Agustín.

Map no: 22   Entry no: 254

Molino Santisteban

A366 km 52-53
Guaro
Málaga

Tel: 95 2453748
Fax: 95 2453748
E-mail: info@elmolinosantisteban.com
Web: www.elmolinosantisteban.com

Frits Blomsma & Gisèle Gerhardus

Frits and Gisèle left Holland just last year with a dream of warmer, more southern climes. It is easy to see how this old mill fitted that dream: it lies to one side of the lush valley cut through by the Río Grande, just half an hour back from the 'Costa', and is surrounded by willow, eucalyptus, citrus, roses and virtually every kind of climber that you can imagine. Olives were once milled here and the old race adds much life, for both ears and eyes, to the pretty garden. The main building has the feel of a rather diminuitive hacienda; the six bedrooms give onto its sheltered inner patio where a fountain gurgles; a wooden balcony wraps around its upper floor. The bedrooms are a good size, are attired with mostly antique furniture and the nicest have French windows which look out across the river. Just across the way is the old mill itself which has become the breakfast room; you eat round a long table sat on ornate leather-backed chairs; they came from a monastery. Your hosts are well-travelled, easy and cosmopolitan and they speak near-faultless English. There is a simple restaurant just yards away and more sophisticated eateries just down the road in Coín.

Rooms: 6 with bath & wc.
Price: Double/Twin 8500-10500 incl. VAT.
Breakfast: Included.
Meals: None available.
Closed: Never.

From Málaga airport towards Torremolinos/Cádiz on N340. After just 200m turn right for Coín/Costa del Golf on A366/C344. From Coín continue on A366/C344 towards Ronda. Santisteban is betwen km posts 52 and 53 on the right, just before Venta Gallardo.

Entry no: 255

Map no: 22

Santa Fe

Carretera de Monda km3
Apartado 147
29100 Coín
Málaga

Tel: 95 2452916
Fax: 95 2453843
E-mail: info@santafe-hotel.com
Web: www.santafe-hotel.com

Warden & Arjan van de Vrande

Two young, enthusiastic and multi-lingual Dutch brothers have begun to make a name for themselves since taking over at Santa Fe. Warden and Arjan's old farmhouse sits among the citrus groves of the Guadalhorce valley, just to one side of the road from Marbella up to Coín: you do hear the rumble of traffic from the hotel. The transformation from farm to guest house has been faithful to local tradition; bedrooms have rustic furniture and terracotta floors (tiles fired with the dog-paw print bring good luck!). Colours used in each of the rooms are different, there are bright bedspreads and the feel is warm and friendly. Guests (the restaurant is popular with non-residents, too) are Spanish and Costa-cosmopolitan. A Belgian chef waves his wand in the kitchen; mention should be made of the spinach with langoustines, the sirloin of pork with cream, raisin, sherry and pine kernel sauce – and the Dutch apple pie for desert. There is an attractive dining room where there will be a log fire in the winter but most of the time you dine out beneath the old olive tree or in the new conservatory. A casual, relaxed atmosphere but plenty of attention to the details too.

Rooms: 5 with bath or shower & wc.
Price: Double/Twin 9500 Pts.
Breakfast: Included.
Meals: Lunch/Dinner 2500-3500 Pts (C).
Closed Tuesdays.
Closed: 2 weeks in November & 2 weeks in January/February. Check!

From Málaga, N340 towards Cádiz. About 1km after airport, right to Coín. In Coín take Marbella road. After 3km Santa Fe is on right (signposted).

Map no: 22

Entry no: 256

El Castillo de Monda
29110 Monda
Málaga

Tel: 95 2457142
Fax: 95 2457336
E-mail: monda@spa.es
Web: www.costadelsol.spa.es/hotel/mond

John Norris & Bruce Freestone

Caesar and Pompey fought it out at Munda and ever since historians have argued (remember the beginning of Mérimée's *Carmen*?) as to where the place really was: many would have the battlefield in the plain beneath the village of Monda. It's been an important strategic site over the centuries: your hotel has parts of 8th-century Moorish fortifications wrapped into its fabric. And what a position! High up above the village, reached by a series of steep switch-backs, the matchless panorama takes in the Sierra Nevada and the Ronda mountains. The hotel owes much to the Moorish tradition: there are fountains, wafer-bricked arches, ceramic tiles and much use of *muqarna*, the delicate stucco bas-relief which is the delight of the Alhambra Palace in Granada. But there are some English touches as well: prints along corridors and a collection of tankards in a smaller dining room suggest a certain nostalgia for Blighty. The main dining room evokes a medieval banqueting hall with its arches and flags. The classical Andalusian mix spills over to bedrooms too: four-posters and Moorish arches, terracotta and snazzy fabrics, and marbled and heated bathroom floors. Luxurious and fun.

Rooms: 24 with bath & wc; 2 suites.
Price: Single 14000 Pts; Double/Twin 16000-19000; Suite 25000-28000 Pts.
Breakfast: 1600 Pts (full English).
Meals: Lunch/Dinner 3250 Pts (M), 5000-6000 Pts (C).
Closed: Never.

From Málaga N340 towards Cádiz/Algeciras. Shortly before Marbella (don't turn off N340) right towards Ojen/Coín. After 16km right into Monda and follow signs.

Breakers Lodge Hostal

Avenida Las Mimosas 189
Linda Vista Baja
29678 San Pedro de Alcántara
Málaga

Tel: 95 2784780
Fax: 95 2784780

Sharon & Mark Knight

Although no longer the little fishing village of yore, San Pedro is one of the Costa villages that has managed to retain its Spanishness. This modern villa is in one of its residential areas on a quiet road that leads straight down to the beach. Mark and Sharon have been in southern Spain for many years and, though widely travelled, would live nowhere else. You'll be greeted with a smile here; they are sociable, talkative types, but know that your privacy is precious. An electronic gate pulls shut behind you, reminding you that things have moved on since Laurie Lee arrived, fiddle in hand. The style of the place is very 'Marbella': a bit ritzy with Doric columns, white cane furniture, a corner bar, padded headboards in the bedrooms. Some of the rooms give onto the pool at the back of the house; there is also a terrace area for sitting out with tea, or a beer. Give Sharon advance warning and her maid will come in and prepare you a *paella*. If not, walk into San Pedro and ask for Fernando's fish restaurant. You'll bless us for sending you there...

Rooms: 6 with bath & wc.
Price: Double/Twin 10000-14000 Pts.
Breakfast: Included.
Meals: None available.
Closed: Never.

From Málaga N340 towards Algecíras. Through San Pedro de Alcántara, under arch across road and exit shortly after for Benahavis. Back towards Málaga, under arch again and turn immediately right. House on right after approx. 200m.

Map no: 22

Entry no: 258

Amanhavis

Calle del Pilar 3
29679 Benahavis
Málaga

Tel: 95 2856026
Fax: 95 2856151
E-mail: info@amanhavis.com
Web: www.amanhavis.com

Leslie & Burkhard Weber

Benahavis is well known with Costa residents because of a string of eat-alike restaurants which stretch all the way through the village. But it remains a pretty place and it caught Burkhard Weber's eye when he came searching for the right place to set up his 'small-is-beautiful' hotel and eatery. Less than a year after opening Amanhavis is already popular with the Marbella set thanks to what he calls his "creative Mediterranean cuisine". When designing the guest rooms space was at a premium but he cleverly managed to fit nine guestrooms round the hotel's ivy-clad inner courtyard where in the warmer months you dine by the central plunge pool. Bedrooms are a flight of decorative fantasy with themes which hark back to Spain's Golden Age like *The Astonomer's Observatory*, *The Spice Trader's Caravan* or *The Philospher's Study'* with decorative elements matching the theme. Satellite TV, safes and Internet access speak of a different age. In winter the rooms feel 'snug' but in high summer Casablanca-style fan may struggle to deal with the heat. The prices may seem high compared to other places in this guide but remember that you're close to Marbella's beaches. Ideal for golfers.

Rooms: 6 with bath & wc; 3 suites.
Price: Double/Twin 17500-22500 Pts; Suite 27500 Pts.
Breakfast: 1750 Pts.
Meals: Dinner 4950 Pts (M). Restaurant closed Sunday & Monday.
Closed: Never.

From Málaga towards Cádiz. Just past San Pedro turn right for Benahavis. The hotel is on the far side of the village, signposted.

Entry no: 259

Map no: 22

Hotel Polo

Mariano Soubirón 8
29400 Ronda
Málaga

Tel: 95 2872447/48
Fax: 95 2872449
E-mail: hotpolo@clientes.unicaja.es
Web: www.andalucia.com/polo

Rafael, Javier, Marta & Blanca Puya García de Leaniz

The Polo is one of Ronda's oldest hotels; the Puya family have been receiving guests here for nearly three decades. A sober, almost austere façade is softened with simple mouldings; some of the tall stone-framed windows have authentic *cierros* (the *mudéjar*-inspired observation window enclosed in decorative wrought iron work). The elegant lines of the building are echoed inside where the marble floors, antiques and deep sofas promise cool comfort. Brothers Javier and Rafael and sisters Blanca and Marta have taken over the family business; they are warm, generous and welcoming. Bedrooms are large and light with a blue-and-white theme and on the top floor some have views across the rooftops to the mountains beyond. One of the best even has a bathroom with a view. The decoration is classically Spanish with wrought iron bedheads, Mallorca weave curtains; carpeted throughout, mattresses are brand new and double-glazing cuts out the noise from the surrounding street life. In the lively and animated centre of Ronda (it can be noisy at the weekends so light sleepers should ask for a quiet room), with a congenial bar and excellent restaurant, this is a real Andalusian experience.

Rooms: 34 with bath & wc.
Price: Single 5000-6300 Pts;
Double/Twin 6750-9500 Pts.
Breakfast: 750 Pts.
Meals: Lunch/Dinner 1300 Pts (M),
3000 Pts (C).
Closed: Never.

In centre of Ronda, very near Plaza del Socorro (best place to park is underground car park; only 1000 Pts daily for hotel guests).

Map no: 22

Entry no: 260

Alavera de los Baños

Calle San Miguel s/n
29400 Ronda
Málaga

Tel: 95 2879143
Fax: 95 2879143
E-mail: alavera@ctv.es
Web: www.andalucia.com/alavera

Inmaculada Villanueva Ayala and Christian Reichardt

A small hotel at the heart of *el barrio de las Curtidurias* or the Tanners' Quarter: they established workshops here because of the abundant supply of water. *A-la-vera de* means 'by the side of' – your hotel is right next to what was the first hammam (or public baths) of the Moorish citadel. Christian and Inma are young, brimming with enthusiasm for their (second) hotel and restaurant and the nicest hosts imaginable. The brief to their architect was to create a building which was in keeping with the Hispano-Moorish elements of its surroundings: thus terracotta tiles, wafer bricks, keyhole arches without and in the bedrooms a deliberately oriental feel: kilims, mosquito nets, colour washes of ochres, blue and yellow. The rooms are smallish, the shower rooms likewise, but it all works. The dining room is evocative of the desert with its sandy tones. Its eight metre height is cut across by an arched central walkway leading to the rooms at either end; light sleepers should ask for one of the rooms away from the dining room. You eat well: lamb is the speciality (a change from the ubiquitous pork) and there is tasty veggie food too, nearly all of it organically grown.

Rooms: 10 with shower & wc.
Price: Single 7000 Pts; Double/Twin 9000 Pts; Double/Twin (with terrace) 11000 Pts.
Breakfast: Included.
Meals: Lunch/Dinner 1800 Pts (M), 2500 (C).
Closed: 2 weeks in November. Check!

In Ronda, directly opposite the Parador, take Calle Villanueva. Right at end and down hill to Fuente de los Ocho Caños. Here left and first right to Arab Baths; hotel next door. Park here.

La Goyesca

Calle Infantes 39
29400 Ronda
Málaga

Tel: 95 2190049 or 608 954063
Fax: 95 2190657
E-mail: hotelgoyesca@ronda.net
Web: www.ronda.net/usuar/hotelgoyesca/

José María Orozco

Don't be put off by the shabby entranceway which leads from the street to La Goyesca. You emerge in a magical inner courtyard whose rich foliage is made up of plumbago, medlar, virginia creepers, ferns, jasmine and a host of other plantery. A stay here is as much about the amiable and loquacious owner as about the hotel itself. José María has a huge love of the home which has been owned by his family for more than three generations and will tell you the history of the place – once a convent's garden, then a small factory of quince jams, later a grain store and then saved from the bulldozer by your host – over several cups of coffee at breakfast and, quite probably, over *tapas* and glasses of sherry in the evening. His guest apartments are wrapped round the patio. Each has lounge, bedroom and kitchenette: big spaces for the price. Decoration is rather 'Spanglish': hand painted dressers and bedside tables, geometric tiles in the bathrooms – and rather kitsch theme-pubbish English prints. But they are warm and comfortable and, unusually for Ronda, they are quiet; you'll only hear the chirruping of the caged canaries or perhaps a rather garrulous thrush who sometimes drops by.

Rooms: 6 apartments.
Price: Apartment (for 2) 12000 Pts incl. VAT.
Breakfast: Included.
Meals: None available.
Closed: Never.

From Málaga towards Cádiz on N340, then A376 to Ronda. Here take first right for Ronda. Follow road through old town, cross bridge, pass bullring and then turn first right. Straight past Hotel Polo and Hotel Goyesca is in fourth block on the left.

Map no: 22

Molino del Santo

Bda. Estación s/n
29370 Benaoján
Málaga

Tel: 95 2167151
Fax: 95 2167327
E-mail: molino@logiccontrol.es
Web: www.andalucia.com/molino

Pauline Elkin & Andy Chapell

Pauline and Andy moved south in search of the good life, restored a century-old mill in a spectacular area of the Grazalema National Park and are now thoroughly part of local life. Water rushes past flower-filled terraces, under willows and fig trees, into the pool (heated for the cooler months). Rooms and restaurant all wear local garb – terracotta tiles, beams and rustic chairs. Some rooms have private terraces. Fresh flowers are everywhere and the Molino's reputation for good Spanish food is made; most hotel guests are British but the Spanish flock in at weekends to enjoy local hams and sausages, rabbit and fresh fish as well as imaginative vegetarian cooking. Staff and owners are generous with advice on walks out from the hotel. From the sleepy little station you can take a train to Ronda or in the other direction past some of the loveliest 'white villages' of Andalusia. The Molino is one of the Sierra's most popular small hotels – and has been for more than a decade. It seems to get the balance just right between friendliness and efficiency and old-timers come back again and again. It is worth paying the extra for a superior room with a terrace. Book well in advance!

Rooms: 14 with bath or shower & wc; 3 junior suites.
Price: Standard double/twin 11340-15230; Superior double/twin 13050-16820; Junior suite 15510-19500 incl. VAT. High season half-board only: 24790-29050 Pts for two.
Breakfast: Included.
Meals: Lunch/Dinner 3000-3500 Pts (C).
Closed: 14 December-mid-February.

From Ronda, C339/A473 towards Seville; just after km118 post, left towards Benaoján. After 10km, having crossed railway and river bridges, left to station and follow signs.

Entry no: 263   **Map no: 22**

Banu Rabbah

Calle Sierra Bermeja s/n
29490 Benarrabá
Málaga

Tel: 95 2150288/2150276
Fax: 95 2150208
E-mail: hotel@hbenarraba.es
Web: www.hbenarraba.es

Jesús García

Benarrabá is named after the Berber tribesman who first settled here with his family: the Banu Rabbah of the hotel's name. The hotel, built on the initiative of the local council, is in the capable hands of a group of six young people from the village. What makes this place special is its exhilarating position: almost 2,000 feet up with a magnificent sweep of mountain, white village and wooded hillsides. The building has a rather cumbersome design but wins points for its bedrooms: their best feature is the generous terraces. The hand-painted wooden beds, writing desks and the bright bedspreads add a merry note and their French windows bring in the light and the view. The restaurant, open to non-residents, features local produce: try the *saltavallao*, a sort of hot gazpacho and perhaps one of the local almond cakes for desert. After dinner do take a stroll through the village: you are unlikely to meet other foreigners (not so in Gaucín). And if you're feeling more energetic, hike down to the Genal (route notes provided by the hotel) where you can swim in the warmer months. Local legend has it that the Moors built a secret tunnel between here and Gaucín.

Rooms: 12 with bath & wc.
Price: Twin 7000-8000 Pts.
Breakfast: 450 pts.
Meals: Lunch/dinner 1450 Pts (M) inc. wine; 2700 Pts (C).
Closed: Never.

From Málaga N340 towards Cádiz. Then A377 via Manilva to Gaucín. Here towards Ronda on A369 and after 4.5km right to Benarrabá. Signposted.

Map no: 22

Entry no: 264

Hotel Casablanca

Calle Teodoro de Molina 12
29480 Gaucín
Málaga

Tel: 95 2151019
Fax: 95 2151019

Susan and Michael Dring

Gaucín is one of Andalusia's most spectacular mountain villages. Its labyrinthine, whitewashed streets huddle against a hillside beneath a Moorish castle; eagles wheel overhead, the views are glorious. But the town lacked anywhere decent to stay until Mike and Sue – they once ran another of the delectable places included in this guide! – came across this grand old village house and set about creating the hotel of their dreams. You too will soon fall under its spell; pass through the enormous wooden doors to emerge into the bar. Beyond is a walled garden where palms, magnolia and jacaranda lend colour and shade – a fountain murmurs beside the pool. Terraces on different levels look out across terracotta rooftops to the castle and all the way to the distant Rif mountains of Morocco; the sunsets from here are amazing! Most rooms have their own private terrace; there are parquet or terracotta floors, good beds, and bright colours jazz up the bathrooms. Dine in at least once; the food is spicy and cosmopolitan, following the dictates of what's in season. And the included breakfast is properly generous.

Rooms: 7 with bath & wc; 2 suites.
Price: Double/Twin 10000-12000 Pts; Suite 14000 Pts incl. VAT.
Breakfast: Included.
Meals: Light lunches approx. 1500 Pts; dinner 3000 Pts. Closed on Mondays.
Closed: End October-beginning of March.

From Málaga N340 towards Algeciras. After Estepona right on MA539 via Manilva to Gaucín (don't take Casares turn!). Here into centre and to street of San Sebastián church; follow one way system right towards Ronda; hotel on left, signposted.

Entry no: 265

Map no: 22

El Nobo

Apartado 46
29480 Gaucín
Málaga

Tel: 95 2151303
Fax: 95 2117207
E-mail: info@elnobo.co.uk
Web: www.elnobo.co.uk

Sally Von Meister

Gaucín has long been popular among the more adventurous of the ex-pat community; eat at one of its village-centre restaurants and although your waiter won't necessarily speak your lingo you can be almost certain that you'll hear some (R.P.) English being spoken. The Von Meisters live in one of the area's most beautiful homes: you may just have read about it in an interior design mag, its 'that' sort of place. The position is amazing: from the shaded terrace you can see Gibraltar, the Strait and the mountains of Africa. It seems impossible that just a decade ago there was only a lowly farm building here; the gardens are awash with colour and the house feels as if it has always been anchored to its rocky hillside. The drawing room is the most memorable space paying full homage to that view-of-views thanks to enormous French windows: an enchanting spot at both breakfast and dinner. Sally's food is Good; she organises cookery courses and describes her culinary thing as 'very Mediterranean'. She uses lots of fish, whatever veg are in season and Tuffy's selection of wines is excellent. The bedrooms at El Nobo are stylish and comfortable and Sally is gregarious and entertaining.

Rooms: 3 with bath & wc; 1 cottage.
Price: Double/Twin 18000 Pts;
Cottage 18000 Pts incl. VAT.
Breakfast: Included.
Meals: Lunch 3000 Pts (M);
Dinner 4500 Pts (M) incl. wine.
Closed: 20 December-3 January.

From Málaga N340 towards Cádiz then right to Manilva. On through village to Gaucín. As you arrive in village, right opposite petrol station. Follow street into village to square by a 'farmacía' (chemists) and here turn back on yourself and take small road downhill (sign for La Fructuosa). El Nobo on left of track after 1km.

Map no: 22

Entry no: 266

La Almuña
Apartado 20   **Tel:** 95 2151200
29480 Gaucín   **Fax:** 95 2151343
Málaga   **Web:** www.andalucia.com/gaucin/almuna

Diana Paget

The old farmstead of La Almuña sits high up on a mountainside beside ancient
footpaths used in former days by smugglers and *bandaleros*; later, officers and their
mounts would pass by en route from Gibraltar to Ronda. Views from the house's
terrace are dreamlike; the eye reaches across the last foothills of the Sierra, white
hilltop villages, all the way down to the coast and on to Africa. Diana's is a warm,
relaxed home; she greets you with a smile and always the offer of tea or something
stronger. Her cooking is legendary in the area; expect to be dining in company.
Much of her food has come from the estate and what doesn't is carefully chosen
locally; you may be treated to smoked salmon, lamb, partridge or quail. Veg are
fresh, herbs straight from the garden and wine always *à volonté*. Diana and her
mother busy to and fro from kitchen to table; four Staffordshire bull terriers look
on. The drawing room (see photo) is utterly homely; bedrooms are a happy
marriage of 'English-country' and 'Spanish rustic'. Come to La Almuña to walk,
talk and dine in the most congenial of company. And there are four horses just
waiting to be saddled for exploring this beautiful area.

Rooms: 4 with bath & wc.
Price: Single 8000 Pts; Double/Twin
16000 Pts.
Breakfast: Included.
Meals: Dinner 4000 Pts (M);
lunch by prior arrangment.
Closed: Never.

From Gaucín take A369 towards Algeciras.
At km 44.8, turn left at a white and ochre
post at entrance; La Almuña 2nd house to
right behind cypress trees.

Cortijo El Papudo

11340 San Martín del Tesorillo
Málaga

Tel: 95 2854018
Fax: 95 2854018
E-mail: papudo@mercuryin.es

Michael & Vivien Harvey

The old farmstead of El Papudo lies in the fertile valley of the Guadiaro river. The area's exceptionally mild climate and its rich alluvial soils means that it has long been a place where fruit trees have flourished: everything from citrus to custard fruit, from avocados to pomegranates is grown here. More recently plant nurseries, too, have sprung up: the Harveys set up one of their own and it has become an obligatory shop-over for the coastal ex-pat community. They are, of course, highly knowledgeable about all things botanical and organise garden tours in Andalusia. Their own garden is a multi-coloured Ode to southern flora. It laps up to the high, solid old Cortijo which was recently converted to a guest house. The decoration of the bedrooms is comfortable rather than remarkable: they are furnished with simple pine furniture and have Casablanca-style ceiling fans for the summer, central heating for the colder months. The nicest have views across the farm to the surrounding citrus groves. The dining room is in the original kitchen and has a handsome flagged floor and a woodburner. Phone, fax or e-mail the Harveys for details of their week-long Garden tours.

Rooms: 11 with bath & wc.
Price: Single 7000 Pts; Double/Twin 10500 Pts.
Breakfast: Included.
Meals: None available.
Closed: Never.

From airport N340 then A49 m'way and then again N340 towards Algeciras. Shortly after signs for Puerto Sotogrande right at r'bout for San Enrique/San Martín del Tesorillo. Just before San Martín at sharp left-hand bend go straight ahead on dirt track signposted 'Viveros Papudo'. House on left after 1.5km.

Map no: 22   **Entry no: 268**

Hacienda de San José

Buzón 59   **Tel:** 95 2119494
Entrerrios   **Fax:** 95 2119494
29650 Mijas   **E-mail:** haciendasanjose@yahoo.co.uk
Málaga   **Web:**

Nicky & José García

There are still some quiet spots on the southern coast, especially if you travel a
mile or two inland. Hacienda de San José is far from the concrete buildings in
what is known locally as 'Avocado Valley', between two golf courses on a hill with
views out to Mijas and the sea. Nicky opened one of the first small, country hotels
in Spain nearly 30 years ago. In this, her second hotel, she and husband Pepe have
created an immensely attractive, hugely comfortable and truly *Andaluz* hotel
which would provide a memorable beginning or end to a holiday in Spain.
Although it is in its first year the smell of woodsmoke and beeswax, the terracotta
floors (with heating beneath), the high wooden ceilings and heaps of antiques give
the building a much older feel; so too the exotic trees and plants of the garden
whose age you would never guess. Your bedroom will be vast and have every
creature comfort imaginable: separate bath and shower, double sinks, the same
underfloor heating as in the rest of the house. Your hosts show great sensitivity in
the way they treat guests; they are mindful of your intimacy but there when you
need them. Come for the riding or just to relax.

Rooms: 5 junior suites.
Price: Double 19500 Pts.
Breakfast: Included.
Meals: Dinner 2800-3500 (M).
Closed: 1 June-31 August

From Fuengirola towards Marbella on the N340. In
Cala de Mijas turn for La Cala Golf. At first roundabout
right and at next fork right again for Entrerrios. 1.8km
from here to hotel; signposted.

Entry no: 269   **Map no: 23**

Casa Aloha

Playa El Chaparral
CN.340 km.203
29648 Mijas Costa
Málaga

Tel: 95 2494540
Fax: 95 2494540

Trisha & Ray Goddard

Caught between the devil and the deep blue sea? Well, perhaps, because Casa Aloha has the N340 coastal road to one side and the sparkling Mediterranean on the other. But the focus at Casa Aloha is certainly seawards, both from poolside and your restaurant table. The Goddards have many loyal fans who would stay nowhere else. Décor is certainly 'Costa-fancy' with a lacquered dining room suite, stuccoed ceilings, thick-pile carpets and an abundance of marble; the villa was owned by a wealthy middle-eastern gentleman. Ray (he played first division football) and Trisha (she "once had a farm in Africa") are a great partnership; he busies over the barbecue whilst she is front-of-house with guests. If you like your steaks big, eat here – and when it comes to *paella* Trisha says it's "hunt the rice!". The Beach room takes first prize with the swash of the waves just yards away; watch them from the *chaise longue* before slipping into your corner tub (yes, the taps are gold-plated!). Although you hear the rumble of traffic from the side bedrooms Casa Aloha is most certainly special. There is also a self-catering villa next door to Casa Aloha (118000-156000 Ptas weekly).

Rooms: 4 with bath & wc; 1 Suite.
Price: Twin 18500; Suite 22000 Pts. Minimum 2 nights.
Breakfast: Included.
Meals: Light lunches/Paellas/ dinner 5000 Pts (M).
Closed: Never.

From Málaga N340 towards Cádiz/Algeciras. Do NOT branch onto A7 toll road but keep on N340 and just past km202 post exit for Cala de Mijas. Follow signs for Fuengirola/Málaga back onto N340. Keep hard to right and take first slip road off to right at km202. Casa Aloha on beachside with yellow walls.

Map no: 23

Entry no: 270

Finca Blake

Carretera de Mijas-Fuengirola km 2 **Tel:** 95 2590401
29650   **Fax:** 95 2590401
Málaga

Amélie Pommier

Finca Blake is at the bottom left of the photo. It is just beneath Mijas, a village of
narrow whitewashed streets just far enough back from the sea to have escaped the
development that has left such deep scars on Spain's southern coast. It was built by
one Major Blake, an RAF pilot who retired to Mijas. In 1961 his was the very first
car in the village! The present owner, Amélie, is a hospitable, multilingual and
sympa and runs her B&B in the best tradition of *mi casa es tu casa*. She has nursed
an already spectacular garden into something more precious still; so far she has
catalogued more than 1000 species. Sit and contemplate this botanical wonderland
from the terrace which looks out to the glittering Med'. Then return to one of
Yves' magical guest rooms which are the antithesis of those made-to-measure
'formula' hotel rooms. They are crammed with oil paintings, rugs, lamps, books
and have bathrooms which invite you to preen yourself with every imaginable
'aide-toilette'. The breakfast room is deliciously intimate; sip your tea (from
Harrods or Fortnum and Mason), abandon yourself to the contemplation of the
paintings and then, perhaps, go for another wander in the garden.

Rooms: 2 with bath & wc; 1 cottage.
Price: Double/Twin 10000-12000 Pts;
Cottage 12000 Pts incl. VAT.
Breakfast: Included.
Meals: None available.
Closed: Never.

From the airport take N340 then A7 towards Algeciras.
Exit 213 for Mijas/Fuengirola then A387 up towards
Mijas. Just after Restaurante Molino del Cura on the
right, Finca Blake is on left, easily spotted because of
blue 'B&B' sign. Ring bell and Yves will open gates.

La Fonda

Calle Santo Domingo 7
29639 Benalmádena Pueblo
Málaga

Tel: 95 2568273
Fax: 95 2568273

José Antonio García

There *are* places on the Costa that have retained their identity and dignity through all those years of unbridled development. One of them is whitewashed, geranium-clad Benalmádena Pueblo; don't confuse it with Benalmádena Playa, which is best avoided. In a quiet street just off the pretty main square, La Fonda is a perfect place for a first or last night in Spain – it is just a quarter of an hour from the airport. The Fonda was the creation of architect Cesar Manrique; he is known for his lifelong battle to show that old and new buildings CAN look well together, providing the latter respect local custom. And this building is a hymn to the south; there are cool patios shaded by palms, potted aspidistras, geometric tiles, fountains, pebbled floors, all set off by glimpses of the glittering sea. Rooms are large, light, airy and marble-floored. Downstairs are wicker chairs and a shaded terrace. La Fonda's restaurant doubles as a Cookery School; treat yourself to a southern gourmet meal at half the cost elsewhere. Or wander along to the square and watch the night in with a plate of olives, a glass of sherry and the gaiety of Andalusian street-life.

Rooms: 26 with bath & wc; 7 in adjacent 'annex'.
Price: Single 6000-9400; Double/Twin 9000-13000 Pts incl. VAT.
Breakfast: Included.
Meals: Lunch/Dinner 4500 Pts (M), 6000 Pts (C).
Closed: Never.

From Málaga take N340 towards Algeciras. Exit 223 for Benalmádena/Arroyo de la Miel.
Follow signs to Benalmádena Pueblo; signposted in village.

Map no: 23   Entry no: 272

Casa Rural Domingo

Arroyo Cansino 4
29500 Álora
Málaga

Tel: 95 2119744
Fax: 95 2119744
Web: www.casaruraldomingo.com

Domin & Cynthia Doms

Domin and Cynthia once stayed at one of the small hotels which we recommend in this book. They were so taken by the experience that they left Belgium, headed south and opened their own B&B. Meet them and you'll understand why they were bound to succeed; they are the friendliest of folk with a highly infectious *joie de vivre*. They were inspired when they chose the land where Casa Domingo would be built: high above Álora it has marvellous views of the eastern ranges of the Ronda Sierra. Their guests can choose between B&B or self-catering apartments. Our choice would be one of the B&B rooms; they are large with comfortable beds, bright rugs and terracotta floors, and mix Habitat style furniture with antiques. Life in the warmer months centres on the poolside terrace and the atmosphere is very relaxed; guests mingle easily, perhaps for a game of *boules*, or tennis and are welcome to prepare a barbecue. Domin and Cynthia don't cook but Álora is a few minutes away by car and has one particularly good restaurant. This would be a great place to spend time at the beginning or end of your holiday in Spain. And children are liked rather than tolerated.

Rooms: 2 with bath & wc, 1 apartment sleeping up to 5 & 2 studios.
Price: Double 8000-9000 Pts; Apartment 80000 Pts weekly; ✆
Studio 60000 Pts weekly.
Breakfast: 1000 Pts.
Meals: None available.
Closed: 7-31 January

From Málaga N340 towards Algeciras. After 500m right towards Churriana. At second set of lights right to Cártama. Here A357 towards Campillos. After 16km right towards Álora. At T-junc right and after 200m left. At next junction follow track to farm; signposted.

Entry no: 273

Map no: 23

La Posada del Torcal

Carretera La Hoya-La Higuera
29230 Villanueva de la Concepción
Málaga

Tel: 95 2031177/2111983
Fax: 95 2031006
E-mail: laposada@mercuryin.es
Web: www.andalucia.com/posada-torcal

Jan Rautavuori & Karen Ducker

Jan and Karen lived on the coast before they discovered the harsh beauty of the mountains north of Málaga. The fruit of their conversion from 'Costa' to 'Sierra' is a fetching small hotel, a short drive from the weird, Dalí-esque limestone formations of the Torcal Park. The hotel's base elements – tile, beam and woodwork – are true to local rustic tradition; inside and out it feels first and foremost *Andaluz*. Bedrooms are dedicated to different Spanish artists; the oils are copies of originals painted by Karen's brother. Many of the trimmings come from further afield like the beds, some brass, some Gothic, some four-poster, which were shipped out from England. The open-plan bedrooms allow you to sip your drink from a corner bath tub yet not miss a second of the amazing views beyond. Underfloor heating warms in winter; Casablanca-style fans cool in summer. Many of the dishes on the menu are local/Spanish but there are a number of more familiar-sounding ones, too and a good selection of wines and spirits. This could be a good place for a splurge: staff are friendly, there are good walks in the vicinity and horses to ride, too.

Rooms: 9 with bath & wc; 1 suite.
Price: Single 12000-16000 Pts;
Double/Twin 17000-24000 Pts;
Suite 32000-36000 Pts.
Breakfast: Included.
Meals: Lunch/Dinner 4800 Pts (M).
Closed: Never.

From Málaga N331 towards Antequera; take exit 148 for Casabermeja/Colmenar. In Casabermeja right (signed Almogía) then at next junction left to Villanueva de la C. At top of village, left at junction; after 1.5km right for La Joya/La Higuera. 3km to hotel; on left.

Map no: 23

Entry no: 274

Casa de Elrond

Barrio Seco s/n   **Tel:** 95 2754091 or 689 939840
29230 Villanueva de la Concepción **Fax:** 95 2754091
Málaga   **E-mail:** elrond@mercuryin.es

Mike and Una Cooper

This is a favourite stopover in Andalusia and the reason why I'm such a fan is that Mike and Una are such genuinely <u>nice</u> people. A friend and I were there while on a walking holiday and Una made such a fuss of us that we were loath to leave! The mostly modern house is set back from a quiet road, surrounded by a carefully tended garden and has an amazing view down towards the Mediterranean. Don't miss sundown when range after range of mountains take on every imaginable hue of blue and purple. There are just three bedrooms leading off a small guest lounge: Mike, immensely practical, has just added a woodburner. The rooms have modern pine furniture and duvets; one of them is large enough to sleep three people. It's a perfect place for walkers: return after a day in the remarkable Torcal Park to one of Una's vegetarian suppers (be sure to let her know in advance because ingredients are always market-fresh): you eat out, of course, in the warmer months and in the kitchen-diner the rest of the year. Dinner includes a house red but you're welcome to bring your own if you prefer. Excellent value: do give it a go.

Rooms: 3 with shower & wc.
Price: Single 4500 Pts; Double/Twin 6500;
Triple 9000 Pts.
Breakfast: Included.
Meals: Dinner on request 2000 Pts incl. a half-litre of wine.
Closed: Never.

From Málaga N340 towards Antequera and Granada. At km241 post N331 to Casabermeja and to Villanueva de la C. Here left at junction; Casa de Elrond on right after 3km.

Entry no: 275   **Map no: 23**

Hotel Humaina

Parque Natural Montes de Málaga
Ctra de Colmenar s/n
29013 Málaga

Tel: 95 2641025
Fax: 95 2640115
E-mail: hotelhumaina@activanet.es
Web: www.hotelhumaina.es

Juan María Luna

If your idea of hotel heaven is somewhere way, way off the beaten track then come here; Hotel Humaina is hidden deep in a forest of oak and pine, at the end of a mile and a half of steep track, at the very heart of the Montes de Málaga Park. It was a hunting lodge before being reborn as a small hotel; the area was popular with the shooting brigade but its new status as a Natural Park means that the deer, rabbit, foxes and hares that you see are more likely to be of this world than the next. What strikes you when you arrive is the utter tranquility of the place and it seems fitting that the hotel's manager, Juan María, should greet you in such a quiet yet friendly manner. The dining room and bedrooms are simply furnished with modern furniture and fittings and their best feature is their peacefulness. The hotel's nicest room is the small lounge which has a chimney and books on the walking, flora and fauna of the area. The food is trad-Andalusian at its simple best: try the *plato de los montes* if you like fry-ups, perhaps followed by a glass of the local (sweet) raisin wine (*vino de pasas*) and set aside time to hike along the waymarked trail which leads out from the hotel.

Rooms: 12 with bath & wc; 1 suite.
Price: Double/Twin 9500-10500 Pts;
Suite 14600-16800 Pts.
Breakfast: Included.
Meals: Lunch/Dinner 2400 Pts (M),
3500 Pts (C).
Closed: Never.

From Málaga centre take the C345 northwards towards Casabermeja: the road is known locally as 'La Carretera de los Montes'. After 18km turn left at signs for the hotel. 2km of good track take you down to Humaina.

Map no: 23

Molino de Santillán

Ctra. de Macharaviaya km 3
29730 Rincón de Victoria
Málaga

Tel: 902 120240 or 95 2400949
Fax: 95 2400950
E-mail: msantillan@spa.es
Web: www.costadelsol.spa.es/hotel/msantillan

Carlo Marchini

Carlo Marchini, tired of the cut and thrust of business in Madrid, has moved to the softer climes of Andalusia, bought an old farmhouse and, after years of careful restoration and planting he is – literally and metaphorically – harvesting the fruits of all his efforts. The building is inspired by the hacienda-style architecture of the New World: an arched patio opens at its southern end to catch the light and the view down to the sea. One of its wings is given over in its entirety to the restaurant where many ingredients come straight from the farm gardens. There's an interesting menu: especially popular with guests are aubergines stuffed with hake or loin of pork in honey and apple sauce; there's a good *paella*, too, if you ask Carlos in advance. Both the arched terraced area looking seawards and the ochre-coloured dining room are attractive backdrops for your feast. Rooms feel properly Andalusian. Stencilling and interesting colours add zest and there are Casablanca fans to keep the temperatures down and netting on windows to keep the mosquitoes at bay. Both Carlos and his daughter Adriana speak excellent English and are a winning combination.

Rooms: 8 with bath & wc; 2 suites.
Price: Single 10900-12900 Pts;
Double/Twin 14900-16900 Pts:
Suite 20900-24900 Pts.
Breakfast: 1300 Pts (buffet).
Meals: Lunch/Dinner 3500 Pts (M), 5000 Pts (C) by
prior arrangement.
Closed: 10 January-1 March.

From Málaga towards Motril on N340. Turn off for
Macharaviaya and turn right at signs to right before you
reach village. 1km of track to hotel.

Entry no: 277

Map no: 23

Villa Turistica de la Axarquia

Carril del Cortijo Blanco s/n
29710 Periana
Málaga

Tel: 95 2536222
Fax: 95 2536222
E-mail: vtaxarquia@ctv.es
Web: www.ctv.es/USERS/vtaxarquia/

José Antonio Garcia

La Axarquia is another of the little known parts of the Costa hinterland: it's just beginning to make waves among those happy to trade beach for mountain. Head for Periana then follow a winding track up to this holiday village which is taking root down among the much older olive groves surrounding it. This is a place which children would like; horse-riding, volley ball, mountain-biking and canoeing – as well as swimming and walking – are all on tap. The hotel's architects have tried to create a villagey feel; houses are staggered along the different streets, colours vary, paths zigzag between the different levels. The interior décor is 'rustic-comfortable' and nearly all the rooms have views. The restaurant (open to non-residents) gets busy but staff still cope well. Breakfast is buffet-style whilst at lunch and dinner emphasis is on simple, time-tried dishes like roast kid and delicious cold *gazpacho* and *ajo blanco* (made with almonds and olive oil). Out of season, relax with a good book or two and let the long, long vistas work their magic but be aware that things get much busier during the holidays when lots of the Spanish gather *en famille*.

Rooms: 14 with bath or shower & wc;
6 Studios & 20 houses.
Price: Double/Twin 10700-12200 Pts;
House (for 2) 10700-12200 Pts;
House (for 4) 18000-20500 Pts incl. VAT.
Breakfast: Included (buffet).
Meals: Lunch/Dinner 1875 Pts (M),
3000 Pts (C).
Closed: 7 January-10 February.

From N340 to Torre del Mar and here exit for Vélez Málaga. Bypass village, on towards Alhama, then left at signs to Periana; from here La Villa Turistica is signposted.

Map no: 23

Entry no: 278

Casa La Piedra
Plazoleta 17
29754 Cómpeta
Málaga

Tel: 95 2516329 or
     657 056166
Fax: 95 2516329
E-mail: casa@2sandra.com
Web: www.2sandra.com

Sandra Irene Costello

Casa La Piedra is an old house in the tiniest of squares right at the top of Cómpeta. This pretty white village is cradled by the Sierra de Tejeda and looks out across vine-covered hillsides to the Mediterranean: their Moscatel grapes are used to make the sweet wine for which the village is famous. Accommodation here is self-catering but if you don't fancy preparing your meals there are masses of bars and restaurants a short walk away and Sandra can deliver all the ingredients you need for breakfast. The house's design and decoration has a warm, organic feel: Sandra's aesthetic sensitivity is reflected in the paintings by local artists, framed photographs, books and bright fabrics. A beautiful stairway with 1920s tiles twists up to the bedrooms. The best is at the top of the house and has a lounge and rooftop terrace, but the twin beneath it is also nice and it too has its own lounge and terrace. Beneath them is a small dining room/library and a compact, kitchen. Sandra is both a reflexologist and an aromatherapist and can give good local advice. *Minimum stay 2 nights.*

Rooms: 1 house with 3 bedrooms.
Price: Double/Twin 8000 Pts; Room for 4 12000 Pts; Room for 6 16000 Pts.
Breakfast: Self-catering.
Meals: None available.
Closed: Never.

From Málaga airport towards Málaga and then almost immediately pick up signs Motril/Almería on N340. Exit for Algarrobo. At roundabout left for Algarrobo and Cómpeta.

Hotel Paraíso del Mar

Calle Prolongación de Carabeo 22
29780 Nerja
Málaga

Tel: 95 2521621
Fax: 95 2522309
E-mail: info@hispanica-colint.es
Web: www.hotelparaisodelmar.com

Enrique Caro Bernal

Nerja is one of the better known resort towns of the Costa del Sol, hardly an auspicious beginning when searching for that 'special' hotel; but the Paraíso is just that. In a quiet corner of town, well away from the main drag of bars and restaurants, it stands at the edge of a cliff looking out to sea. The main house was built some 40 years ago by an English doctor, the other part is more recent and it has all been thoroughly revamped thanks to the hotel's charming young manager, Enrique, who really seems to care for each and every one of his guests. Most remarkable, perhaps, are the hotel's terraced gardens which drop down towards the beach; jasmine, palms, bougainvillaea, bananas, morning glory and a washingtonia give it all an utterly southern air. Many guest rooms have a view and some their own terrace. They are large with mostly modern furniture and all the trimmings; some have jacuzzi baths, all have bathrobes and good towels. Beneath the hotel are a sauna and a hot-tub, dug out of solid rock. It is all run on solar energy and it could be just the place to recharge your batteries and still survive on the 'Costa'. And there are six new suites being finished as we go to press.

Rooms: 10 with bath & wc; 7 suites.
Price: Single 7000-14000 Pts;
Double/Twin 8000-14500 Pts;
Double (with sea view) 10500-15500 Pts;
Double/Twin (with jacuzzi) 11500-16000
Pts; Suite 14500-19500 Pts.
Breakfast: Included.
Meals: None available.
Closed: Mid-November-mid-December.

From Málaga N340 towards Motril. Arriving in Nerja follow signs to Parador; the Paraíso del Mar is next door.

Map no: 23

Entry no: 280

Cortijo Alguaciles Bajos

km 3.4 Ctra SE-445
41710 Utrera
Sevilla

Tel: 630 561529
Fax: 91 5641071
E-mail: alguaciles@inicia.es

The Management

Looking for the complete antithesis to those chain hotels where a credit cards opens the door and switches on the lights? Your search could end at this deeply rural B&B. It is lost in the rolling wheatlands of the Sevillian hinterland and you arrive by roads where you might pass the occasional tractor or flock of goats but rarely another motorist. Head up a palm-lined drive, round a corner then pass into a cobbled courtyard whose whitewashed walls are offset by ferns, geraniums and jasmine. "Aah", we sighed, "Andalucía". Encarna, the housekeeper, greets you and shows you to one of four guest rooms which are furnished with beds and tables and dressers which all form part of the collective memory of the Mencos family (they live in Madrid for most of the year). Our favourite is the massive *naranjo* whose bathroom alone would house a bijou studio in London or Paris. No meals are served apart from breakfast but there are two utterly authentic roadside restaurants a short drive away. The silence at night is all-enveloping and after staying here you are somehow closer to understanding the elusive Andalusian character.

Rooms: 4 with bath & wc.
Price: Twin 7000 Pts.
Breakfast: Included.
Meals: None available.
Closed: Never.

From Sevilla NIV towards Cádiz to Cabezas de San Juan. There at crossroads left on A371 towards Villamartín, then after approx. 6.5km left again on SE-445 towards Montellano. Farm on left after 3.4km.

Entry no: 281

Map no: 22

Hacienda de San Rafael

Apartado 28
Carretera Nacional IV (km 594)
41730 Las Cabezas de San Juan
Sevilla

Tel: 95 5872193 or 020 85632100 (UK)
Fax: 95 5872201 or 020 85632300 (UK)
E-mail: hsr@lineone.net

Kuky & Tim Reid

As southern Spanish as can be. Handsome San Rafael lies contentedly amid the gently undulating farmlands of Seville's hinterland. Half a mile or so of olive-lined drive leads to its cheery main façade, doors and windows picked out against the white with a simple band of ochre paint. Andalusia! Olives were once milled here; Kuky remembers it all from her childhood. She could scarcely have imagined that one day she and an English gentleman husband would be at the helm! Guest rooms give onto a cobbled central patio, the inner sanctuary of any true *cortijo*; the glorious bougainvillaea is just three years old. Each room has a shady, veranda with cane furniture for sitting out – you can dine here should you prefer. They also have a mezzanine sitting area beneath high ceilings, 'Casablanca' fans and open-plan bathrooms beyond an open arch and antique dresser. There are two lounges where oriental furnishings and prints collected on trips to the East go well with more local pieces. But the tranquility of the place and the vastness of the views from the house are what we most remember. We liked Tim and Kuky's enthusiasm for their home and their role as hosts.

Rooms: 11 with bath & wc.
Price: Double/Twin 30000 Pts.
Breakfast: Included.
Meals: Lunch 4000 Pts; Dinner 7000 Pts.
Closed: 16 November-9 March.

Leave Seville following signs for Cádiz. BEFORE you get to motorway branch off onto the NIV. Just past km594 post and over brow of hill (keep well to right here!) right into main entrance to farm.

Map no: 22

Casa Nº 7
Calle Virgenes 7
41004 Sevilla

Tel: 95 4221581
Fax: 95 4214527
E-mail: info@casanumero7.com
Web: www.casanumero7.com

**Gonzalo del Río y
Gonzalez-Gordon**

The idea of a hotel with the feel of a private home is a rare thing in Spain, but this exceptionally kind aristocrat from Jerez has a great fondness for Britain and the British. And perhaps it was memories of England's country houses which inspired the conversion of his home to a hostelry. It was no rush job; he preferred to spend "an extra year or two" so that every last inch should evoke a mood of privileged intimacy, in keeping with Sevilla's Moorish architecture. Bedrooms are regal affairs; fabrics, furniture, lighting and bathrooms are all top-notch and the photos of famous forebears, books (*Who's Who*!) and magazines help create the mood of home-from-home. Three first floor reception rooms give into the patio-bedrooms. The cool and elegant drawing room is a perfect spot for a pre-dinner glass of sherry; it will be from the family's Jerez *bodega*, of course. In a quiet dining room there are scrambled eggs for breakfast served by one of the hotels two butlers. You are in a quiet Santa Cruz street (you can see the Giralda from the roof terrace), Gonzalo knows all the best places to eat and drink and nearby is a great flamenco bar. An exceptional small hotel.

Rooms: 6 with bath & wc.
Price: Double/Twin 25000 Pts.
Breakfast: Included (full English).
Meals: None available.
Closed: Never.

At heart of Santa Cruz quarter. Park in Aparcamento 'Cano y Cueto' at junction of Calle Cano y Cueto and Menendez Pelayo (next to the Jardines de Murillo). Tell attendant you are staying at Casa Nº 7.
From here 5 minutes walk to hotel (or take taxi).

Hotel Simón

Calle García de Vinuesa 19
41001 Sevilla

Tel: 95 4226660/4226615
Fax: 95 4562241
E-mail: hotel-simon@jet.es
Web: www.sol.com/hotel-simon

Francisco Aguayo

Just a stone's throw from the Cathedral the Simón is a friendly, unpretentious little hotel and ideal for those travelling on a tighter budget. Gentle-mannered Francisco ('Frank') Aguayo García enjoys receiving guests and practising his (excellent) English. The hotel is utterly Sevillian; you pass through the main portal, then a second wrought iron door and on into a cool inner patio. Tables are laid out amid aspidistras and ferns, the perfect escape from the throbbing heat; in Seville temperatures can creep into the 40s in summer. The dining room has old mirrors and ceramic-tiled walls, period tables and chandeliers: a reminder that this was a grand, bourgeois residence. The bedrooms are set around the patio and reached by a marble staircase. They are clean, simply decorated, and are air-conditioned: you'll appreciate it if you're here in the summer. Many of the rooms have just recently been refurbished: Frank constantly strives to make the Simon a better place to stay. There are plenty of restaurants and bars nearby and the Simon's friendly staff will advise on where to find the best *tapas*. Light sleepers should note that at weekends local bars stay open late.

Rooms: 24 with bath & wc; 5 suites.
Price: Single 6500-8000 Pts;
Double/Twin 9500-13000 Pts;
Suite 13000-17000 Pts.
Breakfast: 600 Pts.
Meals: None available.
Closed: Never.

From Plaza Nueva in centre of Seville take Avenida de la Constitución (if closed to traffic tell police you are going to hotel) then right onto Calle Vinuesa (one way).

Map no: 22

Entry no: 284

El Triguero

Carretera Carmona-El Viso del Alcor km 29   **Tel:** 955 953626 or 91 4116974
41410 Carmona   **Fax:** 955 953626
Sevilla

Teresa Mencos

El Triguero is cradled by low hills looking out across the rich farmlands of Sevilla's hinterland: fields of wheat and sunflowers are interspersed with pastureland where beef cattle and fighting bulls are reared. Although you are very close to beautiful Carmona and Sevilla too, the setting couldn't be more bucolic. As you enter the grand reception hall and are shown up to your room by the cheery housekeeper, a veil of silence seems to wrap around you. We stayed in the amazing tower room: the views from here are, of course, the best and we loved its warm colours and collection of old prints and were happy with just a small shower room. Other bedrooms are larger with family antiques, old writing desks, carved figurines of the Saints, probably cut flowers, maybe a brightly painted rush-seated chair. It feels just like a grand family home, not a mite studied but with a simple elegance just the same. Both meals and rooms are brilliant value and the dining room, looking out across a citrus grove to the pool, is heavenly: just birdsong to accompany you at breakfast. Be sure to let the housekeeper know if you want to have dinner.

Rooms: 9 with bath or shower & wc.
Price: Single 5000 Pts; Double/Twin 8000 Pts.
Breakfast: Included.
Meals: Lunch/Dinner on request 2000 Pts (M).
Closed: Never.

From Sevilla towards Cordoba on NIV then right to Carmona. Here take N392 for El Viso del Alcor (signs too for LIDL). Hotel entrance is on left at km29 post. Signposted.

Entry no: 285   **Map no: 22**

El Esparragal

Carretera de Mérida Km 795   **Tel:** 95 5782702
41860 Gerena   **Fax:** 95 5782783
Sevilla   **E-mail:** elesparragal@sistelnet.es
                                    Web: www.elesparragal.com

The Oriol Ybarra Family

Monks of the San Jerónimo Order built a monastery here in the 15th century in a setting of isolated, rare beauty; later, a *cortijo* was carefully grafted on to the religious edifice when Disestablishment sent the Brothers packing. At the end of the nineteenth century came reform and embellishment; thus was created one of the most beguiling buildings of southern Spain. The main façade will raise a sigh with its ceramic tiled tower, Roman arched windows and bougainvillaea: beyond it are two main patios (one of them the original cloister) and the guest rooms and suites; you will travel far to find any that quite match them. Approach them past fountains and arches; Spain's best-known designers have created a southern miracle in salons, dining room and guest suites; the whole hotel is a 'Who's Who' of fabric, tile, and furniture 'names'. There are oil paintings, *mudéjar* doors, gilt mirrors, tapestries: elegance that permeates every corner. Ride out into Esparragal's 3,000 hectares on Andalusian thoroughbreds, dine on game or estate-raised beef; treat yourself to an Arabian night that you'll never forget. (The simpler rooms are perfectly decent but have no AC).

Rooms: 14 with bath & wc; 4 more basic ('inferior') rooms.
Price: Double/Twin 18000-20000 Pts; simpler Double/Twin 8000-10000 Pts.
Breakfast: Included.
Meals: Lunch/Dinner 3500 Pts (M).
Closed: Never.

From Seville N630 north towards Mérida. After 21km left towards Gerena (having earlier passed another turn for Gerena). Signposted on left after 1.5km.

Map no: 22   Entry no: 286

Cortijo Torre de la Reina

Paseo de la Alameda s/n
41209 Torre de la Reina (Guillena)
Sevilla

Tel: 95 5780136
Fax: 95 5780122
E-mail: info@torredelareina.com
Web: www.torredelareina.com

D. José María Medina Contreras

We were instantly won over by the silence of Torre de la Reina and have clear memories of a wander through its gardens at night with the courtyard, gardens and old watchtower all delicately lit. Originally this was a medieval house-fortress until it was converted into a fully fledged Renaissance hacienda; you'll understand why it was recently declared a national monument. The gardens are a southern feast of huge palm trees, bougainvillaea and scented jasmine. The house is just as peaceful and elegant inside. In what used to be the granary is a vast guest lounge with antique furniture, lovely *estera* matting, chess sets and plenty of books. Yellow, ochre and white combine to give warmth to this light airy building and in winter a log fire burns in the great old hearth. Bedrooms come equipped with mini-bar, satellite television and super-plush bathrooms. But it still feels homely thanks to the warm earthy colours, old prints, bright rugs and fireplaces (in the suites). An elegant and utterly southern hostelry, just a shake away from beautiful Seville, whose staff are very kind and welcoming.

Rooms: 12 with bath & wc; 7 suites.
Price: Double/Twin 16000-27000 Pts; Suite 20000-27000 Pts.
Breakfast: 1200 Pts.
Meals: Lunch/Dinner 3500 Pts (M).
Closed: Never.

From Sevilla N630 towards Mérida. After Itálica ruins, right to Algaba. At r'bout in Algaba take C341 towards Alcalá del Río. After about 1.5km left to Torre de la Reina. On left as you enter village (white and yellow gate). There is no sign for hotel.

Entry no: 287

Map no: 22

Hotel Cortijo Aguila Real

Carretera Guillena-Burguillos, km 4   **Tel:** 95 5785006
41210 Guillena   **Fax:** 95 5784330
Sevilla   **E-mail:** hotel@aguilareal.com
                                       Web: www.aguilareal.com

Isabel Martínez

Aguila Real is every inch the classic *cortijo*: an elegant whitewashed building, surrounded by fields of cotton, sunflowers and wheat, and only a dozen miles from the narcotic charms of Sevilla (you can just see the Giralda tower from the gardens). Passing under the main gate you enter the huge inner courtyard where there is bougainvillaea in profusion; the old dovecote and a water trough remind you that this was once a working farm. The public rooms are decorated in pastel colours with heavy old tables, paintings, hunting trophies and lots of books – and beautiful barrel-vaulted ceilings. Silver cutlery and classical music in the dining room are in keeping with the food, which, in the words of the housekeeper, could best be described as 'good, well-presented, regional food'. Most vegetables are home-grown, portions are generous, the wine list is long and *tapas* and *raciones* (see our introduction) are available at lunchtime. Bedrooms are set around an inner courtyard and have hand-painted furniture, huge double beds and double-sinked bathrooms; some have their own terrace. The palm-filled garden, carefully lit at night, is enchanting.

Rooms: 10 with bath & wc; 4 suites.
Price: Double/Twin 15000-18000 Pts;
Suite 20000-25000 Pts.
Breakfast: 1500 Pts (buffet).
Meals: Lunch/Dinner 3500 Pts (M).
Closed: Never.

From Sevilla N630 towards Mérida. After approx 9km right on SE180 to Guillena. Through village and at second traffic-lights right on SE181 towards Burguillos. Go straight across at r'bout: hotel signposted after 4km on right.

Map no: 22   Entry no: 288

Casa Montehuéznar

Avenida de la Estación 15
41360 El Pedroso
Seville

Tel: 95 4889000/4889015
Fax: 95 4889304
E-mail: hueznar@arrakis.es
Web: www.arrakis.es/~hueznar

Pablo García Rios

This could be a great place to stay if you want to combine walks in the Sierra Morena with day trips to Seville; from El Pedroso you can take a train to the city mid-morning and then back early in the evening and thus avoid driving through the city's snarled up suburbs. This grand town house was built at the end of the last century, when mineral extraction briefly brought wealth and fame to the area. It is all utterly *Andaluz*: a sober façade with the original wrought iron balconies and window grilles; a weighty door leads through to the central patio, where ferns, aspidistra, geraniums, palm tree and fountain make it the spot to breakfast or dine when the weather is right. The original tiled and bannistered staircase leads to the rooms; they have attractively carved wooden furniture and each is named after one of Andalusia's provinces – Seville being the biggest. Food is regional/family with deer, boar and rabbit the specialities; Riojas and Ribera del Duero are the right accompaniment. Kind staff and kind prices too: light sleepers should know that you do hear passing traffic from the rooms at the front of the hotel.

Rooms: 8 with bath & wc.
Price: Single 4000 Pts; Double/Twin 7500 Pts.
Breakfast: 300 Pts.
Meals: Lunch/Dinner 2300 Pts (M), approx. 3000 Pts (C).
Closed: Never.

Arriving in Seville from Madrid take SE30 ringroad towards Mérida. Exit off ring road at signs for C433 La Rinconada. Follow C443 towards Cazalla to Pedroso; hotel is opposite railway station.

Las Navezuelas

A-432 km 43.5
Apartado 14
41370 Cazalla de la Sierra
Seville

Tel: 95 4884764
Fax: 95 4884594
E-mail: navezuela@arrakis.es
Web: www.arrakis.es/~navezuela

Luca Cicorella & Mariló Tena Martín

A place of peace and great natural beauty, Las Navezuelas is a 16th-century olive
mill on a farm set in 136 hectares of green meadows, oak forest and olive groves.
Water streams down from the Sierra, often along Moorish-built channels. Boar and
deer roam the Aracena range to the north and pretty Cazalla is two miles away.
The house is pure Andalusia with beams and tiles while the garden is a southern
feast too with its palms and orange trees and rambling wistarias and jasmines. The
rooms are fresh, light and simple with old bits of furniture: nothing in excess yet
nothing missing. There are two sitting rooms and a welcoming dining room with
log fires in winter. The menu includes delicious local dishes made almost
exclusively with ingredients from the farm – from veg to chicken, lamb and ham.
And there's home-made jam for breakfast. The friendly young owners go out of
their way to help and give advice on expeditions on foot, horse or bicycle and
where best to watch birds; the whole area is an ornithologist's dream. Many of our
readers have written to say how much they like it and we can't wait to return.

Rooms: 4 with shower & wc, 2 suites & 4 studios for 2.
Price: Double/Twin 8000-8500 Pts;
Suite 9500-11000 Pts; Studio 10000-11000 Pts.
Breakfast: Included.
Meals: Lunch/Dinner 2000 Pts (M).
Closed: 7 January-20 February.

From Sevilla A431 to Cantillana. Here take A432
towards El Pedroso/Cazalla. Pass km43 post and after
500m right at sign for Las Navezuelas.

Map no: 16

Entry no: 290

La Cartuja de Cazalla

Ctra Cazalla – Constantina A455 km 55.2
41370 Cazalla de la Sierra
Sevilla

Tel: 95 4884516
Fax: 95 4883515
E-mail: cartujsv@teleline.es
Web: www.skill.es/cartuja

Carmen Ladrón de Guevara Bracho

An exceptional place, an exceptional owner. The 15th-century Carthusian monastery, one of only four in Andalusia, lay empty for 150 years until Carmen Ladrón, visiting in the 1970s, knew she had discovered her mission. She founded a Centre for Contemporary Culture which now includes both an art gallery and a ceramics workshop where the crockery once used by the Brothers is being faithfully reproduced. The rooms are decorated with works by artist guests; painters, sculptors or musicians can sometimes give their art in exchange for their stay. The guest rooms (they finance the centre) are in the old monastery gatehouse and the former cells. The former has been originally restored with light streaming in through a huge skylight. These bedrooms have modern furniture and bathrooms and no telephones or TVs to spoil the peace; others have more recently been added in what were once the monks' cells. Dine with Carmen in her home next door and give importance to the *tertulia* (chat-cum-debate), a forum for sharing knowledge and ideas. Uncannily peaceful, we have happy memories of wandering through the monastery's grounds in the early morning light. A truly remarkable place.

Rooms: 8 with bath or shower & wc;
4 suites.
Price: Single 9000 Pts; Double/Twin
12000-15000 Pts; Suite 20000 incl. VAT.
Breakfast: Included.
Meals: Lunch 1800 Pts (M), 3000 (C);
Dinner 3500 Pts (M), 4000 Pts (C).
Closed: 24 & 25 December.

From Sevilla C431 to Cantillana then A432
to El Pedroso & Cazalla. There, right onto
A455 towards Constantina. La Cartuja is at km2.5 post.

Entry no: 291

Map no: 16

Ibiza
•
Mallorca
•
Menorca
•
Lanzarote
•
Tenerife
•

The Balearic &
Canary Islands

"If we are always arriving and departing, it is also true that we are eternally anchored.
One's destination is never a place but rather a new way of looking at things"
– Henry Miller

C'an Jondal

Apartado de Correos 369
07800 Ibiza

Tel: 971 187270 or mob 619 321478
Fax: 971 187270
E-mail: beashab@aol.com

Beatriz Olivares

Hidden among the stands of pine and carob of Ibiza, C'an Jondal stands in deep seclusion on a spur looking out across terraced hillsides to the glittering sea. As you approach along a long dirt track the smell of juniper, pine and wild herbs is reminiscent of Provence. Beatriz discovered the farm some 20 years ago and has planted three hectares of vines and apricot trees which she farms organically. Her house feels warm, authentic and peaceful. You may be met by the friendliest of dogs, while on the small 'reception' desk in the subtly-lit lounge a cat might be sleeping. This place is the antithesis of a large, chain hotel; here the evening meal is discussed over breakfast according to what is in season. Yours might be a French, Arab, Chinese or Ibizan meal and it will be eaten *en famille*. Bedrooms have the same homely and cared-for feel as the rest of the house; no two are the same and they are decorated in warm, earthy colours. A beautiful walk takes you down through the forest to one of the island's loveliest beaches from where you can sail with Beatriz in her yacht. Aromatherapy, meditation and reflexology can also be arranged at the hotel.

Rooms: 6 with bath & wc.
Price: Double/Twin 11000-16000 Pts;
Double 'Special' 13000-18000 Pts.
Breakfast: Included.
Meals: Dinner 1500-3000 Pts (M) incl. wine.
Closed: Never.

From Ibiza towards Sant Josep. After approx. 6km left towards La Caleta/Cala Jondal. After 1.5km right at sign for C'an Jondal. 1.5km of track to the farm.

Pikes

PO Box 104
07820 San Antoni de Portmany
Ibiza

Tel: 971 342222
Fax: 971 342312
E-mail: pikes@ctv.es
Web: www.ibiza-hotels.com/pikes

Anthony Pike

Cut away from the busy road from Ibiza town to San Antonio, follow a twisting road through ancient olive, almond and citrus groves and you reach Pikes, the island's oldest and most famous country hotel. The thing that first strikes you is the hotel's rampant vegetation: this verdure broken up by bougainvillaea, natural stone walls and the organic lines of its buildings which have the feel of both village and souk. Tony Pike has worked miracles since buying the original 500 year-old old farm; he provides a hotel with every conceivable comfort in each of its guest rooms and suites. To adequately describe them here is impossible; each is different, many have an eastern theme, most have enormous beds, vast bathrooms, private terraces, perhaps a view across the valley. In the Chez Fez restaurant many of the flavours, too, come from the East but there is also a first-class international menu. The staff are attentive and treat the famous (many come here) and the not-so-famous as equally valued guests. A spicy hotel with buckets of razzmatazz whose guests can enjoy everything from gym to jacuzzi, sauna to spa, sailing to scuba.

Rooms: 27 with bath & wc incl. several suites.
Price: Double 22000-30000 Pts; Junior suite 28000-40000 Pts; Suite 35000-54000 Pts; Luxury suite 42000-60000 Pts. Marrakech suite 77000-120000 Pts. Prices for other sites on request.
Breakfast: 1200 Pts.
Meals: Lunch/Dinner 4000-6000 Pts. Restaurant closed in winter.
Closed: Never.

From airport cross island following signs for San Antoni. 1km before you reach Sant Antoni about 50m before a petrol station turn right and follow signs.

Map no: 20

Entry no: 293

La Colina

Ctra Ibiza a Santa Eulalia
07840 Santa Eulalia del Río
Ibiza

Tel: 971 332767
Fax: 971 332767

Ellen Trauffer

Ellen Trauffer came on holiday 14 years ago and was soon back with the idea of creating a small country hotel. Times were different then: tourism was decreasing but she was so determined to 'get things right ' that now a telling seven out of every ten visits to La Colina are repeat bookings. Ellen went for comfort rather than superfluous luxury; don't expect a radio or TV in your room in this 400 year-old farmhouse but do assume that it will be a beautifully furnished, light and spotlessly clean living space. The organic, almost minimalist cut of house and rooms is in the true tradition of Ibizan architecture. Unlike other hotels of the 'pack-them-in' school La Colina's restaurant is for guests only. It is has a very intimate feel and although the food is from the international recipe book nearly all ingredients – fish, meat, fruit and veg – are fresh from the market. Breakfast is a big buffet spread and the muesli a welcome import from Ellen's native Switzerland. Once a week she gets all of her guests together and takes them out to a local restaurant! This is a hotel with a huge heart and the price of rooms and food is very reasonable:

Rooms: 12 with bath & wc; 3 apartments.
Price: Double/Twin 12800-14500 Pts;
Suite 20100-22600 Pts; 2-bedroom
Suite 26100-28600 Pts incl. VAT.
Breakfast: Included.
Meals: 2800-4000 Pts (M).
Closed: November & December.

From Ibiza towards Santa Eulalia. After 10km on right-hand side you will see a Swiss flag. Right here and up the track to La Colina.

Les Terrasses

Ctra de Santa Eulària km 1
Apartado 1235
07800 Ibiza

Tel: 971 332643
Fax: 971 338978
E-mail: lesterrasses@interbook.net
Web: www.lesterrasses.net

Françoise Pialoux

Françoise Pialoux has crafted, planted and furnished a remarkable vision in this hidden corner of Ibiza. She is an immensely likeable, vivacious woman and her character seems to infuse every corner of Les Terrasses. The farm stands alone on a knoll in the island's centre surrounded by terraces of fruit trees and exotic plants. In the sitting room there are deep sofas, lace curtains, books and a piano; hammocks await you in the shade outside and two secluded pools, one of them heated, are hidden away behind stands of bamboo. The bedrooms are on different levels, some in the main house and others in the converted outbuildings. No two are alike and nearly all the well-known design mags have run articles on them; the rich colours, hand-embroidered bedspreads, bamboo-shaded terraces, open hearths, candelabras, wooden and terracotta floors are a photographer's dream. Choose where and when you'd like to breakfast – by one of the two pools, in the house or in your room. Stay for dinner, too: fish is usually a strong feature. But do book well in advance to be sure of a room; there is no better place to unwind.

Rooms: 7 with bath & wc; 1 suite.
Price: Double/Twin 18000-22000 Pts; Suite 24500-30000 Pts.
Breakfast: Included.
Meals: Lunch 2500 Pts; Dinner 4000 Pts (M).
Closed: 15 November-26 December.

From Ibiza towards Santa Eulària. After 9km on right-hand side you will see a rock painted cobalt blue. Right here, on up the track and Les Terrasses is on your left.

Map no: 20

Entry no: 295

Hotel Hacienda

Na Xamena
07815 San Miguel
Ibiza

Tel: 971 334500
Fax: 971 334514
E-mail: hotelhacienda@retemail.es
Web: www.hotelhacienda-ibiza.com

Alvar & Sabine Lipszyc

Few hotels in the world have a setting quite as heart-stoppingly beautiful as this: Hotel Hacienda is high above the Mediterranean on Ibiza's north-eastern coast, in a spectacular cliff-top cradle, wrapped round by indigenous forest with not a building visible for miles. Come here for the Big Relax: it would be tempting to do nothing but lounge on its terrace-of-terraces, by its enormous pool, gazing out to cliff, sea and sky. Being realistic you'll want to eat and sleep, too. Choose between the *Entre Mar y Cielo* grill (Between Heaven and Earth): lobster from the vivarium if that's your thing, the *Las Cascadas* restaurant whose menu lists the very best of the Mediterranean recipe book or the cosier, more intimate *Sueño de Estrellas* (Dream of Stars) gourmet restaurant. Brilliant design has ensured that all rooms and suites get a share of that view; many have whirring tubs which massage you as you watch the sun dip below the horizon. The rich and famous come, so too does Vogue for fashion shoots, and film directors galore. This five-star hotel recently celebrated its 30th birthday and is still characterised by the way that it cares for *all* guests. Extraordinary.

Rooms: 47 with bath & wc; 18 suites.
Price: Double/Twin 28400-45500 Pts; Double/Twin 'Superior' 33900-52600 Pts; Junior suite 37700-55600 Pts incl. VAT.
Breakfast: 2600 Pts.
Meals: 'Entre Mar y Cielo' 7500 (M), approx 10000 Pts (C); 'Sueño de Estrellas' 12600 Pts (M), approx 15000 Pts (C).
Closed: November-12 April.

From Ibiza to San Miguel. Here continue towards Puerto de San Miguel. Just before village turn left and follow signs to Na Xamena.

Entry no: 296   **Map no: 20**

Son Siurana

Ctra Palma-Mallorca km 45
07400 Alcudia
Mallorca

Tel: 971 549662
Fax: 971 549788
E-mail: sonsiurana@ctv.es
Web: www.sonsiurana.com

Montse Roselló

The Roselló family have been in residence at Son Siurana for over two hundred years and the latest two generations – Montse, Sofía and their mother – have given the estate a new lease of life as a luxurious rural retreat. Although you are close to Pollensa Port and Alcudia their mansion-house is deeply rural, surrounded by more than 100 hectares of fig and almond groves and pastures where sheep still graze. The main house is a long, low and graceful stone building with doors and windows highlighted by lighter-coloured *marés* surrounds. Life in summer centres around a large terrace which looks out to a pool which has been sculpted in among the rocks. Beyond, the estate has ancient pines, lakes and a vegetable and herb garden which supplies Siurana's kitchen: guests can pick their favourite vegetables! You stay in one of eight cottages which have been slotted into the farm's outbuildings. Decoration follows the dictates of local tradition with hand-painted tiles, terracotta floors and antiques; perfect for the design mag photographers who have flocked in to write about the place. Breakfast is served in the main house, on the terrace or in your cottage. *A Rusticae hotel.*

Rooms: 8 houses/apartments.
Price: Apartment (for 2) 18000-23500 Pts; House (for 4) 28000-34000 Pts.
Breakfast: 1500 Pts.
Meals: Dinners twice weekly. 3500-5000 Pts (C).
Closed: Never.

From Palma towards Alcudia. Turn left for Son Siurana directly opposite km 45 post.

Map no: 20

Entry no: 297

Ets Albellons

Calle Binibona s/n
07314 Caimari
Mallorca

Tel: 971 875069
Fax: 971 875143
E-mail: albellons.rese@jet.es

The Vicens family

Drive through the sleepy back lanes of Alaró to the tiny hamlet of Binibona, on past mind-boggling feats of ancient terracing, twisting and turning all the way up to a spur dominating a vast swathe of Mallorca's centre. Ets Albellons feels as if it's always been here but Juan and Vicente totally rebuilt the old farm house – taking four long years to get things just right. It is now a home of comfort, elegance, seclusion and style from which you gaze out across 30 acres of olive, pine and carob. Visitors' books, we all know, only get handed to those who sing songs of praise, but this spot comes close to meriting its description as a "little piece of paradise". Bedrooms and suites are pampered and preened: hand-crocheted bedspreads, high ceilings, big spaces, cut flowers, grand Mallorcan wooden beds, terraces and swish bathrooms. You could send a fax, blow-dry your hair, zap on the air-con or soak in your whirlpool bath. You should enjoy your food: local cheeses and sausage, bread from the village and Mama's recipes for dinner with most vegetables farm-grown. Try and take the time to accompany Juan on one of his half-day rambles out to Lluc through this extraordinary countryside.

Rooms: 9 with bath & wc; 3 suites.
Price: Single 15500-16800 Pts; Double 21000-23500 Pts; Double 'Deluxe' 27800-30500 Pts; Suite 28400-31600 Pts; Suite (with terrace) 29600-33000 Pts.
Breakfast: Included (buffet).
Meals: Dinner 3300 Pts (M).
Closed: Never.

From Palma towards Andratx. Exit for Inca. Here towards Alcudia, and at 2nd r'bout left via Selva-Lluc to Caimari. Turn right at Banca March, left at church, right by next church to Binibona. Signposted.

Can Furiós

Camí Vell de Binibona 11
Binibona
07313 Selva
Mallorca

Tel: 971 515751 or 971 515492
Fax: 971 875366
E-mail: canfurios@nexo.es
Web: www.can-furios.com

John Hughes

Can Furiós is one of the smartest Mallorca's small hotels and although it only recently opened its doors it already has a name for both its rooms and its food. It is in the tiny hamlet of Binibona on the sheltered, eastern flank of the Tramuntana Sierra. Terraced gardens with palm, olive and citrus trees have been beautifully sculpted round the swimming pool and the main building (parts date back to the Moorish period). The restaurant is in what was once the farm's almond press. Formally dressed tables and chairs are what you might expect given the prices of the menu; the food is excellent with fresh seafood the house speciality. Rooms are in the main house and the three suites in what were the farmworkers' cottages. Each is different from the next, some have four-posters and the best English mattresses. Open your window to catch the scent of rosemary and jasmine on the breeze. It is amazing to think that there was just a ruin here five years ago; this building pays homage to the skill of local masons, the memory of an elderly Mallorquín lady who once lived here and to the determination of John Hughes to get things right. *The hotel does not accept children.*

Rooms: 3 with bath & wc; 4 suites.
Price: Double/Twin 26000 Pts; Junior suite 28000 Pts; Suite 35000 Pts; Bridal suite 38000 Pts.
Breakfast: 2000 Ptas.
Meals: Lunch/Dinner approx 9000-10000 Pts (C).
Closed: January.

From Palma m-way to Inca. Here left to Selva, here right to Moscari. At church, turn left and follow road towards mountains. After approx 1km at a fork, go right. Straight over next x-roads and on for 1km to Binibona; hotel ahead of you as you arrive.

Map no: 20

Entry no: 299

C'an Reus
Carrer de l'Auba 26
07109 Fornalutx
Mallorca

Tel: 971 631174
Fax: 971 631174
Web: n-reus.html

Tomeu Arbona

Few villages in Southern Europe have quite such a heart-stopping natural setting;
Fornalutx is in the middle of Mallorca's rumpled spine, the Tramuntana Sierra,
sandwiched between the craggy loveliness of the Puig Major and the Puig
del'Ofre. Artists, sculptors and writers discovered the village long ago – and then
so did the tourists – but the place has kept its identity. C'an Reus is at the bottom
of the village, a light and elegant house, built by a returning émigré without any of
the ostentatiousness that some of the so-called *Casas de Indianos* were wont to
display. It must feel a million miles from the poorer parts of Palma where Tomeu
worked as a social worker. He is the kindest of hosts with a deep knowledge of his
native Mallorca. The bedrooms are to-die-for with their original tiled floors,
wonderful beds and linen, antique dressers and perhaps an old print of the Sierra.
Breakfast is a feast; local cheeses and sausages, home-made marmalades and tarts
are laid out for you to indulge in whilst you gaze at that view-of-views from the
steeply terraced garden. Tomeu is keen that you experience the best of Mallorca;
the home-from-home that he has created is just that.

Rooms: 6 with bath & wc; 1 suite.
Price: Smaller twin 12000 Pts; Double
14000 Pts; Twin 14000-16000 Pts; Suite
18000 Pts.
Breakfast: Included
Meals: Dinner occasionally available on
request approx. 4000 Pts (M).
Closed: 15 December-6 January.

Round Palma on Via Cintura (ring-road)
then branch off towards Soller. Through
(toll) tunnel and on round Soller towards Puerto de Soller. At 2nd r'bout right at
signs for Fornalutx. Park as you arrive in village and walk to hotel; C'an Reus is in
lowest street in village.

Scott's Hotel

Plaza de la Iglesia
07350 Binissalem
Mallorca

Tel: 971 870100
Fax: 971 870267
E-mail: scotts@bitel.es
Web: www.scottshotel.com

George Scott

Whatever the star rating or reputation of a hotel, experience doesn't always quite equate to expectation. Not so at Scotts. Your genial, immensely cosmopolitan hosts have created a stylish and intimate small hotel after carefully and imaginatively restoring a grand seigniorial townhouse in the centre of old Binissalem; visit in the knowledge that you'll be very well looked after and blissfully comfortable. To this end enormous beds were handmade in England, goose-down pillows brought from Germany, cotton percale sheets from New York. "Pretty came second" says George but pretty Scott's most certainly is and a night here is an experience to remember. Suites have any number of exquisite decorative touches and the feel is fresh, light and elegant; here an 18th century Japanese print, there a grandfather clock, perhaps a Bokhara rug or a *chaise longue*. Breakfast in the gorgeous patio-courtyard (at any time you like) with Mozart to accompany perhaps poached or scrambled eggs, freshly squeezed orange juice and the best local sausage and cheeses. And buy a copy of George's novel, a whodunit whose action takes place right here: its called *The Bloody Bokhara*!

Rooms: 12 with bath & wc; 5 suites.
Price: Double/Twin 28000-33000 Pts;
Suite 40000 Pts.
Breakfast: Included.
Meals: Light suppers on Monday,
Thursday and Saturday nights. 2000 Pts
(M) incl. wine.
Closed: Never.

From the airport towards Palma and then follow PM-27 motorway towards Inca/Alcudia. Exit at km 17 for Benissalem. Scott's is next to the church marked by discreet brass plaque beside entrance.

Map no: 20   Entry no: 301

Mofarès

Avenida Capdellá s/n
Apartado de Correos 17
07184 Calvía
Mallorca

Tel: 971 670242
Fax: 971 670071

Antonio Rotger

'Mofarès' comes from the Arabic; there was an estate here at the time of the Reconquest in 1229. It still is a working farm; the house and cluster of outbuildings stand amid neatly tended groves of olive and carob, beyond which a flock contentedly ruminated the day we passed by. Life looks inwards to a cobbled central patio (*clastra*) where exotic plants offset the dazzling lime-washed walls. Antonio has brilliantly succeeded in creating comfort in an historical setting; he'll eagerly show you the old olive mill, the bakery and his collection of agricultural instruments in the old stables. The lounge has old photos of the farm and a wood-burner but better still is the dining room in the old kitchen with vaulted ceiling, old ceramic tiles and space to pull up a chair beside the hearth. At breakfast and dinner Antonio has a simple rule-of-thumb: you have whatever you like! Profit from his love of wine and choose a bottle from his *bodega* which has carefully compiled maps of Spain's wine regions. Bedrooms (more like suites) vary in size and shape; all are pleasant, with elegant repro Mallorcan beds, *yengo* weave curtains and bedspreads and most creature comforts.

Rooms: 9 with bath & wc.
Price: Double/Twin 24000 Pts incl. breakfast.
Breakfast: Included.
Meals: Dinner occasionally on request from 3000 Pts (M).
Closed: 1 December-7 January.

From Palma towards Andratx. Exit for Palma Nova. From here to Calvía. There take road towards Capdellá. Mofarés is on the right just 700m after leaving Calvía.

Son Xotano

Ctra Pina-Sencelles km 1.5
07220 Pina
Mallorca

Tel: 971 872500
Fax: 971 872501
E-mail: sonxotano@mallorcanet.com
Web: www.mallorcanet.com/sonxotano

Cristina Ramonell Arbona

Eight generations of Ramonells have farmed the fertile lands of Son Xotano that lie deep in Mallorca's little-known central region. Philoxera put paid to once large vineyards; Spanish thoroughbreds are now raised among groves of almond and carob. Your first sight is of Xotano's cherry-coloured frontage half hidden behind a huge stand of oleander. In the house the lounge's *estera* matting, family portraits, gilt mirrors and potted aspidistra are a perfect backdrop for occasional *soirées musicales* when guests feast then dance the bolero. But, grand balls excepted, this is a blissfully quiet place and birdsong and a distant horse's whinny are about all you'll hear. Each bedroom is named after Mallorca's different winds. They are guardians of fine Mallorca weave fabrics, rugs and family heirlooms (like grandfather's trunk). You dine in the old *bodega* with a high vaulted ceiling, enormous oak vat and inglenook. Choose between two set meals: lamb *a las finas hierbas* may be on the menu or duck in a red wine and grape sauce. After your meal retire to the cosiest of lounges in the old kitchen with a glass of Xotano's own carob liqueur.

Rooms: 8 with bath & wc; 8 suites.
Price: Double/Twin 19950-25200 Pts; Double/Twin (with terrace) 23100-29400 Pts; Suite 24150-29400 Pts; Suite (with terrace) 28350-32550 Pts.
Breakfast: Included (buffet).
Meals: Snacks at lunchtime; Dinner 4000 Pts (M). Closed Mondays and Tuesday lunchtime.
Closed: Never.

From airport towards Palma then follow signs for Santany on motorway. Exit for Manacor, on towards Manacor to Algaida turn towards Pina. Here towards Sencelles. Signposted on left after 1.5km.

Map no: 20

Entry no: 303

Finca Perola

Finca Rafael Genas
07640 Ses Salinas
Mallorca

Tel: 971 121143 or 971 649313
Fax: 971 121143

Micaela Oliver Vaquer

Four generations of Micaela's family have tended their flocks on the land
surrounding Finca Perola. But then milk prices fell drastically and she and her
husband were on the point of selling up. That was before people began to tire of
overcrowded beaches and rural tourism became fashionable: this quiet, unaffected
couple now have a constant flow of guests, many of them German, to their
peaceful farmhouse. The farm is rather monolithic but its lines are being softened
by cacti, palms and bougainvillaea. Life at Perola is mostly lived out on a large, airy
terrace which looks across a huge pool to groves of almond and carob where sheep
graze; it was lovely to wake to the sound of their bells clunking in the distance.
Bedrooms are enormous (ours had a 6m high ceiling!) and have been slotted into
the old grain and machinery stores. They are functional rather than chic with a few
knick-knacks here and there. Forgive a touch of the kitsch for they are wonderfully
clean and comfortable. Do make the trip up to the nearby sanctuary of Santa
Magdalena which you see from the farm and then return to dine with your hosts.
The lamb and beef are from the farm.

Rooms: 5 with bath & wc.
Price: Double/Twin 16000 Pts incl. VAT.
Breakfast: Included.
Meals: Dinner approx. 3000 Pts (M). On
request but not at weekends.
Closed: November & December.

From Palma towards Santayani to
Llucmajor. Here at 3rd roundabout
towards Porreres. Finca Perola is
signposted on the left after 5.5km.

Es Torrent

Ctra Campos – Sa Rápita km 5
07630 Campos
Mallorca

Tel: 971 650957
Fax: 971 650957
E-mail: estorrent@wmega.es
Web: www.todoesp.es/torrent

Eulalia Sureda y Toni Bujosa

Es Torrent is in the best tradition of rural tourism; come to stay at a working farm rather than a made-to-measure countryside hotel. The building is far from the crowded beach resorts for which the island is infamous, reached by a long drive which cuts up to the warm, sandstone frontage of the farm. Yukka, palms, oleander, prickly pears and olive trees give it masses of southern allure; the clipped lawns could have been lifted from a garden in Surrey. In the main farmhouse are most of the bedrooms as well as the lounge and dining room. The former has a large open hearth, chequered table cloths, a collection of old plates and old prints depicting scenes from the Old Testament. Rooms are bright, clean and cosy and the food follows the island's best culinary traditions; bread is baked daily by Eulalia and fruit, veg, eggs and meat all come from the farm. The decoration of the bedrooms strikes a nice balance between the old (beams, tile, and dressers) and the modern (smart bathrooms, central heating). Many guests are German who discovered this type of holidaying several years ago. The beach is just 5km away and it is a lovely ride: bikes are available right here.

Rooms: 7 with bath & wc; 1 house for 5
Price: Single 15500 Pts; Double/Twin 25000 Pts. House prices on request.
Breakfast: Included.
Meals: Dinner 2800 Pts (M).
Closed: Never.

From Palma towards Santanyi to Campos. There right towards Sa Rápita. Es Torrent is signposted on the right after 5km.

Map no: 20

Es Passarell

2a Vuelta No. 117
07200 Felanitx
Mallorca

Tel: 971 183091/557133
Fax: 971 183091/557133
Web: www.todoesp.es/es-passarell

María Dolores Suberviola Alberdi

Far from the madding crowds of the beach resorts, Es Passarell is testimony to the boundless energy of María Dolores ('Lola') who saw in these old stones a vision of better things to come. Outbuildings were converted, gardens were planted: you now approach this isolated farm through a swathe of colour made up of palm and vine, honeysuckle and geranium, almond, fig and citrus. No two bedrooms are alike and size and configuration follow the dictates of the old farm buildings. Choose between house, apartment, suite or double room, between self-catering and catered-for. It's all been converted and decorated with a designer's touch; the mix of antique furnishing and modern art feels good and you can understand why some of Europe's most prestigious magazines have featured the place. There are bright rugs, dried flowers, unusual angles, intimate terraces for *al fresco* thinking and a delicious whiff of the linseed used to treat beam and tile. Breakfast is buffet and big; four types of bread, mountain-cured ham, fresh fruit salads, cereals and eggs. Twice weekly there are gourmet dinners; Monday's is meat-based while on Friday salmon is the main theme.

Rooms: 11 with bath & wc (incl. some apartments).
Price: Double (bath) 16000-18000 Pts; Double (shower) 12000-14000 Pts; Apartment 18000-24000 Pts incl. VAT
Breakfast: Included.
Meals: Lunch/Dinner approx. 2500 Pts (C). Three times weekly special 'gourmet dinners' 4500 Pts (M). Book ahead.
Closed: Never.

From Llucmajor to Porreres. Here continue towards Felanitx. Between km2 and km3, at sharp bend in the road, turn right and follow road for approx 2.5km. House to right, signposted.

Son Mercadal

Camino de Son Pau s/n
Apartado de Correos 52
07260 Porreres
Mallorca

Tel: 971 181307 or 610 758332
Fax: 971 181307
E-mail: son.mercadal@todoesp.es
Web: www.todoesp.es/son.mercadal

José Roig Ripoll

If you are looking for a peaceful and bucolic setting, a blissfully comfortable bed, good food and kind hosts – then look no further. It is just three years since the Ripoll family welcomed their first guests to their beautifully restored and renovated farmhouse. Every last corner of the house has been carefully considered; the house is a 'painting', as the Spanish would say, a measured still-life of things old and rustic. José's son, Toni, a graphic designer by profession, is responsible for the decoration and his artistic eye has created a warm, harmonious mood throughout the house. Most of the beautiful antique pieces were already in the family: the grandfather clock, piano, old washstands, a complete Art Deco bedroom set , the engravings of Mallorca. And the food is of the best the island has to offer: Toni is keen for you to try the local specialities. So at breakfast you are fêted with local sausage, cheeses, eggs from the farm and wonderful bread and at dinner perhaps with a *tumbet* (the local meat-and-veg delicacy) and in the *bodega* is a selection of the island's very best wines. Much of what graces your table will be straight from the farm.

Rooms: 7 with bath & wc.
Price: Double/Twin 16500 Pts incl. VAT.
Breakfast: Included.
Meals: Lunch/Dinner approx. 3000 Pts (M) on request.
Closed: Never.

From Palma towards Santyani. Here, on far side of town, left to Porreres. Here towards Campos. After approx. 1.5km left at sign Son Mercadal/Son Pau. 2km of track to house.

Map no: 20   Entry no: 307

Son Porró

Diseminados
Poligono 3º, Parcela 233
07144 Costitx
Mallorca

Tel: 971 182013
Fax: 971 182012

Pilar Sánchez

You are at the heart of the 'Plá', the vast plain which lies in the lee of the great Tramuntana range. The area has a unique beauty with ancient farmhouses and ancient groves of fig and almond. Son Porró's stone walls look old, too, but the house was just recently completed. It owes its existence to Pilar Sánchez who greets you as she would an old friend and when you leave you'll feel as if you are just that. Nothing is too much trouble for her: when guests arrive late she'll cook them a meal at midnight, if that's what they want. Her bedrooms are large, functional and comfortable: some lead off a quiet, jasmine-filled courtyard, others are in two stone-built houses in a grove of fruit trees beyond the pool. In Son Porró's vast lounge the bright Mallorcan *lenguas* weave fabric of the curtains adds zest: black leather sofas feel rather more sombre. What makes this place special are Pilar's lunches and dinners: in summer there are barbecues out on the patio. She tailors her cooking to suit her guests and uses local ingredients. And friends of hers can take you out on a guided walk or riding.

Rooms: 3 with bath & wc, 5 suites & 2 houses.
Price: Double/Twin 16000-20000 Pts; Suite 20000-25000 Pts incl. VAT. House (for 7) 35000 Pts; Bungalow (for 3) 20000 Pts. Self-catering.
Breakfast: Included.
Meals: Lunch/Dinner 2500 Pts.
Closed: Never.

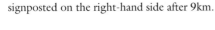

From Palma towards Alcudía on motorway.
Exit for Inca and at second roundabout follow signs for Sineu. Son Porró is signposted on the right-hand side after 9km.

Entry no: 308   **Map no: 20**

Finca Predio Son Serra

07440 Muro   **Tel:** 971 537980
Mallorca   **Fax:** 971 860540

Sr Reinke Sussman & Dieter Gustavo

Dieter worked with a large tour company in Spain and the USA before striking out on his own and setting up his dream hotel in the north of Mallorca. The main building of Son Serra is over a hundred years old, built for two Sisters of a local Order who taught the local *campesinos* (farm labourers) how to bake bread (yes, we found the idea puzzling, too!). The handsome building has oodles of southern allure thanks to the sweep of palm-filled garden that leads up to its old portal and the bougainvillaea that festoons the main façade. The terrace out beneath these palms and an enormous pine is the hub of life at Son Serra; when it is warm this is where you breakfast (a big buffet) and where the evening meal is served. This is a highly sociable and enjoyable occasion when guests, many of them German, eat together round two vast tables. Your bedroom is in one of the farm's outbuildings, a good insulating distance away beyond the vast swimming pool. The rooms' best feature are their shaded terraces. There are ten horses for riding along the nearby beaches, the Albufera Nature reserve just 5km away, guided hiking weeks in the Spring and water-skiing with Dieter.

Rooms: 15 with bath & wc.
Price: Double/Twin 20000 Pts.
Breakfast: Included.
Meals: Lunch/Dinner 3500 Pts (M). Snacks also available at lunchtime.
Closed: 1 November-12 December, 9 January-5 February.

From airport on m'way towards Palma then right towards Andratx. Take second exit for Inca. Through Inca then at r'bout follow signs to Sa Pobla then on to Muro. Here follow signs for Can Picafor on PM 3431. Finca signposted on right between km 6 and 7 posts.

Map no: 20   Entry no: 309

Hotel Fínca Son Gener

Carretera Artà-Son Servera   **Tel:** 971 183612 or 971 183736
Apartado de Correos 136   **Fax:** 971 183591
07550 Son Servera
Mallorca

Angelika Senger

A few years ago this 18th-century farmhouse in the quiet north-east of the island, far away from the bronzing crowds, lay in ruins. But a minor miracle has been worked thanks to handing the project for renovation and decoration to an architect-designer of immense sensitivity – and creativity. When you first see the building you are struck by its luminosity with the white *marés* stone of its façade, framed between the greenery of the surrounding lawns and the blue of the sky. The interior of Son Gener is a celebration of light and form, too; nothing in excess, just carefully selected sculptures and sofas, plants, tables and lamps that seem to create a backdrop for the walls and the structure of the building – and not the other way round. It feels both deeply relaxing and uplifting and the same holds for the guest rooms (all suites with their own terraces) where every corner, lamp, tap or vase seems 'in synch' with the spirit of the place. You breakfast overlooking the peaceful gardens which have beauty and composure as the rest of the house. If you like understated elegance, that Japanese way of saying so much with such simplicity, then you would love Son Gener.

Rooms: 10 junior suites.
Price: Junior suite 35000 Pts incl. VAT.
Breakfast: Included.
Meals: Lunch light snacks available; Dinner 4000-5000 Pts (M).
Closed: December & January.

From Palma to Manacor. There continue towards Artá. Through Sant Llorenc and 2km before reaching Artá turn right on the 403-1. Son Gener signposted on left after 3km.

Alcaufar Vell

Ctra de Cala Alcaufar km 7,3
07710 Sant Lluís
Menorca

Tel: 971 151874 or 659 901393
Fax: 971 721508
E-mail: fincaalcaufar@navegalia.com
Web: www.alcaufarwell.com

Jaume de Febrer

An entry in Alcaufar Vell's guest book reads "We came for one night and then booked for four, we stayed for eleven... need we say more?". Places to stay are rather like friends; you get to know them gradually and however much you plan things, you should let your heart decide the ones you choose to keep. There is a lot of heart in the family home which María Angel and her son Jaume run in the best Spanish tradition of *mi casa es tu casa*. The house is old; in 1773 the present building was wrapped around a 14th century Moorish tower and six generations of Jaume's family have lived here. The house has three guest lounges, one with a vast inglenook; not a TV in sight but instead you'll find books, old farm instruments and a delicious feel of uncluttered comfort. The dining room is grander with beautiful blue and white stucco and Art Nouveau floor tiles. At breakfast feast on fruit and honey from the farm, local sausage, bread from a wood-fired oven and gaze out to the sparkling sea. And at dinner try the best of what the Menorcan cookery book has to offer before retiring to your bedroom which is every bit as enchanting as the rest of this wholly magical place.

Rooms: 2 with bath & wc; 2 junior suites.
Price: Double 11500-13500 Pts; Suite 13000-15500 Pts incl. VAT.
Breakfast: Included.
Meals: Dinner 2500 Pts (M).
Closed: Never.

From airport follow signs for Maó and then Sant Lluís. Just before Sant Lluís turn for Cala Alcaufar. Pass turning for Punta Prima then take second turning to the right. Signposted.

Biniarroca Hotel

07710 Sant Lluís
Menorca

Tel: 971 150059
Fax: 971 151250
E-mail: hotel@biniarroca.com
Web: www.biniarroca.com

Sheelagh Ratcliffe & Lindsay Mullen

Biniarroca once was a working farm; although parts of the building date back to the 16th century the place is now 21st century-smart thanks to four years of restoration work by its English owners. Sheelagh, a designer, had already run a small guest house on the island; Lindsay is an artist and you'll see her light-filled creations in oil on display in the hotel's antique-filled lounges. Thanks to their combined artistic nous Biniarroca already is taking root on this flat tract of land which leads down to Menorca's southern coast. A solitary palm stands sentinel over the cobbled courtyard; just off to one side is a pool with a shaded terrace where plumbago and bougainvillaea are already softening the façade of the beautiful *marés* limestone. Each guest room's decoration is different; all come with extra-large beds, antiques and oils and with full optional extras. We marginally preferred those in the old stables for their extra privacy. You'll also remember the hotel for its food: with the Mediterranean so close the fish, of course, is excellent and most vegetables are organic and come fresh from the farm gardens. The silence at night is enchanting.

Rooms: 13 with bath & wc; 3 suites.
Price: Double/Twin 15000-28000 Pts;
Double deluxe 18000-32000 Pts; Suite
28000-47000 Pts incl. VAT.
Breakfast: Included.
Meals: Light lunches approx 3000 Pts;
dinner 6000 Pts (M) or 6000-7000 Pts (C).
Closed: Never.

From airport towards Maó and then on
towards Sant Lluís. Here follow signs
towards Alcaufar then take first left towards Es Castell. Biniarroca signposted on
left after 2km.

Hotel del Almirante (Collingwood House)

Ctra. de Villacarlos
07720 Es Castell
Menorca

Tel: 971 362700
Fax: 971 362704
E-mail: hotel.almirante@menorca.net

Enrique Pons

A Georgian-style mansion with the glittering harbour of Mahón on one side and palm fronds and an enormous ficus on the other: an attractive if curious sight. This was the residence of an English gentleman, Nelson's second-in-command at Trafalgar, Lord Collingwood. Francisco, Enrique's father, is a real gent too; he opened his hotel in 1964 and has been at the helm ever since. Nearly all guests are British; many come through tour operators then return under their own steam. The best rooms have antiques and period bathrooms and are in the main house. Collingwood's was No.7: from here he could keep vigil over the fleet. Others are in a hacienda-style outbuilding that horseshoes round the pool – less memorable but good value. In public rooms, maritime paintings (even a Titian), potted aspidistra, a grandfather clock, faded Art Nouveau painted panels, a piano and a stuffed grey heron all create an atmosphere of home-away-from-home. The dining room looks out across the harbour, lovely in the morning light, but the coffee was disappointing; perhaps we should have ordered tea! Francisco gives a weekly lecture on Collingwood and on Fridays there's a dinner-dance.

Rooms: 41 with bath & wc.
Price: Double 5125-7885 Pts;
Twin 7640-13115 Pts incl. VAT.
Breakfast: Included (buffet).
Meals: Lunch/Dinner 1400 Pts (C).
Closed: 1 November-30 April.

From airport towards Mahón (Mão).
Follow signs to Es Castell (Villacarlos) and at 6th roundabout right. Hotel is on left after 300m.

Map no: 20

Entry no: 313

Finca Las Salinas

La Cuesta 17
35570 Yaiza
Lanzarote

Tel: 928 830325 or 928 830326
Fax: 928 830329
E-mail: FSALINA@santandersupernet.com
Web: www.fincasalinas.com

Santiago Espada & María Carmen Lleó

Yaiza is one of Lanzarote's prettiest villages, the complete antithesis of the concrete sun, sea and pizza resorts of the north of the island. The creation of the beautiful Timanfaya park close to the village saved a whole swathe of the island from development: walk here and you'll discover some of the islands most extraordinary landscapes and beaches where you needn't worry about staking a claim with your towel. And book your room at Las Salinas, a flamboyant eighteenth-century mansion whose exotic lines, earthy colours and palm-graced grounds could have been inspired in the palaces of Morocco or the hunting lodges of Rahjastan. The keynotes of a stay here are privacy and tranquility. Guest rooms are vast with private terraces; their decoration mixes antique and modern furniture. Your Big Relax could begin with a walk in the wonderful gardens, a swim in the heated pool, or a session in the jacuzzi or sauna; there's also a gym for the muscle-pumpers. The Finca's restaurant is painted in cheerful washes and divided into a number of separate dining areas; 'canariense' and international recipes are a celebration of the fish which come fresh from the Atlantic. *A Rusticae hotel.*

Rooms: 16 with bath & wc; 3 suites.
Price: Winter: Double/Twin 28000-36000 Pts; Junior Suite 36000-44000 Pts; Suite 46000-54000Pts. Summer: Double/Twin 17000-22000 Pts; Junior Suite 21000-29000 Pts; Suite 27000-34000 Pts incl. VAT.
Breakfast: Included.
Meals: Dinner 3800 Pts (C).
Closed: 1-31 July.

Leaving airport follow signs for Yaiza/Playa Blanca. You'll see hotel as you arrive in Yaiza, easy to spot beacuse of its red façade.

Hotel San Roque

Calle Esteban de Ponte 32
38450 Garachico
Tenerife

Tel: 922 133435
Fax: 922 133406
E-mail: info@hotelsanroque.com
Web: www.hotelsanroque.com

Familia Carayon

Ravishing – by the brochure alone you will be lured straight to the Canaries, dumping en route your prejudices about mass-tourism and the ruin of the islands. The old mansion has been metamorphosed – with astonishingly good taste and no little magic. Wood and steel, old and new, geometric shapes and warm, earthy colours have all been included with a flourish. Nothing is overdone; all is muted, bold and interesting. White-covered beds may float on a sea of dark-polished timber, a modern rug on the floor and a vast painting behind the bed. Each of the rooms is different; just expect anything that is beautiful. If you don't love every modern detail your eye will be drawn away to something that is, quite simply, breathtaking – like the courtyard, transformed by its all-round wooden balcony and ochre walls into an outside room with white armchairs and potted plants, and a soaring steel sculpture. Puritans will be unsettled for there are far too many opportunities for decadence: sauna, pool, music galore, tennis, food to long for and breakfast as late as you want. Garachico is, apparently, an insider 'tip' – ancient and intimate. Mountains and sea – there is everything, and nothing, to do.

Rooms: 16 with bath & wc; 4 suites.
Price: Double/Twin 26000-29000 Pts;
Junior suite 32000-35000 Pts;
Suite 38000-41000 Pts.
Breakfast: Included.
Meals: Snacks available throughout day;
Dinner 3300 Pts (C).
Closed: Never.

From the southern airport take the motorway past Santa Cruz, La Laguna and Puerto de la Cruz. Continue on past San Juan de la Rambla and Icod de los Viños to Garachico. Here take the fourth left into a cobbled street and then first left again. Hotel on right.

Map no: 21

Useful vocabulary

Before arriving

Do you have a room free tonight?	*¿Tiene una habitación libre para hoy?*
How much does it cost?	*¿Cuánto cuesta?*
We'll be arriving at about 7pm.	*Vamos a llegar sobre las siete.*
We're lost.	*Estámos perdidos.*
We'll be arriving late.	*Vamos a llegar tarde.*
We're in the 'La Giralda' bar in...	*Estámos en bar 'La Giralda' en ...*
Do you have animals?	*¿Tienen animales?*
I'm allergic to cats/dogs.	*Tengo alergía a los gatos/los perros.*
We'd like to have dinner.	*Queremos cenar.*

On arrival

Hello! I'm Mr/Mrs Sawday.	*¡Hóla! Soy Señor/Señora Sawday.*
We found your name in this book.	*Le hemos encontrado en este libro.*
Where can we leave the car?	*¿Dónde podemos dejar el coche?*
Do you have a car park?	*¿Tiene aparcamento propio?*
Could you help us with our bags?	*¿Podría ayudarnos con las maletas?*
Could I put this food/drink in your fridge?	*¿Podría dejar esta comida/bebida en su nevera?*
Could I heat up a baby's bottle?	*¿Podría calentar este biberón?*
Can you put an extra bed in our room?	*¿Es posible darnos una cama supletoria?*
How much extra will that be?	*¿Cuánto más costará?*

Things you need/that go wrong

Do you have an extra pillow/blanket?	*¿Podría dejarnos otra almohada/manta?*
A light bulb needs replacing.	*Es necesario cambiar una bombilla.*
The heating isn't on.	*No está encendida la calefacción.*
Can you show us how the AC works?	*¿Nos puede enseñar como funciona el aire?*
We have a problem with the plumbing.	*Tenemos un problema de fontanería.*
The room smells.	*Nuestra habitación huele mal.*
Do you have a quieter room?	*¿Tiene una habitación más tranquila?*
Please could you ask the man in the room next door to stop singing!	*¡Dígale al hombre de al lado que deje de cantar!*
Where can I hang these wet clothes?	*¿Dónde puedo colgar esta ropa mojada?*
Where can I dry these wet boots?	*¿Dónde puedo secar estas botas?*
Could we have some soap, please?	*¿Hay jabón por favor?*
Could we have some hot water please?	*¿Podría darnos agua caliente, por favor?*
Do you have an aspirin?	*¿Tendría una aspirina?*
Could you turn the volume down?	*¿Podría bajar un poco el volumen?*

How the house/hotel works

When does breakfast begin?	*¿A partir de qué hora dan el desayuno?*
We'd like to order some drinks.	*Queremos tomar algo.*
Can the children play in the garden?	*¿Pueden jugar fuera los niños?*

Useful vocabulary

Can we leave the children with you?	*¿Podemos dejar los niños con vosotros?*
Can we eat breakfast in our room?	*¿Es posible desayunar en nuestra habitación?*

Local information

Where can we get some petrol?	*¿Dónde hay una gasolinera?*
Where can we find a garage to fix our car?	*¿Dónde hay un taller de coches?*
How far is the nearest shop?	*¿Dónde está la tienda más cerca?*
We need a doctor.	*Necesitamos un médico.*
Where is the nearest chemist's?	*¿Dónde está la farmacía más cerca?*
Where is there a police station?	*¿Dónde está la comisaría?*
Can you recommend a good restaurant?	*¿Podría recomendar un buen restaurante?*
Where is the nearest cash dispenser?	*¿Dónde hay un cajero automático?*
Can you recommend a nice walk?	*¿Podría recomendar algun paseo bonito?*
Do you know of any local festivities?	*¿Hay alguna fiesta local en estos dias?*

On leaving

What time must we vacate our room?	*¿A qué hora tenemos que dejar libre nuestra habitación?*
We'd like to pay the bill.	*Queremos pagar.*
How much do we owe you?	*¿Cuánto le debemos?*
We hope to be back.	*Esperamos volver.*
We've really enjoyed our stay.	*Nos ha gustado mucho nuestra estancia.*
This is a wonderful place.	*Este es un lugar maravilloso.*

Eating in/or out

Could we eat outside, please?	*¿Podemos comer fuera?*
What is today's set menu?	*¿Qué tienen hoy de menú?*
What do you recommmend?	*¿Qué es lo que recomienda usted?*
What's that person eating?	*¿Qué está comiendo aquel hombre?*
We'd like something with no meat in it.	*Queremos comer algo que no tenga nada de carne.*
What vegetarian dishes do you have?	*¿Qué platos vegetarianas hay?*
We'd like to see the wine list.	*Queremos la lista de vinos, por favor.*
This food is cold!	*¡Esta comida está fría!*
Do you have some salt/pepper?	*¿Hay sal/pimienta?*
Where is there a good tapas bar?	*¿Dónde hay un bar con buenas tapas?*
Which tapas do you have?	*¿Qué tapas hay?*
We'd like a plateful of that one.	*Una media ración de aquella, por favor.*
A plate of that one, there.	*Una ración de aquella, allí.*
Please keep the change.	*La vuelta es para usted.*
Where are the toilets?	*¿Dónde están los servicios?*
The toilet is locked.	*El servicio está cerrado con llave.*
It was a delicious meal.	*Estaba muy rica la comida.*
I'd like a white/black coffee.	*Un café con leche/un café solo.*
We'd like some tea, please.	*Quisieramos tomar un té, por favor.*

Quick reference indices

WHEELCHAIR

These owners have told us that they have facilities suitable for people in wheelchairs. It is essential that you confirm what is available.

Galicia
4 • 8 • 14 • 16 • 18

Northern Spain
28 • 37 • 38 • 41 • 42 • 47 • 49

Basque Country
53 • 55

Aragon-Catalonia
63 • 84 • 90 • 94 • 101 • 102 • 115

Eastern Spain
118 • 119 • 128

Western Spain
131 • 133•144

Central Spain
150 • 153 • 154 • 158 • 164 • 168 • 171 • 173 • 186 • 192 • 195

Andalusia
198 • 199 • 200 • 226 • 229 • 232 • 236 • 245 • 251 • 260 • 262 • 267 • 268 • 270 • 276 • 277 • 287 • 288

The Balearic & Canary Islands
291 • 303 • 306 • 307 • 310 • 311 • 312 • 314

WINE

A selection of places of particular interest to wine buffs.

Galicia
1 • 6 • 8 • 10 • 16 • 18

Northern Spain
51

Basque Country
55 • 63 • 64

Aragon-Catalonia
66 • 70 • 76 • 78 • 82 • 99 • 103 • 109 • 111 • 112 • 113 • 114

Eastern Spain
123 • 124

Western Spain
132 • 141 • 146

Central Spain
148 • 150 • 166 • 175 • 194

Andalusia
226 • 238

The Balearic & Canary Islands
302 • 307

WALKING

The following places have good walks close by and owners who are knowledgeable about them.

Northern Spain
31 • 38 • 41 • 42 • 43 • 46

Basque Country
55

Aragon-Catalonia
76 • 84 • 88 • 89 • 94 • 97 • 100 • 101 • 102 • 104 • 105 • 115

Eastern Spain
120 • 121

Western Spain
133 • 136 • 137 • 139 • 142 • 144

Central Spain
161 • 166

Andalusia
199 • 200 • 209 • 210 • 211

Quick reference indices

GREAT VALUE

The following places offer rooms at less than 7500 Pts (excluding breakfast) for two in high season.

RIDING

These are a selection of places where riding can be be arranged, often with the owners and using their horses.

A short history of the Company

Perhaps the best clue as to why these books have their own very particular style and 'bent' lies in Alastair's history.

After a law degree, a stint as a teacher in Voluntary Service Overseas led to a change in direction. He became a teacher (French and Spanish) and then a refugee worker, then spent several years in overseas development work before settling into environmental campaigning, and even green politics. Meanwhile, he was able to dabble - just once a year - in an old interest, taking clients on tours of special places all over Europe. This grew, eventually, into a travel company (it still exists as Alastair Sawday's Tours, operating, inter alia, walking and biking tours all over Europe).

Trying to take his clients to eat and sleep in places that were not owned by corporations and assorted bandits he found dozens of very special places in France - farms, châteaux etc - a list that grew into the first book, *French Bed and Breakfast*. It was a celebration of 'real' places to stay and the remarkable people who run them.

So, this publishing company is based on the success of that first and rather whimsical French book. It started as a mild crusade, and there it stays. For we still celebrate the unusual, the beautiful, the highly individual. We have no rules for owners; they do things their own way. We are passionate about rejecting the ugly, the cold, the banal and the indifferent and we are still passionate about promoting the use of 'real' food. Alastair is a trustee of the Soil Association and keen to promote organic growing especially.

It is a source of huge pleasure to us that we seem to have pressed the right button: there are thousands and thousands of people who, clearly, share our views and take up our ideas. We are by no means alone in trumpeting the virtues of standing up to the monstrous uniformity of so much of our culture.

The greatest accolade we have had was in *The Bookseller* magazine, which described us as 'head and shoulders above the rest'. That meant a lot. But even more satisfying is that we are building a company in which people matter. We are delighted to hear of new friendships between those in the books and those using them and to know that there are many people - among them artists, farmers, champions of the countryside - who have been enabled to pursue their unusual lives thanks to the extra income the books bring them.

Of course we want the company to flourish, but this isn't just about money; it is about people, too.

Alastair Sawday Publishing
Special Places to Stay series

Tel: **01275 464891**
Fax: **01275 464887**
www.sawdays.co.uk

The Little Earth Book

The Little Earth Book

Alastair Sawday, the publisher of this book, is an environmentalist. For over 25 years he has campaigned, not only against the worst excesses of modern tourism and its hotels, but against environmental 'looniness' of other kinds. He has fought for systems and policies that might enable our beautiful planet - simply - to survive. He founded and ran Avon Friends of the Earth, has run for Parliament, and has led numerous local campaigns. He is now a trustee of the Soil Association, experience on which he draws in this remarkable new book.

Researched and written by an eminent Bristol architect, James Bruges, *The Little Earth Book* is a clarion call to action, a mind-boggling collection of mini-essays on today's most important environmental concerns, from global warming and poisoned food to economic growth, Third World debt, genes and 'superbugs'. Undogmatic but sure-footed, the style is light, explaining complex issues with easy language, illustrations and cartoons. Ideas are developed chapter by chapter, yet each one stands alone. It is an easy browse.

The Little Earth Book provides hope, with new ideas and examples of people swimming against the current, of bold ideas that work in practice. It is a book as important as it is original. One has been sent to every M.P. Now you, too, can learn about the issues and join the most important debate of this century.

Oh - one last thing: *The Little Earth Book* is a damned good read! Note what Jonathon Porritt says about it:

"The Little Earth Book is different. And instructive. And even fun."

Did you know.....

- If everyone adopted the Western lifestyle we would need five earths to support us.

- 60% of infections picked up in hospitals are now drug-resistant.

- Environmental disasters have already created 80 MILLION refugees.

Order Form UK

All these books are available in major bookshops or you may order them direct. Post and packaging are FREE.

	Price	No. copies
Special Places to Stay: **Portugal**		
Edition 1	£8.95	
Special Places to Stay: **Spain**		
Edition 4	£11.95	
Special Places to Stay: **Ireland**		
Edition 3	£10.95	
Special Places to Stay: **Paris Hotels**		
Edition 3	£8.95	
Special Places to Stay: **Garden Bed & Breakfast**		
Edition 1	£10.95	
Special Places to Stay: **French Bed & Breakfast**		
Edition 6	£13.95	
Special Places to Stay: **British Hotels, Inns** and other places		
Edition 2	£10.95	
Special Places to Stay: **British Bed & Breakfast**		
Edition 5	£12.95	
Special Places to Stay: **French Hotels, Inns** and other places		
Edition 1	£11.95	
Special Places to Stay: **Italy** (from Rome to the Alps)		
Edition 1	£9.95	
The Little Earth Book	£4.99	

Please make cheques payable to: **Alastair Sawday Publishing**   **Total**

Please send cheques to: Alastair Sawday Publishing, The Home Farm Stables, Barrow Gurney, Bristol BS48 3RW. **For credit card orders call 01275 464891 or order directly from our website www.sawdays.co.uk**

Name:

Address:

Postcode:

Tel: Fax:

If you do not wish to receive mail from other companies, please tick the box ❏   Sp4

Order Form USA

All these books are available at your local bookstore, or you may order direct. Allow two to three weeks for delivery.

Special Places to Stay: **Ireland**	Price	No. copies
Edition 3	$17.95	

Special Places to Stay: **Portugal**		
Edition 1	$14.95	

Special Places to Stay: **Paris Hotels**		
Edition 3	$14.95	

Special Places to Stay: **French Hotels, Inns** and other places		
Edition 1	$19.95	

Special Places to Stay: **French Bed & Breakfast**		
Edition 6	$19.95	

Special Places to Stay: **Garden Bed & Breakfast**		
Edition 1	$17.95	

Special Places to Stay: **British Bed & Breakfast**		
Edition 5	$19.95	

Special Places to Stay: **British Hotels, Inns and other places**		
Edition 2	$17.95	

Special Places to Stay: **Italy (from Rome to the Alps)**		
Edition 1	$14.95	

Shipping in the continental USA: $3.95 for one book, $4.95 for two books, $5.95 for three or more books. Outside continental USA, call (800) 243-0495 for prices. For delivery to AK, CA, CO, CT, FL, GA, IL, IN, KS, MI, MN, MO, NE, NM, NC, OK, SC, TN, TX, VA, and WA, please add appropriate sales tax

Please make checks payable to: The Globe Pequot Press   **Total**

To order by phone with MasterCard or Visa: (800) 243-0495. 9 a.m. to 5 p.m. EST; by fax: (800) 820-2329, 24 hours; through our Website: www.globe-pequot.com; or by mail: The Globe Pequot Press, P.O. Box 480, Guilford, CT 06437.

Name: Date:

Address:

Town:

State: Zip code:

Tel: Fax:

Report Form

Comments on existing entries and new discoveries.

If you have any comments on entries in this guide, please let us have them. If you have a favourite house, hotel, inn or other new discovery, please let us know about it.

Report on:

Entry no: _____ Edition: _____

New recommendation: _____

Name of property: _____

Address: _____

_____

Postcode: _____

Tel: _____

Comments: _____

_____

_____

_____

_____

_____

_____

From: _____

Address: _____

_____

Postcode: _____

Tel: _____

Please send the completed form to: **Alastair Sawday Publishing, The Home Farm Stables, Barrow Gurney, Bristol BS48 3RW**

Thank you.

Booking form

Atencion de:
To:
_____

Fecha: Date:
_____

Estimado Señor/Estimada Señora,

Le(s) rogamos de hacernos una reserva en nombre de:
Please make the following booking for (name):

Para	*noche(s)*	*Llegando día:*		*mes*	*año*
For	night(s)	Arriving: day		month	year
		Saliendo día:		*mes*	*año*
		Leaving: day		month	year

Necesitamos   *habitacíon(es),*   :
We would like   rooms, arranged as follows:

Doble		
Double bed	Twin beds	
Triple	*Individual*	
Triple	Single	
Tipo Suite	*Apartamento*	*obien*
Suite	Apartment	or other

Requeriremos también la cena:	*Si*	*No*	*Para*	*persona(s)*
We will also be requiring dinner	yes	no	for	person(s)

Les rogamos de enviarnos la confirmacíon de esta reserva a la siguiente dirección:
Please could you send us confirmation of our reservation to the address below
(esta misma hoja o una fotocopia de la misma con su firma nos valdrá).
(this form or a photocopy of it with your signature could be used).

Nombre: Name:
_____

Dirección: Address:
_____

_____

Tel No: E-mail:

Fax No:

Hoja de Reserva - Special Places to Stay: Spain

Index by house name

Index by house name

Index by house name

Index by place name

Index by place name

Index by place name

Exchange rate table

Pts	Euro	US $	£ Sterling
50	0.29	0.25	0.18
100	0.59	0.50	0.36
500	2.95	2.50	1.80
1000	5.90	5.00	3.60
1200	7.08	6.00	4.32
1500	8.85	7.50	5.40
2000	11.80	10.00	7.20
5000	29.50	25.00	18.00
10000	59.00	50.00	36.00
15000	88.50	75.00	54.00
20000	118.00	100.00	72.00
25000	147.50	125.00	90.00
30000	177.00	150.00	108.00
40000	236.00	200.00	144.00
50000	295.00	250.00	180.00

Rates correct at time of going to press December 2000

Spoofs

All our books have the odd spoof hidden away within their pages. Sunken boats, telephone boxes and ruined castles have all featured. Some of you have written in with your own ideas. So, we have decided to hold a competition for spoof writing every year.

The rules are simple: send us your own spoofs, include the photos, and let us know which book it is intended for. We will publish the winning entries in the following edition of each book. We will also send a complete set of our guides to each winner.

Please send your entries to:

**Alastair Sawday Publishing, Spoofs competition,
The Home Farm Stables, Barrow Gurney,
Bristol BS48 3RW.
Winners will be notified by post.**

Symbols

Treat each one as a guide rather than a statement of fact and check important points when booking:

 Pets are welcome but may have to sleep in an outbuilding or in your car. There may be a supplement to pay or size restrictions.

 Vegetarians are catered for with advance warning.

 Full and approved wheelchair facilities for at least one bedroom and bathroom and access to ground-floor common areas.

 Credit cards accepted; most commonly Visa and MasterCard.

 You can either borrow or hire bikes here.

 Good hiking or walking from the house.

 Air conditioning in bedrooms. It may be a centrally-operated system or individual apparatus.

315 Entry numbers in green means premises are uninspected.